In League Against King Alcohol

In League Against King Alcohol

Native American Women and
the Woman's Christian Temperance Union
1874–1933

THOMAS J. LAPPAS

UNIVERSITY OF OKLAHOMA PRESS : NORMAN

Publication of this book is made possible through the generosity of Edith Kinney Gaylord.

Library of Congress Cataloging-in-Publication Data

Names: Lappas, Thomas J., 1974– author.
Title: In league against king alcohol : Native American women and the Woman's Christian Temperance Union, 1874–1933 / Thomas J. Lappas.
Description: Norman : University of Oklahoma Press, [2020] | Includes bibliographical references and index. | Summary: "The story of how Native American women joined forces with the Woman's Christian Temperance Union to move their own goals and objectives forward. Subtly but significantly they altered the welfare and status of American Indian communities in the early twentieth century"—Provided by publisher.
Identifiers: LCCN 2019033226 | ISBN 978-0-8061-6463-2 (hardcover) ISBN 978-0-8061-8970-3 (paperback)
Subjects: LCSH: Woman's Christian Temperance Union—History—19th century. | Woman's Christian Temperance Union—History—20th century. | Indians of North America—Alcohol use—History—19th century. | Indians of North America—Alcohol use—History—20th century. | Indian women—Political activity—United States—History—19th century. | Indian women—Political activity—United States—History—20th century.
Classification: LCC E98.L7 L38 2020 | DDC 305.48/897—dc23
LC record available at https://lccn.loc.gov/2019033226

The paper in this book meets the guidelines for permanence and durability of the Committee on Production Guidelines for Book Longevity of the Council on Library Resources, Inc. ∞

To Rebecca and Natalie, and to my mother, Fayne Lappas

Contents

Illustrations

Figures

Map

Preface and Acknowledgments

This book's existence may be surprising to many readers. Over the past decade, whenever people asked me about my research project and I replied, "The Woman's Christian Temperance Union (WCTU) in Native American communities," I received quizzical looks, which I took to mean, "I have no idea what you are talking about." If I had said, "alcohol in Native American communities" or "women who fought for prohibition," my audiences would probably have been less perplexed. Many Americans are familiar with the very real, but overly stereotyped problem of alcohol abuse in Indian country.[1] Most know about the Prohibition Era and its titillating images of flappers, bootleg liquor, speakeasies, organized crime, and the also stereotyped, humorless, self-righteous reformers who promoted the Eighteenth Amendment. The popular image of women activists being the primary factor in the passage of prohibition legislation contrasts with the view of most historians, who have argued for the greater effectiveness of the all-male Anti-Saloon League (ASL) in securing passage of Prohibition, despite the earlier, fervent efforts of the WCTU.[2]

It seemed that few of my friends and colleagues had considered the possibility that Native American women fought to keep alcohol out of their communities, and to outlaw it throughout the United States, alongside their non–Native American counterparts. Many people then asked, "How did *you* get interested in that?" This innocent question made me hyperaware of my position vis-à-vis my subjects. Since I am not a woman, nor Native American, nor a devout Protestant (as nearly all WCTU members were), some might find it surprising that I would be interested in such a topic, much less be the author of a book-length study on the WCTU in Indian country—an endeavor that has consumed over a decade, hundreds of hours of research, and thousands of road miles to libraries and archives around the country. Others may question the motivation of a historian who is an outsider to every one of his subject groups. Therefore, I should provide some explanation of how this project came about. The people who have made this book possible, and my gratitude to them, are part of that story.

In the fall of 2004 I was beginning my second year of teaching at Nazareth College in Rochester, New York. The city straddles the Genesee River—the heartland of the Seneca, the westernmost nation of the Haudenosaunee, "The People of the Longhouse," commonly known as the Iroquois. The Iroquois confederacy originally consisted of the Senecas, Cayugas, Onondagas, Oneidas, and Mohawks. In the early eighteenth century the Tuscarora moved up from the Southeast, becoming the sixth nation. Knowing that I was at a college with a heavy teaching load and I would be hard-pressed to travel far for research, I began looking for a local project. The present work began as an investigation into the possibility of Iroquois labor on the Erie Canal—the artificial waterway whose construction contributed to Iroquois displacement by white Americans.[3] That project ultimately did not go very far, but during preliminary research I came across numerous primary sources that mentioned the Six Nations Temperance Society, a Christian-based organization founded in the 1830s.

Although I knew about the Seneca Prophet, Handsome Lake, I had never heard of other temperance work among the Haudenosaunee. Learning about the presence of multiple Iroquois temperance efforts compelled me to visit the Onondaga Historical Association in Syracuse, near the Onondaga Nation, where I came across newspaper articles about the founder of the Onondaga WCTU, Elizabeth "Eliza" Pierce, an Onondaga woman who will be an important character in the upcoming story. Spurred on by the sense that Native American temperance activity may have been a bigger story among the Haudenosaunee and, possibly, Indian nations throughout the country, I expanded my research in ever widening circles, with visits to the Tonawanda Historical Society where Terry Abrams helped guide my search, and the Tuscarora Nation, where my then-student Bethany Printup-Davis arranged a meeting with current members of the Six Nations Temperance Society, Dale Henry, and Florence and Kenneth Patterson. I became convinced of the worthiness of investigating temperance efforts in Native American communities, but especially the WCTU's involvement, considering the scale of the national women's organization. The WCTU's connections with Native American communities were partnerships—not egalitarian ones in terms of power, nor equally reciprocal in terms of cultural exchange, but ones where both groups of women shared the goals of community sobriety and well-being. Many progressives, traditionalists,

Christians, "Pagans," full-bloods, mixed-bloods, and people with a combination of those identities expressed an interest in temperance activities.

As I considered the nationwide implication of Native American WCTU activity, I began reading the microfilmed rolls of the WCTU's *Union Signal* and *Annual Meeting Minutes*. Through these, I learned of another Onondaga woman named Lydia Pierce (no relation to Eliza), who lived on the Seneca Allegany Reservation in western New York. In 2012, through a grant from the Phillips Fund for Native American Research from the American Philosophical Society and funding from Nazareth College, I was able to travel to Haverford College to use their Quaker and Special Collections, which contain materials about the Tunesassa boarding school at Allegany, where Lydia Pierce attended and where a children's temperance group was active. That same year, I made my first trip to Evanston, Illinois, where Janet Olson, the archivist at the Frances Willard Archives, and Lori Osborne, director of the Frances Willard House Museum, guided me through the collections. There I also met the historian Leslie Dunlap, who had been working for years in the Willard Archives and on the WCTU's connections with African American and Native American women.[4] Their knowledge of the archives and insights into the women of the WCTU have been invaluable and this book would not exist but for their help.

The initial outcome of all this was a 2017 article in the *Journal of Women's History* where I argue that, although both Onondaga women were Christians and supporters of Euro-American educational practices and participation in the market economy, they worked to preserve many Iroquoian traditions, notably women's participation in the political and familial realms.[5] Thus, Haudenosaunee WCTU members both defended and redefined tradition while asserting their place in the twentieth-century United States. The question that was always lingering was, How unique was the Haudenosaunee example?

While combing the national WCTU materials for information on New York State, I began collecting materials relating to the WCTU's activities among Native Americans throughout the country. This led to an expanded set of questions: How did Native Americans across the United States participate in the WCTU? How did the WCTU affect broader federal and state Indian policies? Considering the longevity and wide readership of the *Union Signal* among American women, what patterns or changes occurred in white women's views of Native Americans? In order to answer these questions, I needed to pay attention not only to national publications but also to state-level WCTU records around the country, which were scattered throughout states with significant Native American populations.

There are three reliable places to look for state-level information on Native Americans and the WCTU: the state or territorial annual meeting minutes (sometimes called "reports" or "proceedings"), the state or regional WCTU newspapers, and the official state histories, which are often hagiographical treatments of past state officers but nonetheless provide essential background information about otherwise obscure women. Guided by this method I visited almost every state where there is evidence of a WCTU presence among Native Americans. The national research began in the summer of 2016, funded by the A. A. Heckman Endowed Fellowship Fund from the Hazelden–Betty Ford Foundation. Stops on this trip included the University of Michigan, Central Michigan University, the Minnesota History Center, the Hazelden-Pittman Archives, the Wisconsin Historical Society, the University of Wisconsin–Madison, the State Historical Society of North Dakota, the South Dakota State Historical Society, and a second trip to the Frances Willard Archives in Evanston. In 2017–2018, with a generous Louisville Institute Sabbatical Grant and funding from Nazareth College, I tracked down state records in California, Colorado, Idaho, Montana, Nevada, Oklahoma, Oregon, Washington State, and Wyoming. (Records for New Mexico, Arizona, Kansas, Nebraska, and Alaska are in Evanston or information about them is embedded in the national publications. These states' repositories do have limited WCTU sources.) The national and state records form the foundation of this book. Supplementing the WCTU materials are boarding school records, including student newspapers and yearbooks, missionary organization records, local newspapers from surrounding counties, towns, and cities, and memoirs and other writings from Native American women and men. *The Annual Reports of the Commissioner of Indian Affairs to the Secretary of the Interior* provide essential context.

Many other individuals and institutions have helped me during this project. Nazareth College not only granted me a sabbatical but helped cover research costs at various stages. At Nazareth, Jennifer Harman and Debra Matthewson offered guidance in managing grants. Dean Dianne Oliver, Associate Dean Yousuf George, Director of the Library Catherine Doyle, and Vice President for Academic Affairs Sara Varhus all were very supportive. The History and Political Science Department has been an academic family that has supported me in myriad tangible and intangible ways: thank you to Nevan Fisher, Paul Kramer, Paul Morris, Sharon Murphy, Olena Prokopovych, Georgette Viteri, and Noël

Wolfe. Special thanks to Isabel Cordova, Timothy Kneeland, and Timothy Thibodeau who read parts of the manuscript and reassured me of the worthiness of the project. Others at Nazareth attended campus talks and asked difficult questions. My unending gratitude goes to Christine Sisak and the entire Interlibrary Loan staff at the Lorette Wilmot Library.

While I was on the road, innumerable other archivists and librarians were partners in this project. While I cannot name all of them, a few must be mentioned. Leah Digman at the Southern California WCTU helped me navigate the collection, fed me lunch, and reminded me that the WCTU is still doing important work today. Heckman archivists Barbara Weiner and Amy Barr were wonderful hosts, pointed me in the right direction in the collections, and introduced me to several important resources. Thanks to Evan Hoffner and family, Rudy Verner, Rhett Elliott, Tay Newendorp, and Matt Olins for housing and/or provisions along the way.

Throughout the years, others have provided support and feedback. When the project began in New York State, I was supported by an Anna K. and Mary E. Cunningham Research Residency at the New York State Library. In the writing process, Michael Oberg and Lori Daggar read early versions of some sections. Others who shared their knowledge through informal conversations or formal academic routes include Catherine Cocks, Glenn Crothers, Jack Ericson, John Fadden, Denis Foley, John Gibson, Perry Ground, Laurence Hauptman, Bartosz Hlebowicz, Peter Jemison, Jeanette Miller, Larry Naukam, Mary Jane Smith, and Rose Stremlau. Skyler Poel helped with follow-up research. At the Louisville Institute, Don Richter and our whole winter seminar cohort including Lisa Bowens, Peter Capretto, Elena Lloyd-Sidle, Devin P. Singh, Victor Thasiah, Nathan Walton, and Martin Wickware reminded me of some important ways to think about Christianity at the turn of the century. From the very early stages Alan Shackelford and Stephen Warren have offered words of encouragement and guidance.

I am especially grateful to Kathleen Kelly, acquisitions editor, and Emily Jerman Schuster, manuscript editor, at the University of Oklahoma Press. Pippa Letsky was a superb and patient copyeditor. They and the whole OU Press team have been consummate professionals: prompt and insightful with feedback and reassuring at every step. I could not have asked for a better experience. Valerie Sherer Mathes, Phil Brigandi, and the anonymous reviewer provided detailed criticisms and suggestions and saved me from several embarrassing errors. I am sure there are errors or oversights that remain. Those are my fault alone.

My largest debts are to my family for making my life's work possible. Mom, Karen, and Carly, I am grateful to have you all in my life and for your support over the years. Natalie, thank you for keeping me company in the writing process and for always asking the most difficult questions, like "Daddy, when is your book going to be done?" Rebecca, thank you for covering the home front while I was in the archives, reading the entire first (and much longer) draft, and still having confidence in the book's value. You are the world's greatest travel companion, cheerleader, and critic—and an inspiring teacher and partner. Thank you for everything.

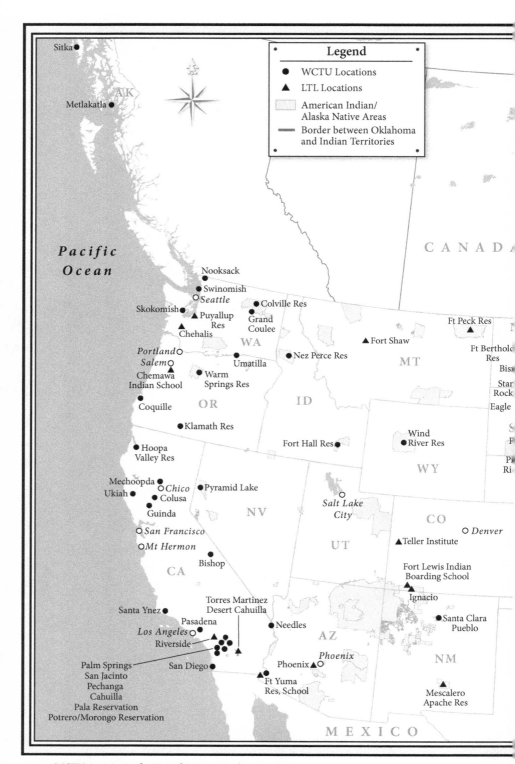

WCTU Activity in the United States. Map by Gerry Krieg.

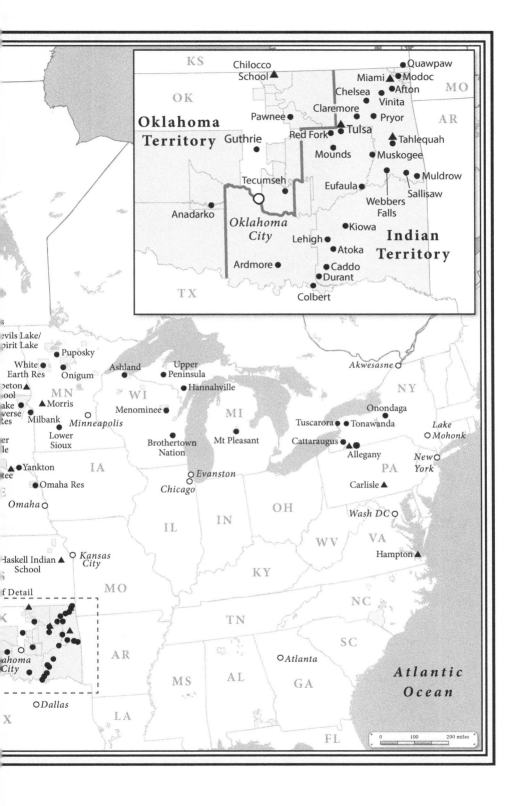

In League Against King Alcohol

Introduction

It is hard to work when you are drunk. This was as true at the turn of the twentieth century as it is today. Whether someone was a farmer, factory worker, accountant, student, parent, or housekeeper, that individual became less productive, more injury prone, and more likely to get fired if inebriated. At a time when women and their families were often entirely dependent on their husbands' wages for their food, shelter, clothing, and medical care, a husband's drinking threatened a family's survival. Working-class women from all racial and ethnic backgrounds often lacked the resources to escape poverty or abuse precipitated by drinking. In that way, temperance was a women's rights issue in the nineteenth and twentieth centuries. Since so many Native American communities were poor and individuals were often on the lower rungs of the market economy's hierarchy, an inability to succeed in school, on the farm, or in other workplaces due to drunkenness could become an existential threat.

From the 1870s through the Prohibition Era, Native American women partnered with white women in the Woman's Christian Temperance Union (WCTU) to promote abstinence and legal prohibition in Indian country. They worked to instill a temperance ethos in the young, to punish bootleggers, and to encourage US citizenship, Euro-American-style education, and commercial agricultural development, all of which they believed would reinforce the temperance effort. Thousands of Native American women were involved in this campaign, on dozens of reservations and in non-reservation Native American communities. Thousands of white women supported, responded to, or guided their efforts. Other women and men—both inside and outside the temperance movement—resented, doubted, and even resisted their efforts.

These years also saw profound changes in the political lives of American women of all backgrounds. Woman's suffrage gained ground, first in the states and then at the national level with the passage of the Nineteenth Amendment.

Anti-alcohol legislation also proliferated. Almost every state tightened regulations. Then came national prohibition via the Eighteenth Amendment and the Volstead Act, which ended with repeal thirteen years later. The WCTU was at the forefront of these suffrage, prohibition, and other reform efforts.

The heyday of the WCTU was also an era of drastic change in the lives of Native Americans and in federal Indian policy. The last stages of the Plains Wars, President Ulysses S. Grant's Peace Policy, the implementation of Indian boarding schools, allotment policies, the General Citizenship Act of 1924, and the first rumblings of the Indian New Deal and Indian Reorganization Act all occurred during this era. Allotment was the process of breaking up tribally owned reservation lands and distributing plots and titles to individual Native Americans, and some Native American women in the WCTU were skeptical of or even resistant to the process. White officials and many white WCTU members claimed that accepting an allotment promised the allottee various legal rights: citizenship, voting rights for male allottees, and economic independence. But there were often significant waiting periods, dependent on the tribe's agreement with the federal government or within the wording of the applicable law passed by Congress. Surplus lands—those not allotted—could be sold to whites, which created a notorious checkerboard effect leaving many communities fragmented geographically, socially, and culturally.[1]

Native American women in the WCTU saw the perils of citizenship as it related to both land and alcohol well before their white counterparts did. Status as individual citizens of the United States threatened to make obsolete the very federal and state alcohol laws that prohibited the sale of alcohol to Indians. Despite the WCTU's support for policies that threatened tribal societies, Native American women joined the WCTU in sizeable numbers, all across the country, as they saw more benefits than downsides to the organization.

Discussions about the future of Native Americans along with fund-raising and advocacy campaigns occurred in thousands of pages of temperance publications printed by the WCTU. Local newspaper reporters, officials from the Department of the Interior and the Office of Indian Affairs (OIA), missionary societies, and local, state, and national politicians all recognized the WCTU's efforts and acknowledged the influence of the organization on their thinking about Indian affairs. With a few exceptions, however, the role that the WCTU played in the lives of Indian women—and vice versa—has largely been ignored by historians.

Simply telling the story of the WCTU and Native Americans is valuable. Native American women were deeply involved in the WCTU. It was one of the largest women's reform organizations in history, and knowing about Native women's involvement informs our understanding of the diversity of America's political and social movements. Within the contours of this story we will also see a brand of Native American activism led by Christian and Euro-American-educated Native American women who connected with a progressive reform organization largely consisting of politically disenfranchised white women— who had developed methods of pressuring the governmental system from which they were excluded. Native American women advocated what they saw as the best path for their communities, which they often tried to hold together despite the devastating effects that boarding schools, allotment, and other policies had on them. Native American WCTU leaders drew upon intertwined Indigenous elements, too—dance, music, religion, and metaphors from long-standing oral traditions—to drum up support for their ostensibly progressive ideas. Not all Native American women came from communities that had matriarchal or matrilineal traditions, but for those who did, there was nothing new about women participating in politics, nurturing future leaders through education, or using behind-the-scenes methods to influence male political leaders. Despite attacks on these traditions from churches, policy makers, and schools, Native women in the WCTU tapped into symbols, ceremonies, and values that both "traditional" and "progressive" (to use shorthand for the moment) divisions would understand and appreciate.

The WCTU members were not the first messengers who combined temperance with a spiritual vision. While there were many Native American leaders in the colonial era who did so, one of the most enduring messages came in the Early Republic from the Seneca Prophet, Handsome Lake. Beginning in 1799 Handsome Lake became one of the most successful temperance organizers in Iroquois territory. While other tribal leaders noted the effects of alcohol on their people and attempted to work with colonial governments to limit alcohol distribution to their tribes, Handsome Lake's promotion of abstinence fit into a whole system of spirituality that spread across the western New York tribes in the subsequent decades. Handsome Lake, who suffered personally from alcohol abuse, received a series of visions from the Creator. One of these visions was a vivid picture of the effects of alcohol on individuals and Iroquois societies. His first vision indicated that four evils, "whiskey, witchcraft, love magic, and abortion-and-sterility medicine," were to be banished from Iroquoia. In one of his visions, those who insisted on drinking in this world were punished in the afterlife by being forced to drink "molten metal." Handsome Lake's message did not emphasize individual moral reformation, alone, but encouraged communities to promote sobriety among the people. Tribal councils on each of the reservations were often accompanied by public harangues of abusers and commands to stop drinking. After Handsome Lake's death, his relatives formalized his message into a set of rituals that are still performed regularly in Iroquois country.[2] Handsome Lake was an inspiration not only to Haudenosaunee people in the nineteenth century and beyond but also to non-Iroquois Native Americans and non–Native Americans in the WCTU.

Christianity, which existed alongside traditional beliefs and practices, had been part of the landscape in the colonial Northeast for about two centuries when Handsome Lake's messages began to take hold in Iroquoia. Scholars have pointed out subtle Christian elements embedded in Handsome Lake's visions and the Longhouse tradition's practices. However, the Six Nations Temperance Society directly adopted practices that resembled those of Protestant-based Euro-American temperance groups such as the American Temperance Society, founded in 1826. In 1830 at least three Christian Temperance Society chapters sprang up: one on Tuscarora, another among the Senecas at Cattaraugus, and yet another on the Six Nations Reserve in Canada. In 1832 these organizations merged into the Six Nations Temperance Society, which has met annually through the present day.[3] Led by Christian ministers such as the Tuscarora Baptist pastor James Cusick, members of the Six Nations Temperance Society signed pledges, played in and listened to brass bands, sang hymns, and read passages from Christian scripture that were interpreted as warnings against alcohol abuse. The Longhouse traditions and the Christian temperance societies were not mutually exclusive. In subsequent decades temperance meetings often began at the church, with hymns and Western music, and then proceeded to the longhouse where cow horn rattles and drums were the chosen instruments.[4]

These were not the only temperance efforts in Iroquoia that combined Christianity with total abstinence. Many Onondagas had been involved in the Six Nations Temperance Society, but there was also a branch of the Independent Order of the Good Templars (IOGT), an international temperance group formed in Utica, New York, in 1851. The broader IOGT even elected a Canadian Mohawk physician as a key officer in the organization: Oronhyatekha (Burning Sky), known also by his English name, Peter Martin.[5] Elizabeth "Eliza" Pierce was an Onondaga woman who seemed to be involved in several temperance efforts, including the IOGT and the WCTU. She was featured in numerous local newspaper articles, and she founded a WCTU chapter on the Onondaga Nation at the turn of the century. The WCTU did not eliminate these smaller organizations, but it began to overshadow many of them, and the national organization and its reach gave the WCTU tremendous influence. It is essential to understand how the WCTU disseminated ideas through the organizational structure and spread the message to Native Americans, and how Native Americans themselves fit into the organizational structures and culture of the WCTU. Therefore, we must examine the organization and its framework for attracting and incorporating Native Americans.

Structure of the WCTU

The WCTU was founded in 1874 in Cleveland, Ohio, immediately following the Woman's Crusade, a local initiative against saloons in Hillsboro, Ohio, between 1873 and 1874.[6] Frances Willard was the second president of the WCTU (1879–1898) and expanded the organization's purview to include a wide array of activities beyond temperance work. Emblematic of her leadership was her "Do Everything" policy, which asserted that the organization should be involved in any issue that even tangentially helped the temperance cause. Willard's strategy increased the visibility of the WCTU and thrust its members into working for a variety of reforms. Aside from anti-alcohol initiatives, their primary associated issue was supporting women's right to vote. They fought child labor, polygamy, cigarette smoking, and other immoralities, often through the creation of dedicated departments whose leaders were dubbed superintendents. The *Annual Meeting Minutes* recorded the debates about creating, eliminating, or merging national departments such as Anti-Narcotics, Work Among Colored People, Work Among Lumbermen, and Work Among Indians, which would focus their efforts on a single issue or on a particular segment of the population.

The WCTU's policies toward Native Americans reflected turn-of-the-century progressive ideas about the responsibility of an activist government to uplift the living conditions of poor people at home and around the world.[7] There was a basis for paternalistic and protective alcohol laws in place, which had banned the sale or distribution of alcohol to Indians, beginning in the colonial period, sharpening in the Jeffersonian Age, and again in the Jacksonian period. Not surprisingly, historians' coverage of women's role in shaping these policies has been light; this should not be seen as a deliberate avoidance of women's historical roles but, rather, as a result of the silence in the sources used in such policy studies. The often male historians of Indian policy have put forth some good faith efforts. In his treatment of Indians and alcohol in the colonial era, for example, Peter Mancall notes that the sources associated with temperance efforts at this time were almost entirely authored by male colonial officials or missionaries. He observes that Native American women involved in temperance efforts "tended to try to limit its worst consequences," especially "violence during drinking sessions," by hiding weapons rather than seeking outright prohibition.[8] Since restricting trade would almost always involve negotiations with traders or colonial officials, it is quite possible that the traditional gender roles for most northeastern tribes would have emphasized women's management and protection of the internal community while male roles entailed negotiations with outside nations and colonies.

In *White Man's Wicked Water*, William E. Unrau ably argues that federal legal restrictions were largely useless in the western United States and even counterproductive in Indian country, especially when surrounding whites drank to excess and encouraged heavy drinking among Native Americans. However, his account admittedly fizzles as it gets closer to the end of the nineteenth century, which rules out coverage of the WCTU in Indian country.[9] A major figure in federal Indian policy studies, Francis Paul Prucha dedicates substantial portions of his numerous works to federal laws regarding alcohol and Native Americans and even emphasizes the role that missionaries and religiously minded Indian service officials played in shaping federal alcohol regulations. Although he mentions the cofounder of the Women's National Indian Association (WNIA) Amelia Stone Quinton, he disconnects her WCTU work from her work "in Indian reform." Other temperance-leaning Indian Department officials, including Hiram Price, Clinton Fisk, Daniel Dorchester, and Thomas Jefferson Morgan, are noted for their connections to missionary organizations—but not to their often personal connections to women's auxiliaries of those missionary societies, and not at all to the WCTU leaders with whom the same officials often corresponded.[10] James Edward Klein's work on prohibition in Oklahoma is dismissive of the WCTU's impact at the territorial, state, and national levels. As do many other traditional political histories of the rise of prohibition, Klein emphasizes the role of the Anti-Saloon League (ASL) over the impact of the longer-standing WCTU. He comments that the women's organization "set up temperance day programs in the American Indian schools, funded a special evangelist to local American Indians," engaged in prison work, and handed out coffee at polling places. Unfortunately, he deemphasizes the impact that this work had on changing the mind-sets of men and the political expectations of Indian men and women. He goes so far as to say that their "activism gained notoriety for the union, though its impact on the liquor issue is dubious because drinking remained common despite the federal liquor ban in the region." If the reckoning of the commonness or rarity of drinking was the final measure of impact, then the ASL, constitutional amendments, and the Volstead Act were equally "dubious," since drinking remained common, though slightly diminished, during prohibition.[11] However, aside from the impact on drinking or even the availability of liquor (though the present work certainly covers these topics), there are other impacts we can observe for the WCTU's work among Indians, including the effects on Indian education, on social and cultural interaction between Native and non-Native women, on religious life, and in numerous other arenas.

While non-Native WCTU members thrust themselves into the affairs of Native Americans, Native American women also reached out to the WCTU in order to curtail alcohol abuse in their communities. Since Native-initiated connections occurred locally, with town, county, or state unions as their point of contact, a national institutional commitment to Native Americans was not always necessary. That is, Indian WCTUs did not require the existence of a national department, though it certainly made Indian work more effective. That institutional commitment to Native Americans wavered frequently. Within the WCTU organizational structure, Native American work could take a variety of forms. For instance, a union in a community close to a reservation might bring Indian women into their chapter or organize a union on a nearby reservation and help the woman become self-sufficient. These were localized efforts, however. The gold standard was to have a national department dedicated to Indian work. Although some departments were constitutionally required, it was usually the national executive committee that created, consolidated, or eliminated departments as the committee members saw fit. The executive committee would nominate superintendents, who were then elected by the delegates at the national annual meeting.[12] Other departments also had a strong hand in Indian work. The desire to target Indian children had long pervaded missionary work since the colonial times and continued through the Indian educational efforts of the late nineteenth century. Therefore, the

WCTU's children's and young adults' wings—the Loyal Temperance Legions (LTLs) and Young People's Branches (YPBs)—often took a leading role in Indian work.[13]

Indian work was sometimes bundled with other WCTU initiatives in curious ways. In 1879 it was proposed at the annual meeting that work among Indians be undertaken in a subcommittee entitled "Indians, Chinese, and Colored People," which was housed in the division called Evangelistic Work. This grouping reflected a general desire to help nonwhites but failed to account for the vastly different experiences, goals, and legal statuses of the different groups. According to the historian of economics Thomas C. Leonard, Progressive Era reformers believed that "the savage races were like children, their development arrested at an evolutionary stage that the superior races had progressed well beyond. And, like children, the savage races were incapable of self-government, requiring the paternalistic protection of their betters."[14] The coupling of Indians and Chinese in the same office reflected the eugenicists' logic that the non-Christian background and the Asiatic origins of the groups made them similar. Adding African Americans to the configuration made sense in this logic due to their being nonwhite.[15] The ineffectiveness of this bundling would become apparent soon enough.

Once a national department was established, it was expected that the states would each create their own department of the same title, if the state deemed it applicable to their circumstances. The state department would, in turn, write reports to the national office describing their activities and accomplishments. National and state superintendents sent out questionnaires or "blanks" soliciting specific information from their subsidiaries. These often formed the basis of the national leaders' reports, assuming they received responses. The first instinct among national WCTU leaders was to connect with the leadership of the Five Tribes in Indian Territory and to encourage the "federal government to see that liquor laws were enforced on the reservations."[16] The Five Tribes (Cherokee, Choctaw, Chickasaw, Creek, and Seminole) were well known to reformers; they were comparatively populous, had organized governments and written constitutions, and were thus good candidates to promote temperance work and suffrage. The executive committee separated the groups from within the Indians, Chinese, and Colored People Department, and Indians received their own department. In 1881 Mary Stapler, Cherokee and daughter of the future superintendent Jane Stapler, was appointed superintendent of Work Among Indians.[17] In 1882 the office was discontinued after Mary's untimely death.[18] But then, in what was becoming a sporadic ritual, it was re-created in late 1883 or early 1884.[19]

The new superintendent was Harriet Calista Clark McCabe, of Delaware, Ohio, who was a member of the Woman's Home Missionary Society of the Methodist Episcopal Church, the editor of their newspaper *Woman's Home Missions*, and secretary of their Indian department. At the time she took the position in the WCTU she was also the chairman of the Western Religious Press for the WNIA, and shortly thereafter the WNIA even created a "Committee on Friendly Relations with the National Women's [sic] Christian Temperance Union," with Mrs. J. R. Jones as chairman. By 1885 the WNIA had changed the title of that office to "Fraternal Relations with WCTU," and McCabe was chairperson of the committee.[20] She was knowledgeable about the Oklahoma Methodist missions and was a reasonable choice for the position in the WCTU.

In 1886 the WCTU abolished the department, determining that it was "wiser to conduct the work through the Woman's [sic] Indian Association and by circulation of literature."[21] Yet, in 1901, the department was born again. The *Union Signal* noted, "this is one of the newest lines of work adopted by the National WCTU, the department having been adopted at the Ft. Worth Convention in 1901."[22] The promoter for the new manifestation of the department was Dorothy Cleveland of Oklahoma Territory. She was a very capable leader, but she passed away in 1903, leaving a vacancy for the next two years. While work among Indians went on between 1903 and 1905, there was weak national leadership owing to her death. The department was listed in *Annual Meeting Minutes*, but no superintendent was listed and no reports were submitted.[23] Another writer suggested again in 1905 that an office entitled "Work among Foreign Speaking Peoples, Colored Peoples, and Indians" be established, apparently unaware that the vacant office still existed on paper.[24] After 1905 the department was taken over by the energetic and effective Dorcas J. Spencer who greatly strengthened the department, expanded its activities, and wrote thorough and detailed reports and pamphlets. Work Among Indians existed as its own department until finally being absorbed by the Department of Christian Citizenship in 1916, reflecting the drive to get Congress to declare all Native Americans citizens of the United States and an assumption about the Christian origins and destiny of the United States.[25]

Despite the chaos in the administration of the various American Indian-oriented departments at the national level, much activity occurred at the state and local levels. The national leadership encouraged the state chapters to mimic the departmental structure of the national organization, but they could also add and subtract departments as needed. The same held true for county and local unions. Therefore, a county or municipality with a measurable Native American population might have an active Department for Work Among Indians even if the national department was inactive or nonexistent. Furthermore, Native American women's efforts could be as effective as any outreach by the local or national officers. Native American women themselves often initiated the creation of chapters, although by definition this meant connecting to the WCTU's primarily white state and national officers, since they were expected to pay dues (unless exempted due to financial hardship), submit reports, and respond to various surveys. That is, Native American women who joined the group and especially those who led chapters or took up other offices gave themselves a good deal of work to do: collecting dues, writing reports, cajoling others for their reports, garnering support for meetings and events, and completing dozens of other administrative duties that might be a headache if there was no reward. Yet, they joined the WCTU and took up leadership roles. This book begins by looking at how and why Native American women chose to put their efforts into this framework.

In chapter 1 we look primarily at Native American women's own words for why they joined the WCTU and what they hoped to accomplish through joining or supporting the organization. These words, however, were usually recorded in official reports to state or national headquarters, in interviews with reporters, in WCTU pamphlets, or in public speeches delivered to white or mixed audiences. In them we can discern the differences between Native American and Euro-American women's views on temperance, Indian citizenship, the prospect for tribal survival, and other matters; however, there was pressure on Native leaders in the WCTU to keep the tone diplomatic if not downright deferential. Native American commentary on alcohol, temperance, and politics are present in the first person, but other times were recorded through the filters of white reporters—who were sometimes men, sometimes women. More radical and critical perspectives may have lain below the surface of the documents. With these journalistic filters there is also the perennial problem of cross-cultural communication, where the recorder may have missed subtle metaphors or muted deviation from what he or she expected or wanted to hear. Nonetheless, the argument in chapter 1 is that Native American women's attraction to the WCTU reflected a path of acculturation and assimilation that many had already been on but, at the same time, revealed a desire to protect their communities, assert women's roles in politics, and develop Native American boys and girls who would become political leaders in their communities in ways that reflected community traditions.

On the one hand, Indian women who assumed WCTU leadership positions resembled their white counterparts. They were Protestant Christians and often well educated. Some were missionaries or teachers and saw citizenship, Euro-American-style education, and participation in the industrial or commercial agricultural economy as important for Native Americans moving forward and at times even vocalized beliefs in racial hierarchy. Yet, their sense of urgency about the alcohol problem in Native American communities was more personal than that of white women, though both groups shared a belief in a peculiar Indian "thirst for firewater." Both groups of women agreed on the historical roots of their communities' susceptibility to alcohol abuse along with a knowledge of key Indian leaders' historical temperance efforts. Native American women differed from white women in their commitment to maintaining the identity of Native American communities and their greater tolerance for traditional religions and Native revitalization movements. They had an understanding of historical wrongs that was deeper than even those whites with a keen sense of the past injustices of the United States toward Native peoples could appreciate. Outside of WCTU leadership, Native American WCTU unions had some particular traits and even peculiarities. In some tribes there seemed to be more male involvement in the WCTU chapters or "unions." Indian unions had particularly strong participation in the children's LTLs and their related medal contests and temperance musical bands. Many elements of WCTU material culture generally—medals, banners, ribbons, and other items—also seemed to have been especially important in Native American WCTU chapters. These traits indicate how Native American tribes participated in the WCTU differently; the subtle nature of those differences indicates how much Native American women and white women had in common.

In chapter 2 we will discuss Native American women's activities and involvement in the WCTU, particularly their work in improving enforcement of existing legislation, influencing state and federal policies, their role in the Oklahoma Territory–Indian Territory merger, and the effect their participation had on women's lives as political actors in benevolent organizations and government. In order to get at the ideas of tradition, I employ ethnographic and theoretical writing about particular tribes or nations, employing Native and some non-Native authors to explain themes and traditions that illuminate the cultures of the historical authors under study.

If understanding the Native authors' perspectives and biases is important, so too is considering the perspectives of the white women who captained the organization. In chapter 3 we examine the white-authored WCTU literature, with an emphasis on the viewpoints, biases, and prejudices contained therein. There was a range of visions that white leaders had for Native Americans in the United States from 1874 through 1933. One strain was reminiscent of the vicious racism and exterminationist tendencies from the eras of westward expansion and the Plains Wars. Another strain was part of the assimilationist bent of many progressive reform organizations that sought preservation of individual Indians and their individual identities, but that also sought to squash tribal cohesion, community identities, traditional religious practices, and Native American languages. Yet there was a third, subtle strain of white reformers that encouraged protection for Native land bases, disclosed historical wrongs, and showed tolerance for some religious traditions and innovations. A desire to prohibit alcohol in Indian communities held these three competing strains together, but the three overlapping strains caused tension when it came to considering how to include Native Americans in Indian work and how to support other Native-centered policies. These competing visions motivated, shaped, and restrained WCTU workers' policy efforts and activities on the ground in Native American communities.

In chapters 4 and 5 we cover the WCTU's efforts to organize unions on reservations and to affect state and national Indian policies, especially pursuing legislative protections for Indians and employing Indian men and women in national and state-level suffrage fights. The WCTU was committed to connecting with Native American youth, and its leaders were well connected to the various types of Indian boarding and day schools across the nation, including federal, state, tribal, and denominational facilities. Documents coming out of boarding schools, essential information for chapter 6, were produced under the watchful eyes of white administrators and so make it difficult to discern the students' deeply held views. However, their essays and assignments, the OIA reports, and other boarding school records reveal how the WCTU interfaced with the Indian schools and tried to shape Native American students into sober and industrious US citizens.

The story concludes with a series of events that made the WCTU less relevant to Native Americans and in the United States, generally. The 1920s and

1930s were an era of transformation in Indian policy, capped by John Collier's Indian New Deal in 1934, which largely ended the practice of allotment and the official goal of complete assimilation, at least temporarily. WCTU workers who wrote and acted during the 1920s reflected the competing trends in envisioning Native Americans: complete assimilation versus self-determination and cultural preservation, the eugenicist approach versus a cultural pluralist approach. While the trends were never 100 percent mutually exclusive (elements of each could be found in some policies), the WCTU, as part of a broader group of women Indian reformers, helped both those factions that sought self-determination and preservation and those factions that sought complete annihilation of tribal identities. Thus, within the WCTU, we can view the political, social, religious, and cultural ambiguities in the minds of both whites and Native Americans who would shape Indian policy.

One limitation to uncovering the experiences of Native American women in the WCTU is the secrecy that was maintained surrounding domestic violence, a corollary of alcohol abuse. Domestic violence is a common theme in WCTU literature. Cracking the role that incidents of domestic abuse played in individuals' participation in temperance organizations is an ethically sensitive endeavor and poses some epistemological problems. But abuse often lies beneath the surface of many first-hand accounts. When speaking to Native American people who know of their family histories it is fairly easy to get at things like occupations, accomplishments, and church affiliations. It is more dangerous to pose the seemingly innocuous question: Why did a relative get involved in temperance organizations? Had she been abused by a drunken spouse or other relative? Was she a witness to it within her family? There are more practical problems when discussing domestic violence from deeper in the past. Most published studies of domestic violence in Native American communities tend to focus on more recent eras. Those like women's studies scholar Kimberly Robertson's (Mvskoke) study of Lakota efforts to stop domestic violence look primarily at the last quarter century.[26]

Earlier historical examinations of domestic violence focus mostly on white communities where court records may capture violence that reached the legal process. Prosecution of domestic violence was rare in those communities, and rarer in Native American communities. Sometimes in historical sources the story of domestic violence lies right beneath the surface, even if it bubbles up only occasionally with a probing newspaper interview or other document.[27] Religious studies scholar, Michelene F. Pesantubbee, describing alcohol-fueled violence in the colonial period, suggests, "although little information is available on the effects of the trade in alcohol on Choctaw women, it is reasonable to assume that increased violence also included violence toward women." However, the historical record is still plagued by unsatisfyingly vague information regarding alcoholism, disease, and violence resulting from abusive drinking as experienced by women.[28] Investigations into temperance societies offer a lens to get at the historical roots of domestic violence in underrepresented groups, particularly Native Americans. It was almost certainly a reason for women's decisions to join the WCTU, if only a few people said so publicly.

Relationship to Previous Scholarship

A quarter century ago, the historian Donald Parman referred to the turn of the twentieth century through World War I as the "crest of unchallenged assimilation."[29] Parman was right that World War I was a tipping point in the federal government's assimilative goals, but his assertion that "the Indian was primarily a bystander, seldom a participant, often a victim, and rarely a beneficiary of the progressive reforms" is less convincing.[30] What the current examination of the WCTU and its white and Native American leadership shows is that even among those Native Americans who adopted Christianity, borrowed a Euro-American style of dress, learned English, and attended boarding schools, there existed a powerful impulse to preserve the central elements of their traditions. Thus, while Native Americans may have been "rarely . . . beneficiar[ies] of the progressive reforms," they were also rarely "bystander[s]," and they were, most assuredly, "participant[s]" in their own histories.

Recent historians studying Native American women during the Progressive Era have been more conscientious of the complexities of Native women's assimilationist veneers and their desires to shape their own futures. In part, the underlying *complexity* of Native American women's responses had to do with the apparent *invisibility* of the progressive Indian women's resistance. In her study of the writings of Native American and white reformers, the literary scholar Siobhan Senier argues that "recovering resistance to Indian assimilation is difficult . . . because the artists who addressed assimilation critically were not primarily concerned in representing tribal practices for the non-Indian readers who comprised much of their audience." Instead, she explains, "assertions of Indian sovereignty and legitimacy . . . exist in women's work . . . alongside moments that seem to advocate or accept assimilation or at least to accept non-Indian values and practices."[31] The WCTU was an influential part of the

Figure 1. Lilah Denton Lindsey (Creek) (1860–1943). Last Indian Territory WCTU president before the merger of Indian Territory and Oklahoma Territory unions in 1908. (Unknown photographer. Courtesy of Tulsa Historical Society, Tulsa, OK. Photograph number 2012.003.154.)

Figure 2. Harriet Calista Clark McCabe (1827–1919). Founder of the Ohio WCTU. Superintendent of the Department of Work Among Indians for the national WCTU, 1884–1886.
(Unknown photographer. Courtesy of Frances Willard Memorial Library and Archives, Evanston, IL.)

Figure 3. L. Jane Stapler (Cherokee) (1825–1895). Vice president of Indian Territory WCTU, 1883–1887, and first president of the Indian Territory, 1888–1895. (O. W. Osborn, Photographer. Courtesy of Frances Willard Memorial Library and Archives, Evanston, IL.)

Figure 4. Dorothy Cleveland (1857–1903). President of Oklahoma Territory WCTU and superintendent of Work Among Indians, 1901–1903. (Unknown photographer. From Abbie Hillerman, *History of the Woman's Christian Temperance Union of Indian Territory, Oklahoma Territory, State of Oklahoma, 1888–1925* [Sapulpa, OK: Jennings Printing and Stationery, 1925], 35. Courtesy of Frances Willard Memorial Library and Archives, Evanston, IL.)

Figure 5. Dorcas Spencer (ca. 1841–1933). Superintendent of the Department of Work Among Indians, 1905–1916. (Unknown photographer. Courtesy of Frances Willard Memorial Library and Archives, Evanston, IL.)

Figure 6.   Annie K. Bidwell (1839–1918). Officer in WCTU of Northern California.
Spearheaded WCTU efforts in the Mechoopda Indian village. (Photographer: Marceau.
Courtesy of Frances Willard Memorial Library and Archives, Evanston, IL.)

progressive tide. However, beneath the surface, Parman's "wave of assimilation" was a more complicated, contested, and incomplete process than we often
recognize. As demonstrated in chapters 1 and 2, the longevity of some Native
American women's commitment to the WCTU will provide even more opportunities to witness these assertions of sovereignty and identity within an organization that had an air of unadulterated assimilation.

This work is not only interested in Native American women's roles in
creating the twentieth-century world but is also interested in the roles and
influence of white women as shapers of Indian policy and alcohol legislation in
the Progressive Era. Women reformers' roles in federal Indian policy have been
brought to light in some fairly recent scholarship. However, the interplay of the
WCTU with Native American lives and federal policy has not been sufficiently
emphasized or even acknowledged, despite the well-established historical relationship between Native American alcohol use and federal prohibitory schemes
to curtail Indian drinking. In her 2009 article on John Collier's forbearer Stella
Atwood, the historian Karin L. Huebner describes her as "the major force
behind the national GFWC [General Federation of Women's Clubs] campaign
for Indian policy reform." She argues that women reformers of the 1920s and
1930s played a prominent role in pushing against allotment of Indian lands.
Huebner notes, "previous scholarship on both the women's clubs and on Indian
reform has seriously underestimated the importance of the women's clubs in
the passage of the New Deal Indian reform legislation."[32] A similar claim could
be made against scholarship on the WCTU and their role in Indian policy. Their
members were involved in letter-writing campaigns to elected officials, appeals
to Indian agents and missionaries, and outreach to tribal governments. They
even initiated undercover operations against bootleggers. A few WCTU members were involved in the GFWC in the same regions where Atwood was active
and may have been involved in influencing Collier's New Deal ideas, too, since
his intellectual mentor had been deeply involved in places like Riverside,
California, which had a strong WCTU presence.[33]

Women's involvement in Indian reform efforts have been discussed by historians, most thoroughly by Cathleen Cahill and Valerie Sherer Mathes, especially regarding women in the federal Indian service and the WNIA. In this
coverage, the WCTU, if it is mentioned at all, has generally been cast as playing
an ancillary role to the WNIA, despite substantial shared membership. Aside
from the fact that WNIA cofounder, and onetime WCTU organizer, Amelia
Stone Quinton, and the WCTU "were closely allied . . . on many issues," the

WCTU has not been seen as a driver or shaper of Indian policy or the lives of individual Native Americans.[34] However, with a much wider membership, earlier start, longer duration, and nearly equivalent political and church connections, the WCTU often partnered with these groups to participate in legislative and enforcement activities that affected laws, policies and personnel decisions in the Indian office, and law enforcement methods. WCTU members responded to federal circuit court and even Supreme Court decisions, sometimes seeking legislative remedies to those decisions with which they disagreed. Not only were they often the *primary* lobbyists and activists in some matters (especially those related to alcohol), they helped shape the thinking of tens of thousands of women about Native Americans. One advantage of the WCTU materials is that we do see Native American perspectives in them, albeit filtered ones. This contrasts with a limitation on using the WNIA to get at Native American ideas about progress. According to Mathes, "from the researcher's perspective, one finds little Indian voice in the WNIA literature, making it impossible to measure individual Indians' responses to the efforts of these women reformers."[35] The WCTU's wide array of publications, in addition to the unpublished writings of Native American women in the WCTU, communicate a select group of Native American women's ideas about their futures.

Although some trends changed over time in a linear fashion, there were often contradictory and competing messages held by group members at any given time, which created a basket of conflicting ideas within the WCTU. While there was a fairly constant faith in assimilation, citizenship, the promise of political equality, and private property manifested in allotment, beneath the surface (and presaging the end of "unbridled assimilation" of the 1920s) was another current, one that recognized the necessity and justice of an Indian land base, protection of Native spiritual traditions, and respect for Indian languages. The latter current was created or at the very least influenced by the presence of a substantial number of Native American women, not just as members but also as leaders in the WCTU with access to its resources, especially its communication and lobbying mechanisms.[36] Ultimately, this work delves deeper into the WCTU sources to amplify the muted role of the WCTU in Indian reform efforts and of Native American women in the WCTU, to correct the limited coverage of the WCTU in discussion of Progressive Era's Native American reform movements.

This work also fits into a broader discussion about the institutional history of the WCTU and of temperance movements in general. In 1991 Ian Tyrell, author of *Woman's World/ Woman's Empire: The Woman's Christian Temperance Union in International Perspective, 1880–1930,* noted that "the WCTU's Indian reform activities have not been closely studied." With few exceptions, his claim still holds true today. One important exception is the historian Izumi Ishii, who has written extensively on temperance efforts among the Cherokee. Ishii's book, entitled *Bad Fruits of the Civilized Tree: Alcohol and the Sovereignty of the Cherokee Nation,* traces the complex ways in which the Cherokee tried to claim control over the management of alcohol in their communities. She explains the role that certain Cherokee women, especially Jane Stapler, played in the WCTU in Indian Territory and Oklahoma, and she rightly points to Oklahoma statehood in 1907 as a watershed year for Native Americans' activity in the WCTU. In a more recent chapter on the subject, she prematurely sounds the death knell for WCTU's Indian activity in Oklahoma when she indicates that, in the process of merging Oklahoma Territory and Indian Territory into a single state, "the WCTU eliminated from its own organization a significant voice for reform."[37] Native American women, especially the Creek woman Lilah Denton Lindsey, remained active in the WCTU in the new state of Oklahoma for several more decades. Hundreds, and probably thousands, of others remained active through the Prohibition Era around the country and used the WCTU as a mouthpiece for a variety of reform efforts. Of course, since Ishii's work focuses on the Cherokee, other Native American communities are outside the scope of her project. In contrast, the present work seeks to widen the lens geographically and temporally on the WCTU but relies on the foundation Ishii has established.

Ishii also explains how some leaders such as the WCTU president Frances Willard, changed personal views over time: "While the WCTU was having a major impact on the Cherokee Nation and its citizens, the growth of the temperance movement in Indian territory changed the image of Native people among temperance reformers." Many changes in perspective were the result of involvement with Native American communities for the first time. Ishii continues, "National organizers who visited the Indian territory had all acquired a better understanding of Indian life, and they became defenders of Native people, especially Native women." From the white WCTU members' perspective, the Indian women's participation changed some of their minds, but Ishii overestimates how deep into WCTU circles the "enlightened view of Native American women" extended. For instance, in response to Stapler's speech at the convention in Atlanta in 1890, Ishii claims, "with her passionate address, Stapler had enlightened all white-ribboners present."[38] It might be more accurate to state that a certain number of women with close interactions with Native American women adjusted their rigid views on the level of literacy, material accomplishments, and racially based limitations on the abilities of Native Americans. Other white-ribboners clearly did not modify their racial animosities, prejudices, and respect for Native women's perspectives at all. This divide will be fleshed out in chapter 3.

Coinciding with what some scholars have described among Native Americans working in white-led organizations, some Native women internalized the same racial and cultural biases that white women possessed in a process of self-colonization. Cahill describes the thousands of American Indian employees, educated in boarding schools, who came to work for the federal Indian service and then aided in the colonial process, promoting acquisitiveness, Christianity, and the English language. These Indigenous Indian service employees also aided in creating a pan-Indian sentiment as people from one tribe then worked on the reservations of other tribes where they discussed their shared experiences.[39] The presence of educated Native American women, working for the schools, the federal government, or the churches did not eliminate anti-Indian sentiment. Many WCTU women—even those in Indian work—maintained the stereotype of drunken Indians and their inferiority as voters and citizens when compared to white women. They were skeptical of their religious traditions and religious innovations like the Ghost Dance, influential among the plains tribes, and the Indian Shaker Church, popular in the Pacific Northwest.

Other scholars have overstated the WCTU's institutional ignorance of their own organization's Native American efforts. The historian Patricia A. Schechter touches on the WCTU's use of banners and went so far as to claim that "the twenty-year existence of Indian Territory WCTU was subsequently ignored by the organization's official histories and has only just emerged in scholarly treatments of the otherwise well-studied WCTU." While her latter claim is true, the former is a slight overstatement. The jubilee year history by Elizabeth Putnam Gordon discussed the fear among the WCTU members of the end of an independent Indian Territory, though as Schechter rightly points out, the Indian chapters or "unions" in Indian Territory were not explicitly mentioned. However, the WCTU chronicler implies their existence. In a laudatory description of WCTU activity in the western states, Gordon mentioned the positive role that temperance instruction in Indian schools (an important WCTU achievement) had on Native American children. Helen E. Tyler's 1949 official history also discussed the establishment of the various manifestations of the Department of Work Among Indians. She included a list of the officers of Indian Territory, within an appendix of state and territorial officers, under the heading for Oklahoma. Included in the list of Indian Territory officers is "Mrs. Jane Stapler" followed by "(Cherokee Indian princess)," the stereotypical moniker for Native American women leaders at the time.[40] Official WCTU publications covered Native Americans extensively, though not always accurately or sympathetically (see chapter 3).

Another role that the WCTU's Department of Work Among Indians played in American history involves the history of Christianity in North America, especially the missionary organizations that were often the WCTU's means of entering Indian country. The Presbyterian, Methodist, Quaker, Congregationalist, Baptist, and Episcopal missionaries were prominent among the WCTU members who reached out to Indian communities. The ecumenical nature of mainstream Protestant denominations—and the downplaying of denominational difference or at least denominational division or conflict—was one effect of the WCTU's Indian work. Christian women, Native and white, expressed commonality rather than denominational distinctions. This ecumenical impulse did not extend to Catholics, Mormons, or Muslims, who were still seen as problematic in WCTU writing. It is no accident that the era of the fundamentalist critique of modern Protestantism coincided with the inclusionary efforts of the WCTU. The ecumenical nature of both the WCTU and the American Indian missions lent itself to a blurring of denominational lines between what would become known as mainline Protestant churches and played a role in the creation of new factions in Protestantism between fundamentalists and reform-minded, liberal, evangelical Protestants.[41]

There are some other considerations in terms of acculturation level of Native American WCTU participants that we must keep in mind. By the 1880s there were serious efforts on the part of the WCTU to reach out to Native American communities and complementary efforts on the part of Native American women to join and participate in the organization's many activities. However, many communities had long histories of missionary activity, intermarriage with whites, and the production of mixed-blood/full-blood and progressive/traditional factions. For some communities this process was just beginning; for others this process of colonization had been underway for centuries. When it comes to determining why Native American women joined the WCTU and the meaning of their participation, we must recognize these factions and understand that membership and leadership lay heavily (though not exclusively) on the side of the progressive and/or mixed-blood factions. However, as many recent Indigenous scholars have worked to point out, often controversially, Native American identity is not necessarily diminished or diluted by having mixed biological ancestry or by becoming Christian. Yet, the presence of Native American Christianity made people's identity—as Indigenous or American Indian or Native American or as a tribal or clan member—more complicated.

The thesis of this work is that the Native American women in the organization embraced a type of social, economic, and political progress that their white counterparts supported and recognized, but which held onto elements of sovereignty, self-determination, and cultural preservation that made Indian individuals and nations distinct—and they asserted their identities as Indigenous women, albeit as Christian and progressive Indigenous women. A secondary contention is that the WCTU's Indian work shines a light on multiple facets of white women's views of Native Americans and the spectrum of beliefs they held about Native Americans' place in the United States, politically, legally, culturally, and spiritually. In this we can see that progressive women, who were becoming increasingly politically influential, helped shape federal, state, and local Indian policies. By petitioning and personally persuading officials and legislators, encouraging temperance among tribal members and governments, and expending tremendous efforts on the education and development of children, the members of the WCTU were part of the wave of reformers that shaped Indian country in the late nineteenth and early twentieth centuries.

Chapter 1

Native American Women
and the WCTU

In 1905 Carrie Kendall Easterly provided the "First Annual Report for the Suffrage Department of the WCTU" in Indian Territory. She indulged in some common biases against Indians as she welcomed the WCTU members with a dose of sarcasm: "Dear Sisters, who have for your political equals, all the insane, the idiots, the criminals and the indians [*sic*] who are about to beat you in the suffrage race, greeting."[1] On the one hand, Easterly's ignorance of Native American women's role in the suffrage and temperance movements is understandable; American Indian women in the audience had been over-whelmed as white populations flooded the area. On the other hand, her choice of words is baffling. Not only was she in *Indian* Territory, but Lilah Lindsey, an enrolled member of the Creek Nation, would soon be elected president of the territorial WCTU and was hardly the first self-identified "Indian" woman who held a leadership position in the Indian Territory WCTU. Other Native American women, Tennessee "Tennie" Fuller (Cherokee), Jane Stapler (Cherokee), and Stapler's daughter Mary were all pioneers of the organization and were respected by other members. Upon Jane Stapler's death, the *Union Signal* published fond reminiscences of her visits to the annual conventions in Boston in 1891 and Denver in 1892, noting "her sons were accomplished young men and merchants, married to white ladies of high standing."[2] The Indian Territory union reported with great pride in 1897 that they had paid money to "have the name of our pioneer president, L. Jane Stapler, placed in the Temperance Temple at Chicago."[3]

While some leaders like Easterly made racist, exclusionary comments, others wrote admiringly about Native women and sought their inclusion in the WCTU. In such mixed company, how did Native American women navigate the organization? Why did they join in the first place? How did they view the suffrage campaign, considering that most Native Americans—whether men or women—lacked citizenship and the right to vote until 1924? Considering the particular challenges of alcohol in Native American communities, did they feel more urgency in their fight for national prohibition or for enforcement of the extant federal laws against selling alcohol in Indian communities? In this chapter and the next, we will see how Native women's activism within the organization changed the minds of white women and spurred changes in laws and enforcement practices.

Native Americans in this vanguard articulated various crimes and hypocrisies of white Americans toward Native Americans, recently and historically. Western civilization offered some attractive trappings (or trappings that they had been acculturated to value): Christianity, literacy, more comfortable housing, Victorian-era musical culture, and dress. Yet, these cultural elements had often been introduced in cruel and hypocritical ways. Alcohol was the greatest symbol of Euro-American hypocrisy, and it seemed omnipresent in the various frauds perpetrated by whites. The WCTU—with its emphasis on prohibition, voting rights for women, education of the young, Christian morality (meaning monogamy and sexual "purity")—seemed to be a reliable and reasonable partner in pursuing the best for the Native American communities while pushing back the worst of Western civilization.

Native American members shared some commonalities. In places like Indian Territory, Oklahoma Territory, and eventually the state of Oklahoma, participants tended to be of mixed ancestry; Cherokees and Creeks, especially, had family histories of intermarriage with white Americans. This imbalance in membership resembled what was described at the time as a divide between "mixed bloods" and "full bloods." Outside of Oklahoma, the primacy of mixed-bloods in WCTU leadership was not necessarily as pronounced, but the Native American WCTU leaders tended to have had comparatively positive, lifelong connections with the Euro-American community, particularly with missionaries, teachers, or other white philanthropists. These white connections were often WCTU members or supporters.

There were some points where Indian women and white WCTU members differed. While white WCTU members were often critical of US treatment of Indians, Indian women experienced more acutely the violence, the corrupt agents, the withheld annuities, the failure to protect communities from alcohol traders, and other law enforcement problems. Of course, white WCTU women's views varied, too, particularly in how they assessed the prospects and desirability of long-term survival of tribal governments and tribal identities. White women sought various means to dissolve those things, with few exceptions. Indian women generally sought to preserve those same things, while simultaneously promoting Christianity, citizenship, and full inclusion in US government, economy, and society.

Native American women revealed, explicitly and implicitly, their reasons for joining and the goals they hoped to accomplish. First, they saw drinking tearing apart the social fabric of their villages and towns and simply sought to stop it. Second, Native American women, and male educational leaders, were particularly attracted to the Loyal Temperance Legions and their promise to stem the tide of alcohol abuse, domestic violence, and social disruption at the earliest stages of development. Since older women led the LTLs, they may have been a substitute for matriarchal elements otherwise challenged under assimilationist efforts by whites, or perhaps they served as a way of reinforcing those matriarchal elements. Third, many Native American women were already Christians and were attracted by the ecumenical Christian message of the organization. Many female missionaries, or wives of male missionaries, were WCTU members, and they introduced Indian women to the organization and its methods. Fourth, other Native American women saw the WCTU's techniques for influencing legislation, liquor and non-liquor related, as a primary reason for joining. Influencing laws was a primary function of the broader WCTU.

In an ideal world, historians would have a journal entry for all the Native women involved in the WCTU, in which they discussed their reasons for joining, their hopes and goals, and their differences of opinion with white leaders. Instead, historians have an incomplete and not quite random sample of Native women from whom we can derive this information. Leaders who articulated their thoughts in writing were limited to those who were literate; however, non-literate people sometimes shared their opinions indirectly through Indian agents, reporters, or their literate Native American community leaders. Literate or not, their ideas were further filtered through white gatekeepers—editors of the *Union Signal*, local newspaper reporters, and occasionally translators. Many of the WCTU Indian members were anonymous; they are mentioned only as groups of people in the WCTU reports and other literature. Therefore, in this chapter and the next we rely heavily on the writings of (or interviews with) Lilah Lindsey (Creek), Jane Stapler (Cherokee), Tennie Fuller (Cherokee),

Martha Tunstall (non-enrolled Cherokee), Sophia Alice Callahan (Creek), Lydia Pierce (Onondaga), Eliza Pierce (Onondaga), and on some selections from anonymous members from the Warm Springs Reservation and other communities. Some Native American women who were closely allied with white women, like Maggie Alfonso (Mechoopda), displayed actions and motivations that are described through the pens and typewriters of deeply committed white WCTU members. There are also Native American men's accounts, which were shared in WCTU literature and thus echo or illuminate Native American women's concerns and struggles with alcohol and other WCTU agenda items. Together, these sources provide an imperfect picture of the reasons that Indian women joined the WCTU, but they do offer a picture worth considering, nonetheless.

Indian Roots of Temperance and the WCTU's Understanding of History

Native American temperance women did not appear from the ether; there were many Indigenous precedents in trying to curb alcohol consumption in or distribution to Indian communities. While late nineteenth-century Native American women might not have known about every temperance effort by earlier Native Americans, they collectively knew about many of them, including leaders and movements outside of their own tribal or regional traditions. Local histories were likely handed down orally within their communities. Some leaders, like Handsome Lake, sparked an ongoing ceremonial life in communities. People probably learned about distant movements through WCTU's temperance literature or from reading US history as students in the white-run schools or as adult consumers of popular historical literature. The recurrence and similarities of some of the Indian temperance stories and historical actors suggest that many probably came from WCTU literature. Sometimes Native American women cited previous temperance literature's discussions of Indian temperance efforts as part of their own personal inspiration, especially in the cases of Handsome Lake (Seneca), Cornplanter (Seneca), and Little Turtle (Miami).

One of the most comprehensive discussions of Native American temperance work from a Native American perspective came from Lilah Lindsey, who internalized an appreciation of Indian temperance shared by those deeply involved with WCTU Indian work. She was well educated in the Euro-American fashion and lived a comfortable life in Indian Territory. Lindsey had a long history with the Presbyterian missionaries of Indian Territory. Her mother, Susan McKellop Denton, was a nurse in Indian country. Lilah went to synodical school in Fulton, Missouri, then to the Highland Institute, Hillsboro, Ohio, and "graduated with honors in 1883." She taught at the Wealaka Boarding School northwest of Tahlequah and then relocated to the Tulsa Mission School where she taught from 1886 to 1887. She had married Colonel Lee W. Lindsey in 1884 and gradually "lost touch with the mission" after she stopped working there.[4] She played many roles in the WCTU throughout her career and was very influential in shaping others' views, especially about Native Americans.

The history of Native American temperance efforts informed her view of present and future efforts. Lindsey composed a "History of Indian Territory WCTU" in 1918. In her handwritten essay, probably delivered as a speech, Lindsey provided an acculturated, Christian Native American view of historical precedents. Indeed, her comparatively privileged position allowed her to draw the contrast for the audience between white and Native ways of retelling history: "In writing the history of most countries or organizations, there is usually a definite time or date for the beginning of things, but in dealing with any thing in conjunction with Indian history there appears but few dates or definite times when many important things were undertaken." Yet, as if to placate the audience's need for a tangible linear date, she changed course: "However, as early as Sept. 23rd, 1844, readers of Thorburn's *History of Oklahoma* will find a facsimile of an announcement in the *Cherokee Advocate* as follows. 'Annual Temperance Meeting . . . The Annual Meeting of the Cherokee Temperance Society will be held at Tahlequah, on Friday the 18th of October next: Addresses will be made both in the English and Cherokee languages.'" The meeting featured speeches and songs in both languages, Lindsey shared. She expressed pride at the involvement of children and key Cherokee political figures at the event.[5]

She then brought the audience deeper into the past, and far from eastern Oklahoma, to show the deep roots of Indian temperance efforts. She quoted from a 1916 issue of the *American Indian Magazine*, published by the Society of American Indians, a progressive Native Americans' group that included figures such as Dr. Charles Eastman/Ohiyesa (Santee Sioux), Dr. Carlos Montezuma/Wassaja (Yavapi), Luther Standing Bear (Oglala Lakota), Arthur Parker (Seneca), Laura Cornelius Kellogg (Oneida), and others. The issue contained two features dealing with temperance and Indians. One, the "Editorial Comment" section contained a piece entitled "The Temperance Issue" and served as the source of her insights into the long history of Indian temperance. She began by declaring, "we learn that during the sixteenth century the

American Indian endeavored to have prohibition of the sale of intoxicants to their people." Following suit, Jacques Cartier, Henry Hudson, the Pilgrims, and the Jesuits had tried to keep liquor from Indians. The second feature in that issue was a piece by the national WCTU Work Among Indians superintendent Dorcas Spencer entitled, "Indians and Prohibition," which discussed current temperance efforts across Indian country.[6] Lindsey quoted heavily from both, while interjecting her own commentary. Quoting from the editorial piece she shared that colonial and early national interactions between whites and Indians "awakened the taste of the red men and marked the beginning of a savage conflict. The use of rum by white men and by red men led to excess and bloodshed. Tens of thousands of native [sic] Americans perished because of the Evil drink. Of a keenly keyed nervous nature, and unused to resistance to the alcoholic poison the blood of the Indian surged wild when rum was spilled into it." This compelled Indian leaders to institute various protective experiments. She mentioned the Seneca prophet Handsome Lake, who "preached temperance" and Little Turtle, the Miami chief who "appealed to the legislature of Kentucky to pass laws restricting the infamous traffic."[7] Such stories of Indigenous political actors were most likely intended to encourage the audience members to unleash their own temperance activism.

Another favorite temperance advocate was Cornplanter, the half-brother of Handsome Lake.[8] New York superintendent of Work Among Indians Marian G. Peckham referenced Cornplanter "of temperance fame" in one of her reports. Dorcas Spencer's letter to the *Union Signal* of June 29, 1911, discussed a medal contest among the Senecas, whom she described as "the remnant of old Chief Cornplanter's tribe." Offering a generous interpretation of his role in temperance history Spencer implored the reader: "Let it not be forgotten that Cornplanter was the first itinerant temperance lecturer and teacher of total abstinence on this continent."[9]

The Indian precedents that Native American and white women both wrote about and whose stories were reprinted frequently formed a shared font of inspiration from which all temperance women could draw. Yet, white women rarely claimed a direct line of historical influence between their temperance origin stories and Native American temperance efforts. Northeastern, white, Protestant women usually traced their intellectual origin to Benjamin Rush's "An Inquiry into the Effects of Ardent Spirits upon the Body and Mind," first published in 1791. They claimed as their organizational ancestor the American Temperance Society, founded in 1826.[10] For them, American Indian temperance antecedents were admirable parallel trends from a different tradition. For Indian women these historical figures had been protecting the communities of their ancestors. Thus, the social fabric torn asunder through drinking, which those predecessors were trying to fix, was not just a distant, colorful, historical inspiration but, rather, of a more intimate nature. When Indian women joined the WCTU to save the social fabric of their community from the centuries-old scourge of abusive drinking they were participating in a long-standing tradition.

Drinking and the Social Fabric

Abandonment of and violence toward women and children, anathema to traditional values of almost all Native American cultures, went hand in hand with alcohol abuse, triggering cycles of generational trauma that were difficult to stop. Alcohol abuse in Native American communities by the 1870s was a serious problem, probably a greater one than in white communities (for whom it was also a challenge). But this historical truism deserves some interrogation, though the evidence seems overwhelming. Nearly every published tribal history that covers any period from the colonial period through the 1920s will have an index entry for "alcohol" or "whiskey" or covers the issue somewhere in the text. Assumptions about a physiological cause behind an Indigenous predilection for drinking were born in the colonial age and have persisted through the present. Recent interdisciplinary scholars have downplayed genetic or other biological causes of alcohol abuse. In Stephen J. Kunitz and Jerrold E. Levy's work, *Drinking Careers: A Twenty-Five-Year Study of Three Navajo Populations*, the authors demonstrate that education, access to wages, proximity to sources of alcohol, family context, and other factors were more important than inherited traits in shaping the "drinking careers" of Navajo individuals.[11]

In the present work there is no claim one way or the other about genetics and alcohol abuse. Psychologists, sociologists, anthropologists, and historians have engaged in many debates over the causes, nature, and extent of Native American drinking, some claiming that drinking has been overestimated or underestimated in historical ethnographic accounts. The debate often hinges on who was doing the observing in these writings. Some have claimed that drinking to the point of drunkenness was a method of resistance to colonialism. In this interpretation, drunkenness could actually be a method of defiance of Euro-American missionaries' and officials' expectations of drinking and thus was an anticolonial gesture using a tool of colonial origin. In this calculation, accounts might inflate the number of imbibing incidents that tribal communities themselves might have defined as socially acceptable drinking.[12] While defiance may have been a conscious or unconscious element of Native Americans' thinking about their drinking, even if true the defiance at times backfired or went too far and further tore apart families and tribal communities. Certainly, Native American women in the WCTU and even children saw drinking as a problem. If people within the community saw it as a problem and described it as such with overwhelming frequency, further theoretical gyrations are not really needed for us to conclude that alcohol caused social problems.

Native American women attempted to stem these problems, especially when they affected them directly, but histories of the attempts to curtail the illegal whiskey trade and such variations almost always take a male-centric approach. It was the chiefs and religious leaders who made the legal, political, or spiritual appeals to develop ways to prevent *outsiders* from introducing alcohol. While their role was undoubtedly essential, what lies below the surface is the women's responsibility in protecting their communities *internally*. When we scratch the surface, this is exactly what we find persisting into the twentieth century. The aversion to domestic violence—indeed it disqualified men in Haudenosaunee government from being chiefs—was a driving force behind participation in the WCTU. Especially when we consider the matrilineal and matriarchal aspects of so many tribes (especially the Iroquois, Cherokee, and Creek that are so prominent in the temperance record), one finds, unsurprisingly, women playing an active role in protecting family and community.[13] One woman's story highlight's this role.

Around 1904 Eliza Pierce, the founder of the WCTU on the Onondaga Nation, was interviewed for a local Syracuse paper. The topic was her seemingly dying husband, Jairus Pierce, who had been prominent in New York State Indian affairs. The issue was a complicated one: the disposition of his property after his looming death. There had been a dispute between his first wife, Lucy Two Guns, and his present wife, Eliza. The reporter explained that "[Jairus] Pierce was at that time [of his separation from his first wife] living in a small cabin upon the site of his present house. . . . [A]fter a time, he took unto himself another wife, Mrs. David Webster, *whose previous husband had treated her badly*, she says [emphasis added]."[14] Mrs. David Webster was now Eliza Pierce, and the article went on to praise Eliza's upbringing in a white family who taught her thrift, Christianity, and all the other trappings of Euro-American civilization that led to the couple's rise within the Onondaga Nation. Fortunately, Jairus survived his illness and lived another nineteen years until he died in 1923 at age eighty-eight.[15] Another newspaper account went further, stating that the separation between Eliza and David Webster was because "he was abusive to her."[16] Around the time of her separation from Webster, she joined the Onondaga Nation's branch of the IOGT called the Konoshioni Lodge, which had been founded in 1877. Eliza even became "Vice Templar" of the lodge.[17] Why temperance? Why soon after her separation from her first husband? The answer seems self-evident.

Legal protection from domestic violence was probably not Eliza Pierce's expectation when she joined the IOGT. Prosecution of domestic violence was rare in white communities, rarer still in Native American ones. A more likely expectation was the personal reformation of drinkers. The IOGT emphasized redemption and opened its leadership to women, a break from previous temperance organizations. IOGT members mimicked Masonic rituals, sang both hymns and popular songs, and performed elaborate ceremonies, all of which attracted the working classes, the young, and the otherwise disenfranchised. Unfortunately for the IOGT, many members left in the 1870s and 1880s for other temperance groups, including the WCTU, which moved beyond redemption of the drinker and mustered social pressure to encourage laws against alcohol sale and distribution, which it saw as the cause of most domestic violence.[18]

The WCTU's answers to violence, alcohol abuse, and poverty in Native American communities were Christianity, capitalism, and citizenship. While authors sometimes noted the irony of acculturation being coupled with drinking, they tended to blame drinking on poorly behaved whites who set a bad example with their drinking habits, which was why state and national prohibition laws were essential. If no one drank, no one could be a bad influence. They often overlooked the trauma of acculturation that was part of the reason people drank. The *Union Signal* told the story of Sam Morris, a Carlisle Indian School graduate who had been charged but acquitted of forging checks in Seattle, Washington. His troubles began when his father encouraged him to acculturate. "When I was very small my father said to me: 'It is no good to continue in the Indian way. The Indian must follow the white man's way.' So we gave up the tepee. We dressed as white men and white women dress. My father did not hunt as his fathers had done. He bought land, and ploughed it, and raised crops, and sold them." Then, in line with the WCTU upbraiding bad whites, he concluded, "And I—because I wanted to follow the way of the white men—drank whisky."[19] Although Morris would not have used the more recent language of "generational trauma," this was precisely what was beneath the surface in his testimonial. Embedded in his passage is a clear statement how each generation stepped away from their traditions, culminating in the boarding school experience, which itself had a poisonous effect and sparked abusive drinking.

And yet, there was the expectation that the WCTU, a firm supporter of acculturation and boarding schools, was inviting for Indian women. The assumption was that their identities as women and as witnesses to alcohol abuse would supersede their identities as members of Native American communities, ignoring that it was precisely the kind of attitudes toward Native Americans that led to the isolation, anomie, and depression that contributed to that alcohol abuse. Indeed, they were expected to take a step away from their traditions to receive the benefits of Christianity, civilization, and WCTU sisterhood.

Witnessing domestic violence and generational trauma led Native American women to try to stop the cycle in their children for the future. A generation earlier than the Morris case, developments on the Warm Springs Reservation in Oregon demonstrated how concern for children stimulated temperance activity. Warm Springs is home to three distinct but confederated tribes, the Warm Springs proper, the Wascoes, and the Paiutes. By the end of the nineteenth century, children's lives were very difficult on the reservation. Children were dying of tuberculosis at very high rates and people feared for their health. The WCTU offered some hope.[20] Oregon's state Indian work originated before the second phase of the national department in the twentieth century. Although there was no state Department of Work Among Indians until 1895, in 1889 the Department of Young Women's Work began to reach out to Native American communities.[21]

In 1892 the Oregon WCTU chose to have the annual convention in the remote town of Pendleton, near the Umatilla Reservation.[22] In 1895 they established a department of Indian work and the Presbyterian field missionary, Jeanette C. Alter, of Warm Springs, was named superintendent. Although she apparently did not attend the convention that year, she submitted a letter that was read at the meeting. The Warm Springs community had already developed a union of their own in 1894, and the letter contained their sentiments. By 1895 they had fifty-five members, making it the third largest single union, white or Indian, in the entire state. The convention agreed that "a letter of greeting be sent them from 'The Great Meeting' and that we send to them badges enough so that each Indian may have one; this by a rising vote."[23] The letter—reprinted in the minutes and signed by Lizzie Kants, secretary of the Warm Springs union—apparently contained translations of the words of Warm Springs' WCTU members. Alter explained, "these are extracts from the speeches of some of our prominent Indian men and women—not one of whom can read or talk English. . . . The star on their banner is no unmeaning symbol—the light *has* reached them [emphasis in original]." Generational concerns attracted them to that light: "They tell us that we are a dying race, but whiskey will kill us faster than anything else. It is killing all the tribes. I am glad that our people are taking a stand against whiskey; we do not want our young people to become drunkards." Another woman expressed her fear for her children. She linked the promise of protection of the children with Christianity: "Whiskey is bad enough for us, but I am thinking what it might bring upon my children. Let us teach them what the Bible says about whiskey." Aside from the fact that the distillation of alcohol had not been popularized when any of the Bible's books were written (and thus whiskey did not yet exist), it is clear the women had become positively disposed toward Christianity, even though the scriptures and sermons would have to be translated.[24]

The Warm Springs union continued to succeed in recruiting members. Handwritten minutes from the state convention in 1896 indicate that WCTU officers Lucia H. Faxon Additon and Helen D. Harford had been active at Warm Springs. The Indian union "had sent an elegant banner to decorate the convention room." The white attendees, recognizing the impressive growth of the Warm Springs union, "resolved that greetings be sent *to the largest Union in the state* from this convention with this message 'Blessed is that Nation whose God is the Lord, and the people whom he hath chosen for his own inheritance,' Psa. 33–12 [emphasis added]." The committee made appropriations for Indian work amounting to three dollars.[25]

The messages within Kants's letter contained symbolism that was common in Indian messages about temperance. One speaker declared, "years ago we were at war with our enemies, but we have found whisky our worst enemy and more to be dreaded than anything else."[26] The association of the war on whiskey with historical intertribal conflicts, clashes with the US army, and mythical battles against evil forces were common in Indian temperance speeches and imagery. After a visit to the Tuscarora Nation, Niagara County president Emma Graves Dietrick described a banner, which was interpreted by a Mr. Mount Pleasant. The county convention had been held on the reservation that year. The banner, reflecting the founding of a Tuscarora Temperance Society in 1844, contained stars representing each of the Six Nations, and then:

> a row of pictures of animals, bear, tortoise, beaver, wolf, eel, and plover. These were the clans of the tribe and each was in danger from the strange animal above it, for in the center of this banner was an octopus or devil fish, with eight arms reaching out for its prey. This our friend called "the liquor beast" and said. "It is always trying to get my people." Perhaps the most remarkable feature of the banner was an American eagle which was standing on the body of the "liquor beast." "This," said Mr. Mount Pleasant, "is American government; it must kill the liquor beast and save my people." The eight arms of the beast were named, "hard cider," "beer," "gin," "whisky," etc., and strong emphasis was laid on the power of the "American eagle" to kill the "liquor beast."

The stars and the clans effectively symbolized the political entities of tribes and the familial entities of clans. Alcohol was a threat to both, and Dietrick explained that the Tuscaroras hoped for governmental protection in the anticipated constitutional amendment: "We were impressed by the fact that National Constitutional Prohibition was thus symbolized by the 'Tuscarora Temperance Society' seventy years ago. Was this not indeed a prophetic banner?"[27]

The symbol of a violent enemy representing the alcohol scourge and its damning effects on polity and family was common in Native Americans' temperance discourse, and these Native American women wanted to rejuvenate their communities. The WCTU promised a means to patch this broken social fabric. Both Native and white women agreed that doing so required beginning with the children, and the WCTU's front line in the fight against alcohol was the martially named Loyal Temperance Legion.

Loyal Temperance Legions

Loyal Temperance Legion came about in 1886 largely through the effort of Anna A. Gordon, the personal secretary to Frances Willard and future WCTU president. LTLs were small, local temperance unions of school-aged girls and boys, led by adult WCTU members. While they offered wholesome activities to keep children away from drinking, there was a longer-term strategy behind them. The LTL's motto was "Tremble King Alcohol for We Shall Grow Up," meaning that boys would reach maturity, vote for prohibition candidates, or run for office themselves. Young girls who reached majority age would do the same if universal suffrage passed but, in the meantime, would join the WCTU as full members. Men could only become honorary members of the WCTU. The most celebrated activities of the LTLs were medal contests, in which participants delivered a memorized speech before a crowd of other members, parents, and community residents. Depending on the complexity of the speech and the children's previous experience these could either be silver medal contests for beginners or gold medal contests for more advanced students. Gold medal contests drew crowds from neighboring unions and offered entertainment in small rural communities. For Indian reservations, these events took on special meaning. Prominent local people were invited; businessmen, ministers, and politicians were regaled with the accomplishments of the civilization process. Speeches were often on temperance-related topics but could also deal with social justice, religious themes, or current Native American matters.[28]

For Indigenous women, and especially those from matriarchal political cultures, this idea of grooming young males to become future political leaders had a long precedent. This becomes extra clear when we consider how LTLs functioned in Haudenosaunee communities. In March 1903 the *Union Signal* commented favorably on the Onondagas' work under Eliza Pierce and especially on their formation of LTLs. The *Union Signal*'s authors claimed that the Syracuse Union No. 2 was

> finding a field for its efforts, and the reward of accomplishment, in work among the Onondaga Indians. The members have been assisted in this work by the Methodist pastor and the superintendent of the day school on the reservation. The Hiawatha union has just celebrated its first anniversary and the meeting was attended by visitors from all the other Syracuse unions. A concert was given by the Indian children, and at its close a Junior L.T.L. was organized.[29]

The LTLs struck a deep cultural chord with Haudenosaunee adults. "Their leader, the principal of their school, read of the L.T.L. in *The Union Signal* and at once realized that it was just what his young people needed. He called some W.C.T.U. members to help him organize. This legion is prosperous and we are hoping to have their male quartette at our state convention."[30] Marvin Crouse, the prominent Methodist pastor referred to, was also the head of the Onondaga chapter of the Six Nations Temperance Society.[31] This system of future male leaders of the society being groomed by the elder women in the community

Figure 7. "A local W.C.T.U. of Indian women in western New York." Likely Seneca Allegany Reservation WCTU women members along with LTL medal contest participants, boys and girls. (Unknown photographer. Courtesy of Humboldt County Collection, Photo #1999.07.3042, Humboldt State University Library.)

tapped into one of the most fundamental elements of the matrilineal system of the Haudenosaunee. For generations clan mothers had selected the men who would act as chiefs, and thus they were already accustomed to influencing the political system through the training of young men. Although the clan system and the Grand Council was operating independently of the WCTU, the persistence of women's influence on political leaders can be seen in this new introduction of the LTLs.[32]

Consider the photograph of the Western New York chapter of the WCTU (figure 7). The photo contains several generations of women and girls (with Lydia Pierce in the center of the three women in the second row), several boys but no men, following the policy of the WCTU for the LTLs. It also reflects the longer-standing Haudenosaunee tradition of the women's role in the preparation of young men within the community. Anyone who looks closely can make out the white ribbons affixed to the clothing of the older women and the medals pinned to the garments of the young medal contest participants.

The oratorical contests, concerts, and even the role of medals should not be overlooked as simply WCTU impositions. Among the Haudenosaunee, where oratorical skills were valued, this was a way of connecting traditions of the children to the contemporary message of Christian temperance. Describing the long-standing importance of speaking skills in Haudenosaunee tradition, Mohawk author Taiaiake Alfred asserts, "in a culture deeply respectful of individual autonomy, the only real political power exists in the ability to persuade. . . . The development of powerful oratorical abilities is imperative."[33] Oratorical skill had long been valued in Haudenosaunee men and would have been fostered in males from the time they were children.

Adding to the power of the LTLs was the use of medals as symbols of success. At one time the LTLs had an explicitly martial tone and included marching and drills for both boys and girls. The pacifists in the WCTU successfully purged those activities, but the medals remained, an artifact of the earlier militarism.[34] Prucha argues that medals were most powerful—spiritually and politically—in the Early Republic. Among the Iroquois, the most salient example of this earlier type of medal was Red Jacket's Peace Medal, given by the Washington administration to Red Jacket in 1792. After the Civil War medals became "simply rewards for good deeds or good behavior, or even prizes for minor accomplishments that had nothing to do with matters of state." Prucha continues, "there was a diminished feeling of the sacredness of the medals."[35] Yet, when we consider the phenomenon of young Haudenosaunee boys participating in the traditional oratorical arts, encouraged by the elder women of their community, it is clear that participants were tapping into something more important than Prucha recognized. While it is tempting to dismiss children's participation in a group as being coerced by missionaries or parents, one cannot discount the power of the temperance message, solidarity of like-minded youth, and perhaps even safety and protection of the LTLs. In 1908 Peckham reported on a New York medal contest where a Native American "child of a poor drunkard" won the contest. Perhaps children like this medal winner poured their efforts into the oratorical contests to combat the generational drunkenness and despair they witnessed around them.[36]

Other Native American communities also saw success among children. In 1891 the territorial reporter Laura Harsha wrote about Indian Territory, commenting that the region was "gaining ground" with two new unions, Vinita and Afton. She exclaimed that the "Loyal Temperance Legion of Atoka is in a flourishing condition. The Loyal Temperance Legion of Tahlequah is doing well, and is preparing for another medal contest."[37] In Hartshorne, "[K. L. E.] Murrow organized a Band of Hope." Bands of Hope were children's temperance organizations, distinct from the WCTU, but precursors and inspirations to the LTLs. They held a medal contest at Baptist Indian University at Bacone with ten participants. While the Tahlequah union was small, it was also energetic, and "The Band of Hope and Loyal Temperance Legion combined are well attended." The Afton members revealed the challenges to Indian unions but promised that the children's groups were the shining successes for organizers. Harsha explained, the "Afton union was organized September, 1890, with eight members; all but two were unacquainted with the work, but seeing the great need of something being done, made a beginning in much weakness, depending wholly on the Lord to show the union what to do, and give it wisdom and strength to do the work as unto Him." There were fourteen members, and they had been successful in getting saloons closed. Harsha wrote frankly of the impediments to their cause: "One great drawback are the corrupt morals of those in authority. Reporting seems to do no good, as the leading business men patronize the saloon and consequently do not use any influence against it." Placing the promise for sobriety back in the hands of youth, she declared, "Afton's stronghold is in its Band of Hope, which numbers forty-five, all under fourteen years of age."[38]

The Indian Territory unions supported its children's educational infrastructure. The Muskogee union accumulated enough funds to begin constructing a two-story building containing classrooms, an assembly hall, and a second-story library. They began with one-third of the requisite funds and were trying to raise the rest. Harsha, the Muskogee president, organized these efforts.[39] The building opened on January 4, 1892, and the *Union Signal* reporters delighted that "the new teacher has declared his belief in the triple pledge and will instruct his pupils in good temperance principles. Intoxicated men and boys are a common sight upon the village streets and cause much anxiety to the earnest temperance workers."[40] The same year Tennie M. Fuller, the corresponding secretary of Indian Territory, submitted the report commenting positively on the work of the "five old unions" whose accomplishments included "two reading rooms . . . the first of the kind in the Territory." They distributed literature, and "one union has its own building where they hold their meetings, have their reading-room and conduct a boys' school." The territorial union had been happy to have the aid of Ellen K. Denny, a dedicated organizer. "She delivered about twenty-five addresses and organized thirteen new unions. Only eleven of these are active, and only one has sent in an official report since first organizing." The hurdles of distance, lack of personnel, and poor infrastructure were the common impediments to longevity of the unions, yet "Nearly all unions are taking up juvenile work with success. We have thirteen Loyal Legions, with pledged membership of about five hundred and twenty."[41]

Native American women's responsibility for their children's preparation for future political life and for assuring their boys' morality as they approached manhood was part of both the matriarchal elements of many Native American communities and the nineteenth-century idea of the woman's domestic sphere being the locus of moral education and development.[42] There was substantial overlap between these notions, despite the more formalized political power and respect reserved for women's roles in most Native American communities. One realm in the Victorian American women's sphere of influence was particularly pronounced in their families' and especially their children's spiritual development. Women's church attendance was higher than men's, and many people saw Victorian women as having a special responsibility to ensure their family's adherence to Christian practice and morality.[43] The WCTU in Native American communities generally followed such assumptions, too.

Christianity: Sewing Together the Social Fabric

Although Native American women referenced their traditions, they were joining forces with a distinctly Christian temperance organization, and their attraction to Christianity and to partnership with Christian missionaries is essential to any understanding of their reasons for joining the WCTU. Native women in WCTU leadership positions all had preexisting, often familial, connections with whites. They identified as Christian and were often professed Presbyterians, Quakers, or Methodists—less frequently Baptists, Congregationalists, Episcopalians, or Catholics. Not satisfied for Christianity to remain only a personal belief system, Native American WCTU leaders saw the introduction or extension of Christianity into their communities as an important goal. Writing specifically about Pentecostalism in Native American communities, the historian Angela Tarango explains the importance of looking at how Native American women practiced Christianity in a way that allowed the colonizer's religion to act as a means of resistance. Tarango advocates moving beyond just the question of the legitimacy of Indigenous people's conversions—a dominant theme in much of the writing on Native American Christianity—and focusing instead on the actual practices of professed Native American Christians.[44]

Tarango's shift away from questioning the legitimacy of their faith is a welcome one, as is the emphasis on understanding religious practice. However, this should not lead us away from considering both practice and theological thinking among Native American Christians. For Native American women in the WCTU, engagement with the churches and the deity was indeed part of doing away with the negative baggage of Euro-American invaders. Their writings convey how much they internalized the specific brand of social gospel Christianity that existed among WCTU adherents. They saw God—not just the *worship* of God—as an essential part of the temperance movement. Many commented on God's providence in their temperance work and used this as a point of connection with their sisters in the WCTU. Indeed, the salvation of their communities from the colonizer's liquor required the assistance of the colonizer's God.

The WCTU's Department of Work Among Indians, the missionary wings of evangelical churches, and Christian Native Americans were practicing a type of social gospel, ecumenical Christianity that was going to be challenged by the emergence of fundamentalism in the 1910s. According to the historian George Marsden, World War I saw an "increasingly aggressive and ambitious character of interdenominational Protestant liberalism in the immediate postwar years" and helped cause a rift with those who rejected such liberalism, especially in missionizing efforts. "Here the suggestion of the more extreme liberals that God revealed himself in non-Christian cultures had profound implications for missionary programs" and was firmly rejected by emerging neo-orthodox Christians. The other idea, rejected by fundamentalists, that was common among social gospel-minded progressives was the idea of encouraging a "Christian Civilization," which would later be manifested in WCTU parlance as "Christian Citizenship."[45] The WCTU turned this concept into a department, which would absorb the Department of Work Among Indians in 1916. This basket of possibilities for the Christian Indian women meant that there was room for them to accept some Native traditions around them—the possibility that God may have revealed himself via the Ghost Dance, the Indian Shaker Church, Handsome Lake's Longhouse ceremonies, and others. Devout Christian Indians saw the social gospel thought of mainline Protestant Christianity and its promise of an improved, just, and sober world as the more attractive faith and practice.

Lydia Pierce, one of the most important Native American women involved in the WCTU, shared her Christianity clearly in her writings. Since she and the Western New York Native American communities were so important to Indian work in the WCTU, we must examine how the WCTU and her participation in it unfolded on the Western New York reservations. Born in 1862 Pierce expressed her faith in God's intervention in the temperance movement, in the spirit of the postmillennial social gospel Christianity. She first connected with temperance at the Quaker-run Tunesassa Boarding School, founded by the Society of Friends in 1852 on the Allegany Seneca Reservation, where she was a student in the 1870s, then known as Lydia Jackson before her marriage to Fred Pierce.[46] She became a member of the students' temperance society and for a time was interested in becoming a full member of the Quaker Meeting, though she apparently remained a Presbyterian the rest of her life.[47] Her close relationship with Christianity fueled her positive relationship with missionaries. The intertwining of the missionaries, Christian Native American women, economic development, temperance, and Native traditions would prove typical in the WCTU movement in Indian country.

Pierce at an early age became a proponent of economic development, as evidenced by her scholastic writings. She connected material success to temperance, linking changing housing styles and cultural development. Following the construction of several log homes in the Old Town area of the Allegany Reservation, "the Indians entirely abandoned their old habits." She then lauded the individual productive efforts of Iroquois men who farmed successfully: "John Mt. Pleasant of Tuscarora Reservation . . . raised last year 1500 bushels of oats and 1600 bushels of wheat, 500 barrels of apples, 300 barrels of peaches, . . . he has a beautiful farm of 200 acres. He owns two reapers, one mowing machine and two threshing machines." She continued, emphasizing the new Victorian-era gender roles, which were a break from the days when Iroquois women did the farming. "His wife who is a Seneca woman keeps the house neat and in order." She then laid out the threats to universal advancement: "I think the worst faults amongst us is [sic] laziness and intemperance. Cider seems to do more harm among men. It seems also to do more harm than whiskey. There we have formed a temperance society that would prevent drunkards to those who would keep the pledge which they have made. For there are many men who have met a drunkard's death."[48]

The center of temperance fervor was the Six Nations Temperance society, which had a strong following on the Tuscarora Nation, adjacent to Niagara Falls. Many white missionaries and federal officials were aware of the society.[49] Officials also commented on the strong temperance feeling among those at Allegany in 1882.[50] The preexisting Native Christian temperance society probably opened the minds of the population to participation in the WCTU. The first reference to an Indian WCTU chapter in New York State was in the *Union Signal*, which printed part of a report from the Cattaraugus County, New York, convention in 1884. "One of the oldest unions in the county is the one at Versailles—the dusky sisters of the forest on the [Cattaraugus] reservation. We hope that the more civilized women of the county will not allow these to lead in human reformation."[51] The last sentence reflects the author's desire to motivate whites to surpass their Indian sisters' work, implying that the lower expectations that white women held for Indian women should propel white women to act quickly in the cause of temperance. In September 1886 the Ontario County, New York, report was reprinted in the *Union Signal*. The convention had been held at the Presbyterian Church in Phelps, led by President Frances E. Perkins. She wrote, bragging of the magnanimity of the white WCTU members: "Even to the Indian reservation, in western New York, has Ontario county [*sic*] stretched out her hands."[52] The recipient of their benevolence was most likely one of the Seneca reservations in the western portion of the state or perhaps Tuscarora. At the Niagara County quarterly convention in 1889 in Hartland:

> A most novel and interesting feature of the convention was the presence of a white-ribbon brother from the Tuscarora Reservation W.C.T.U. and the words spoken to him ought to prove an inspiration to all who have more advantages than he. We are told that he is one of the brothers of the chiefs of his tribe. . . . The white ribbon which he so proudly displayed, was worn over a heart as loyal and true as any which beats under a whiter skin than his. There was a mixture of pathos and humor in the little speech he made, which touched every heart.

The reporter continued, describing the man's reason for joining the temperance fight: "My brothers all die of drink; I left alone; I hear of this convention, and I want to come see what these women doing." He then described the challenges of traveling to the convention, which he walked several miles to attend. The article's author then proclaimed, "we think this man a hero, and are proud to claim him as a brother. Where is the white brother who would do more than this?"[53] These rumblings of WCTU connections with Native American communities in New York took shape in the subsequent decade.

In September 1890 Erie County reported on their departmental work. They had established two new departments, including Work Among Indians.[54] Cattaraugus County elected Marian G. Peckham, of Leon, as its "commander" at the convention held at the Yorkshire Center First Baptist Church.[55] The follow-ing year, in a sign of support, the members of the county WCTU sent "Tele-grams of greeting . . . to the Six Nations Temperance League (Indian) then in session at Tuscarora Reservation."[56] By 1894 the WCTU was firmly entwined with the reservation politics and Iroquois Christian communities. A. W. Ferrin, Indian agent for the Western New York tribes, described the WCTU on Catta-raugus that started a movement "in favor of citizenship and allotment." The movement itself was "started by the WCTU on that reservation." They started a petition, but most on the reservation were opposed to allotment.[57] The impetus for the WCTU and the push for allotment were heavily supported by the Pres-byterian missionary Sarah Trippe. In 1894 the Niagara County convention met at the Methodist Episcopal Church in Lockport, presided over by county presi-dent Ruth A. Frost. "An Indian girl was present and gave a bright paper on phys-ical culture, following it up with an exhibition of the same. She was heartily applauded and obliged to respond to a recall."[58]

In 1896 the Indian agent J. R. Jewell provided a comprehensive roster of missionaries, Christian churches, denominations, and preachers on the west-ern New York reservations and explained how they partnered with the WCTU. Preachers included the Reverend M. F. Trippe Presbyterian minister at Alleg-any, Tonawanda, and Tuscarora, and Baptist minister George Runciman at Cattaraugus. Cattaraugus also had a Baptist church led by an unnamed Native American preacher. The Tuscarora Baptist Church was led by Rev. Frank Mount Pleasant. The Presbyterian Church at Tuscarora was led by Rev. James Gansworth from Tuscarora. The Office of Indian Affairs report pinpointed the establishment of the WCTU on Cattaraugus in 1894, where the group was largely "in favor of citizenship and a division of land in severalty." However, at a vote on January 16, 1894, about citizenship and severalty, the reservation population voted down the initiative, with forty in favor and two hundred against. Notably, the Native WCTU was equally divided, despite the organ-ization having started the movement in the first place. Agent Jewell argued that Indians were not ready for citizenship, which he blamed on their propen-sity for strong drink.[59]

Over the next decade the WCTU became firmly established on the reser-vations. By 1908 there were several unions among the Senecas at Allegany and Cattaraugus, created with the encouragement of missionaries and supported by Native American ministers and their congregants. Lydia Pierce developed a name for herself in WCTU literature around 1909, especially as an enthusiastic organizer of new unions. In 1909 she helped found a WCTU at Indian Falls, on the Tonawanda Reservation, supported by Peckham, who had begun what she called the "initiatory" steps among Native Americans there. Peckham reported approvingly of Pierce's work organizing silver medal contests and forming Mothers' Meetings. The contests, as Marvin Crouse had noticed on Onondaga, were effective ways of getting children involved, but within the context of the Haudenosaunee's value of public speaking these would have been even more powerful. Furthermore, the Mothers' Meetings would have also been picking up on matriarchal elements of the Haudenosaunee traditions. By 1910 there had been six medal contests sponsored by the Tunesassa Union. The Seneca superintendent of Mothers' Meetings, Ella Jamison, had spoken at the WCTU's county meeting. According to Peckham, Jamison had "spoke[n] eloquently on The Right Education of Mothers, as it meant so much for the future prosperity in the home, the church, and the nation."[60]

The WCTU wove its way into other temperance efforts and into Christian Indian communities. In 1910 Peckham provided an "excellent report" on New York providing the current state of affairs. She estimated a population of five thousand people with three unions, the first of which was started by the missionary; the other two were started by the Indians themselves. She described Charles Doxon, a fifty-year-old Hampton alumnus as head of the Six Nations Temperance Society. The unions, located at Cornplanter, Tunesassa, and Red House, all attended the Six Nations Temperance Society's annual event on October 4–7, 1910, at Allegany. In the three years of its existence Tunesassa awarded six silver medals. "Indian Maiden" Lorene Neffew gave an address. Indian Minister Rev. Asa Hill delivered a sermon entitled "Christianity and Purity."[61] In some descriptions, Lydia Pierce was described as an American Purity Association Representative, and the WCTU had its own Department of Purity Work that fought against sexual immorality, which was not only a Christian concern. One of Handsome Lake's tenets dealt with ending "love magic" or promiscuity.[62]

By 1911 New York's Indian work was winning praises from the national leaders, who may have hoped that the Senecas would serve as a model for other Native American communities. Superintendent Dorcas Spencer noted that "the Senecas in Western New York have done excellent work in [medal] contests."[63] The first two state superintendents of the department were the white missionaries Marian G. Peckham and Sarah L. Trippe. The first was Peckham, from Gowanda, New York, who left the position in 1911. Sarah Trippe of Salamanca, located on the Allegany Reservation, succeeded her. In 1914 Pierce would take up that position "at the recommendation of Mrs. Trippe."[64]

In December 1911 Emma Graves Dietrick, a national WCTU organizer, traveled to New York and met with Lydia Pierce, "The Indian president of the Tunesassa W.C.T.U. of the Allegany Reservation." Together, they traveled to Tuscarora, where they had been in correspondence with Nancy Printup. Dietrick was disappointed that there were only six people at the meeting, one a wife of the principal. "Were we discouraged? No, indeed; we formed a union of five members, chose Mrs. Printup as president." She continued, "in January another meeting was held at the council house. This, I attended. An audience of nine had gathered." A few others were not able to attend. Three attended the county convention in June, paying their dues but also chipping in an additional two dollars for the Willard fund, which apparently "astonished the white delegates" and "dues for an L.T.L. of eleven members." They had since chosen a secretary, a Mrs. Williams. Dietrick went on to describe myriad temperance efforts by this small union and explained, "that little handful of Indian women is tremendously wide awake. . . . I decided that it had been wonderfully worthwhile to start that tiny union among our Indian sisters."[65]

In her 1914 report on Work Among Indians Spencer declared, of New York, "this is our banner state." She intimated how and why the state, with a comparatively small Native American population, had become so successful in the WCTU: "The Society of Friends has maintained an Industrial School on a reservation for a hundred years, and trained their pupils in intelligent and capable leadership. One is the active, thoughtful president of a local W.C.T.U., who lately planned a successful temperance rally and picnic with Young Campaigners and a fine program."[66] This alumna was, of course, Lydia Pierce. Also in 1914, the *Union Signal* printed a story about the Tunesassa meeting, occurring on New Year's Day. At the meeting, with speeches made by the men in Seneca and in English by Pierce and others, they voted to endorse the Hobson Resolution. Pierce gave a speech entitled "A Saloonless Nation in 1920." Pierce, asking rhetorically how they were going to get the bill passed, explained, "First, by prayer; second, by prayer, and third, by prayer." She then went further: "but let us not think that by praying we shall have done our duty and wait idly for an answer. Let us work and join those who have banded themselves together to fight the liquor traffic by education, agitation, and organization," echoing Willard's motto for the WCTU.[67] The social gospel's marriage of prayer and sociopolitical action found a mouthpiece in Lydia Pierce.[68]

Eliza Pierce had a dedication to Christianity similar to Lydia's, but she did not have the same tight connection to specific missionaries and white WCTU leaders. In many ways Eliza was a typical WCTU leader for the time. She belonged to a mainstream Protestant denomination, the Episcopal Church. She valued Western education and encouraged her children and grandchildren's schooling on and off the reservation. She joined other temperance groups, having already been a member of the Onondaga Nation's branch of the IOGT and was a longtime member of the Six Nations Temperance Society.[69] Yet, as potentially the first Native American founder of a WCTU in the East, she was also distinctive.[70] In a July 1902 profile of Pierce, Victor Gage Kimbert, a reporter from the weekly Syracuse, New York, newspaper the *Sunday Herald*, characterized her as an energetic grandmother in her early sixties. She had formed the union with the aid of several generations of younger relatives. Although membership never exceeded a few dozen, her organization had tripled in size since she founded it in 1901.[71] That same year New York State had over eight hundred unions with over twenty-two thousand members.[72] Eliza's family life was tumultuous, and the WCTU helped her mitigate the challenges she faced. Born Eliza Billings in 1839 to Rev. John Billings and Sally Jameson, she was sent to live with a white family near Binghamton, where she was exposed to Christianity, domestic work, and English literacy.[73] She returned to the Onondaga Nation, where she became an organist for the Episcopal Church, yet she continued speaking Onondaga and married an Onondaga man named David Webster, with whom she had three children. She ultimately separated from him.[74]

Her remarriage to Jairus did not end conflict in her life. Although their relationship seemed to be harmonious, Eliza was his second wife. Jairus had been married previously on the Cattaraugus Seneca Reservation to a Cayuga woman named Lucy Twoguns in 1854. By some accounts, the wedding was conducted by a Presbyterian minister. Other accounts suggest that their marriage was a traditional, not church, wedding and was thus more easily dissolvable according to Haudenosaunee tradition and state law.[75] Jairus and Lucy moved to Onondaga around 1873 and then split up three years later. The separation was made messier by the fact that they had a son, Ulysses, and two older daughters. When Jairus married Eliza Pierce, Lucy accused him of bigamy and took her anger out on Eliza. The women fought, allegedly hurling milk pails at each other. Jairus threatened to contact state authorities for Lucy's assault on his new wife until Lucy threatened to respond in kind for his alleged bigamy.[76] The incident left Eliza resentful of the Cayuga presence in Onondaga territory. Though the Haudenosaunee had historically been a confederacy, each nation maintained its identity and asserted its sovereignty, which sometimes led to intertribal conflict within that confederacy.

Jairus and Eliza's partnership lasted four decades. Jairus became a successful farmer and a temperance supporter in his own right. He was not elected to the Chiefs' Council by the clan mothers but was respected in the community and worked on land claims cases, especially when federal allotment policy threatened the Nation's sovereignty over their territory.[77] When the Six Nations Temperance Society met at Onondaga, in the customary rotation, he was often a speaker. He traveled around New York performing traditional dances while Eliza was a featured singer and dancer.[78] As Oneida musician Joanne Shenandoah notes, "Nowhere is the Haudenosaunee appreciation for women better reflected than in their music and dance. When the women dance, they form a circle around the drum; they move with the Earth, counterclockwise, their feet caressing the Earth as they shuffle to one of the hundreds of verses sung in their honor."[79] In Eliza's involvement in Haudenosaunee performances, we can see not only the persistence of cultural forms but also the continuation of honoring women within the community.

Despite the Pierces' community involvement, life was not placid. Conflict erupted with Eliza's sister-in-law Charlotte Thompson, a Mohawk woman from the St. Regis Reservation/Akwesasne who had married Eliza's brother David Billings. According to Pierce, they had a long-standing animosity, and Thompson threatened her with violence around 1900.[80] In 1905 David died, leaving his Mohawk wife and six children living on the Onondaga Nation, in the home he possessed. According to Onondaga inheritance custom, the property of the deceased male would go back to the eldest females of his clan, in this case, his sisters, who would redistribute the real property and personal possessions. The distribution of property occurred at a "Dead Feast," hosted by the female relatives, with the approval of the Council of Chiefs. Pierce and her sister did this, redistributing the property to other family members as custom dictated. This action left the widow and her children without a home on the reservation. Incensed by another slight from her sister-in-law, Thompson and her children sued Pierce. Judge William S. Andrews ruled that New York had jurisdiction to decide the case, but barring some pressing interest of the state, the Onondagas' traditional inheritance practices were protected, and the suit stopped there.[81] As with the WCTU, the New York State Supreme Court was a resource outside the borders of the Onondaga Nation that could protect Onondaga tradition and self-determination, in this case against the intrusion of Mohawk individuals and the Euro-American inheritance laws they attempted to employ. While Pierce did not bring the suit, she ultimately prevailed in the courts, where she, through her attorneys, upheld traditional practices.

How did Eliza Pierce first come into contact with WCTU leaders and why did she found the organization? There is no obvious answer in the documentary record, but there are a few possibilities. First, the New York State WCTU established a Department for Work Among Indians in 1897. The first two superintendents of Work Among Indians in the state, the missionaries Peckham and Trippe utilized reservation churches as mouthpieces for temperance.[82] However, they were both associated with Allegany and Cattaraugus Reservations and had a much closer relationship with Lydia than with Eliza Pierce. Yet, they may have contacted Eliza Pierce's church, since Eliza founded the organization shortly after the department's founding. Second, Eliza may have independently come into contact with WCTUs earlier, during her travels around the state. In the 1880s and 1890s, it would have been hard *not* to hear WCTU speakers or see their advertisements. A third possible inspiration was at the New York State Fair, which was an occasion for heavy drinking among people of all ethnicities. To combat this revelry, the Onondaga County WCTU targeted fairs not only to get organizers to establish and enforce anti-alcohol rules but also as a place to recruit new members. At the fair, Haudenosaunee people and especially Onondagas performed dances and music and sold souvenirs to fairgoers. Eliza may have come into contact with the WCTU there.[83] A fourth possibility for Pierce's initial contact with the WCTU could have been during trips to Syracuse, where she may have visited WCTU branches. Indeed, once the Hiawatha WCTU disbanded as an independent union, Pierce and other Onondaga women became members of Syracuse Union Number 2. Earlier interactions with the women in Syracuse might have inspired Pierce, perhaps during her IOGT activities. The off-reservation women may have even reached out to her.

A fifth point of origin may have been the boarding schools where, by the 1880s, "scientific temperance instruction" (STI) had become part of the curriculum. Scientific temperance was the collection of ideas from the fields of medicine, phrenology, and anthropology that decried the physiological destructiveness of alcohol and created a scientific basis for total abstinence. Getting STI into all US schools, including Native American boarding schools, was one of the goals of the national WCTU and especially the national Department for Work Among Indians. One of their victories was when Commissioner of Indian Affairs Hiram Price agreed to insert STI into the federal boarding schools throughout the country. In 1881 Price wrote to the WCTU indicating that their request met his "hearty approval, and books of this character will be included in the supplies for Indian schools to be purchased next spring." By 1894 the federal government had made it mandatory in all federal schools.[84] Jessie Waterman, Pierce's niece and the branch's secretary, graduated from the Hampton Institute, which had active student temperance organizations. Frances Cook, her granddaughter and WCTU member, attended the Lincoln Institute in Philadelphia.[85] Perhaps the idea for an Onondaga branch of the WCTU came back with these young women. Ultimately, we cannot say for sure how and why Eliza decided to form the union. These influences likely compiled in her mind over time, but whatever sparked Pierce's actions, the organization she spearheaded and its activities offered the community something they found useful, and its influence spread.

Far to the west, Creek temperance leader Lilah Lindsey explained her inspiration more directly in her history of the Indian Territory WCTU. She was adamant about God's necessary role in temperance, and in her recounting of Indian temperance heroes she emphasized the role of Christianity in Indian Territory. She wrote particularly fondly of Samuel Worcester who not only preached the gospel but "endeavor[ed] to protect their rights when the white man was robbing the Indians of their rights." She described his well-known arrest and incarceration for refusing to take a loyalty oath, culminating in the US Supreme Court decision in *Worcester v. Georgia* (1832), which overturned his conviction. Being persecuted for fighting against removal was one of the trials facing all missionaries, she noted. The missionaries "passed through many trying experiences and sacrifices to befriend the Indian and take to him the Gospel."[86]

She mixed the spiritual with the legal realm of prohibition. Revealing a willingness to share her mystical imagination, she noted that "the writer has often in her temperance talks told her hearers, that the souls of hundreds of devoted missionaries are scattered all over Indian Territory, and those lovely silent spots are keeping vigils as it were over the rights of those they died to save . . . and we pledge to these silent vigils that we will never allow a legalized saloon on this hallowed soil." She described the voyage from the Cherokee homelands in the Southeast to Oklahoma and the development of various institutions among the

Five Tribes, especially their temperance efforts: "Until 1885–1886 the Temperance movement among the Indians seems to have been headed and carried on altogether by the men, which was very commendable since it was the men who were most benefitted from the temperance movement." However, the "National Woman's Christian Temperance Union with its usual alertness, was not neglectful of the Indians. They prepared a program for temperance day to be used in all the Government Schools. Attractive and appropriate pamphlets also were supplied to every teacher in the Government Schools."[87]

Lindsey moved beyond the temperance-educational contributions and explained the political aid that the WCTU was able to bring to bear on behalf of Indian communities, but she did so with a messianic viewpoint. Referring to Dorcas Spencer's work with the Hupas and the removal of the military bases near their communities, Lindsey exclaimed, "the wronged Hoopas of Northern California had no more faithful friend or Angel of Mercy than Mrs. Dorcas Spencer the National W.C.T.U. Superintendent of Indian Work. Thus the temperance seed has been sown in various sections of the country until a mighty wave of righteousness swept over our fair land and better things are yet to come, in the way of temperance reforms." She even wrote to the WCTU president, Anna Gordon, asking for her recollections of her early visits to Indian Territory in the 1880s with Willard. Gordon sent her excerpts from the *Union Signal* but was able to recall few additional details. After transcribing the excerpts, Lindsey summarized their work in covenanted terms: "Thus these women of God struggled along with brave hopeful hearts, and a faith and trust in their heavenly Father, knowing full well, if they were faithful to their trust in laying this first temperance foundation, that in his own good time, workers would increase, friends for the cause would arise and the good works would grow and prosper." This foundation helped the organization last over the years, through good times and bad, waning interest, and failures, until, "finally, in latter years it became a power for good all over Indian Territory and was the means of reclaiming many a wayward man who had had [sic] been addicted to drink." These early women scraped to pay for organizer Emma Molloy's visit. "Can we be surprised at the result of her visit? Not if we believe in earnest consecrated prayer followed by works. We are told that the whole country is stirred on the subject of temperance and religion; for the two go together hand in hand."[88]

Lindsey emphasized the WCTU's multidenominational approach, meeting at one church then the next, "the paramount desire being to see drunkards reclaimed and souls saved. This was fulfilling God's word, 'Behold, how good and how pleasant it is for brothers to dwell together in unity.'" She continued, "but don't fail to observe that in that little Presbyterian Church [sic], they 'envoked [sic] the help of the great Father, <u>for whom they were Engaged in labor.</u>' They never for one moment left God out of their plans, but depended on him to lead." She explained that the ten women who addressed the council were not known to her anymore—an uncharacteristic memory lapse for the WCTU members, who rarely waivered in their knowledge of their own local unions. She provided earlier historical precedent of white man's malfeasance, using an example when Native Americans went to St. Louis for trade and Christian instruction. Instead, they witnessed drinking and debauchery. She imagined a harangue by one of the Native American returnees: "You did not give us the White-man's book, so we return to our waiting people empty handed, with no light from the civilized nation. So it always has been, Indians pleading for more *light to help them to be the ideal citizen* [emphasis added]."[89] For the devout social gospel activists, citizenship and Christianity went hand-in-hand and stemmed from a belief that creating a just Christian society would usher in the second coming of Christ. Lindsey's assertion coincided with the coming change in WCTU structure placing Indian work under the Department of Christian Citizenship.

One of the most devout white WCTU officers who dedicated themselves to Indian work was Annie K. Bidwell. She was not a missionary, per se, to the Mechoopda Native Americans who lived on her and her husband's property at Rancho Chico, California. However, the Indian village there served as an incubator for Indian Christianity and temperance activity in Northern California and she and her husband were de facto missionaries for the Presbyterian Church. Although there are some brief writings from Mechoopda women from the era, the majority of what we know from Rancho Chico comes from Bidwell's own diary or public writings, detailing events from the Indian village and discussing her activities in the WCTU and as western vice president of the WNIA and member of its auxiliary, the Northern California Indian Association.[90] Bidwell was undoubtedly sympathetic to Indigenous Californians' land loss and demographic tragedies, and she and her husband attempted to create a haven for the Mechoopda.

However, as the historian Margaret D. Jacobs reminds us, the entire Rancho Chico enterprise was coercive. John Bidwell owned the vast property where the Mechoopda village sat, and although most California Native Americans outside of Rancho Chico had less stable housing and employment, the Native

Americans who lived on the Bidwell property had to conform to the Bidwells' rules, which included mandatory church attendance, abandonment of traditional religious practices, restrictions against seeking outside employment, and abstention from alcohol. By any count Annie Bidwell was one of the defining matriarchs of Indian work. She was such a devout Presbyterian that she refused to marry her Methodist beau until he converted to Presbyterianism. John's temperance credentials were pristine, too; he eventually ran for president on the Prohibition Party ticket in 1892. Despite the uneven power relationship and Annie Bidwell's intrusions into their private lives, the Mechoopda were able to maintain some religious ceremonies, including dances and burial practices, under the Bidwells' very noses. Jacobs observed that Annie Bidwell flexed her stringent Presbyterian expectations for gender roles and took on some male responsibilities requested by the Indigenous women to whom she ministered.[91] The WCTU and other temperance efforts brought together Native American women, Bidwell, and other white women, though Jacobs only briefly mentions temperance.[92] Bidwell's temperance work among the Native community at Rancho Chico could have been as coercive as other acculturative efforts, but it also responded to a real social problem articulated by Native women.

In 1891 one of the fullest early reports of Indian work in Northern California came from the superintendent of that department, Ella M. Priddy of Ukiah, Mendocino County, though Emily Hoppin read the report at the convention. Priddy did her best to reach out to her white WCTU sisters near Indian communities, but when she sent out a questionnaire to inform her report, only Bidwell returned a completed form. Bidwell noted that at Rancho Chico, "Liquor is sold to the Indians . . . but the guilty parties are fined when detected. But about six take it to excess." Twenty years before, according to Bidwell, the drinking was worse. Nearly all Indians drank heavily. By 1891 almost all the women abstained. The Presbyterian mission was active and many Native Americans were members. They even donated money for other Indians around the state for their WCTU and mission work. According to Priddy, "The Klamath and Hoopa Indians are begging for missionaries to come over and help them," and the Mechoopda were part of a nationwide effort to missionize Native Americans in California.[93]

The Bidwells had an exceptional commitment and a unique opportunity to enforce alcohol laws. First, it was their property, and they could authorize an investigation or threaten Indian or white violators with eviction. Second, they were very devout, committed to temperance, religiously and politically, and motivated to enforce the law. It is telling that the Mechoopda women were the first wave of abstainers, since male excessive drinking and violence was a common trend. In Eliza Pierce's story, the general pattern of Protestant conversions in the nineteenth-century United States and the WCTU's general popularity in itself all suggested temperance fervor was strongest among women. However, Mechoopda men were soon involved in temperance, and both the women's and men's group meetings occurred before or after worship services, sometimes in the Indian chapel.

The temperance swell did not subside after the death of John Bidwell in 1900. From Annie's diary we learn that Sunday, January 5, 1902, was a particularly busy day at the Indian village. The national prohibition advocate, "Quincy Lee Morrow addressed Indians this P.M.—12:15 to 12:40—and organized a Prohibition Alliance of 24 members. W[illia]m Conway made address in behalf of the same. Austin [M.] Leau interpreted Mr. Morrow's plans to the older Indians. Lafonso, then Billy Preacher, [and other men Following]; Amanda the first woman to raise hand; then other[s]. Result—Men 11. Women 9. Children 4." The talk and the organization work were followed by spiritual entertainments: "Maggie Sang twice & Austin once."[94] The services served as another way of communicating the successes of the civilization efforts of activists. The following week, on Sunday, January 12, 1902, Bidwell brought several visitors "from the East" to services in the Indian Village. They "expressed great surprise & pleasure at Indians' advancement, singing, & services."[95]

On Thursday, January 21, 1902, Bidwell went "to the Indian Village with their Alliance papers rec'd last evening." The Indian WCTU and non-Indian Prohibition Alliances were to collaborate on several future endeavors. She had also received some Demorest medal contest materials from Dorcas Spencer, Northern California WCTU recording secretary, including eight contest books and three contest journals.[96] On January 23, 1902, she sent the Prohibition Alliance charter to Maggie [Lafonso] which would formalize the groups' partnership.[97] On January 25, 1902, she sent one dollar to Dorcas Spencer for the "Medal Contest books" and postage. Bidwell attended and paid her dues to the Prohibition Alliance as required.[98] She wrote enthusiastically on Sunday, January 26, "Dedicated at last. The Indian W.C.T.U. Free Reading Room & Library Also the Gymnasium." After the service the Indian congregation went to the reading room and gymnasium where there were dedication ceremonies, hymns, and the singing of the Doxology. Bidwell was sure to point out that there were men, women, children, and infants present. Every step and space involved in the formation of the temperance alliance was consecrated with prayers and hymns, and family connection with the temperance vision was affirmed.[99]

By 1903 Maggie Lafonso had solidified her position in the WCTU chapter at Rancho Chico and continued to develop her relationship with Bidwell. In the annual report that year, superintendent of Indian work Ada Campbell began by noting the lukewarm activity in Northern California, generally. In Mendocino County, at Ukiah, there were two hundred Indians, all of whom still had access to alcohol; yet, they welcomed temperance work. In Butte County, where Rancho Chico was located, the outlook was more promising: "The report from the Mechoopda Indians of Butte County is always very encouraging. They number eighty-five. They sustain their own W.C.T.U., Prohibition Alliance, and L.T.L. and take six copies of the *California Voice*." The officers at Mechoopda were all Indigenous leaders: the president, Nellie Conway; secretary, Maggie Lafonso; and treasurer, Amanda Wilson. Membership in the WCTU was twenty (out of eighty-five total).[100] At the second annual Zayante Indian Conference, a major Indian reform event with a strong temperance bent spearheaded by the Northern California Indian Association, Maggie Lafonso was the only Indian woman in attendance.[101]

There was mutual fondness between Bidwell and the Mechoopda in the WCTU and its allied organizations, despite the structural power imbalances. In the winter of 1907 Maggie Lafonso decided to get married and asked Bidwell to perform the ceremony. Bidwell declined, explaining that it would not only be a violation of Church rules but would also be illegal under California law for a laywoman to perform a marriage. However, she was not opposed to pushing the boundaries of the roles of women in the church. The previous year she agreed to perform a baptism. Despite some misgivings about the propriety of women performing baptisms, she had done three by May 1906, at the specific request of the recipients who preferred her to the male ministers.[102]

In March 1909 Bidwell was ill and on March 7 could not conduct the service at the Indian Village, but she did attend services. William Conway "led singing, [Martha?] at piano. . . . And Maggie conducted [the] service." Maggie "[a]lso appealed for cooperation of every Indian in L.T.L. work." The following Sunday, William was leading the song service when Bidwell arrived. They were waiting for Maggie to return from a Sunday school meeting to take over leading the service. On Wednesday, March 24, the Indian Village hosted a WCTU institute where the state WCTU president Sara Dorr presided. All of the local WCTU unions and the LTLs attended, dining, intermingling, singing, and playing music together; especially enjoyable was the Indian Brass Band.[103] The Mechoopda WCTU had clearly become part of the broader community.

The WCTU leaders described above were not typical California Native Americans. They were devout Christians, literate in English, materially better off than most Native Americans, and they had direct access to sympathetic, sometimes powerful, white women. In each of their unions, there were other Native American women who did not have these attributes—hence the need to translate Morrow's speech for the older Mechoopda at the previously discussed 1902 meeting. Jacobs noted that some of Bidwell's Christianization efforts contributed to a generational divide, but one can also see that the WCTU, with its expressed commitment to linking children with older women, offered the possibility of reunification of elders with the young people.

Not all Indian women's connections to missionaries eased their paths to women's reform groups. In Indian Territory Martha Tunstall, who identified as Cherokee and was identified as Cherokee by the WCTU more broadly but who was not an enrolled member of the Cherokee Nation, shared some of the impediments to participation, one of which was her preacher husband. Prior to becoming deeply involved in WCTU work in Indian Territory, she sent a letter to Frances Willard, who shared it in the *Union Signal*. Tunstall, forty-seven-years old, wrote from the border town of Baxter Springs, Kansas, and told her story. She had been a vice president of the "Woman's National Suffrage Association for Texas," appointed by Susan B. Anthony herself. Yet she resigned the position, because, as she explained, "my husband is so opposed to suffrage that I dropped everything connected with it. I have never been in a woman's meeting of any kind." She volunteered her services, however, to the WCTU. "I see you have no one to operate in Indian Territory. My husband is a preacher here; I am going a great deal with him this winter, spring, and summer."[104] Tunstall eventually became an organizer for the WCTU, overcoming her husband's initial reluctance, perhaps because the Christian emphasis distinguished the WCTU from what he may have considered the more radical woman suffrage movement.

As Angela Tarango stated regarding studies of Native American Christianity, scholars sometimes get stuck on belief and questions of the "legitimacy" of conversions made under coercive or hegemonic pressures. "Legitimacy" or genuineness is difficult if not impossible to determine because of its internality and amorphousness.[105] However, if outside behaviors, hard work, and their own words are indicative of internal commitment to Christianity—even if blended with traditional beliefs and practices—then the Christianity in the WCTU was a powerful factor in drawing people to and informing WCTU work for Native American women. Alongside the religious aspect of the WCTU mission and culture, Indian work had a pragmatic legislative and law enforcement agenda. The concrete WCTU activities that Native American women engaged in as members of the Christian temperance organization was the other side of the temperance coin.

Chapter 2

Native American Women in the WCTU
Activities and Effects

Once they were connected to the WCTU Native American women engaged the organization to improve their communities in various concrete ways. First, they sought improved enforcement of federal, state, and tribal laws or OIA policies. Second, in line with typical WCTU strategies, and despite being unable to vote, they tried to nudge politicians toward prohibition. Some legislative or policy goals were distinctive to Native American WCTU workers, which included resisting allotment or at least informing sympathizers about its negative consequences. While resisting allotment may seem to mean they were at odds with whites in the WCTU, Native American women increased their temperance pledge signing efforts during allotment threats because citizenship, which usually came with allotment, was often accompanied by a loss of legal protections from alcohol. Third, some Native American women saw WCTU work as an opportunity for improvements in educational, economic, and living conditions, and they sought to make gains in these realms.

Fourth, aside from seeking assistance regarding alcohol, acculturation, and other arenas that fit into WCTU's overall pattern, Native Americans reached out to the WCTU to use their infrastructure, petitioning methods, and lobbying abilities to help with developments arising from particular challenges faced by Indians in the United States—especially, navigating the legal system both as victims of crime and as accused criminals. Fifth, the WCTU was intimately invested in the struggle over the merger of Indian and Oklahoma Territories. The WCTU initially opposed the merger, and many Native women opposed combining the unions of the two territories upon statehood. Although Native American WCTU members lost both these battles, they won the continued prohibition of alcohol in what had been Indian Territory for a period of years after statehood. Sixth, a secondary effect of their participation in the WCTU, especially for those who were leaders and ran their own unions, was their exposure to "parliamentary usage," or the systematic management of meetings, which contributed to the long-term civic participation of many women in their tribal communities. In all of these arenas, the WCTU promised Native American members tangible rewards for their efforts, some of which had concrete results.

Expansion and Enforcement of Prohibition

Motivated by a desire to improve their communities, steeled by their belief in God, and introduced to the WCTU by missionaries or by some other route, members of the Indian WCTU leadership sought first and foremost to expand prohibition laws. They saw the WCTU as the mechanism to do it, since they could not run for office or vote for elected officials. There were a variety of federal, state, and tribal laws governing alcohol sales to Indians. At key moments and key places Native American women sought to expand or clarify prohibition laws in ways that closed loopholes or strengthened laws that were otherwise easily evaded.

One of the first arenas where Native American women had the opportunity to participate in lobbying or legislative activity was in Indian Territory. They had a leg up on women's political work especially since the Cherokee and Creeks were some of the first Indian nations with democratically elected tribal governments and written constitutions, in the American fashion, but also with traditionally strong matriarchal elements in their political cultures.[1] Because of the long history of colonialism, boarding schools, trade and other interactions with whites, the Native leadership in Indian Territory was intertwined with white women earlier than was the leadership of many other Native American WCTUs. Native American women's comparative power in Indian Territory decreased precipitously in the late 1880s and through the twentieth century as the territories were flooded with whites who increasingly outnumbered Native Americans.

One of the earliest references to Indian Territory in national WCTU materials is in the 1877 annual meeting minutes when "Mrs. Joseph Wind" is listed as vice president of Indian Territory. (The WCTU used the title "vice president" of a given state until replacing it with "state president").[2] This was Matilda Wind, "Aunt Tildy." Born in Canada in 1851 she came to the territory "from Kansas in 1861, received her education at an Indian mission, married a full-blood Ottawa Indian—Joseph Wind and devoted the greater part of her life to teaching in Indian schools at Chilocco, Wyandotte and Quapaw. She was a quarter-blood Indian." She was long affiliated with the Tuttle mission at Ottawa and lived in the general vicinity the rest of her life.[3]

In 1879 the new vice president, Emeline Tuttle, submitted a thorough annual report from Indian Territory. She explained that there was a "Christian Temperance organization" at the Quapaw Mission, located in the far northeastern corner of Indian Territory. "About 400 have signed the pledge, and most have kept it faithfully." She continued, "there are several other temperance societies in the Territory, also juvenile Temperance organizations in many of the schools." Tuttle explained the peculiarities and shortcomings of alcohol laws for American Indians. "The No-License law prohibits the manufacture and sale of intoxicating liquor in the Territory. The Indians on the borders and along the railways, however, suffer very much on account of liquors being smuggled in by designing white men." The liquor trade in close proximity to the roads and railroads connecting the eastern states to the Far West was especially destructive and had a long history in Oklahoma, Tuttle explained. "[A]n effort was made to carry on a Woman's Union, but it was found best to unite their strength with the men, in order to succeed. The Indian men are more developed than the women and better able to carry on the work of reformation."[4] Federal officials noticed these efforts. In 1879 the agent J. M. Haworth, after a typical critique of alcohol abuse in Indian Territory and calls for enhanced legal protections, reported positively on temperance efforts: "The Indians have a very good temperance organization, which meets each Sabbath at the Ottawa School buildings; most of the Ottawas and Modocs and some Shawnees are members of it."[5]

In 1879 A. C. Tuttle, the Quaker missionary to Quapaw and Modocs and husband of Emeline Tuttle, wrote a letter rich in religious imagery, which was reprinted in the annual meeting minutes. He assured the readers that Emeline would discuss at length the "shameful difficulties by way of bribery and temptation on the part of the pretend civilized men upon the border States in laying waste that which we so honorably build up." He reminded the readers that whites were on the verge of flooding into Indian Territory, overwhelming the tribes. Thus, Emeline was to meet with representatives from the Cherokee Nation in November 1879 in order to coordinate their efforts to increase protections from alcohol.[6] The Tuttles along with Sarah P. Morrison traveled throughout the territory "and held meetings at different points." They attended an "International Temperance Convention" in Tahle-quah, with a large portion of the attendees coming from the tribes. Indian Territory advocated multiple avenues in the fight against alcohol including legislation and enforcement but also spiritual revitalization. In 1880 the Annual Meeting Minutes noted that gospel temperance was being taught among the Five Tribes.[7] According to the author A. J. Birrell, gospel temper-ance was "a remarkable attempt to bring the power of the Gospel and under-standing love to the aid of those who were struggling with alcoholism."[8] The commitment to the Christian redemptive message of gospel temperance sug-gests that the movement in Indian country was in part about saving those who had been lost through personal transformation, not just through pre-vention and the legal system, though reaching out to federal officials remained essential.

At the Tahlequah convention, the minutes describe how a "committee was appointed to correspond with the commissioner of Indian affairs, and ask him to instruct the officers under his care to be more faithful in enforcing United States laws, and thus prevent the introduction of liquor into the Territory." The committee apparently worked quickly and effectively: "This was attended with good results, and six liquor-dealers have been convicted within the past few months." However, the report ended with a final lament: "The work in the Ter-ritory is not systematized, nor is it possible that it can be under existing circum-stances, as the Territory itself is not organized."[9]

Indian Territory's WCTU would have to wait a few more years before they attained stability in their organization. In 1883 the Indian Territory WCTU leadership changed again. After a trip to Indian Territory, Frances Willard lamented in November 1883 that the "Modocs' friend" "Eliza" H. Tuttle had moved to Dover, New Hampshire, leaving the vice presidency vacant. The Rev-erend W. C. Duncan, a Cherokee Presbyterian from Tahlequah, apparently influenced the WCTU to appoint L. Jane Stapler (Cherokee) as vice president of Indian Territory. Jane Stapler's vice presidency was a sad accident, however. "It was the daughter of Mrs. Stapler [Mary Stapler] who was, by Mrs. Tuttle's sug-gestion, appointed as [Tuttle's] successor, but the young lady died soon after, and her sister has since died, so that the chastened mother's heart is most sorely bereft. But like other Christian women in our heroic band, she will find in work for the grieved and bewildered humanity heaven's most sacred antidote for individual sorrow and loss." During the trip, Willard wanted to go to the Cher-okee Legislature, but she passed up the opportunity in order to make it to the

Texas WCTU annual convention, settling for a visit to a WCTU meeting at the Presbyterian Church in Muskogee.[10]

In 1884 the *Union Signal* recording secretary, Katie Ellett, summarized the national organizer Emma Molloy's activities in Indian Territory. Ellett provided few details but delighted that "many drunkards have been reclaimed" and that there was much hope for the future.[11] In 1885 Ada Archer (Cherokee) was listed as vice president of Indian Territory.[12] In December 1886 the *Union Signal* reported that Martha Tunstall, who had been shut out of women's organizations by her husband, had recently organized the Tahlequah Union, where she was accompanied by her husband in the initial meetings. Based on her previous accounts, one wonders whether he was being supportive, meddlesome, or a little of both. However, at the WCTU meeting the women encouraged the signing of temperance pledges among the members and also sought enforcement of current law and the creation of new ones. They organized a group of ten women to visit the Cherokee National Council and petition them to pass a law against drunkenness, not just sale or distribution of spirituous liquor, and to fund enforcement of the law.[13] In 1887 the national organization was devoid of an office of Indian work, but this did not mean members ignored Native Americans altogether. The national members agreed "that Mrs. Cairns be invited to represent the W.C.T.U. in Indian Territory, $100 having been appropriated for the work."[14]

The February 17, 1887, *Union Signal* reprinted the WCTU president of the Cherokee Nation Martha Tunstall's address to the Cherokee National Council. The editor introduced the address, explaining that the paper was breaking a tradition of not reprinting addresses but making an exception for an Indian woman's speech: "They and we are one in this work" (suggesting that all readers are "us," or white; the Indians are "them"). Tunstall's reprinted speech claimed that Indian Territory "is the first and only body politic that excludes by legislation from her precincts 'firewater,' and refuses to allow to be set up as a temptation, and vended as a drink, 'wet damnation by the glass,' whereby sobriety is cherished among the present generation, and a traditional hate is fostered in posterity against this king of evils." She described the challenges in Indian Territory, including the crafty techniques used by smugglers and their determination to circumvent the law, even resorting to the assassination of enforcers of prohibition. Aside from pushing the council for the passage of a law against drunkenness, she also called for the introduction of scientific temperance instruction in Cherokee Nation–run schools, which were not directly controlled by the federal government. (Federal schools would have already come under federal STI law by this time.) She blended "next generation" and messianic thinking seamlessly: "And so your children will be brought up in the temperance line, and if we do not win the fight in this generation, the next generation will; and so we will conquer at last. Let us work and pray, and wait and watch, for the good time coming."[15]

In 1887 Tunstall reported that there were "*five* auxiliaries . . . with a membership of *three hundred* with seven Loyal Legions, having *three hundred fifty* members [original emphasis]." Tunstall tried to work with the Tahlequah Union and through the Cherokee National Council and explained the result of her memorial regarding drunkenness: "She influenced the Talequah [*sic*] Union to present a memorial to the council asking the passage of a law making drunkenness a misdemeanor. It passed the council, but there was a tie in the Senate and the President gave his vote against it." Both Native American and white women were deeply disappointed at the Cherokee men for failing to pass a new level of restriction, but they continued to strategize for other legislative campaigns.[16]

That same year Mrs. J. A. Rogers, secretary of Indian Territory, submitted some "Interesting Notes" regarding the history of the Tahlequah Union, founded a few years earlier by Molloy. The union was dwindling until it was reinvigorated by Tunstall. Then a Miss Sweet led it, but she left because of ill health and now it was in trouble again, though it continued to meet "the third Saturday afternoon of each month; The Band of Hope meets every Sunday." Apparently, there had been too much reliance on the missionaries who had church work obligations so they were requesting a white ribbon worker to help with organization. The residents explained that June and July were the best times to come to Tahlequah because the teachers from "all parts of the Cherokee Nation" were there for an educator convention and they could most effectively influence the children. The second-best time was in November and December, when the Cherokee National Council was in session. The article mentions the unfortunate failure of the petition to have drunkenness criminalized. Muskogee, "the leading town of Creek Nation" had a substantial white population and "There is no interest in temperance work there." On the other hand, "Vinita is a leading town. Atoka, in the Choctaw Nation, is a point of influence. Webber's Falls is also influential. There are places in the country at which branch societies might be formed. These men and women are not ignorant, yet not intelligent on this subject." The report closed with an invitation for an organizer for a few weeks to come to Tahlequah to remedy the weak activity there.[17]

In 1887 Martha Tunstall spoke at the national WCTU convention. In a reprise of her address to the Cherokee National Council, she described in even greater detail some of the creative mechanisms used by smugglers to hide alcohol. They put it in emptied eggshells, in sacks of flour, inside firewood, and in kerosene cans. The legislative effort to outlaw drunkenness was intended to be a way to counteract these wily and successful smugglers. She explained the insidious forces that had led to the failure of their petition. It passed the Council of the Cherokee's bicameral legislature, but it failed in the Senate because of opposition from the Speaker, whom she described as "a drinking man." She proposed an all-out assault on the next Council and chief, as there was to be turnover of elected officials in the coming year. She promised to speak and wanted to solicit WCTU women to address the Council with her. She mentioned the suffrage-oriented mentality of the Tahlequah women and herself—reflecting a newly tapped assertiveness when compared to her prior writings. She closed with a vivid picture of how the *Union Signal* became an inspiration to her. She was living in the "backwoods" when Rose Philips of Missouri first sent her the *Union Signal*. When she read about the convention and speeches there, she explained, "my heart was fired with the idea—the grand incomprehensible idea that women had ever dared step out and make such brave, grand and noble utterances."[18]

No description of her speech's reception is provided. But when she returned home to Watalula, Arkansas, Tunstall wrote a letter to the *Union Signal* complimenting the staff on the "splendor and magnificence of the assemblage." She provided a suggestion that the WCTU seek a national bill "prohibiting the issuance of license to manufacture and sell intoxicating liquors in any of the states where the state constitutions do now prohibit the same. The doctrine of states rights would seem to demand this much."[19] By 1888 Tunstall had found her voice and become emboldened. She wrote to the *Union Signal* to thank the various state unions that had sent her their annual meeting minutes, which she studied carefully in order to make her own work more successful. She desperately wanted to "attend the Woman's Congress at Washington in March, adding woefully, 'I've been shut out of the world for forty-nine years, and would love a small airing as I near Beulah Land.'"[20]

Apparently, Tunstall's requests for additional national support were heard. Mary E. Griffith, a national organizer from Salina, Kansas, wrote to the *Union*

Signal on June 13, 1888, about her experiences during six weeks of organizing unions and LTLs in Indian Territory. She described the physical beauty of the region and talked about the prohibition laws of the Cherokee and Creek Nations, which included strict confiscation acts, restrictions against "Jamaican Ginger," and even a potential death sentence in Creek Nation for certain unnamed "baser crimes." She mocked the federal government's civilizing efforts as self-defeating at best: "our national, paternal government (?) desiring to 'protect the people against Indian outbreaks' sends down detachments of the standing army supplied with such civilizing influences as come with ammunition and liquors (?)." She described one woman who had her door shot full of holes from a drunken soldier at Fort Gibson. Despite all of this, Griffith claimed she saw "only one WCTU in the Territory" at Tahlequah, but she made up for it by organizing new unions wherever she went.[21]

In 1888 the *Union Signal* announced that there was to be a convention in Indian Territory on July 25 and 26, 1888. The notice was signed by Sarah Perkins (national organizer), Tunstall (no office listed), L. Jane Stapler (president), and Tennie Fuller (corresponding secretary). A later article by Perkins suggests the territorial convention had actually taken place on July 18 and 19.[22] This earlier date was confirmed in Julia A. Rogers's recounting of Perkins's visit. After Perkins's departure from Indian Territory, Rogers commented positively on her impact. The Tahlequah union was unable to attend the convention in Muskogee, but "one of our number, Mrs. Jane Stapler was elected president." Perkins had described Stapler as, "a fine, cultured woman, who presides over a large household with the dignity and grace of a Roman matron."[23]

In May 1889 Willard herself made another tour of the South, including an extensive visit of Indian Territory. She was impressed with Stapler, "niece of Chief Ross, who was the George Washington of the Cherokees." She provided a detailed description of the convention and leadership at Tahlequah. K. L. E. Murrow from Vinita was secretary; "Mrs. M. T. Watson of Muscogee, a leading spirit, as was Mrs. Rev. Miller, a beautiful woman, wife of the Presbyterian pastor; Mrs. John Stapler, Mrs. Thompson, Mrs. Covel and others. Ex-Chief John Ross, a graduate of Princeton College, and an accomplished gentleman, spoke to the convention. He is a nephew of the great chief." In her description Willard demonstrated a better understanding of Indian country and the law and Native American leadership—revealing that she had learned something about US jurisdiction and its limits in Cherokee Territory, which caused challenges when it came to enforcing alcohol laws.[24] In other places in Indian country Native women also fought for tougher laws.

On the Allegany Reservation, Lydia Pierce wove together various threads, including desires for new laws, enforcement of existing laws and treaty obligations, and hope for the full political participation of Native Americans, all while appealing to both Christianity and Native traditions. Allegany was particularly vulnerable to the kinds of enforcement problems plaguing Indian communities abutting white towns. Salamanca, New York, was (and is) on the Allegany Reservation but has a majority white population. By the 1900s it looked a lot like towns in Indian Territory, Oklahoma, and other municipalities where a Native community was overwhelmed demographically by a flood of whites. In their interdisciplinary study of Navajo drinking, Kunitz and Levy describe similar towns near the Navajo Nation in the Southwest. The towns offered wages, alcohol, and the kind of abusive drinking that was common in the white community, especially among the laboring classes.[25] Salamanca was notorious for the same reasons. Indeed, the local liquor purveyors there banded together to fight any legal restrictions of their operations.[26] The fact that they were politically organized and connected made it necessary for Haudenosaunee women who wanted to protect their community to interface with the American political system. The question was, how?

It seems that one of the forces attracting Pierce to the ranks of the WCTU was the promise of the political link it could help forge with the broader temperance machine, allowing Native Americans to fight the liquor lobby at the local and national level. In the opening lines of one of her first annual reports she declared hopefully, "The New York Indians are not yet citizens of the state but I believe the time is drawing near when they will be and will vote with the white man. Therefore, they need all the help the W.C.T.U. can give them, for creating sentiment for State and National Prohibition."[27] Legislative efforts extended beyond the realm of prohibition and voting laws and into the realm of education, at both the state and federal levels as jurisdiction indicated. She promoted the Gulick Hygiene Series of textbooks on scientific temperance, writing to the New York State superintendent of Indian schools to convince them to use them in the state's Indian schools.[28] The desire to insert scientific temperance and the Gulick Series was a curious one, especially when we consider the vigor with which she pushed this issue. The series included inaccuracies and stereotypes of Native Americans that were common at the time.

Confusing Eastern Woodland homes for those of the Plains tribes, one volume described "an Indian in his wigwam on the prairie" as an example of a decentral-ized population that did not need to be as particular about hygiene as twentieth-century urban dwellers. In contrast, the majority of presumably white Americans needed to be more fastidious.[29]

The Gulick Series was one of the sources from which WCTU leaders learned about historical temperance proponents such as the Miami Leader Little Turtle. The series used his 1801 meeting with the Committee on Indians in Baltimore as an example of early Native American temperance efforts, reflective of the noble savage trope common in the era.[30] WCTU literature also frequently invoked Little Turtle and the Seneca leader Cornplanter in order to emphasize the long duration of Native American temperance socie-ties.[31] Perhaps Pierce was able to overlook the inaccuracies because the series seemed downright enlightened for the era in its inclusion of Native American precedents. It conveyed a powerful message of temperance, which was at times embedded in Native traditions as well as evangelical Christian ones.

Pierce was able to engage in national politics while appealing to Haudeno-saunee traditions. In 1914 the Tunesassa meeting was New Year's Eve, one of the two traditional dates of the meeting of the Tuscarora or Six Nations Tem-perance meeting. Men and women made speeches in Seneca. Pierce spoke in support of the congressional "Hobson Resolution," which promoted a consti-tutional amendment prohibiting alcohol.[32] Soon after, Trippe, the state super-intendent of Work Among Indians, was ailing, and she asked Pierce to assume her duties at the state meeting, which she did. By then the Tuscarora had a Young People's Branch and an LTL, were regularly receiving copies of the *Young Crusader*, and were paying annual dues.[33]

By 1915 Lydia Pierce, now state superintendent of Work Among Indians, crisscrossed the state giving speeches; she even made her way to Akwesasne/St. Regis Reservation, almost four hundred miles away. One speech, given at Tuscarora to the Six Nations Temperance Society, was reprinted in a nation-ally distributed pamphlet entitled "From an Indian to Indians." Pierce opened with honorific references to the Six Nations Temperance Society, paralleling its history with the foundation of the Haudenosaunee: "The 'Six Nations Tem-perance League' is a great organization. It means a great deal to the Indians of this state. The tribes of the state of New York, centuries ago, banded them-selves together for the purposes of defending themselves and their families from the tribes living south, north, and west of them whom they took to be their enemies." Linking the violence of their ancient enemies with the evil liquor purveyors, she continued, "Then it was the old league of the Iroquois tribes against their neighboring foes, and afterwards at their council fires in the old Long House, it became a Temperance League to conquer their last and worst enemy."[34]

She invoked the mandate to consider the impact of actions today on the seven generations in the future. Alcohol sellers and drinkers in the community "are leaving to their children down to the third and fourth generation the evils that liquor brings on a nation."[35] Such a phrase might be attributed to general concern for future generations—the kind of sentiment that any WCTU leader might express. This would underestimate the depth of meaning of generational thinking to the Haudenosaunee. Tuscarora writer Richard Hill states, "as Iroquois, we are told to think of the seventh generation to come when we deliberate on our future. In making our decisions and choosing our paths, we are to consider not our needs or the needs of our children but the welfare of the generations to come."[36] Pierce was articulating the need to undo the errors of past generations and prepare a healthier path for future generations.

She advocated the program of the WCTU: "The best thing, then, is to surround our children with better environment, give them a good education, teach them to be self dependent and industrious, to respect themselves, and above all, teach them the religion of Jesus Christ." The final paragraphs of the pamphlet encouraged western Native Americans, specifically those Native American men in South Dakota who could vote legally, to do so and to support those leaders who would support national prohibition.[37] To Pierce, and to many other Native Americans, traditional beliefs, Christianity, and even some of the values of democratic and industrializing America were at least partially compatible. Indeed, there was substantial overlap. To WCTU pamphleteers Pierce's published speech promised to inspire all Native Americans to further the WCTU platform.

Legal Enforcement

With the mixed success of getting new laws established, Indian WCTU leaders sought enforcement of existing laws as another means to help their communities. Native American women took pride that Indian Territory had longstanding prohibitions against alcohol. On September 24, 1891, the *Union Signal* reported on the front page that the president of the United States had issued his proclamation that Indian Territory was open to white settlement. The author declared, "the opening of the Oklahoma lands was attended by such scenes of ruffianism as promises poorly for good citizenship in that territory."[38] Beginning with the land rush of 1889, both Indian and Oklahoma Territories saw a flood of whites, overwhelming the Indian population.

For both territories the Indian population went from 24.9 percent to 5.3 percent of the total population from 1890 to 1907.[39] With an Indian population of 61,925 people in 1907, Oklahoma was a center of Native American life in the United States, but this population was scattered in small towns and rural regions throughout the state. Although exact statistics for Indian members in the WCTU do not exist, the anecdotal evidence suggests that whites overwhelmed the state, county, and local unions, many of which had white majorities even prior to 1890. With changing demographics and the chaotic emerging transportation networks, enforcement of existing federal and tribal laws became very difficult and was one of the primary complaints of white and Indian WCTU officeholders. Later in life Lindsey recalled the shock of the land rushes. On November 18, 1941, she did a radio interview with KTUL radio for Tulsa high school students. She recalled statehood coming and explained, "we Indians had our Government, churches, schools[,] well-organized and funct[ion]ing toward the well-fare of the masses, and were happy. . . . The change was a shock; and at every sound of the whistle, every toll of the bells, we realized, all that we held dear, was slipping away, and we love them yet."[40] As Lindsey's sentimental statements indicate, Native American women knew they needed to do something to respond to the inevitable flood of alcohol and mischief that accompanied the influx of whites.

One way the WCTU attempted to gently encourage enforcement was by marshaling a group of well-respected women to share their well wishes with leaders positioned to support enforcement. Stapler's third annual convention report noted, "Mrs. Acheson, president of the Texas W.C.T.U. was made a delegate." She listed the other delegates and officers and then provided a series of resolutions, which were often boilerplate suffrage and temperance goals. However, they warmed up to federal officials, newspaper editors, and local property owners. They offered their "thanks to our Indian Agent, Dr. Leo E. Bennett, for his cordial co-operation and help. Also we tender the heartfelt thanks of the whole convention to the Muskogee, *Phoenix* and *Brother in Red*, for their kindness in printing notices, tickets, and use of paper for temperance purposes. To C.W. Garrett, for his generous donation of a lot for a reading room to Muskogee union."[41] The use of good manners and diplomacy was one way of getting things done, or at least of keeping the support going.

In 1890 Indian Territory president Jane Stapler addressed the annual meeting, thoroughly describing how alcohol abuse, coupled with racial bias against Indians, conspired to make the suffering even greater for Indian people. Leaders firmly challenged officers of the law to enforce new or existing laws, based on the peculiarities of Indian drinking. Stapler applauded the fact that she, as a member of an Indian nation, was speaking: "It is perhaps well that added to what has already been said, the representative of a race that has suffered more from the evil effects of liquor than any on this continent should give some expression encouraging you in the good work that you have so steadily and heroically under-taken." Aware that some readers may have overestimated the predisposition of Indians to alcohol abuse or that the WCTU members thought that Indians' experiences with alcohol may have been evidence of physical defect, she continued: "When I say my race, the Indians, have suffered more from intemperance than any others, it does not necessarily imply that they have been the hardest drinkers." She explained that the legal system was part of the problem. "Too often the innocent among them have suffered, because some lawless white, regardless of consequences has sold or given liquor to the wild Indian, and while both were intoxicated, they have come to blows and perhaps a deadly conflict. Then friends of both parties have joined in the fray, and from that a rush to the frontier post with an alarm that 'The Indians are on the War-path' has caused a hasty parade of troops which has been met by an ambitious chief with his warriors."[42]

According to Stapler, this common phenomenon had gone underreported. "Perhaps God in his wisdom has prevented their going on the pages of history to tarnish the glory of the greatest nation on earth." She explained fully the legal restrictions on Indians. It was illegal to sell into Indian country or to sell to Indians "under the charge of an Indian agent" meaning, the restriction only affected an Indian "who has not severed himself from his tribe." This limitation was potentially a problem, since the forthcoming allotment process indicated that those who accepted allotments and were deemed competent would effectively be outside the reach of this law. Although the Dawes Act of 1887 did not cover the Five Tribes and excluded several other tribes, the pressure was on to allot all the Indian lands and terminate their governments. The allotment and termination of the Five Tribes would not be accomplished until the Curtis Act of 1898. In 1890 the fear of the change in status was palpable.[43] Stapler's inspiring speech did not fix things.

In 1892 there was a new union at Ardmore, led by Josephine Carr. Yet, drinking in Indian Territory and especially at Muskogee seemed worse than ever. National prohibition seemed to be the only answer to the loopholes in the law that kept the alcohol supply flowing.[44] In June 1892 the territorial reporter Sarah Ford Crosby submitted the report from the May 1892 territorial convention, in which she lamented the widespread violations of prohibitory laws. She shared the activities of organizer Ellen K. Denny of Vincennes, Indiana, who held a medal contest that was won by "Miss Florence McSpadden, a beautiful Indian girl of eighteen, who personated, 'The Martyred Mother.'" Crosby then shared the bad news. "I wish to add a word about the terrible condition of affairs in Muscogee. One beer saloon has been clearing hundreds of dollars and now four more have opened. We have petitioned the chief of this (Creek) nation, the judge and Congress, and we are praying without ceasing. Our jail is full, over eighty in six cells, and reeling men on the streets at all hours, because a judge has decided that beer is not intoxicating."[45]

This unfortunate turn of events stemmed from a recent decision by the US Commissioner Judge David Ezekiel Bryant, for the Eastern District of Texas in 1891. Julius Kahn, a merchant, was arrested for selling a low alcohol malt beverage in Ardmore, Indian Territory. Kahn's defense argued that the low alcohol drink, a "pale malt tonic," was not intoxicating. The judge agreed, ruling that beer, and other comparatively low alcohol beverages, were not intoxicating and were thus outside of federal law, which only outlawed "intoxicating" or "spirituous" beverages. This effectively meant that one could legally sell malt liquors— meaning beer and lower alcohol fermented beverages—to Indians in Indian country. The Chickasaw Nation, where Ardmore is located, was immediately overrun with saloons. One of the loopholes in the judge's decision was that Indian agents, who were authorized to regulate trade with tribes under their jurisdiction, could legally stop deliveries. Agent Leo E. Bennett ordered Indian police to seize beer in Indian Territory and turn it over or destroy the bottles. Bennett ultimately closed twenty-eight beer saloons. Commissioner of Indian Affairs Thomas Morgan, a devout Methodist and temperance supporter, advocated destroying beer based on the commissioner's and his agents' authority to regulate trade.[46] However, the lack of statutory prohibition against beer left the situation tenuous.

The WCTU launched a campaign to clarify the law, removing the agents' or the commissioner's personal proclivities from the equation by campaigning against all beer sales in Indian Territory, including low alcohol beverages. The WCTU's platform was to get people to consider beer, wine, and cider all as intoxicating liquors, and women fought to have them prohibited wherever a law or policy banned "liquor." This position obviously brought them into conflict with Judge Bryant who had "declared [low alcohol beer] was not illegal." According to Tennie Fuller:

> Our women circulated petitions to local authorities to stop the sale of hop tea and beer, which resulted in the spilling of these intoxicants in many of our towns. We also, under the leadership of Mrs. J. S. Murrow, of Atoka, I.T., circulated a petition throughout the Territory, to the President of the United States, praying him to have the sale of beer in our country prohibited. Our President also wrote a prominent lawyer in Washington City, asking his assistance in getting a bill through Congress prohibiting beer in our country. Such a bill did pass Congress and is now in effect here.[47]

The revised law, *US Statutes at Large* 27 (1892), modified the language, prohibiting "'ardent spirits, ale, beer, wine or intoxicating liquors or liquors whatsoever kind.'"[48] Territorial president Jane Stapler sent word to the *Union Signal*, who reprinted the joyous news on August 11, 1892. The church bells rang in Tahlequah. The territorial union claimed that their creation of "fourteen new unions means a relentless stand for 'home protection' on the part of the territorial W.C.T.U."[49] A year later, the enforcement of the laws appeared to Fuller to be effective.[50]

The brakes on the beer sales did not mean that the WCTU removed their pressure from the federal government when enforcement activity seemed lackadaisical. In January 1893 Crosby explained how Stapler, Fuller, and another delegate had returned from the national convention feeling reassured that "we now feel more than ever that we are part and parcel of the great National union, and we hope the committee on legislation will give the United States Attorney General no rest till he does order the head marshals of our territory to change their instructions to deputies, as provided in this resolution." "Resolution Six," introduced by the delegation from Indian Territory and passed by the national organization, dealt with restrictions against selling bitters, tonic, and other alcoholic fluids that had ostensible nonbeverage purposes.[51] Some success was evident. On December 6, 1894, in South McAlester, "the district attorney has issued an order which calls for the arrest by the United States marshal of all druggists and store-keepers in Indian Territory who sell bitters, tonics, and other patent medicines containing alcoholics."[52] The WCTU's success in tightening enforcement revealed an ability to affect government officials' sentiments, even if they were not the only reason laws and policies were changed. Minimally, they perceived their power to affect authorities. Moreover, their quick responses to judicial decisions and to the sneaky methods of obtaining alcohol through "bitters, tonics, and patent medicines" reveal that they were astute observers of nefarious activity. The WCTU of Indian Territory would receive a setback after their string of small victories. On March 23, 1895, President Stapler died at her home in Tahlequah.[53]

In the Northeast other Native American WCTU women fought for stricter enforcement, too. For Eliza Pierce, on the Onondaga Nation, enforcement was a problem not just because of white interlopers but also because of Haudenosaunee ones. While the Six Nations Temperance Society brought together the nations of the confederacy, there were limits to Pierce's patience with intraconfederacy relations. She was a member of that organization and hosted visitors who came for meetings. She traveled to other reservations for conventions, enjoying her hosts' hospitality. Yet she blamed incursions by non-Onondagas not only for her personal travails but also for the presence of alcohol at Onondaga. According to the reporter Victor Gage Kimbert: "She deplored bitterly the fact that in a population of only 600 [on the Onondaga Nation], nearly one-third were aliens and the sympathy and counsel of the sister unions was sought that some mode of relief might be found." In Kimbert's estimation, Pierce was attempting to get the WCTU to interpose itself between other Iroquois nations and the Onondagas: "The State guards its Indian wards against the greed of the white man to a great extent, but it is not always practicable to shield him from that of his brother Indians." The source of debauchery was not the Onondagas but other members of the Six Nations: "Mrs. Eliza Pierce declared that the Oneida and St. Regis [Mohawk] Braves had been particularly obnoxious in lowering the standard of morals, and firewater the chief instrument."[54] The WCTU brought together members of her family and other Onondagas, putting them in control of this issue, which had often been disruptive to women's lives. She saw personal and social issues being exacerbated by violations of Onondaga sovereignty—bringing alcohol into other people's communities and attacking her and other family members. Furthermore, the Council of Chiefs seemed unable to prevent the incursions. The activities of the Six Nations Temperance Society and the IOGT were insufficient. Thus, she concluded that New York State should be compelled to uphold its responsibilities to the Onondagas.

How, though, was she to get the ear of people in power? Doubly disenfranchised in New York State as a Native American and as a woman, she was neither a citizen nor able to vote. In the broader society the WCTU had been developed by women to solve just such problems. Women could not vote, but they could speak, publish, persuade male voters and leaders with moral and scientific arguments, educate the young, and appear at voting booths in hopes of influencing the political process.[55] One element that must have made the WCTU attractive to Haudenosaunee women was that the WCTU's methods of influencing the male world of electoral politics through persuasion echoed the matriarchal elements of the Haudenosaunee social and political organization.

The Iroquois clan system rests on the idea that one's family line, manifested in a clan, is traced through the mother. Clan mothers then wielded influence within the immediate community and in confederacy politics by selecting the chiefs who met to discuss matters of importance to the Haudenosaunee. The system had much in common with that of the WCTU. However, Iroquoian societies were infused with the assumption of equality between men and women, who had distinct but equally important roles. The white WCTU members were working in a power structure where women had decisively less power. Yet, as Iroquois women had lost some of their traditional roles since the American Revolution and the resultant onslaught of Euro-American civilization, the WCTU's methods of influencing male leaders, with the accompanying hope of eventually being voters and elected officials themselves, would have met both traditional expectations and the realities of power in the early twentieth century. This political pragmatism of Native American WCTU women came at a cost, however, in their internalizing some of the racial stereotypes and insecurities that were both consciously and unconsciously encouraged by white women in the organization.

Race, Citizenship, and Allotment

In her "History of Indian Territory WCTU," Lilah Lindsey revealed she had internalized white racial expectations and hierarchy for Native Americans and African Americans, while at the same time leveraging for a better position for Indians in the eyes of white audiences. "The Indian possesses not only a superb physique but a remarkable mind in mental capacity even without education he ranks high holding a place somewhat lower than the Caucasian but much higher than the Negro."[56] Lizzie Kants, from Warm Springs Reservation, Oregon, seemed to share a sense of racial difference and implied Indian inferiority. She declared, "There is a great difference between a white woman and an Indian woman unless both are drunk, and then they are both on the same level."[57] These words were shared with the national corresponding secretary who celebrated what she believed to be the first Indian WCTU in the state of Oregon.[58] The presumption of white women's superiority—racially, culturally, or socially—may have been a self-effacing comment from someone seeking to please the missionaries or WCTU workers on the reservation. On the other hand, they may have represented the views of someone reconciled to the acculturation process she was a part of. It is also possible that this phrase may have been at least partially invented by the translator and transcriber to match her own sentiments, particularly about the evil-yet-leveling qualities of alcohol. Although these homages to racial hierarchy were common enough among Native American authors, this did not mean that Indian women were ashamed of their heritage or attempted to hide or even downplay it.

WCTU leaders often celebrated the Native American backgrounds of its members and leaders. Indian women such as Lindsey often capitalized with good humor on their ancestry. It is unclear how genuine this humor was or if it was a survival mechanism, though it was likely a bit of both. At the World's WCTU convention in Boston in 1906, National President Stevens called Lindsey to the podium, proclaiming, "I want to introduce one of our dependable workers, tried and true, and the *only real American* representing Indian Territory. She is an Indian of Creek and Cherokee blood." Lindsey, upon reaching the podium, addressed the audience saying she was "glad *her* ancestors were on the receiving line when your ancestors came to America."[59]

This example of making light of the tragedy of colonialism may have been a way for Indian women to endear themselves to an audience whose full approval they sought for various political or pragmatic reasons. Lack of US citizenship was a problem when it came to promoting state or federal legislation, but many Native American individuals resisted it. US citizenship was the legal imprint that one was no longer going to belong to a truly sovereign Indian *nation* in the same sense that Indian nationhood existed during the treaty-making era. In 1871 President Grant and Congress ended treaties as the means of negotiating with tribes. Along with Grant's Seneca commissioner of Indian affairs, Ely

Parker, they came to think of treaty making with tribes as no longer befitting the weakened position of once truly independent tribal nations.[60] Others saw the lack of citizenship as an impediment to their progress and material success. In one example, John W. Staples, a Cherokee man, was replaced as postmaster of Tahlequah Indian Territory and replaced with a postmistress, "Mrs. L. Adair" a white woman who was married to a Native American man, because the attorney general thought that Indians, being noncitizens, would not be allowed to hold the position.[61]

In an undated draft of an essay written around the time of American entry into the Great War, Lindsey laid out her view of citizenship clearly. She not only presaged the absorption of the Department of Work Among Indians by the Department of Christian Citizenship and the increasing nativism of the WCTU, but she also argued that Native Americans should be privileged in their position in the nation, not second-class citizens. "My conception of citizenship is that there are three classes; The natural or original citizen the Indian, who received the pilgrim, and welcomed them on the bleak Atlantic sea shore, the hunter of the plains hills and vallies [sic] the true hearted, country loving men and women, who later as this country became thickly infested with the pale faces had to meet these same people with the fleet arrow, the tomahawk, and the American made gun." The second was "the citizen born in this country of Foreign parents, who have always been loyal men [and] women, the law makers of our country, the defenders of our country such as Washington, Webster, Lincoln, John A. Logan." Third was "The Naturalized Foreigner, who came here and took the oath of Allegiance, to our Constitution + Flag." Some of these, she continued, "came here for selfish purpose, make money + when the call comes to defend our country returns to his Foreign land and takes up arms for his own showing his loyalty is to his own foreign land. He disceminates [sic] communism in this country undermining our Government spreading his ideas in our Public Schools + Even dares to stand in our pulpits of Protestant churches and fo[i]st their ideas on an unsuspecting people."[62]

Her language loudly echoed the nativist sentiments of many whites around World War I and afterward—a sentiment that would allow the Department of Christian Citizenship to absorb Indian work. Furthermore, it clearly placed her within the anti-communist Red Scare that was emerging and insinuated her approval of allotment, since reformers often criticized tribal ownership of land as emblematic of communistic thinking. Yet she began her essay asserting the unique citizenship status of Native Americans. One wishes that Lindsey might have laid out exactly what citizenship would look like for the Indians if they accepted both US citizenship and private property. How did she envision the future functions and powers of tribal governments, assuming they would still exist, moving forward? How would specific protections against alcohol distribution to Indians work if there were no specific Indian territories? Or, would there be some kind of residual boundary surrounding Indian-owned private properties—a sort of Indigenous municipality—that would still be offered protection? For now, these questions were left unsatisfyingly unanswered. Indigenous Americans were, according to Lindsey, distinct, special, and superior to the hordes of disloyal immigrants who supposedly fled back to their home countries to fight against the United States.

Native American women involved in the WCTU linked allotment, citizenship, and prohibition in their minds and in their political and social temperance strategies. For those who feared that allotment was inevitable and would bring a freedom wrought with fewer protections from alcohol, the WCTU's pledge-signing efforts and mobilization for national prohibition offered solutions. For those who opposed allotment outright, joining the WCTU gave Indian women a political voice through the existing WCTU lobbying and educational channels by which they might resist its implementation.

While most acculturated Native leaders thought that citizenship and voting rights were essential to any future for Native Americans in the United States, traditionalists often rejected US citizenship. Native American reformers diverged among themselves in their views on allotment. At its most benevolent the policy meant *equality* and not political distinctiveness. Many Native Americans saw extended protections as the federal government's obligations, based on treaties, historical precedents, justice, and morality. The Creek novelist and WCTU member Sophia Alice Callahan played this out in her novel *Wynema: A Child of the Forest*, often billed as the first novel by a Native American woman. In it, Callahan promoted the WCTU, prohibition, and women's suffrage wholeheartedly through the title character along with other heroines like Genevieve, Wynema's *Mihia* or "teacher." In one scene Wynema is reading a paper that discusses the question "Shall We Allot?" Unfamiliar with the topic, she turns to Genevieve for clarification, who explains, "Some United States Senators are very much in favor of allotting in severalty the whole of Indian Territory, and, of course, that would take in your country also. I don't like the idea, though it has been talked of for a long time. It seems to me a plan by which the 'boomers' who were left out of Oklahoma are to be landed. . . .

Note the matter assumes a serious aspect, for even the part-blood Indians in favor of allotment; and if the Indians do not stand firmly against it, I fear they will yet be homeless."[63]

Wynema temporarily acted as the foil for the pro-allotment position: "so long as our land remains as a whole, in common, these lazy Indians will never make a move toward cultivating it; and the industrious Indians and 'squaw men' will inclose [sic] as much as they can for their own use. Thus the land will be unevenly divided, the lazy Indians getting nothing because they will not exert themselves to do so; while if the land were allotted, do you not think these idle Indians, knowing the land to be their own would build up their homes?" Genevieve, who eventually wins Wynema over to her side, responds by explaining that the process will more likely result in the winnowing away of Indian landownership as whites would scheme to get title to the land from individual Indians who would be disadvantaged in the US legal system. Although Wynema's momentary naïveté is remedied by the realism of Genevieve, Callahan succeeds in explaining how incentivizing productivity could be a seductive rationale for reformers' supporting allotment. Other Native American WCTU members fell on the other side of the issue.[64]

One of the most prominent Native American reformers at the national level was the Omaha activist Susette La Flesche/Inshata Theumba, "Bright Eyes," who helped shape Frances Willard's thinking and the WCTU's general commitment to allotment. The *Union Signal* published one of Willard's letters in 1887 after she had been in Boston and heard a speaker discuss "The Indian Question" (allotment), which was about to become policy on most Indian reservations. She was impressed when "Mr. Cook introduced 'Bright Eyes,' who has done so much for her people with voice and pen. She is a dark, handsome Indian, of rather fragile figure, and voice so slight that it was wonderful how even her earnestness and forceful words held that great audience, while she read her experiences and observations on 'Reservation Life' and the curse of politicians in Indian affairs." She went on to note the connections of the WCTU to the WNIA and Clinton Fisk, "president of the general movement, and hence there are links not a few between us and this cognate cause."[65]

Willard certainly expressed respect for La Flesche, but she seemed to be a novelty to Willard, despite the fact that she had earned a name for herself as a journalist in the late 1870s, covering the crisis with Standing Bear and the Poncas and had become established as a serious reformer after acting as Standing Bear's interpreter in 1879. Susette La Flesche had married *Omaha World-Herald* editor Thomas H. Tibbles a few years before she met the WCTU president. Willard delighted in the fact that La Flesche "signed our pledge at my request and I divided my white ribbon with her. So she is now a [WCTU] member, and I advise 'our folks' at editorial headquarters to get an article from her, giving the temperance question from her point of view." When Willard left the encounter she was firmly convinced of the need for allotment of land in severalty, equal treatment for all races, and citizenship for American Indians. Willard noted explicitly the multiple links between the WCTU and the Indian reform organizations: "Our own Mary Lowe Dickinson is president of the Women's [National] Indian Association, of which Mrs. [Amelia Stone] Swanson Quinton, once associated with our work in Brooklyn, is secretary."[66] It was clear that the WCTU would continue to cover the "Indian Question" and to support allotment, in part because of Willard's encounter with La Flesche.

Outside of Indian Territory and Oklahoma, new federal legislation regarding allotment of lands to individual Indians was a major threat when it came to alcohol distribution. If protected status as a tribe was lost, alcohol could be sold in the community previously legally protected by the reservation boundary. As the legal protection was threatened, a demand for alternatives to prevent drinking among the population became desirable. One solution was individual abstinence through pledge signing. The WCTU conducted one successful pledge drive at the White Earth Reservation in Minnesota. The community had a long tradition of legal alcohol restriction going back to at least 1882; removal of federal protection threatened this.[67] In 1906 Minnie Green, superintendent of the Young Woman's Christian Temperance Union (YWCTU or "Y") work, went to schools at White Earth and at "Orrigan" (probably Onigum on Leech Lake) "and held three meetings, which she addressed through an interpreter." She explained that Indian citizens were being declared "free moral agent[s]" excluding them from protections against alcohol laws, which would cause "another fight with the liquor traffic and a greater need of redoubled energy along this line of work." She advocated that Native women, along with the WCTU on the whole, move "'on to the legislature' for our law makers should seek to protect these brothers of ours from their greatest foe."[68] Although we do not have the specific words of the pledge, White Earth signers' widespread participation is suggestive of the hope for sobriety that the WCTU provided through social, religious, and political means, and through their promise to appeal to the state legislature, in the face of allotment threats.

The national superintendent of Work Among Indians Dorcas Spencer recognized the tangle of differing citizenship statuses and voting eligibilities of
Native Americans. In 1916, in an effort to inform potential Native American
voters of the prohibition candidates, she drafted a circular letter to send to all
voting Indians. She relied on the WCTU president of each state to inform her
of the exact number of letters to send, since voting laws and the status of
individual Indians varied. To her, citizenship and voting rights were entirely
positive developments. "It does the Indian good to be recognized as a possible
political factor," she wrote, and she spoke optimistically of the "new law granting citizenship to every Indian who is properly certified to be qualified for its
responsibilities." Secretary of the Interior Franklin K. Lane visited South
Dakota and noted that 186 "men [have] the right to vote," which yielded control over resources from leases owed them by the government.[69] Such financial
freedom was often a selling point for allotment, but in practice it often made
those resources vulnerable to opportunistic whites.

For the Onondaga WCTU president, Eliza Pierce, allotment was more of
a threat than an opportunity. Following the 1887 Dawes Allotment Act the
federal government attempted to initiate the same policy on Iroquois lands.
Allotment would have placed tribally owned lands in the hands of individual
Iroquois landholders who could then, after a fixed period of time, sell their
land to whites or other Native Americans, whether they were Onondaga or
not.[70] If lands were opened up to allotment, the threat of land loss was not just
from whites but also from people she saw as illegal non–Onondaga Iroquois
settlers. Based on her experience with her husband's ex-wife, she might think
that non-Onondagas would benefit from white authorities' plans to open land
to individual ownership. Her husband, Jairus, opposed allotment, too, and this
factor seems increasingly important in Eliza's desire to use the WCTU to pressure outside authorities to push non-Onondaga influence off the reservation.
Haudenosaunee communities had always had residents from the constituent
nations living within them. Yet, Pierce put conflicts about alcohol into intertribal terms. Most of the problems with disharmony that she saw stemmed
from "alien" Iroquois on the Onondaga reservation.[71] Pierce came from a tradition where clan mothers held tremendous power, through their appointment
of chiefs and in many other ways. Thus, the WCTU and the Iroquois matriarchy
had many similarities. These similarities should not be overstated, of course.
The WCTU developed within the context of the industrializing United States. It
was organized hierarchically, used printing presses and mass distribution of

literature, and was specifically seeking women's inclusion into the democratic and capitalist system of the nation—these made it quite different from the matriarchal elements of the Haudenosaunee. However, the Iroquois tradition of protecting and preserving the community persevered into the early twentieth century, in this case filtered through the mechanisms of the WCTU.

In the Southwest, similar connections of the WCTU to political participation for the sake of enforcement occurred. The first New Mexico state WCTU convention was in 1911. A year earlier, Clara True left her post as an Indian agent in California and moved to Española, New Mexico, where she "was a member of the convention." She brought five Native Americans from the Santa Clara Pueblo, located adjacent to Española. The author of the article in the *Union Signal* described them: "These Indians were all prominent men in the Santa Clara pueblo [*sic*], one being the governor, a young man and a conservative, and another, the ex-governor who is eighty-two years young (and he looks it) and is leader of the progressives." Despite their differing views on acculturation, they all had, "taken the total abstinence pledge more than a year ago and had kept it." There were "297 total abstaining Indians back home. The men were respected and helpful members of the convention to its close." Although their support for the WCTU was probably genuine, there were pragmatic reasons these men attended the conference. The article revealed that the ex-governor "Francisco Naranjo . . . gave an address in Spanish, which the governor interpreted, telling how the officials employed by the Government pastured 1,000 head of cattle, belonging to Mexican cattlemen and political 'healers,' thus breaking down the Indians' fences and, devastating their crops and destroying their pasturage." Apparently, Naranjo hoped the WCTU could encourage the government to enforce property rights on the reservation along with alcohol laws.[72]

Acculturation

Aside from the alcohol and allotment-related legal issues, the WCTU promised other possibilities to Native American women, including the economic self-reliance of their tribes and the seemingly contradictory goal of acculturation and its associated literacy campaigns. For instance, independent statehood for Indian Territory would allow voters to pursue state prohibition and women's rights. The authors of the 1903 Indian Territory report articulated a pro–independent statehood platform so they could win suffrage. There was more than just a legislative strategy behind independent statehood. In their resolutions they declared, "Be it further resolved, [t]hat we favor an Indian name for our Indian State such as will recognize and perpetuate the name of the original owners of the Territory." They charged their delegates to convince the national convention "to endorse and work for the furtherance of the interests set forth in the Indian Statehood Resolutions" and asked that Indian Territory become its own state "not attached to Oklahoma or any other State or territory, but be an independent State, as are all States, and to have an Indian name." The Indian name proposed was Sequoyah, after the creator of the Cherokee syllabary, which allowed for literacy in the Cherokee language.[73]

The WCTU saw literacy as key to Indian women's effectiveness as campaigners for suffrage, prohibition, and other causes. The superintendent of "Evangelistic and Missionary Work Among Fullblood Indians," K. L. E. Murrow, provided one of the most honest assessments of Indian Work. She complained that even after twenty years of work, "we do not have one Union composed entirely of fullblood Indians. I am a missionary and go among all classes of Indians and have organized many Women's Mission Societies among fullblood Indians and they are as successfully carried on, as is generally the case, among white people." However, "The majority of our fullblood Indian women cannot read. The young women now coming to the front are able to read." She made a strong recommendation that "women of all denominations take up this work among the Indians on connection with their Women's Mission Societies and introduce the work gradually, giving a part of one meeting each month to temperance, or one whole meeting, teach them the necessity of signing and keeping the pledge and training their children in that line, etc. It seems to me that the only way to accomplish this task is to educate the children and young people along our lines of work. There are in Indian Territory, for Indians, 365 District or day schools and 24 boarding schools." She then provided nation-by-nation enumeration of schools, and encouraged her audience to introduce Scientific Temperance Instruction, which was not mandated for tribally run schools outside of federal jurisdiction. She encouraged medal contests and LTLs "wherever possible."[74] In these ways the WCTU was truly attempting to be a comprehensive aid organization, which would assist Native American women in transforming the communities.

WCTU officers saw the positive temperance effects of transitioning to Euro-American divisions of labor, with men farming and women working exclusively in the domestic sphere and child rearing. In the 1916–1917 Southern California WCTU Yearbook, Mary Fowler declared "Great Progress" in Indian work.

Since men had learned "scientific and successful farming[,] that they have no time for idleness which leads to indulgence in the liquor habit. They are organizing farmers' clubs in the villages." She continued: "Young men and women of Soboba" have a "Progressive Club" that met two times a month "to discuss new ways of living, how to make a living, and the subjects of temperance and morality are not neglected." The village had a Better Babies club; "A Soboba girl, a graduate of the Sherman school, is leader of an Old Woman's club and is making plain to them the necessity for a change from old methods to new. She is bridging the gap between the Indian woman of yesterday and of today. These efforts lessen the friction of the two."[75]

Despite the goal of financial independence, white and Native American women recognized that the required dues could be an impediment to joining or creating unions, despite temperance sentiment among tribal members. The Indian agent at the Santee Agency, Nebraska, commented that, around 1886, residents wanted to "organize with Some state organization, but upon inquiry they found the charter . . . to be more expensive than they anticipated, and concluded to organize under by-laws of their own." They did not hesitate to use financial pressure to secure results, however, instituting a five-dollar fine on those who violated the temperance pledge. They succeeded in recruiting twenty-nine members, who wore a badge of "white metal with the word 'temperance' engraved thereon. . . . One member was expelled, much against his wish, for breaking the pledge."[76]

Petitions and Other Legal Help

Because the WCTU developed a reputation for petitioning elected officials and helping to shift public opinion on various matters, Native Americans found in them an ally for legal matters outside of prohibition, suffrage, and citizenship. In one of the most important cases in WCTU memory, Dorcas Spencer, before becoming the Work Among Indians superintendent, was an organizer in California and ended up in northern California near the Hoopa Valley Reservation. Spencer's Indian experience began with the Hupa Indians in 1889 as an outgrowth of her organization work. Women in Humboldt County, in the far northwestern corner of the state, invited her to come and organize the residents there. During her months-long stay, she connected with a Hupa man, Billy Beckwith, whose initial concerns were not temperance per se but, rather, the general poor condition of life on the reservation, made worse by the presence of Fort Gaston, a nearby army base that was the source of debauchery for Indians.

He had even appealed to his congressman, but to no avail. Fort Gaston was investigated after an extensive letter-writing campaign was initiated by Spencer that eventually reached President Benjamin Harrison who assigned Dr. Daniel Dorchester to investigate the situation further. Eventually, the post was closed in 1892.[77]

In 1911 the WCTU intervened on behalf of New Mexico Pueblo resident Juan Cruz, a temperance worker who was arrested for first-degree murder. Cruz had worked for six months for special agent William Johnson, a specialist in investigating and prosecuting alcohol violations on Indian reservations. Cruz supported Johnson's daring efforts, sometimes for pay and sometimes for free. According to a letter from Johnson, Cruz, "often went with my officers and hid as they did." In one instance, "When a drunken Indian came out of a saloon with a bottle of whisky, Juan took it away from him. The Indian hoodlums set upon him, beating him with rocks. At last, with blood streaming from his wounds, Juan fired in the darkness and Garcia, the worst desperado in the county, fell dead. He fired at random to drive off the mob, just as I have done many times. Had he not done so, he would have met his death." Spencer reassured readers that the "WCTU of New Mexico and elsewhere have contributed funds for his defense."[78] In southern California, Mary Fowler heard about the case and solicited eight letters on his behalf from members "and started San Jacinto Y.P.B.'s on a play to raise money to assist in his defense."[79] The California *White Ribbon Ensign* reported, "it was only through the efforts of the W.C.T.U. of Santa Fe, and an attorney employed by them, that the freedom of the boy was secured." There were consequences for this political maneuver, however: "Assistant Commissioner Abbot and Assistant Secretary Adams who were anxious to have Juan Cruz convicted are now retaliating" by using the Santa Clara Pueblo's land for cattle grazing and giving their land to other, surrounding Pueblo Indians.[80]

In the November 1911 edition of *White Ribbon Ensign*, the author commented on the "Resignation of Chief Special Officer William E. Johnson" and attacked the politicians who failed to support him in his efforts to enforce prohibition laws in Indian country. Johnson's immediate gripe was the issue with the Pueblo Indians in northern New Mexico who were being robbed of their land, which was made much easier when they were kept inebriated. Santa Clara Pueblo, however, "became abstainers almost to a man. They not only did this, but went about securing evidence to prosecute saloon keepers for selling to other Indians. Many of these Indians became my personal deputies. They secured indictments and convictions against most of the saloon-keepers of Santa Fe."[81] In this way, the WCTU tried not only to keep local law enforcers, who were often tied to liquor interests, from unfairly prosecuting Native Americans but also to keep effective federal enforcers in their government positions so as to protect the Indian communities.

As important as their actual material influence was, the WCTU made the most out of these stories for internal and external self-promotion. National and state unions published and republished these stories. The Billy Beckwith story became part of Spencer's biography and part of her rise to prominence within the organization. Such stories endeared the literate Indian women who read them to the WCTU and brought the organization credibility within the communities. The Juan Cruz incident demonstrated the WCTU's commitment to using their networks for the benefit of Native American crusaders against alcohol. The WCTU may have been the best hope to influence decisions at the highest level of government in a variety of ways.

Oklahoma and Indian Territory

What is now the state of Oklahoma was only one place the WCTU was active with Native American communities, but it was the location where the WCTU put its greatest efforts in organizing unions and creating a national legislative campaign in the interest of Native Americans. In response to a questionnaire from the national organization, K. L. E. Murrow described the context in which Lilah Lindsey and other leaders operated. This was then printed in the 1905 Indian Territory annual report under the title "Questions and Replies" and described the diversity of the Native American population in Indian Territory. Murrow estimated the population at sixty-five thousand Indians, forty thousand of whom were mixed-bloods and twenty-five thousand who were full-bloods. These included the "Cherokee, Creek, Seminole, Choctaw, Chickasaw, Delaware, and several other small tribes. . . . They rightfully own all the land in this Territory. As yet they pay no taxes and do not vote." She described the richness of the agricultural land and mineral resources, which formed the basis of their economic potential, but "the full-bloods are being cheated out of it and robbed by wholesale." She deemed the mixed-bloods to be well integrated into the half million whites in the territory. Most spoke English and many were living in nice houses. "Many are refined and cultured."[82]

She continued, "It is different with the twenty-five thousand full-bloods. They live in settlements among themselves, mostly, remote from the lines of travel; not many speak the English language; live in log or frame houses more or less comfortable; they do not mix very much in social relations with either whites or mixed bloods." When it came to schools, there were no US government schools for the Five Tribes. "The Indians have an excellent school system of their own. They have large invested school funds from which they draw plenty of money to educate their children. They have several large, free boarding schools with good buildings and some three hundred, or more, neighborhood or public schools, all free. Of course the mixed bloods being more progressive and aggressive get the most benefit from these schools but the full-bloods are not entirely neglected." She expressed a pessimistic yet prescient view of the "expir[ation]" of the tribal governments, which was scheduled for March 4, 1906. "Then will come the tug of war for the full blood." When they go to school, "It is probable that the full-blood children, not being able to speak English and with their different manners and habits will be ignored, ostracised [sic] and driven out of the schools."[83]

Despite the lack of integration in some arenas, in others, the WCTU was quite pleased with the full-bloods: "The full-bloods have churches and Sunday schools and native preachers of their own. Thousands are faithful, Christian men and women. . . . They have had good missionaries, working faithfully among them, for nearly one hundred years, and the Lord has blessed the labors of these good men abundantly." When it came to alcohol, Murrow reminded the reader that this was a "prohibition Territory. . . . The strict prohibitionary laws are fairly well executed." And there were thousands of "prosecutions under the law forbidding its sale." Temperance instruction was widespread "in churches, schools, and everywhere else." When asked in the questionnaire about reaching out to superintendents of government schools, medal contests, and LTLs, Murrow reminded the reader that "there are no U.S. Government schools in this Territory" but "all the mission schools do this work." There had been many medal contests and lots of pledge signing by Indians. "Rarely does an Indian man or woman or child refuse to sign a temperance pledge." She did not know how many LTLs existed in the territory since there were so many schools.[84]

As the end of tribal governments and the merger of the territories and possible statehood all loomed, Lindsey certainly looked like the model for what progressive, mixed-blood Indian leadership might look like. The national WCTU members certainly perceived her as such. National WCTU president Lillian M. N. Stevens wrote a lengthy and joyous *Union Signal* piece about

Indian Territory and the merger with Oklahoma. Stevens and her companions traveled to Bartlesville, Chelsea, Tahlequah, Muskogee, Calvin, and Tulsa. In Tulsa, she met with Lindsey, whom she described as "proud to be known as a Creek Indian" and a great businesswoman. They visited Tahlequah, capital of the Cherokee Nation and home to first territorial WCTU president, Jane Stapler. They visited Stapler's family and then went to the Cherokee National Female Seminary where the girls sang the popular temperance song "We Are Out for Prohibition" and of the two hundred students who sang for her, Stevens declared many of them "natural musicians." She was excited that "the principal has promised that they will soon organize a YWCTU." At Muskogee, they were entertained by Laura Harsha, and they met Lucy B. Davis, the ex-corresponding secretary. The next day they went to Calvin, a newer town, home to territorial vice president Mamie D. Ware. They saw a WCTU parade, "led off by children," and noted the road improvements made since Willard's last visit. Local support for prohibition contributed to Indian Territory's success, she claimed. In closing, Stevens predicted that Congress would vote for the merger of Oklahoma and Indian Territories and immediate statehood, where prohibition would continue in the new state within the old boundaries of Indian Territory.[85]

At the Indian Territory convention in 1906, preparations for the merger were underway. One of the most interesting discussions involved the choice of a name. Local chapters often took on honorary names beyond just their location. Honorific titles such as Frances Willard Union, Annie Bidwell Union, and Hiawatha Union were typical. If Indian Territory was absorbed into Oklahoma, which was all but assured, what was to become of the Indian Territory Union? Could the two halves of the state remain separate, as was the case with Northern/Southern California Unions, Eastern/Western Washington, or the Southern/Northern Idaho unions? "What name shall we give our W.C.T.U. in case of joint statehood?" one officer queried. "The name Sequoyah was suggested by both our National and Territorial Presidents. Motion made in event of joint statehood that we call new W.C.T.U. work Sequoyah, and that the Executive present this motion to annual convention for their adoption."[86] In their list of resolutions, members resolved to do "all in our power to secure the enfranchisement of women in constitution of the state of Oklahoma, not only for the sake of our homes, but also for the sake of our state." This proposal was made under the leadership of Lilah D. Lindsey, who was chair of the executive committee because of her position as president.[87]

In 1907 at the Indian Territory convention there was a discussion about the merging of the Oklahoma and Indian Territory unions, and "nearly every delegate" and all of the leadership spoke. When it was put to a vote, the tally was "24 for and 27 against." The president of Oklahoma's WCTU "Mrs. [Abbie] Hillerman arose and in a nice manner thanked the convention for their expression and said as far as she was concerned they would consider it closed." The convention proceeded, with the election of territorial officers and delegates to the national convention. Lizzie B. Coval of Muskogee was elected superintendent of the Department of Work Among Indians. Lindsey was elected president of the Indian Territory Union. The election of national delegates was particularly important because they would be representing their unions while discussing the issue of a merger at the national convention. According to the minutes: "There were 13 members of the convention who had Indian blood or had intermarried," out of 51 who had voted on the merger motion and others who may have been nonvoting attendees.[88] The Department of Work Among Indians was listed as an "elective" department, headed by K. L. E. Murrow. Inserted in the directory was Murrow's charge to the readers of the proceedings: "Each Union is requested to give this department special thought. Mrs. Murrow will be glad to furnish information other than that she has given in the suggestive programs. Because of the peril threatening the Indian tribes from drink and tobacco we should do all in our power for the furtherance of this department."[89]

Clearly, there were mixed views about what should happen to the Indian Territory union—and mixed expectations of what was coming. In September 1907 the Indian Territory newspaper *The Helper*, right before the territorial convention, ran a story under the headline "All Indian Territory for God and Temperance." Mabel Sutherland's opening article suggested that the upcoming convention is "the last chapter" of the Indian Territory's WCTU's history and lamented the territory unions' failure to pay dues properly, suggesting that the new arrangement would bring financial stability to all of the unions.[90] WCTU members in Oklahoma Territory assumed such a merger was coming.

The previous year, at the Oklahoma WCTU convention in Norman, the Oklahoma Territory WCTU members had expressed their desire to form a joint union with Indian Territory. The executive committee members agreed that a "Fraternal Committee of three from Oklahoma W.C.T.U. be appointed to visit the Indian Territory convention, to bear greetings from Oklahoma W.C.T.U., and express the hope of an early union of the two territories, that President Abbie B. Hillerman be chairman of that committee."[91] WCTU members in other states looked nervously upon the potential merger of the two territories, fearing that the prohibition that existed in Indian Territory would be undone in the merger. The corresponding secretary of Montana, Matilda Currah strongly encouraged her readers to "send a protest to [Montana] Senator W. A. Clark against uniting Oklahoma and Indian territory as one state (thus, regardless of former treaties, aiding and abetting the encroachment of the liquor traffic among the Indians)."[92] The Missoula union launched a protest of their own against territorial mergers. The Indian Territory–Oklahoma Territory merger and the potential merger of Arizona and New Mexico raised the suspicions of the Missoulians. Both mergers were "discussed with warmth, and a vote was passed to circulate a petition protesting against that portion of the bill threatening injustice to women by classing them with minors, criminals, lunatics and ignoramuses."[93] Despite protestations from many quarters, the two territories merged, and the unions did too, under pressure from the national WCTU.

In October 1908 the *Union Signal* announced the merger of the Indian Territory and Oklahoma Territory unions into the WCTU of Oklahoma. Contrary to the record of events in Indian Territory, the October 1908 story curiously suggested that both had been looking forward to it (despite the Indian Territory voting against it at their previous convention). The national executive committee at the Nashville convention had recommended it and, through subtle pressure, made the union happen. In a loose-leaf handwritten memoir, Lindsey discussed her presidency of Indian Territory in its final days. She and Abbie Hillerman were appointed by president Lillian Stevens "in spring of 1907 . . . to draw up plans for the union of the two organizations into one state W.C.T.U." This occurred in Oklahoma City in 1908. In September 1908 the marriage of the unions was "consummated." The *Signal* author sensed some sadness when each separate union disbanded. Lindsey, "who has given time and endeavor and money to the cause, realized that the name she loved would lose its identity, but gave it up gladly because of the assurance that the union marks the beginning of a greater work in the new state." In the reorganization Cora Hammet was elected president, and Josephine Dorman was elected vice president. Lindsey, the most prominent Native American woman at the national level, was not elected to state office in the new union, but she would soon become president of the Tulsa union and would become state corresponding secretary in 1911.[94]

The WCTU of Oklahoma members met in 1908 and published their proceedings in the yearbook. The superintendent of Work Among Indians and Soldiers was Mary Clark of Fort Sill, Oklahoma, located in what had been

Figure 8.   Nashville WCTU Convention Ribbon, Marked "Indian Territory," 1907.
(Courtesy of Lilah Lindsey Collection, Collection Number 1976-016, The University of Tulsa,
McFarlin Library, Department of Special Collections and University Archives, Tulsa, OK.)

Oklahoma Territory. Fort Sill was also the final resting place of the Apache leader Geronimo. It was a long way from the strongholds of the Five Tribes in the eastern part of the state.[95] Once the merger occurred and the new officers were established, the Oklahoma Department of Work Among Indians and Soldiers began to attack nascent Indigenous revitalization movements that involved intoxicants—including peyote, which many reformers erroneously referred to as "mescal." In her 1908 report Clark, located in Fort Sill and surrounded by the western tribes, indicated that she modified the typical abstinence pledge: "I have had a pledge including mescal with other intoxicants printed for the Indians and many of them have signed it. Have had three pupils' meetings and planned for three others, but failed on account of weather and other things. There is much to do and am planning to do more the coming year."[96]

Opposition to the merger had not been frivolous, and the aftermath confirmed the fears of Indian Territory WCTU members. In 1911 the Cherokee Keetoowah Society, a traditionalist organization of Cherokees, requested the continuation of their ward status because of the lack of federal protections in the new situation.[97] On May 8, 1913, the *Union Signal*'s Washington writer Margaret Dye Ellis reported that since the merger the scamming of Indians of their severalty lands was rampant, according to W. K. Moorehead of the Board of Indian Commissioners. Grafters would buy tax certificates after individuals failed to pay their tax bills.[98] By 1913 Work Among Indians was no longer conflated with the soldiers' department. The superintendent was a Mrs. M. L. McIntosh, of Chelsea, Oklahoma, who was probably of Creek or Cherokee descent, and the department was listed under "Organization."[99] As Native American women in the WCTU navigated the various lobbying efforts, citizenship battles, mergers of complex organization, transitions from statehood to territories, and the development of new constitutions, they were learning through experience something else promoted and valued by the WCTU itself: parliamentary procedure, or as they termed it "parliamentary usage."

Parliamentary Usage and Preparation for Governing
Although it might not have been an initial attraction to join the organization, parliamentary usage was something many Native American women came to value. The WCTU Department of Parliamentary Usage led workshops, printed pamphlets, and otherwise promoted procedures for discussion, introduction and passage of rules, constructing and amending constitutions, and other elements of organizational business. The symbolism behind these activities for

the WCTU as a whole was hard to miss—women who were disenfranchised politically by law, and excluded from the upper echelons of power in the churches by ecclesiastical rules, demonstrated that they could run meetings, follow rules, and accomplish tasks in perfect order. It was proof of their worthiness in the political arena. It was doubly powerful as an exhibition of ability for Native American women, who were doubly disenfranchised because of both gender and race.

Annie Bidwell observed this phenomenon with glee in California. January 28, 1902, was the first "Regular meeting of the Indian Prohib[ition] Alliance" with thirty-seven present. As with separate WCTU unions, members of the Indian Prohibition Alliance made great efforts to operate in an orderly fashion and according to parliamentary rules. The "diagram of position of officers [was] obeyed strictly. Maggie [Lafonso] calling them to their places. President John A[z]bill & Vice Pres. Jas. Nuckel [?], read better than one in a thousand of well-educated white persons. Amazed me! Mothers and babes present." Bidwell, acting as chaplain, offered a prayer for the group.[100] On the other side of the United States, a similar level of diligence prevailed. Lora La Mance, a national WCTU organizer visited Lydia Pierce and the Tunesassa Union and observed what she saw with condescending admiration: "It was a real pleasure to see with what parliamentary exactness these dignified Indian matrons conducted their meetings and how wide-awake they were along all W.C.T.U. lines." She noted that Cornplanter's original treaty with the United States had prohibited liquor being sold to his people. Unfortunately, "sharp lawyers have managed to pick flaws in the instrument, and thus evade the prohibition provision of this treaty." La Mance was optimistic, however, that the City of Salamanca would vote out the saloons from their territory in a referendum in April.[101] Such a victory would require parliamentary exactness, to be sure.

Family, legal rights and protections, Christianity, literacy, and parliamentary procedures were all part of the efforts by Native American WCTU members to walk a wholesome and productive path. The shadows of demographic collapse, violence, alcohol abuse, suffering at the hands of whites, all hung over the path they chose. They participated in an acculturation movement that was more benevolent, perhaps, but nonetheless part of the same colonizers' plan to eliminate distinct tribal governments and identities. They made this path their own as they carved out space to eliminate the most destructive elements of the colonizers' toolkits: alcohol trading, unrestrained military bases, and attacks on Indian land ownership, whether in common or as allotments.

Thus far, we have examined only the most well-intentioned white WCTU women who involved themselves in Indian matters and the Native American women with whom they often became personally close. Unfortunately, the WCTU members from across the nation had a much more conflicted vision of Native Americans. These white WCTU members often ignored the failures of US Indian policy, indulged in harmful stereotypes, and were unaware of the unique legal statuses of tribes. Yet, these biases in turn shaped the impact of the WCTU's work among Indians.

Chapter 3

Representations of American Indians in WCTU Literature

While Native American women were joining the organization, taking up offices, fighting for their futures through the WCTU, white women in the organization were writing about American Indians in conflicting ways. The WCTU's textual construction of Native Americans can be seen in examples from the *Union Signal* and WCTU documents where "Indians" are used as literary embellishments or discussed in terms of current events and historical precedents aside from being part of WCTU activities. These rhetorical constructions affected how the WCTU members thought about Native Americans and thus how they developed their outreach to Native communities. Considering the wide distribution and readership of the *Union Signal*, the WCTU became an important shaper of general public opinion among women about Native Americans and should be seen as both reflector and shaper of popular evangelical Christian, reform-minded ideas.

The WCTU authors used Native Americans as rhetorical devices, as historical examples and inspirations, and as part of the organization's coverage of current events. The varying and sometimes inconsistent ideas about Native Americans and policies toward them preceding or concurrent with the organization's formal work helped to color the policies and practices of the WCTU toward Indian tribes and individuals once they tried to incorporate them and to advocate for national, state, and local Indian policies. These thoughts, beliefs, and misconceptions found their way into publications, including the *Union Signal*, the myriad state WCTU papers, the *Annual Meeting Minutes*, STI manuals, WCTU pamphlets, and even advertisements. Capturing these intellectual or ideological influences on the mind-set of WCTU members sets the foundation for understanding how and why WCTU members proceeded with their work in Native American communities and allows us to understand the racism, biases, and ethnocentrism that Native women suffered through, during their work.

Although WCTU leaders held conflicting positions, there were recurring themes and beliefs that approximate a consensus, and which culminated under the leadership of Dorcas Spencer. (1) There was sympathy for Native American population losses and for their suffering at the hands of the US military, white vigilantes, and alcohol traders. With a few exceptions, there was little commitment to preservation of Native American tribal governments or tribally held land bases, but WCTU leaders concurred that individual Indian landholdings should be protected from unethical transfer to whites. (2) Beneath the sympathy, authors fostered stereotypes of an Indian propensity for violence. They promulgated stories and personal memories of the Plains Wars, massacres, and individual crimes by Native Americans. To some white ribboners, this supposed violent nature made their prospects for full inclusion dubious, and their participation in the political system undeserved. (3) This position, often voiced by women living far from Native American populations, sometimes gave way to a belief in their redeemability through Christ, Euro-American education, abandonment of traditional religious practices, and temperance. (4) Those changes in the Native American mind would then be coupled with citizenship, allotment and private landownership, and general assimilation into the mainstream economy. (5) Authors appropriated historical events, characters, and imagery for their own purposes, sometimes for humorous or dramatic effect, sometimes in a misguided attempt to provide depth and historical precedent, but usually in ways that fundamentally showed the authors misunderstood events from an Indigenous perspective. While each trend influenced the other, there were often tensions between the dramatic, literary uses of American Indians and their more concrete policy statements.

While it may be difficult to disentangle general late-nineteenth-century views from specific strains of thought in the WCTU members, we can identify some people who were influential in shaping WCTU thought. The trend toward having sympathy for the Native Americans and holding a critical view of historical US Indian policies began with two foundational thinkers, Frances Willard and Helen Hunt Jackson. Their early writings about Native Americans expressed views that were later manifested more broadly in WCTU writing.

Frances Willard and Helen Hunt Jackson

Although Helen Hunt Jackson's name became synonymous in WCTU circles with Indian reform, and Willard's name was ubiquitous in all things WCTU-related, both women's words about Native Americans would enjoy longevity decades after they had been "promoted" (the WCTU euphemism for death). Willard, the second president of the WCTU, from 1879 to 1898, vastly broadened the scope of the organization's activity, making Indian work possible at all. Her views on any social issue while not dictatorial were influential to say the least. Jackson, the writer turned Indian reform advocate wrote three directly relevant works that would inform WCTU thinking: the legalistic and historical work, *A Century of Dishonor* (1881), the federally sponsored *Report on the Condition and Needs of the Mission Indians of California* (1883), and a sentimental novel set in the post–Mexican American War era, *Ramona* (1884). These pieces shaped the views of many Americans, but they were particularly popular in women's reform circles. Jackson's pieces engendered sympathy and were a giant leap away from the exterminationist views still held by many in the 1880s, but *Century of Dishonor* explicitly argued against the tribes holding any "fee title" to their land. That is, she denied Indian tribes' claims to sovereignty over their precolonial territories, admitting only a "right of occupancy," coinciding with the overwhelming legal precedent at the time. According to Jackson, it was the United States' continued violation of that more limited right that was the basis of the "dishonor" that the government brought on itself. After Jackson died in 1885, her influence continued in the pages of WCTU literature.[1]

The two women held different places within the WCTU pantheon: Willard *was* the WCTU to many people and she emphasized legal prohibition, the redemptive powers of Christ, Euro-American education, and Western civilization for Native Americans. Jackson was not a temperance advocate, but her fiction and nonfiction contained enough anti-alcohol sentiment that creative WCTU authors, always on the lookout for historical inspiration, were able to spin her works in a way that made her seem like a temperance pioneer. For Willard, temperance was obviously essential to any civilization process. With their biases and the limitations they placed on tribal persistence and future independence, they constrained the possibilities of the WCTU members' mind-sets concerning Native Americans. To understand the depth and limitations of their ideas, we must engage in a closer reading of their own words and of how subsequent WCTU members internalized, perpetuated, and sometimes misconstrued their messages.

Willard's influence came from her position as president, and her "do everything" policy eventually led to tackling Indian policy. She gained most of her experience with Native Americans and state and federal Indian policy from her extensive travels, but she rarely stayed long enough in the communities she visited to develop any in-depth relationships with tribes or even with specific Native American leaders, though she admired women like Jane Stapler and Susette La Flesche Tibbles. Her interactions transformed her thinking, but she transmitted both her educated observations and partially informed judgments to the WCTU publications where her words carried authority. Willard's views would change over time, but some of her earlier impressions helped set the stage for a generally unfavorable impression of traditional Native American cultures and a bias against Native American people—except those who had adopted Christianity, were educated in Euro-American ways, and fit into an overall acculturation campaign. One of the most important historians of the WCTU, Ruth Bordin, tended to be sympathetic to Willard's views: "On her western tours Willard visited reservations and was received enthusiastically." She extended this view to the rest of the WCTU: "There seems to have been little or no prejudice in the WCTU against native [sic] Americans. Oklahoma sent Jane Stapler, a Cherokee, as a delegate to the national convention in 1890. She was received warmly."[2]

Contrary to Bordin's assertions, however, both Willard and other WCTU leaders harbored bias against Native Americans, particularly those in a less than "Americanized" condition, according to Willard's standards. In her 1877 address to the annual meeting, Willard was speaking about the importance of laws protecting the common good. In a long metaphor comparing the need for liquor laws to the accepted wisdom of fire codes, she noted, "bitter experience has taught us that it's a law framed for the greatest numbers' greatest good." She continued, using the Paiutes of the Great Basin region as a symbol of individual self-interest run amok, even aligning them with Satan—and, perhaps even worse in her eyes, the liquor interests: "Civilization, as a general rule, proceeds upon this basis, leaving Piute [sic] Indians, South Sea cannibals, and whisky politicians to act upon the favorite principle of 'every man for himself and his satanic majesty may take the hindmost.'"[3] At the time of this statement Willard's experience with Native Americans was limited and, since she had spent most of her life in New York, Wisconsin, Illinois, and Europe, her knowledge of Paiutes was almost entirely theoretical.

Once president she came into contact with greater circles of members from around the nation, including Native Americans. In 1880 Willard commented on her previous year's visit to Indian Territory. "I remained six weeks, and found that direct information, to say the least, modified previous impressions." She discussed her day-to-day interactions and the locations she visited in Indian Territory. She posited four forces at work on "the Indian": The "Government, the missionary, the intruder, and the Indian himself. And these are sometimes, in effect, interchanged. Were our Government altogether a Christian Government instead of being only in part so, its wise provision of prohibition for Indian Territory would be more perfectly carried out." She issued a powerful call for a more humane Indian policy, for removing government agents and having WCTU women as agents, and she suggested investigating the possibility of doing this and seeing if there were legal restrictions against them seeking offices.[4]

Even by modern standards Willard's travel schedule was impressive. Considering that she did it all without the aid of airplanes or automobiles, often traveling to remote regions of the country, in defiance of nineteenth-century expectations about women, it is hard not to be in awe. The rapidity of her travel and the short duration of some of her stops limited the level of understanding she could attain about any given Native American tribe or individual's perspective on alcohol, education, Christianity, or acculturation. For instance, after her 1881 visit to Indian Territory, Willard commented on Ulysses S. Grant's Peace Policy, which she described as "the happiest Presidential thought of President Grant."[5] Considering Willard's religious proclivities, a superficial look at Grant's policy was a cause for optimism. Missionaries were appointed as Indian agents, presumably bringing in people who would have less material interest in their position and a more benevolent spiritual interest in their supervisees. Grant appointed Ely Parker, a Seneca army officer, as commissioner of Indian affairs, evidence of some desire to have a Native American perspective in the role. However, most historians have been critical of the "policy," because behind the pastoral administrators was the threat of military force if tribes did not comply with the "peaceful" parts of the policy. Indeed, many of the most memorable battles of the Indian Wars occurred during, or even as a result of, the Peace Policy.[6]

The Peace Policy directed the OIA to assign people like the Quakers Asa and Emeline Tuttle as missionaries. The Tuttles supervised the arrival of the Modocs whom the federal government forced to move from the

California–Oregon border to Indian Territory in 1873, following the Modoc War—a violent conflict ending with the execution of several Modoc leaders in an incident commonly offered as evidence of the failure of the Peace Policy.[7] Willard described their arrival at the Quapaw Agency, which was to be the Modocs' new home. Describing an event to which she was not a witness, she surmised that the Modocs were "unkempt, uncleanly, huddled together in squatting attitude, with untaught hands, brains cobwebbed by superstition, and bodies diseased by strong drink; without habits of industry, instincts of home, and knowledge of Christianity; this band of savages is turned over to Brother Asa and Sister Emeline to see what the New Testament and the total abstinence pledge can do for them." However, by the time of Willard's visit in May 1881— with Emeline, who was the vice president of Indian Territory WCTU—she could promise the reader, "this is the last scene of the 'dissolving view' of sloughed-off barbarism—the dawn of a new manhood in Christ Jesus." She assured readers that she had slept "in a community where the hands that used to clasp the scalping-knives had grown familiar with plough-handles and the voices that yelled the lava beds' war-whoop now sang Moody hymns."[8]

Her disregard for traditional religion, which she dubbed "superstition," and her lack of understanding of Modoc resistance to Euro-American encroachment in the Modoc War did not stand in the way of her desire for their continued cultural, educational, and spiritual redemption. She came home with several lessons that would help shape WCTU's policies. She advocated for trade schools to be built on reservations rather than relying on the distant boarding schools, which were far more disruptive to families and communities. She was emphatic that federal prohibitory laws be enforced, beginning with the commissioner of Indian affairs on down to the local agents. She expressed her optimism and editorialized on the politics of the OIA, noting that there was a better chance of enforcement now that the "perfidious Commissioner [Ezra Ayres] Hayt (whose entire wits were absorbed in fraudulent attempts to make money out of his office)" had been replaced by the "thorough, active temperance man" Hiram Price.[9] The WCTU was thus to play a role, according to Willard, in the salvation of the Native Americans, and they were to be partners with the churches and the OIA itself.

The redemptive force of the WCTU (embodied by Frances Willard) and Native American potential for civilization (embodied by exemplary or symbolic Native American figures) could become comingled in curious ways in the writings of WCTU authors. One later WCTU historian, Elizabeth Putnam Gordon, created a simile comparing Willard to Sacajawea, the Shoshone woman who accompanied Lewis and Clark on their journey to the Pacific in 1805, ushering in the spread of US civilization to Indian country and (in the assimilationists' eyes) saving her race.[10] In *Women Torch-Bearers*, the 1924 jubilee-year history of the WCTU, Gordon commented on Willard's arduous 1882–1883 journey throughout the United States. Of her stint in the Pacific Northwest, particularly Oregon, Gordon invoked both Willard's messianic beliefs and the Native American history of the region:

> In her heart of hearts, "a fire burned for a beacon light." Like Sacajawea, the Indian princess, who at sixteen, with her baby on her back, led brave pioneers through the trackless forests to this unclaimed country, so Frances Willard, possessing the brain and brawn of her distinguished pilgrim ancestors, resolved, with God's help, to point out to these privileged people living in the Valley of the Columbia, a still higher civilization, the only sure way of protection for their homes.[11]

At first blush, the reference to Native Americans might seem like an innocuous literary embellishment. However, WCTU flourishes involving Native American historical figures reflected the organization's visions for Native Americans in the temperance movement and in the broader United States. This was a faulty connection between Willard and Sacajawea, who was kidnapped by the Hidatsa, sold into marriage with a white Frenchman, Toussaint Charbonneau, and then dragged across the American West without her consent, only to die young in the Dakotas shortly after giving birth.[12]

The Sacajawea comparison and her frequent manipulation by suffrage and temperance workers have been discussed in public history circles, as her real-life story was altered by early twentieth-century progressives who desperately wanted a Native American heroine to lend credence to their own noble efforts.[13] The WCTU played a role in this, bringing her into their writings as inspiration. On August 24, 1905, Sacajawea even graced the cover of the *Union Signal* itself (see figure 9). To the WCTU, the image of Sacajawea gave historical weight and North American authenticity to their overall project and to their efforts with modern Native Americans.

In the North Dakota WCTU publication *Western Womanhood*, the title of a biography stated it clearly: "Sakakawea: The First Feminist." The piece quoted Professor A. E. Minard, from a paper read at the State Federation of Women's Clubs in Fargo, North Dakota, describing what she symbolized. According to

The Union Signal

Vol. XXXI   EVANSTON, ILL., AUGUST 24, 1905   No. 34

SACAJAWEA

The Indian Woman who led the Explorers Lewis and Clark
through the trackless wilds of the West

Figure 9. Sacajawea *Union Signal*, cover, 1905. Suffrage and temperance organizations frequently used Sacajawea as a motivational image. (Credit: *Union Signal*, August 24, 1905. Courtesy of Frances Willard Memorial Library and Archives, Evanston, IL.)

the speaker, the women who worked to put up her statue at the State Capitol "knew that there was in her character and deeds not only that which was worthy of commemoration in the past, but that which was prophetic of the future." The willingness to take risks, work ethic, pragmatism, and knowledge of languages and cultures were the traits that impressed the Lewis and Clark expedition and were the traits that were needed to guide contemporary women in their quest for the vote and for prohibition. At the end of the two-column metaphor, the author then fabricated Sacajawea's own post-voyage reflections, for which she provided no evidence (none exists) on her conception of the "Voyage of Discovery." The author asked rhetorically, "Was she sorry she had taken the task when the journey was done? On the contrary, did not the memory of it become one of her dearest possessions? How life must have grown broader and deeper for her as she kept beside the captains in their march to the great sea water."[14] Neither the WCTU linking of Willard to Sacajawea nor the characterization of Sacajawea herself had anything to do with the historical woman. The temperance authors' literary manipulations falsely linked an impressive, courageous, and memorable Native American to the cause of temperance, westward expansion, and Euro-American civilization.

Sacajawea was not the only figure whose views were manipulated by the WCTU. Helen Hunt Jackson's catalogue of the cruel treatment of Native Americans deeply affected many WCTU members. After her death in 1885 the *Union Signal* and other WCTU publications paid tribute to her legacy both directly and indirectly. Many subsequent temperance short stories, poems, and aphorisms published by the WCTU had a Hunt-esque sentimentality and romanticism. Alternating between emphasizing their "degradedness" and expressing their "sentimental affection" for Indian women's (and more rarely men's) fidelity, sobriety, and wisdom resulted in a sort of dualistic view of Native people that was only loosely connected to reality and which was, ultimately, never satisfactorily resolved by the WCTU. *Century of Dishonor* is largely organized as a series of case studies of violations of treaties or agreements with specific tribes. Her defense of the tribes' rights stems from a clearly Eurocentric view of the conquest of the Americas. She concedes that the European colonizers held the *right of sovereignty* over the land, which was transferred to the United States upon gaining independence from Great Britain. This stemmed from their *right of discovery*, whereby European nations "discovered" lands occupied by Indigenous people who did not enclose and hold land in ways deemed permanent by European authorities. Those authorities also had an incentive to dispossess the communities that very much occupied and used the lands where they lived. Their sovereignty was in doubt, once the colonial enterprise began, according to the Euro-American inheritors of that colonial legacy. According to this faulty logic, the tribes possessed the weaker *right of occupancy*, which could be extinguished through agreements or treaties between both parties. The basis of Jackson's criticism was that the United States had unilaterally and unfairly violated or terminated those treaties. American Indians, especially her beloved Mission Indians of California, deserved protection of the lands they *occupied*, but they lacked absolute legal sovereignty over the land, which would have reflected a more truly anticolonial stance—one rare among even the most sympathetic and knowledgeable reformers of the nineteenth century.[15]

According to Valerie Sherer Mathes, Jackson was not as energetic in putting forth a comprehensive assimilationist agenda as other WCTU-aligned reformers. Mathes explains that Jackson's criticism of US treatment of the tribes was then picked up by the WNIA and the IRA, who promoted assimilation more directly than she did, but who shared her sense of outrage about past treatments.[16] Helen Hunt Jackson never joined the WCTU or even explicitly advocated legal prohibition, but an anti-liquor strain was present in her Indian works, which later WCTU writers amplified, perhaps overzealously. Among the Winnebagoes, she claimed, "drunkenness is becoming one of the serious vices of the tribe. They are surrounded on all sides by white men who traffic in whiskey, and who are, moreover, anxious to reduce the Indians to as degraded a state as possible." In discussing the Cheyenne she commented on an 1847 federal law "forbidding the introduction of whiskey into the Indian country, and even the partial enforcement of this law had a most happy effect." Writing about the Sioux she quoted the artist George Catlin who declared, "That the Indians in their native state are drunken, is false, for they are the only temperance people, literally speaking, that I ever saw in my travels, or expect to see. . . . These people manufacture no spiritous liquor themselves, and know nothing of it until it is brought into their country, and tendered to them by Christians."[17]

In the introduction to her "Report on the Condition and Needs of the Mission Indians of California" (1883), coauthored with Abbot Kinney, they commented on the dangers of alcohol to vulnerable Native American communities. "Considerable numbers of these Indians are also to be found on the outskirts of white settlements, as at Riverside, San Bernardino, or in the colonies in the San Gabriel Valley, where they live like gypsies in brush huts, here to-day, gone to-morrow, eking out a miserable existence by days' works, the wages of which are too often spent for whiskey in the village saloons." They referred to "Mr. Wilson's report" on Los Angeles, "where every other house was a grog-shop for Indians; and every Saturday night the town was filled with Indians in every stage of intoxication." She continued, describing the unequal punishment for whites and Indians for alcohol law violations. In the closing paragraph of the report portion, she stated: "that drunkenness, gambling, and other immoralities are sadly prevalent among them, cannot be denied." However, in the specific recommendations that follow, not one is specifically focused on the alcohol trade. To Jackson, the observations she made did not lead her to suggest additional restrictions or increased enforcement of existing laws.[18]

In *Ramona* Jackson casts the alcohol trade as being destructive to Mexicans and Native Americans, and it is almost entirely the fault of white alcohol traders who take advantage of the generally naïve Indians manipulating them into drinking and causing mayhem. In one scene, during a summer festival, "disorderly whites took advantage of the occasion to sell whiskey and encourage all sorts of license and disturbance."[19] But for the aggressive tactics of American alcohol peddlers, Indians' behavior would have been much better. This sympathetic view of Native Americans, her critique of the general treatment of tribes by the US government, her limited expectations for tribal sovereignty, and the characterization of alcohol abuse as the manifestation of white greed on a population with the potential for "civilization"—or redemption—would be reflected in explicit and implicit ways by the WCTU literature.

In an 1887 report on a mission to Southern California, Scottish temperance worker Margaret E. Parker explained how the Colton WCTU president's adult son acted as her guide. "He pioneered me to San Jacinto, that beautiful place in the mountains described by Helen Hunt Jackson in her story, 'Ramona.'" Adapting the Hebrews story of Cain and Abel to contemporary circumstances, Parker evoked Jackson: "'She being dead yet speaketh' as I can testify, having seen Indian schools which owe their existence to her inspiration. I visited one at Santa Fe, on my way to California, where Indian girls are trained at the expense of the government. This school is named 'Ramona,' in memory of Helen Hunt Jackson. If the blessed ever look down on their life work, surely she will be made increasingly happy in her seeing her beloved Indians cared for as a result of her labors."[20]

In an 1888 memorial in the *Union Signal* Margaret Spencer provided a biography of Jackson that reflected the "salvation from despair" trope common in all sentimental literature. She noted that Jackson's mental state deteriorated after the deaths of her husband and her children—one in infancy and one at eight years old. "In the blindness and despair, she was left desolate." In part because of the power and prayer of her friends and family she emerged after months of depression. "Out of this deep, dark well of desolation and sorrow she had drawn a new love, a new and greater courage and strength, which has since overflowed into the heart of the world—never from that day withholding one sweet or kindly word. It was a costly gift and sacrifice, but she said 'Our Father gave his only Son for us; what are we, to refuse Him our miserable selves?'" She moved westward with her second husband, "Mr. Jackson," and there her redemptive work involved both temperance and Indians. "She hated intemperance and prophesied 'great things for women in the grand work,' and while in Los Angeles was the means of breaking up several liquor dealers for selling whisky to the Indians." Although there was a gap of over a decade between the death of her last surviving child and the 1879 Standing Bear case that thrust her into Indian work, Spencer compressed this gap in her biography so as to inspire new workers among Indians. To the WCTU reader, work among the Indians was the way that Jackson was redeemed from a world of pain. The reader would also have been reminded of Cherokee leader Jane Stapler, who threw herself into temperance work after the loss of her two daughters in the early 1880s.[21]

Margaret Spencer did not describe Jackson as a formulaic or money-seeking author. Although the sentimental story was a popular form, the sentiments were genuine. Ramona's story was powerful for temperance workers and WCTU readers precisely because it was sentimental—Spencer equated Ramona's maternal experience with Jackson's own. Jackson's life struggles and tragedies, and her early death, however sad to her readers and followers, also served as inspiration for WCTU workers.[22] Such a description of Indian reformers, which included the near absence of actual Native American people or an assessment of the negative consequences of white education and acculturation, was characteristic of much of the WCTU writing about Indians. Writers focused instead on the inspirational nature of those who worked with Native Americans. In their formulation, the salvation that Jackson experienced was then shared with or transferred to the Native Americans. The WCTU picked up on Jackson's redemptive experience, and the association of

Indians with it, and would cast Indians rhetorically as backward and brutish but, at the same time, eligible for social and spiritual redemption. Even though Jackson was never a proponent of prohibition or an advocate of temperance, the WCTU made her into an inspiration in the temperance fight.

Indian Characters, Morality Tales, and Misunderstandings

In the same spirit that WCTU biographers and historians appropriated Sacajawea and conflated her with Willard, *Union Signal* journalists and WCTU authors were fond of juxtaposing civilization with savagery as a lesson for white Christian readers, and they used fabricated scenarios with American Indians for various effects. The impact of these literary contortions went beyond entertainment. The inaccurate rhetorical use of Native American history and culture devalued Native traditions, governments, and tribal persistence. In 1893 the *Union Signal* published a short piece by Samuel Huntington Comings entitled "Savagery vs. Christianity—'Competition' vs. 'Mutualism,'" which served as a morality tale to promote Social Gospel Christianity. The author recounted a dream "of being in a camp full of savages." Prior to missionary contact, the unnamed band divided up a deer according to the principle of "might makes right." The "burly chief at once took the hindquarters on his back, because he was the strongest brave in the party." The distribution continued, in order of physical strength until "an old and decrepit savage . . . gathered up the scanty fragments of the game." The dreamer then projected forward several years, after the introduction of Christianity. In this scene, the powerful hunter lived in a nice cottage and sat in a Windsor chair as he spoke. The "bent and aged warrior" of the previous scene was still living in a "rude wigwam." The message was clear. "I could not find any essential difference between the first exhibition of savage selfishness in dividing the deer, and the present methods prevailing among so-called Christians, where the *sharp* and *unscrupulous* gather in the overwhelming fruits of modern wealth, and become profligate and vicious from the very surfeit of goods not needed for any natural want; while the weak, simple, or unfortunate suffer and die, or are degraded by want and poverty." The author then asked rhetorically, "Can Christianity lead us to a higher life of some sort of 'mutualism' than the savagery of 'competition'? That is one of the most urgent problems that asks solution of the Christian teachers of today."[23] The characterization of Woodland Indian values is horribly fabricated. The real-life "mutualism" of the successful Native American hunters is well borne out in the historical record, whereby

Native American men gained prestige in their communities by distributing their hard-won game to members of their community rather than hording their wealth.[24] While the progressives sought to promote mutualism, they often missed the rhetorical injustices they administered to the Native American cultures they employed.

Other authors tried in clumsy ways to encourage sympathy for Native Americans by making sure white Christian readers knew that Indians were just like them, save for their lack of civilization. The 1891 superintendent for Work Among Indians in California, E. M. Priddy, tried to make a connection between her readership's sense of heritage and the Native Americans of California. Borrowing from Alexander Pope's oft-quoted "Epistle on Man," Priddy wrote, "'Lo! the poor Indian.' Yes, he is low, but is the Indian any lower than our forefathers, who, less than three hundred years ago, ate with their fingers? Give the poor Digger [Great Basin Indian] education and Christianity, and he will eat with a fork in less than three years."[25] Other times Native American societies could be used as a model of the kinds of social and legal reforms the WCTU sought for women across the United States. One story informed readers that "among several semi-civilized tribes the women do all the courting, and among the Zuni Indians, they control the situation after marriage, as the children, inheritance, etc. belong to the wife."[26] The implication was that white Christian American society had something to learn from the gender roles of their otherwise only "semi-civilized" neighbors.

In 1896, despite the complications with Indian policy and the differing levels of acculturation and economic circumstances of tribes, Willard seemed to think the "Indian Problem" was being solved in Indian Territory through acculturation, education, and citizenship. Willard paid Helen Hunt Jackson her due, noting that Indian policy had "never [been] so ably treated as by 'H.H'—a woman—in her novel Ramola [*sic*]." Upon Willard's arrival in Muskogee, she was met by a "fine delegation of white-ribboners." Things had changed since her first visit to Indian Territory in 1881. She was struck by what she perceived as a lack of Indian population in Muskogee—or at least a lack of people who matched her assumption of what it meant to be Indian: visible, racial markers of "Indian-ness." Describing a pleasant scene at the opera house and a "cultivated audience" she noted, "Let no one imagine that an Indian was present. Nay, verily, they have 'died out' or they live in remote places. We saw some wagonloads of them passing through the town, but they were nowhere about save as transients."[27]

At Fort Smith, Arkansas, however, she learned of someone who more accurately met her expectations for the perfidy of a real or unacculturated "Indian." Cherokee Bill, the alias of Crawford Goldsby, was of mixed Native American, African American, and European ancestry, which seemed particularly suspect to Willard: "He was but twenty years old, but such was his nerve (he was of mingled blood—Indian, African, and white) that with his mother and childhood's nurse beside him on the scaffold, he faced the crowd, and when they called, 'A speech!' he answered with surprising dignity. 'I did not come to talk, I came to die.'" A murderer and bank robber, he was executed around the time of her visit, though she did not witness the spectacle in person. As if to redeem herself of being in proximity to the ghoulish event, she spent the next day speaking with inmates who had been sentenced to death, all of whom were "as hard as a nether millstone." Generally critical of the death penalty, Willard found the whole situation in Fort Smith reprehensible. People from Indian Territory were, by federal regulation, dragged to Fort Smith where justice was swift and brutal. She was optimistic that if Indian Territory became its own dry state and if the WCTU could maintain its influence there, a more humane system of crime prevention and prosecution could be developed.[28]

Alongside Willard's unflattering description of the Modocs and Paiutes, the whitewashing of the acculturated tribes of Indian Territory, and the racist coverage of Cherokee Bill, other WCTU authors put American Indians to work as useful examples to spur WCTU activity. They employed Native American figures to shame the comparatively privileged white women to work harder, organize better, and donate more generously. In the early 1890s the WCTU was building a temperance temple in Chicago, which was completed in 1892. Their most direct fund-raising method was to solicit donations directly from members through local chapters. In 1891 Julia Hall, a missionary and WCTU worker, supervised a Modoc union with fifty-six members who, despite their poverty, donated to the temple fund. Hall reported condescendingly, "we are training them that it is better to give than to receive." Matilda B. Carse, a key organizer in the fund-raising campaign, used the Modocs' generosity to motivate more prosperous donors. Carse urged the readers, who would have been familiar with Willard's coverage of the Modocs and other tribes, to "think of the Modoc Indians working for the Temple! Surely after this announcement all white-ribboners who have not sent for a mite-box will do so, and not allow the Modocs to outdo them."[29] Despite the condescension of certain authors toward Native Americans, Native American leaders wrote confidently of their contributions to the WCTU's efforts.

During the fund-raising efforts for the temple, besides direct requests the WCTU engaged in numerous campaigns, including selling inkstands that were miniature models of the temple. Jane Stapler commented glowingly on the objects—symbolic of literacy and the refined, middle-class art of letter writing. Stapler declared, "It is extremely difficult to overrate [the inkstand's] beauty and perfection. I displayed it to our white ribbon sisters and friends. Voices all around said, 'send for one for me.' Please send a dozen by express to my address."[30] Although the quotation was recorded by Carse, the words coming from Stapler suggest a very different role for Native American women: instead of having to be pushed into generosity like children, as characterized by Hall and Carse, the women in Stapler's union had good taste and the financial means to order more, thus being actual contributors in the fund-raising efforts.

It is not just that Native American voices better recognized Native American contributions to the organization; non-Native leaders in Indian Territory who had closer interactions with Native Americans in their daily life understood their contributions better than more distant WCTU members. In 1903 the Indian Territory president Laura E. Harsha spoke in glowing terms of the first territorial president, Jane Stapler, and the early officer Tennie M. Fuller, both Cherokee: "Looking backward over these years of our history, brings memories of our loved and revered Mother Stapler (a true mother in Israel) our pioneer President, and her co-worker, our loved sister, Tennie M. Fuller, who, through our early days held us together; both true as steel and good as gold, and both working for their people." And paying them the greatest compliment in WCTU circles, Harsha continued, "Their lives, like that of our Frances E. Willard, will ever live and their spirits like hovering angels, help lead us on to victory."[31] President of the Oklahoma WCTU, Abbie Hillerman, wrote a president's letter, published in the *Oklahoma Messenger*, describing the recently elected Indian Territory president, Lilah Lindsey, as a "very gracious presiding officer."[32] In 1909, when recounting events surrounding the merger of the two unions in 1907 (when Lindsey was elected vice president), Mary Johnson, Oklahoma WCTU state press superintendent reported that there had been "such an instantaneous outburst of applause, Chautauqua salutes, etc., etc., that there could be no doubt as to the sentiment of the convention upon the subject."[33]

It was not simply that there were more honorific descriptions of Native American leaders coming from Indian country. These descriptions were more realistic in describing how to approach the differences in literacy and culture of Indian Territory and Oklahoma Territory based on a clearer sense of real life in Native America. In Indian Territory, the Literature Department superintendent Martha Gilmore set out a plan for herself to get the temperance tracts published into Native American languages. This had already been done in Cherokee communities where the literacy rates were higher than among the "full bloods" to the west. K. L. E. Murrow, superintendent of "The Evangelistic and Missionary Work Among Fullblood Indians" Department, lamented this comparative lack of literacy and English language skills and applauded the efforts to approach the children in the schools whose English skills were better. Nevertheless, she and her husband "had printed 1000 pledge cards for the Choctaws, 1000 for the Creeks and 500 for the Cherokees." Presumably, these were in the tribes' respective languages or there would be no need to have different versions printed.[34]

Laura Harsha also provided an important corrective for outsiders' views of Indian criminality. Describing jail work in the Muskogee jail, she declared, "We have in it upwards of sixty inmates, of all ages, sizes, colors, nationalities and conditions, 90 per cent of which are in through strong drink." She went on to describe the various WCTU efforts in Indian Territory and in the jails, in particular. The essential goodness of all people came through in her writing, and she turned the exterminationist phrase "No Good Indian but a dead Indian" on its head, replacing it with a new motto: "All are good Indians but drunken ones."[35] This was a reminder to those not familiar with Native American communities that the cause of violence, mischief, and criminality was the same as in the white communities: alcohol. It had nothing to do with racial or cultural inferiority.

While some of the stories in WCTU literature may have been used to motivate the rank and file, this does not mean the authors were disingenuous or that white women's writings about Native Americans were always fabrications of their beliefs or sentiments. Annie Bidwell, in a journal not intended for public consumption, wrote about her mentee William Conway. Conway described dirty theaters when he was away in Sacramento, and the "'peculiar ways of amusing themselves of the Anglo Saxon race.' As expressed in certain low theatres" where a friend had brought him. She assured her diary that "he was 'disgusted'" by whatever he saw there.[36] That is, Native people close to whites expressed their dismay with the whites' own uncivilized nature when they were exposed to alcohol and debauchery. Bidwell was clearly heartened by the sense of respectability and good taste that Conway had supposedly internalized.

Gender, Race, Citizenship, and Alcohol Abuse

WCTU authors also used stories of Indian alcohol abuse as cautionary tales for the destruction of liquor in the broader world. In one case they employed the Native Alaskans. The *Union Signal* quoted the Reverend R. W. Hill who had just returned from Alaska. He claimed:

> "The Indians will give away wife and children," he says, "to obtain liquor, and their carousals are so fierce and reckless that murders and suicides are frequent results." He also believes that unless the progress of ruin is stayed, the end of the Alaska Indians is not far off. Who can remain indifferent in learning such facts, and in watching with these the fearful work going on over the whole world, as the outgrowth of this one deadly business? Our whole being cries out, what shall we call thee, thou enemy of mankind? The great master poet of human nature answers, "Let us cal[l] thee—devil!"[37]

Such personifications of alcohol as the devil incarnate and overselling the level of violence that was an otherwise real effect of alcohol abuse led WCTU writers to indulge in a general characterization of Indian men as threatening and violent, whose citizenship was suspect, even though full US citizenship for American Indians was one of the oft-stated goals of the WCTU. While Indian women were cast as the protectors of their families' morality, Indian men were always a threat to that moral course and their weaknesses made Indian men unfit for citizenship and the franchise.

Recent events in Indian country along with historical examples of Native Americans were employed by the *Union Signal* to stand as a model for the goals of the WCTU, but the organization often relied on some quite unflattering imagery of Native Americans—particularly Native American men. In anticipation of some Native American men in South Dakota getting the right to vote in 1885, the WCTU saw a step toward one of their goals: full inclusion of Native Americans into the US citizenry.[38] But, at this moment of potential solidarity, white women, justly frustrated by their continued disenfranchisement, attempted to delegitimize the Native American men's fledgling citizenship. One commentator declared, "And now it is the Indians who are to have the ballot—it is said. They need it for protection, and it is claimed that if they have the ballot they would enforce the law prohibiting the sale of liquor to Indians. The *squaws* might, but as for the braves, we fear—we fear—!"[39] Yet, after the passage of the Dawes Act and in the immediate wake of a referendum in South

Dakota in which women's suffrage was rejected and Indian male suffrage was approved, WCTU member Helen Gougar revealed the nastier, racist side of WCTU thought: "Men have long conceded the fact that the voice of Pugilist Sullivan in government is more trustworthy than that of Frances Willard. This is cause for mild enthusiasm compared to that of Susan B. Anthony at the feet of Sitting Bull, in war paint and feathers, imploring him for the ballot!" The passage continued with numerous juxtapositions of supposedly civilized, disenfranchised women supplicating in front of caricatures of unqualified Indian men. "In my imagination I can see, in the near future, Elizabeth Cady Stanton making one of her masterful addresses for just divorce laws before Hole-In-The-Day, and Lucy Stone pleading for equal property rights before Cane-In-The-Winds, while Mary H. Hunt humbly pleads with Tail-Of-Black-Horse for the scientific instruction law, and Esther Pugh beseeches Git-Up-And-Git-Over-The-Ranch for her pet anti-tobacco statute while Mary Allen West evolves wise editorials to be read in the electric light of the teepee by Heap Squaw."[40] Such vitriolic responses were commonplace from other WCTU quarters as well.

In 1891 during the California state president's annual address, B. Sturtevant-Peet, was vigorously dispelling male critics of women's suffrage. She provided a list of common objections, decrying "the man who feared illiteracy, and would not vote for the bill except upon an educational qualification." She reminded the audience, "this was not considered when the negro and the Dakota Indians were enfranchised."[41] In July 1899 the *Southern California White Ribbon* printed a column "Indians and Women." The author shared an apocryphal story about Reverend Anna H. Shaw, who having finished giving a suffrage talk in South Dakota, read a local newspaper editorial attacking the suffrage amendment "on the ground that women do not by nature possess the logical minds, the calm and reflective judgments which the weighty duties of citizenship demand." Soon after, while "walking up the street . . . Miss Shaw saw approaching her an Indian, a fine specimen of a recently enfranchised tribe." The man was an imposing and impressive figure, and Shaw thought it would be a great opportunity to ask him how the tribes managed to be so successful in gaining the franchise and how women might follow their strategies to gain similar success. According to the tale, "The Indian gazed blankly at her for a moment, and then uttered the monosyllable 'Ugh!' the only English word, if I may call it so, which he had mastered during his prolonged and successful preparation for citizenship. Disappointed and disheartened, Miss Shaw, the cultivated, University-bred white woman, turned away from her political superior."[42]

South Dakota's Native Americans getting the franchise was a sticking point for decades to come. In 1916 North Dakota's *White Ribbon* provided an "analysis" of Indian male citizenship:

> The Indians never wanted suffrage, never asked for it and they rarely use it except when some crafty politician gives a roast ox barbeque, smuggles in plenty of firewater and winks at gambling and debauchery. . . . The liquor men have a plan on foot to give a series of these disgraceful feasts and get influential wet men to swing the Indians into line. . . . [P]olitics are beyond an Indian's ken, particularly when he is so slightly removed from savagery that citizen Indians bear such names as these which were copied from Tripp county land plats: Joseph Singing Goose, Thomas Walks With the Wind, Moses White House War Bonnet, Thomas Kill A Plenty, John Crazy Horse Fool Bull.

The list went on. While the author's bigotry is undeniable, there was a political calculation going on beyond the base resentment. She claimed that a Cheyenne man promised an unnamed temperance speaker that he would vote for "statewide prohibition . . . but he wouldn't vote for any woman to have a vote. In case of a close vote the Indians would be a powerful factor. South Dakota has more Indian voters than any other state in the union. Tripp county alone has 2,500 Indian land-holders. . . . Not all the men are voters, but there are several thousand that are."[43] When it came to gaining the vote, it appears that women's sense of injustice at their exclusion superseded any joy they might have gained from seeing one of their stated goals for American Indians achieved in the Dakotas. For many WCTU members, the demands of gender equality shouted louder than those of racial parity for Native Americans.

In contrast to places where Indian men had a monopoly on Indian voting, states with more progressive suffrage policies, like California, had passed women's suffrage in 1911 and some Indian women did vote. Such moves toward political and social equality came at the possible price of losing their Native American identities. In 1912 Mary E. Fowler wrote, "The Indian is the child of the past. They are fast becoming what we are—citizens of a great country with all the responsibilities of citizenship." She had spoken at "five unions, four clubs and three missionary societies. [I h]ave helped young Indians in debates on woman suffrage and temperance versus moderate drinking." She noted some progress: "Two years ago there was an average of two arrests for drunkenness in Soboba, a month; this year only two in twelve months—a great gain in morals and sobriety." Women were able to vote in California in "supervisory elections," and twenty-five Indians, four of whom were women, had pledged to do so "against license in the Fifth Supervisory District." "License" was a reference to regulatory licensing of alcohol dealers. "No license" legislation was a compromise with total prohibition that the WCTU platform did not support.[44] With the help of white WCTU leaders, according to Fowler, Indian women could be counted on to vote in line with the WCTU platform when given the opportunity.

Meanings of Racial Difference

Other WCTU members were not as optimistic about social or political integration as Fowler was. In New Mexico in 1884 one WCTU officer stated that in Santa Fe and Albuquerque "we began to see the problem of reform, indeed, of American life among a mixed race. Here are Indians and Negroes and Mexicans, and now and then a pure Castilian." Then, discussing the role of WCTU sisters, she said, "To these the daughters *of our own people* [emphasis added] have carried the doctrine of total abstinence from that which is the enemy of all races and of all conditions." The author indicated that she tried to speak to a mixed audience at the "Presbyterian Synod. The attempt was not very successful, and I have personal appreciation of the apostle's admonition not 'to speak in an unknown tongue.'"[45] Even Fowler could write in bluntly racial terms, despite her desire for political integration. In her 1911 report she warned potential WCTU Indian workers: "In dealing with the Indian in education, in morals and religion one must always recognize, to a certain extent, his racial difference. One must allow him to express himself in his own way or one will never know the real Indian; for he is a man of God's outside world, and he has the simplicity of nature and should not be made artificial by being led to imitate the white race. He must be elevated without crowding out his distinctive racial differences."[46]

Fowler was aware that race played into the uneven numbers of arrests for alcohol traders. Whites tended to get off easily, but Chinese traders were more susceptible to arrest and prosecution. Fowler used this to her advantage: "I reported one Chinaman for selling liquor to Indians in Riverside. He was arrested and punished. Mr. Will Stanley reports eight arrests, six of which were successfully prosecuted." She targeted the Indian youth by distributing literature and "sent the *Young Crusader* to three Indian boys, who are doing good temperance work and are my helpers in the villages."[47] Fowler's dominance of southern California WCTU work suggests the racial attitudes that were probably being communicated to the young Native people with whom she worked. How injurious this was to her young Indian crusaders is incalculable.

Reconstructions of Indian Violence

Some authors allowed their frustrations about failing to gain the franchise to fuel their racism, and other authors wrote about historical violence in ways that cast Native Americans as a persistent danger. In most cases all realistic threats from the Indian Wars had ceased. These authors proposed that what they perceived as the baser nature of Indians was often caused or at least exacerbated by alcohol. Although optimism and potential redemption both seep into the narratives, the authors mostly fostered fear and pessimism about Native Americans' continued presence in the United States. In a state report from Nebraska, Nettie C. Hall recorded that she "had the pleasure of taking tea with Mrs. Steers, who had spent seventeen years teaching the Indians at the mission school, and whose husband, one of nature's noblemen, has charge of the iron shops of the mission, teaching the native boys to mould and fashion everything in that line." Hall was further impressed by a young Santee Sioux musician who "presided at the organ with grace and dignity, and led the large audience in gospel hymns[. She] was one who had grown from a child of the forest to a noble Christian womanhood, under the careful training of the Riggs mission school. I never had a more attentive audience than among those dusky faces upturned to me for an hour and a half." Then, she shifted tone and began reflecting on the so-called Santee Sioux Uprising of 1862 from a decidedly Euro-American perspective. "I shall never forget my feelings as I laid my head on the downy pillow in a nicely furnished, airy room in the Mission Normal Training School, and tried to adjust my bewildered thoughts that would tangle up my flight from Minnesota in 1862, during the massacre of my friends by the fathers of these same students, and the quiet, polite demeanor of these dusky children of the Tepee, as they quickly and cheerfully obeyed the instructions of the Christian teachers."[48]

Missing from Hall's story of the Santee Sioux Uprising was the role played by the federal government in causing it and the vicious American response to the Sioux participants in the aftermath. Indian agents in Minnesota were political appointees with little experience and had withheld annuities that had been stipulated in an earlier treaty. The resulting starvation and suffering led to an impromptu resistance movement, which began with the death of several innocent civilians at the hands of younger warriors. Once the violence began, Little Crow, an established leader, led a series of attacks against local farms and towns. When the attacks were put down, 38 Santee Sioux were executed, though 303 were originally condemned to die after military judicial proceedings.[49] Although the event was no doubt horrifying for the white settlers who survived the event, the initial cause of the violence was a series of disastrous Indian policies that left many people starving.

Other WCTU members were less circumspect. In January 1891 the *North Dakota White Ribbon* approvingly reprinted an interview with Marietta Bones from the *Minneapolis Tribune*. Bones, a vehement suffragist claimed, "the Indian, as you know, is a disturbing element at present. So long as the Indians are allowed to remain in such a wide scope of the country, they will be a menace to our settlers. If their horses and firearms were taken away, and they removed to the Indian Territory—and there provided for and policed—they would be less dangerous." She continued, "If the government is as anxious to do justice to the people of North and South Dakota as it is to the Indians, then it will certainly remove them from these states, and, in fact, from all the western states." Marietta Bones had a reputation for having an abrasive personality, and her characterization was among the most dehumanizing of all WCTU members' statements. It occurred right around the time of settler paranoia about the Ghost Dance and the apex of white fear of Indian uprisings.[50]

One might suspect that a sea change in the WCTU's view on Indian–US relations might have followed the Wounded Knee Massacre of December 29, 1890. Unfortunately, only a slight softening of views occurred. Prior to the massacre, in November 1890, the *Union Signal* printed on its front page a description of the Ghost Dance, a Native American revitalization movement that had begun with the Paiutes and spread to the Lakota reservations in the Dakotas and that would be a contributing factor in increasing the fearfulness of white spectators. The author declared, "A pathetic craze has seized the Indians of our Northwest—that their Messiah was to appear to restore their heritage, and that they must prepare for his coming by the ghost dance. Accordingly they gathered in appointed places, and kept up the weird dances till often strong men dropped down dead. Such gatherings of Indians naturally alarmed the settlers, troops were called out and for days the country was aroused."[51] The military presence and tensions between the army and the Ghost Dancers ultimately erupted in violence. First, Sitting Bull was killed on December 15, 1890. Then the army opened fire on Ghost Dancers at Wounded Knee Creek on December 29, 1890. The *Union Signal* reported a few sentences on "the butchery of women and children at Wounded Knee." A few weeks later, they reported that "The Indian War is virtually ended and a company of Sioux chiefs are to visit Washington for a peace talk with their 'Great Father.'"[52]

WCTU commentary on Sitting Bull tried to discredit the leader, failing to recognize the reason he had become a hero to so many Lakota. In a piece published only a few months after his death, the *Union Signal* shared the experiences of Emeline Whipple and May Collins, both missionaries to the Dakotas. In a description of life on Lakota reservations in that tumultuous time, generally sympathetic to the victims of the Wounded Knee Massacre, they remained critical of Sitting Bull, largely blaming him for the massacre because of his support for the Ghost Dance. "The influence of Sitting Bull was only and always bad, and many prayers had ascended from the little church at Standing Rock, that God would in some way remove his bad influence, convert Sitting Bull or take him out of the way."[53] This coverage was not unique among American newspapers and magazines reporting on Sitting Bull. Communications scholar John M. Coward dedicates an entire chapter of his book *The Newspaper Indian* to discussing the media's treatment of Sitting Bull at the time. He explained, "'good' chiefs were those who adopted civilization or gave in to white demands, 'bad' chiefs were those who did not. For Sitting Bull in particular—a man known for his hostility to whites and their ways—a fair or balanced presentation in the papers was probably impossible." Any Native American leader who fought for the preservation of a traditional way of life, especially those leaders who resisted the US reordering of the Indigenous land distribution into reservations—would be vilified in the WCTU and the mainstream press publications.[54] The contempt for Sitting Bull was present decades later when WCTU workers were organizing in the Dakotas. They went so far as to claim that the Lakota themselves were still vengeful toward the long-deceased warrior: "The grave of Sitting Bull may be seen between the Agency buildings at the fair grounds at Ft. Yates—a pile of stones surrounded by an iron fence. When his body was thrown into the grave a barrel of lime was thrown in upon it, and it has been only through the efforts of the soldiers that the Indians have been prevented from hacking it to pieces."[55]

The fear engendered by white paranoia about the Ghost Dance and by the media overplaying Indian violence continued for years in WCTU publications. In 1892 the *Pacific Ensign* reported that "fear is entertained that there will be another outbreak among the Sioux at the Pine Ridge Agency," and on February 9, 1893, the paper reported that "four cowboys were killed at the Pine Ridge Agency by Indians." When police were sent to the scene of the "massacre" they were fired upon by Indians. They returned fire and killed "three Indians . . . wounding others."[56] There was little editorializing—except to mark the death of the whites as a "massacre" while little sympathy was shown for the dead Indian perpetrators. Philip Deloria provides a compelling interpretation of this incident based on Lakota pictographic histories. The killing of the cowboys was probably based partly on revenge for Wounded Knee, but the Lakota men's charge against the police officers was a deliberate act creating a "culturally appropriate manner" to die; that is, they died bravely, having made a stand against white oppression.[57] Unfortunately, any sympathy from the local papers at the time, or the WCTU publications that relied on their reporting, would have been out of the question, since the violence seemed so close and so threatening.

Other stories allowed for the American Indian to be the personification of the evils of drink. Even in the wake of Wounded Knee, some WCTU members could show remarkable insensitivity. One story involved the annual memorial of the 1886 assassination of anti-saloon leader Rev. George Channing Haddock in Sioux City, Iowa. The event was cosponsored by the local WCTU, and the *Union Signal* editors reprinted a portion of an 1891 speech by George D. Perkins, the Sioux City *Journal's* editor. On cue, he demanded "the enforcement of existing laws against the saloon, which he characterizes as 'a savage in war paint with scalping knife on the thoroughfare of civilization.'"[58] The speech and thus the article kept alive the stereotypical imagery to which the readers of the *Union Signal* had become accustomed, while at the same time the organization was trying to develop temperance efforts among Native American communities.

Native American violence meted out justly could be covered approvingly, at least when the Indians lived in more distant Colombia or Venezuela and when that violence was done for the protection of noble Native American women against, presumably, Hispanic (read: nonwhite) men: "The plan of the Guajira Indians to protect their young girls, while not sanctioned by the moral code, must prove effectual. Three traders who were caught stealing young Indian maidens for the purpose of selling them into servitude, were captured and roasted alive."[59] Preservation of traditions of violence was not always supported in the pages of WCTU publications, even by Native Americans themselves. In one piece, Dorcas Spencer, often an understanding advocate, described the rejection of even constrained violence by the Hupa Indians with whom she was closely affiliated. Describing the success of the Hoopa Indian Reservation football team against the surrounding white schools, Spencer noted that many of the players began to regret their success in the violent sport. They "came to the unanimous decision that it is an uncivilized game not fit to be played by people who are trying to work upward to civilization." One player declared, "'It is taking us back' they argued 'we don't want to go backward.'"[60] Spencer probably wrote this piece to fight against the recurring theme of Native American propensity for violence, which undermined her reform efforts.

Compared to how they viewed the Ghost Dance, WCTU members were more sympathetic toward other Indigenous religious innovations, particularly the Indian Shaker Church. In May 1912 the *White Ribbon Ensign* featured a story on Indian Shakers from the Northwest. The Indian Shaker Church (unrelated to the Mother Ann Lee's eighteenth-century sect) were adherents of the deceased John Slocum; the church is found throughout Washington and Oregon. The story reported approvingly that temperance is a central tenant of the church: "John Slocum, the Moses of the Shakers, though dead, is their prophet. Through him the 'Great Spirit' is directing the work of saving the red men from their greatest curse—whisky." According to the article, the "priests or priestesses" interrogated backsliders and reported bootleggers to authorities. Witnesses had been testifying willingly, leading to convictions for the first time in the Northwest.[61] The WCTU members' reception of Native religious innovations allowed some doctrinal wiggle room for appropriately temperate messages. The WCTU was less tolerant of white supposed Christians, whose behavior counteracted their reform efforts.

White Hypocrisy and Native American Inspirations

Before doing battle with distillers, saloon keepers, and illegal whiskey peddlers, the WCTU stressed Indian weakness for alcohol. WCTU literature consistently characterized Indians as victims of nefarious dispensers of alcohol. Any example of Native American strength in the face of this adversity was a source of inspiration and a cause for celebration. In 1885 one *Union Signal* author quoted a missionary from Indian Territory who noted the disparity in legal consequences for the Native Americans caught drinking and for the white traders who supplied it. "The United States government having made it a penitentiary offence [sic] for an Indian to drink any liquor, allows the post-trader to sell liquor. This is bad for the poor Indian." She continued, "Last winter, while in the

City of Detroit, I went into the prison, and there I found a pleasant-faced Indian boy, spending a year and a half for drinking a little whisky, the first he had ever taken; while the strong-armed post-trader who had sold it to him, still continued his traffic."[62] The WCTU authors carefully noted Indians' efforts to stop such egregious actions, celebrating their resistance efforts: "The Indians of Eastern Washington have taken steps to prevent the sale of liquor among them by unprincipled whites."[63] Gone unchecked, white traders would lead Native Americans into ruin, so word of the Eastern Washington Indians' efforts was good news. Such conscientiousness was not always the norm, however.

Indians' potential to disregard the WCTU's moral imperatives, and the WCTU's anti-Catholicism, come through, too. Under a heading "Fiesta Orgies" Martha Davis reported on the Riverside County convention of 1894. Summarizing a report from the superintendent of the Cahuilla Reservation, she relayed, "Cahuilla is fortunately so far from white and Mexican influence that there is but little drinking on the reservation except at the fiestas and now and then at a 'wake' over the dead." However, when they leave the reservation, "there is drinking. Some drink whenever they can, many at the fiestas. Oh, these hellish fiestas! They are on the saints' days." The description continued painting a picture of the fiestas with Indians, Mexicans, and whites at Temecula and Soboba, stating they were "the worst ever known" in terms of their drunkenness, prostitution, and fights.[64]

Perhaps because the WCTU writers knew of the extraordinary pressures placed upon Native Americans, white ribboners often used them as "good examples" of temperance commitment and thus an inspiration for others. Writing from Sitka, Alaska, Susan S. Winans contrasted the corrupted white Christians with the Native Americans: "it is really lamentable to see those who profess the religion of Jesus, come out here and cast off all restraints and join with those who forget God, and mock at His servants [the missionaries]. The natives set these people a good example. . . . The native temperance band in Sitka is the most flourishing band in the territory." She was not just impressed by their temperance efforts but by their egalitarian gender roles: "in this tribe the woman is not backward about speaking or praying first. The men yield many things to their wives. They cannot sell any game, fish, or property, without first consulting their wives, and gaining their consent. The women do most of the selling."[65] To the south, a reporter noted the financial investment in temperance that people were making: "Indians from the Omaha Reservation have decided to put aside two thousand dollars from their pasture money to be used in temperance work."[66] As it oscillated between staid prudent temperance efforts by tribes and lascivious tales about drunken Indians, the *Union Signal* portrayed an inspirational struggle in its description of Native Americans and alcohol.

Indian country as an inspiration was offset by the way that the *Union Signal* dealt with ongoing Indian resistance movements in the West in a demeaning fashion. It noted in September 1897 that "the government has cut off all rations to the Apache Indians except flour. They are threatening an uprising, and the settlers near the reservation are very much exercised."[67] The following year, in Minnesota, the paper reported on the Battle of Leech Lake/Sugar Point. The article, entitled "An Indian Outbreak" blamed the violence on "the determination of the Indians to prevent the arrest and punishment of their head chief, who is accused of violating the laws that prohibit the sale of whisky on Indian reservations." The next week the story morphed into a satire that amplified many ugly stereotypes in order to highlight the problems with the legal liquor trade in the white community: "The untutored savage has been at it again. . . . An Indian to-day is as big a fool as a white woman. We say this without fear of contradiction. She thinks she is entitled to the privileges and prerogatives of her white brother, and the red man thinks the same of himself." The anonymous author continued, blaming the hypocritical and unevenly applied federal alcohol laws for the violence that had occurred on the reservation:

> Mr. Chief Bush Ear, of Leech Lake, Minn., and all over, is a bad man, no doubt, and he has his limitations. For instance, he can not see why he can not sell liquor to his subjects, especially as he comes of royal blood in his own right, when every pesky nobody that wants to sell it to these same subjects, down in Duluth, in spite of the same law he violated. Why his men should be jerked up and carried away to trial for selling whisky to their fellow men, and then the whites openly sell it to these same dusky warriors is past his benighted comprehension.

That the author of this story was using Chief Bush Ear to spur on universal prohibition became clear to the reader: "Temperance women, alike with the untutored child of the wigwam can not find any line of reason, hair split as they may, for arresting and trying an Indian for the same thing a white man does with impunity. The Indian ought to be arrested. The white man ought to be arrested."[68]

Historical events involving Native Americans infiltrated the advertisements of the *Union Signal*. "Kirk's Soap" advertised for many years with a campaign that drew in readers with the headline "An Indian Outbreak" and suggested that an "uprising" of dirt could be prevented by using their special family friendly "dusky diamond tar soap."[69] The "Indian Outbreak" was a common trope in journalistic writing on violence between whites and Native Americans. Philip Deloria describes its use as reflecting a very real fear of whites that was predicated on the failure of "containment" of Native Americans on the reservation. Belittlingly, advertisers played off both Native American resistance and the frontier whites' fears. The advertisers, as the authors of these rhetorical devices, and the readers enjoyed a distance from the violence and thus could indulge in humorous references while then refocusing on the alcohol problem in other communities. It is unknown how readers viewed such ads, but the advertisers' light-hearted treatment of serious events (and the WCTU editors' tacit approval) suggest that the real tragedies in Native Americans' lives were not given consistent, sympathetic consideration.

History and the Erasure and Manipulation of Native American Experience

The WCTU authors used other allegorical events from more distant history of Native American and European interactions but showed remarkable ignorance of Native American involvement in them. An 1889 poem published in the *Union Signal* around Thanksgiving describes the Pilgrims' ordeals in leaving England and carving out a life for themselves in the Americas. The poem centers on their religious devotions and mentions the role of Native Americans only once, which was to cast them as a threat: "And too often, e'en the bravest/ Felt his blood run cold with dread,/ Lest the wild and savage red man/ Burn the roof above his head." In 1902 a short story on the first Thanksgiving included Massasoit as a character (though it never mentions the Wampanoags by name) but turned the event into a demonstration of Pilgrim generosity and stewardship over the Native Americans. "Early in the morning of the appointed day—about the first of November—Massasoit and ninety of his warriors arrived in the outskirts of the village, and with wild yells announced their readiness to enjoy the hospitality of their white friends."[70] Absent from the tale are the provisions that were brought *by* the Wampanoags to share in the harvest festival, famously described by Edward Winslow in *Mourt's Relation*.[71]

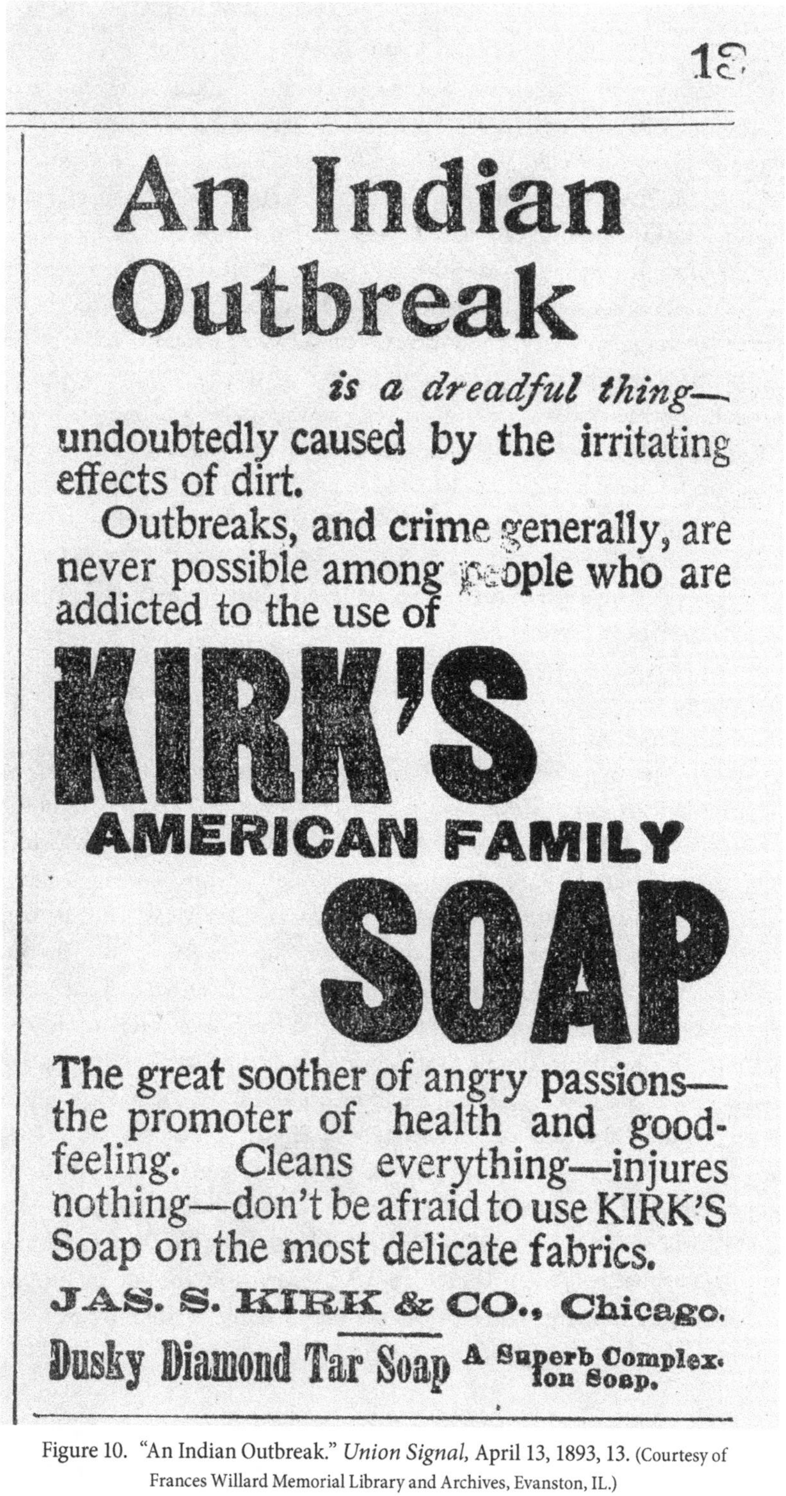

Figure 10. "An Indian Outbreak." *Union Signal,* April 13, 1893, 13. (Courtesy of Frances Willard Memorial Library and Archives, Evanston, IL.)

While the WCTU overlooked the Wampanoags' hospitality, they committed an even greater injustice in their generous coverage of Columbus, the butcher of the Tainos and the harbinger of the alcohol scourge itself. Preparations for the quadricentennial of Columbus's arrival in the New World began years before 1892, and WCTU publications covered the celebrations surrounding that date, almost all of which ignored any Native American perspective on the invasion. An 1889 article proclaimed, "The New World invites the Old to her birthday party in 1892, and 'the best man' of the occasion will be Christopher Columbus. It should be so." The article then went on to editorialize that American women should be sure to remember the important role Queen Isabella played in making the whole voyage possible.[72] The WCTU publishing house even printed a patriotic children's book entitled *Columbus and What he Found*, which it advertised in and sold through the *Union Signal*.[73]

In 1893 the *Union Signal* printed a call by Amos. B. Wells: "Wanted, Other Columbuses" to bravely lead the nation to new lands. One of these new Columbuses would, Wells prophesized, "robed in dazzling white, whose heaven directed rudder will drive straight, some glad day, into the haven of purity, with all our sons and daughters on board. He will have tossed overboard the last whisky bottle, the last opium box, the last quivering, reeking story, the last cigarette, the last instrument of unmentionable vice."[74] Native Americans were absent in these glorifications of the vanguard of colonialism; or, worse, were the happy recipients of his arrival. The emulation that was fostered by the WCTU, especially in its children, offered no critical perspective on European expansion. The modern hero, channeling Columbus, would rescue humanity from vice—and especially alcohol.

This should not be surprising considering the general view of the benevolence of imperialism that was held by progressives. Since the WCTU was very interested in expanding outside the confines of the United States, ultimately creating the World Woman's Christian Temperance Union, it was a logical next step to comment on American imperial endeavors. In these cases, "the Indian" was brought in as symbolic of other global events, often tied to progressive foreign policy. During the Spanish American War, the *Union Signal* frequently published works on the imperialism of the United States. On the front page in October 1898, the authors warned, "Recent results of this government's policy anent the North American Indian do not augur well for its success with other inferior races."[75] What was at stake in American expansion was made clear in subsequent pieces. Frequent contributor Wilbur F. Crafts asked, rhetorically,

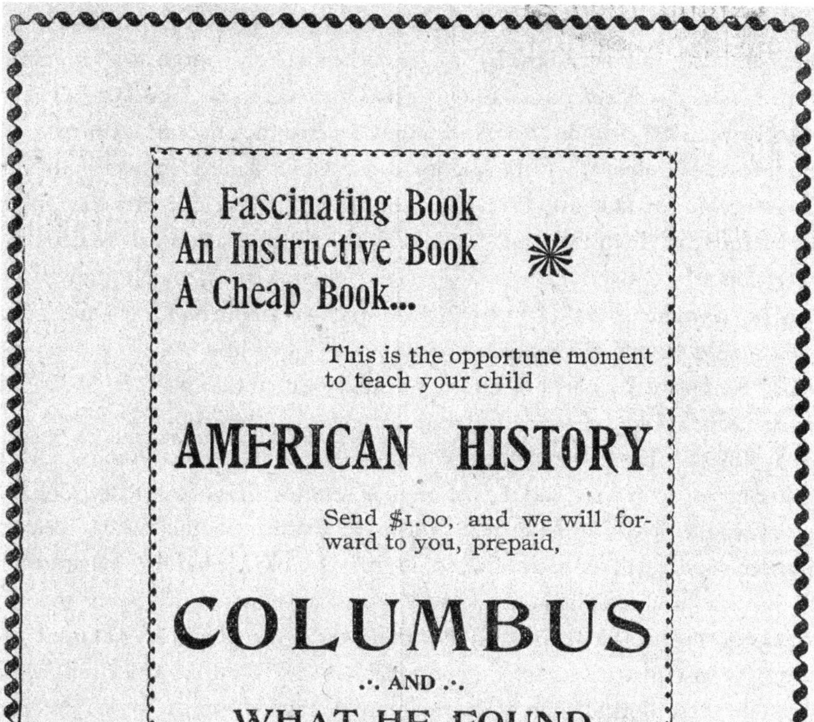

Figure 11. "Columbus and What He Found." *Union Signal,* April 13, 1893, 17. (Courtesy of Frances Willard Memorial Library and Archives, Evanston, IL.)

"Why should we cast aside our Anglo-Saxon traditions to welcome the nude to our literature and homes, when every nation from which we have borrowed it is either dead or dying? . . . The problem of purity is the question of life or death to nations."[76] That is, to Crafts, imperialism's failure was that it had not been imperial enough and had been too inclusive, allowing too much of other traditions into the supposedly pure Anglo-Saxon culture.

There were exceptions to the whitewashing of history and of imperialism. At times WCTU authors revealed some knowledge of Native American traditions, while appropriating them as inspirations for their own goals. In "Hiawatha the Great," a student named Lilah Mae Dutton from Burlington, Vermont, described the Haudenosaunee tradition of Hiawatha spreading the message of Peace among the Five Nations, a journey that resulted in the Great League of Peace and Power in what became New York State. However, she went on to credit him with being "the foremost statesman of his age in the Americas, and was the first advocate on American soil of international arbitration."[77] In what was perhaps a vague reference to the documented punishments for drunkenness in Mesoamerica in the Pre-Columbian period, the "Signal Notes" led off the column that week with the declaration that "The ancient Indians killed their kings if they became drunk."[78]

One fanciful poem captured the broad contours of the Indian alcohol trade. The piece described Wineka, the daughter of a Native American warrior who became a victim to the bottle: "But the white man gave him, with crafty words/ The drink he'd brewed in a viper's nest. For this wrong, O white man, shall ever burn/ Bitter hate, and revenge, in Wineka's breast." The author, Ellen N. Merriman, suggested the piece would be a "pleasing recitation for a temperance concert" in children's temperance education circles. She even went on to suggest some ideas for wardrobe and casting. Whoever plays Wineka might don "a bright-colored shawl or large scarf for the blanket, draped so as to conceal the front of the dress, and a crown made of pasteboard covered with plain silver paper; at the left side fasten a red plume or wing." So as to capture the image of the Indian princess, "The one who assumes the character should have long, dark hair left flowing."[79]

"Civilized" Indian Men and Women

While the literary Indian served the purposes of the WCTU in a variety of ways, imagery and messages were often contradictory. The WCTU also used real-life nineteenth- and twentieth-century Native American leaders to further their causes, though the stories about them revealed a willingness to craft these public figures in ways that were conducive to the WCTU's goals. In one instance, the WCTU's column "Our Library Table" promoted the book of Potawatomi author Simon Pokagon, who wrote a short booklet entitled "The Red Man's Greeting." It was originally titled "The Red Man's Rebuke" and was intended as a retort to the Columbus celebrations of the previous year. It was a "sorrowful requiem for the glory of the Red Man, a passionate protest against the fire-water which they knew only through their white brothers after 'Columbus discovered America' and a bitter prophecy of the punishment that awaits in the 'Happy Hunting Grounds,' the white men whose injustice to the Indian has made him so much grief." Pokagon was a controversial figure among the Potawatomi, but he certainly spoke the language of the WCTU in his work regarding alcohol. In his essay he describes the effects of alcohol on Native American men's ability to be humane and productive in their communities: "the drink habit coiled about the heartstrings of its victims, shocking unto death, friendship, love, honor, manhood—all that makes men good and noble; crushing out all ambition, and leaving naught but a culprit vagabond in the place of a man."[80]

Carlos Montezuma was another favorite of the WCTU. In an 1893 piece commenting favorably on the Carlisle Indian School in Pennsylvania, the authors profiled him briefly. "The resident physician, who is appointed by the government, is Dr. Montezuma, a full-blooded Apache. Taken from the lowest condition of Indian life, his twenty-two years in the Eastern states have made him to-day as cultivated a gentleman as one often meets."[81] Sixteen years later, Montezuma was a featured author in the *Union Signal*. In contrast to much WCTU coverage, he summarized the injustice of the colonial enterprise through its historical trajectory, though he placed the moral quagmire of it comfortably in the past:

> It is too late now to serve any purpose by going into the matter of right and wrong concerning the early and recent relations between the aborigines of this country and the other races—the invaders of the Indians' domain. The barbarous trespasses on the estate of this native son, the ruthless onslaught upon his home and fireside, the demonical attacks upon him and his household, the desperate resistance which he finally came to make against his annihilation, together with the horrible scenes attending his indiscriminate revenge upon the despoilers of his birthright,—are all buried in the ashes of the past.[82]

Despite his assurance that the injustices were put behind him, he implicated European and American greed and failed Indian policy in the subsequent two-page document. But his essay was intended to tout the success of boarding schools and Euro-American education and act as a call for Native American people to leave the reservation and take their place among all the races at the forefront of civilization. This was not an attempt to decolonize oneself. Nor was it a defense of Euro-American treatment of Native Americans. Instead, it was a type of pragmatic response to the economic realities and power relationships of the twentieth century. But it relegated tribal identity and community to a secondary position. This is not necessarily surprising considering Montezuma's own background, which was not firmly rooted in a single Native American community. In many ways, Montezuma's message reflected superintendent of Work Among Indians Dorcas Spencer's plan for Native Americans. She paid much more attention to the views and perspectives of actual Native American people than almost anyone writing for the *Union Signal* or other publications and, with the exception of Jane Stapler, had more extensive experience with Native American people than anyone in her position. Unfortunately for the longevity of WCTU in Native American communities, the dissolution of the Department of Work Among Indians in 1916 also led to a decrease in Native American perspectives in WCTU publications, though Indians were still featured within their pages.

Historical Indian Temperance as Motivator amid Nativist Fervor

Between 1916 and 1924 the WCTU's Indian work became less direct. The WCTU itself adopted a more nativist agenda and tone. Use of American Indians as a rhetorical device continued even as institutional commitment waned. This occurred at the same time that their total assimilation was expected and their sovereignty was increasingly challenged by federal policies and social reformers. One rhetorical device that white and Native American women shared was the historical precedent of Native American figures who promoted temperance in their own communities. In 1927 the California WCTU paper the *White Ribbon Ensign* loosely recalled some other past examples of temperance in the United States. In a column with the title "America First As Usual: This Time an American Indian" the author reported on a statement made by "Miss Bertha Mapes, chairman of the speakers' committee of the Prohibition Educational League of Bronx County, that the first prohibition speech in America was made by an American Indian more than 126 years ago . . . at a yearly meeting held in December, 1801, by the Quakers of Baltimore, an Indian appeared with the Committee on Indians, and in his speech begged the Quakers to use their influence on Congress to induce that body to enact laws forbidding the sale of liquor." The reporter went on to quote the Indian, undoubtedly the Miami leader Little Turtle: "We tell them, 'Brothers, send us useful things, bring goods that will clothe us, our women and our children, but not this evil liquor, that destroys our reason, that destroys our health, that destroys our lives.'"[83] The WCTU made good use of this story, emphasizing Native Americans' desire not only for prohibition legislation but also for trade; that is, absorption into the industrialized US economy.

In 1930 the same publication used examples from even earlier Native American temperance efforts. The *White Ribbon Ensign* published a piece by Senator Morris Sheppard of Texas, the author of what became the Eighteenth Amendment.[84] In the article he referred to the "Alleghany Indians," who, appalled by white traders profiting from human misery, "in 1738 took steps preventing the use of such beverages among themselves. In 1754 a Creek Indian delivered an eloquent and impressive attack on the traffic in intoxicants. He condemned a system which coined its profits from the debauchery of human beings."[85] In this way Native American temperance efforts received recognition from one of the prohibition movement's heroes.

What were the conclusions about Native Americans that a WCTU reader would take away after years or decades of perusing the *Union Signal* and her local state newspaper? What mixed messages would she try to resolve in her mind? Would such resolution be necessary, or could she latch onto some unitary trend that remained uncomplicated in the literature and ignore the other strains of thought? Most likely, she would recognize that larger-scale Indian violence had something to do with mistreatment by the US government but that the more localized domestic abuse or criminality was caused by strong drink. It would require of her a very close critical reading of the sources to be convinced that both types of violence and alcohol abuse itself were results of—or responses to—a Euro-American, Christian, colonialist enterprise that was unjust and socially disruptive at its core. Moreover, if she did consider this possibility even momentarily she would probably conclude, as Dr. Montezuma did, that such deeds were too far in the past to be of much practical importance now. Instead, ending tribal affinities, encouraging Indians to seek Western education—be it industrial or, in certain cases, professional—were important steps. Conversion to Christianity, rather than participation in dangerous traditions like the Ghost

Dance or other "superstitions," was essential for the goals of both civilization and their own salvation. It would be hard for her to rid her mind of the accounts of the latest violent acts committed by Indians or the references to historical atrocities that conjured up a host of fearsome images: the scalping knife, kidnappings, and murders of innocent farmers. Blood curdling tales with Indian villains had been an approved genre, and it would take a lot of mental energy to dismiss what was almost a staple in the *Union Signal*. Furthermore, it was clearly acceptable to tell whimsical tales of Indian figures, fabricated or not, if they communicated an important moral lesson. Indian imagery could be used to sell soap, mineral water, dime novels, and many other things a middle-class white woman would want—often employing the same language and imagery as the titillating stories published in the temperance papers. The ironies or damages caused by such appropriations were not of much concern. Armed with this spectrum of conflicting views, individual women of the WCTU—some nationally known leaders, some only local workers in remote regions—tried to organize Indian country for the temperance cause.

Chapter 4

"Work Among Indians"
Organizing Indian Country

Their various ideas, perceptions, biases, and expectations shaped the WCTU members' organizational approach to Native Americans. While there is risk of overstating the divide between Native American and white women, it is important to keep in mind how much "Indian work" was planned with only a trickle of input from Indigenous women. The WCTU members reached out to Indian reservations, frequently working with missionary organizations to find non-Indigenous WCTU members who could organize in far-flung reservations. They tried to influence Indian agents and officeholders in Washington, DC. Although they were firm warriors against corruption in the Indian Department, WCTU leaders were nonetheless part of the same onslaught by that department against tribal sovereignty, tribal governments, traditional religions, Native religious innovations, and communal tribal landholdings. However, some of those white women entrenched in Indian work developed sympathies for tribal landholdings and sovereignty. Even when the WCTU adopted its most nativist bent after 1916, there were vestiges of this sentiment that would lead into other reform movements beyond campaigns for citizenship, allotment, and assimilation—more akin to those cultural pluralist initiatives during the Indian New Deal under John Collier.

The national department reemerged and expanded under the superintendencies of Dorothy Cleveland and Dorcas Spencer, and the Department of Work Among Indians became an active part of the WCTU and its allied reform groups. Some of the most important pipelines for state leaders and organizers in the department were the missionary wings or boards of the large Protestant denominations—namely, Presbyterians, Methodists, Quakers, Episcopalians, Baptists, and Congregationalists. Other partners in their work were the other white-led Indian rights and reform organizations, such as the Women's National Indian Association (WNIA), the Indian Rights Association (IRA), the Lake

Mohonk Conference of the Friends of the Indian, and the Zayante Indian Conference created by the Northern California Indian Association (NCIA), an auxiliary of the WNIA. These partnerships not only contributed to the WCTU's success but also connected progressive religious and reform organizations across the country, contributing to the rise of ecumenism among major Protestant groups in the early twentieth century.

Through all of these endeavors, the WCTU's progressive efforts resulted in attacks on traditional practices and Native spiritual innovations, like peyote use by the Native American Church, the Feather Religion, the Ghost Dance, and the Indian Shaker Church—though they were sometimes tolerant of the Indian Shaker Church because of its strong temperance emphasis. They sought to use their clout with anti-alcohol sympathizers in government or reform groups who conflated these innovations with alcohol abuse, peyote, narcotics, chaos, savagery, licentiousness, and heathenism. In this sense, the WCTU members proved themselves to be at war not only with alcohol and nefarious whites, which were undeniably destructive, but also with traditional religious practices, non-Christian ceremonial innovations, tribal sovereignty, communal landholdings, and anything else that broke with white Americans' middle-class values and aesthetics.

Oklahoma and the National Department

The renaissance of national WCTU Indian work came out of events in the decade leading up to the Indian Territory–Oklahoma Territory merger and took a major step with the superintendency of Dorothy Cleveland from 1900 until her death in 1903. The WCTU of Oklahoma Territory was established in April 1890, the month before Oklahoma Territory itself was officially established. The region that would become Oklahoma Territory had received the recently nomadic tribes, removed from the plains after the Medicine Lodge Treaty of 1867, which created a testy relationship between the new arrivals and the Five Tribes.[1] Once the plains tribes were confined to new territories in Oklahoma, missionaries were sent there—as federal Indian agents connected to Grant's Peace Policy and in the decades that followed—to help tribes adapt to the sedentary life they were now forced to adopt. In 1892 Oklahoma's territorial WCTU president Mrs. E. J. Roberts commented on work among the western tribes. The Methodist Episcopal Church had recently appointed her "field matron to the Cheyenne and Arapahoe Indians, . . . my work being to teach them to do all kinds of housework." The field matron position was described by

Cathleen Cahill as one of the "two primary adult education initiative[s] on the reservations—the farmer program and the field matron (or female industrial teacher) program—aimed to teach Indian men and women appropriate household skills. Federal employees showed Native people how to farm and keep house by modeling those skills on the reservation and visiting individual homes to provide instruction and encouragement." After her experiences as matron, Roberts lamented, "There is a great deal of drinking among the Indians; the saloon keepers sell to them in defiance of strict laws against it. I have tried to find out from the Indians where they get the liquor, but they, like the white people, refuse to tell."[2]

In subsequent months the Oklahoma territorial reporter, Sue Uhl Brown, continued to decry illegal alcohol sales. By November 8, 1892, Cheyenne and Arapaho men had earned the right to vote, though Brown was quick to point out that none of them spoke English and all political work needed to go through translators. Considering the language of many WCTU members about Indian men who voted before women earned suffrage, such a statement might be interpreted as another slight against non-English-speaking Indian men. However, the fact that the WCTU was sending members to Oklahoma's Indian communities to do political work, accompanied by translators to overcome the language barrier, suggests that there was a willingness to work with these new voters. Although some disenfranchised women may have resented them, others with personal connections to Native Americans saw them as potential as allies in the temperance fight.[3]

In Indian Territory a small convention of eight delegates was held in Claremore on May 15 and 16, 1895, with the noticeable absence of Jane Stapler, who had recently passed away. New officers were elected. Eva Ratcliff, of Vinita, a Presbyterian Cherokee, who had been a teacher, replaced Stapler.[4] In 1895 Indian Territory's WCTU received additional organizational help from outsiders. Corresponding secretary Allenette Cook wrote a brief report, sharing that Clara C. Parrish of Paris, Illinois, and later Kansas came down for ten days to form Young Woman's Branches and to buttress membership in existing unions. As a result, the unions' rosters increased by "about one hundred and eighty-five."[5] As their numbers grew through national intervention, the Indian Territory unions developed their techniques for influencing temperance sentiment in their communities. In 1896 the Tahlequah union was able to persuade one of the local papers to allow them to edit a temperance column, helping them to bend the readers' minds toward temperance and to make sure announcements of meetings and temperance-related news spread beyond WCTU publications alone. Indian Territory reported three new unions that same year. None had faded away, or "died" in the WCTU parlance.[6]

The impediment in Indian Territory that year was not monumental distances or remoteness but "fluctuating populations" because of land rushes. The May 1896 Indian Territory convention held at Muskogee reported "sixteen or seventeen unions," and members began to draft the first territorial constitution, which they produced according to good order and "parliamentary form." Helen M. Stoddard, the state president of the Texas WCTU, had been a "helpful visitor" finishing up a month of organizing work in the territory. Convention members welcomed students from the Baptist Indian School "to welcome and cheer us," the "C.P. College brought out its cultured young women," and "The 'Harold' (M[ethodist] E[piscopal] College) also lent its talent to augment the pleasure of our stay." Neva Traviss of Muskogee won a medal contest.[7] Stoddard assisted in expanding WCTU influence in Indian Territory, and in early summer she organized a union among the Caddo, "with sixteen adult members, besides seven honorary members. They at once elected a delegate to the territorial convention, and gave an ice-cream supper for the purpose of defraying expenses. It proved a success." M. L. Hunter, the territorial reporter from Caddo, reported that within three months their union grew to twenty-three, their LTL from five to thirty-five.[8] "Mrs. Stoddard's month in the territory was helpful, not only in the organization of new unions and increased membership, but also in bringing our principles before the men of the territory, and inspiring the women of the Union to more advanced methods of work." In Creek territory, "the Union of Muscogee has local headquarters. Six medal contests have been held, and Scientific Temperance Instruction and Purity have been the special lines of work."[9] At the executive committee meeting in the1896, "Mrs. Murrow, of Indian Territory, presented the needs of the field and asked for a W.C.T.U. missionary."[10]

In the 1897 annual meeting minutes, the Indian Territory corresponding secretary Allenette Cook issued a very thorough report with a count of "twelve local unions, two of which have been organized during the year. One union has died. . . . One convention has been held. Red-letter days have been observed by two unions." Red-letter days were the commemorations established by the WCTU to celebrate particular milestones in the temperance fight. The observance suggested a high degree of order and commitment by a local union. "The traffic in liquor is said to be diminishing in the Territory." Members circulated

"Petitions against the druggists' licenses" to dispense alcohol; they conducted medal contests and circulated materials on social purity. Mrs. Murrow's request for a missionary from the previous year was heard by the WCTU leaders since, for "part of the year," M. E. Mulnix had been a missionary, appointed by the "general officers" of the WCTU in response to the previous year's request. Mulnix, a deaconess in the Methodist Episcopal Church, had "during the spring and summer months . . . travelled through the territory; held public meetings, and organized two unions. Miss Mulnix is now teaching school in the Territory, but she will give what time she can spare to W.C.T.U. work."[11]

In writing her report Tennie Fuller admitted her physical frailty and inability to attend the convention. She relied on an attendee, a Mrs. Stretch of the Vinita union, for her information. At the convention the work was new for many delegates, and they were not up to snuff with their parliamentary usage. Mulnix sounded like a good-humored parliamentarian, however, and guided them through the proper procedures, including the elections of officers.[12] Tensions were rising in Indian Territory. As the year 1897 closed, the "Indian Agent, [Dew M.] Wisdom, . . . ordered the arrest of any persons found with liquor in their possession, or who are intoxicated. Such persons will have to tell where they got their liquor or be declared in contempt of court for refusing to do so."[13] In April 1898 Fuller gave a rundown of recent events. Ella Haynes of Afton managed the juvenile work, which was "flourishing." The LTL of Afton was just getting ready for "its first bow toward the public by way of an entertainment," probably a medal contest or perhaps a concert. The LTL of Tahlequah was just being reorganized, apparently having becoming inactive. Now it boasted a robust fifty members. President Willard had died that year, and Fuller shared that "we of the Indian Territory feel the loss of Frances Willard in a special manner. She always showed our weak little union the greatest kindness and sympathy, besides having always spoken a word in favor of our people when opportunity allowed." Fuller closed with the news that territorial president Eva Ratcliff had resigned over "ill-health" and had "gone to a southern clime."[14]

In 1898 Corresponding Secretary Cook reported twelve local unions, but "no County or District organizations" and offered the usual updates. She explained that there was great enthusiasm for mothers' meetings and gospel temperance groups. Cook admitted, "our population is so transient that we do not know when we organize a Union that it will be there in six months. Our Unions are nearly all composed of women from the States, as it is nearly impossible to get Indian women identified with the work. Intoxicating liquors are sold in every town although it is against the law, and the people need education on this subject."[15] Apparently, Cook's own 1897 claim that liquor traffic was diminishing had been too optimistic.

In February 1899 Lulu Jones reported on the January convention of Indian Territory. Baptist Missionary for the territory, K. L. E. Murrow had been elected president.[16] In early spring 1899, Rudicil College at Ardmore received Murrow's talk on narcotics.[17] The October 1899 *Union Signal* reported on the September 1899 Indian Territory convention. This was a very auspicious report: "Reports showed considerable increase over last year in organization and increase of membership. Thirteen new unions were organized in a little less than nine months since our last convention." Things were not perfect, the report explained: "Five unions have died during the year. Cause, not enough encouragement and help by way of living messengers to run to and fro."[18]

In 1899 the Indian Territory president, Laura Harsha, "brought good reports from Indian Territory" and revealed a great deal of political activity and "Mrs. Ellis spoke about the efforts to repeal the Prohibitory Law in Indian Territory."[19] Nannie E. Oliver of Sallisaw "reports her Convention as the best in the history of W.C.T.U. of the Territory. The membership was increased by 100." However, suggesting again a lack of stability among both the new invaders and the longer-term Native American residents, Harsha said, "None of the local women were in the field to speak of; the work was done by Mrs. Howe, of Missouri, and Mrs. Stoddard of Texas, and Mrs. Kuhl of Illinois," indicating that there was a lot of national support for outside help in Indian Territory. Convention members were very active legislatively, and they drafted a petition to President William McKinley regarding enforcement of the anti-canteen law. The convention "also petitioned the Councils of the five civilized Indian tribes, asking them to petition Congress to continue the Prohibitory laws of this Territory. We feel much encouraged and are full of hope for the coming year."[20]

In adjacent Oklahoma Territory, Dorothy Cleveland from Anadarko, Oklahoma, had taken over the position of corresponding secretary in December 1898, when the previous secretary moved to Indian Territory. She had not received her reports from all the local unions but stated optimistically, "I am sure the work is better than it seems." She counted 310 members and 130 honorary members, "which is an increase over last year." She continued, "Seven new Unions were organized during the year, making 32 in all. There are also six L.T.L.'s, with a membership of 375. Three conventions have been held; one Conference and four public gatherings of note. Five hundred and ninety-two signatures have been secured to the total abstinence pledge. Contest and organization have been the special lines of work."[21] The flurry of activity in Indian Territory and adjacent Oklahoma Territory, with their shared histories and demographic similarities, compelled Cleveland to try to institutionalize Indian work at a higher level.

At the 1899 national convention in Seattle, Washington, Cleveland "presented a petition to the National Executive at Seattle asking that there might be a Department of Work Among Indians. This was not favorably considered but it was provided that the Indians should be looked after by the department of organization." While the executive committee rejected the stand-alone department, they requested that she "systematize a plan for reaching them in every reservation through local W.C.T.U. women and employees and teachers in the Indian schools." Cleveland explained the urgency: "Ten years hence they will be ten times harder to handle because the class of white people who come to the reservations now are of the worst kind and often bring drinks to the Indians in camp."[22]

Although disappointed that the committee did not approve a department, Cleveland nonetheless devised an educational plan that would come to characterize Indian work in the coming decades. The plan entailed several stages: (1) The first step was to organize employees in Indian schools into small unions. Members should send their dues to the state WCTU. She encouraged wearing the white ribbon to communicate their membership to others. The adornments not only served as conversation pieces to spark discussion of the advantages of temperance but would also provide a tangible symbol of their commitment to the cause and lifestyle and thus set a personal example. (2) The next step should be to organize an LTL among the children. Organizers were reminded not to worry about collecting dues because neither the children nor their family would likely have much money. However, their full inclusion in the organization was essential. She explained, even if Native American communities did not pay their share, the state LTL superintendent should "let them wear the badge and call themselves an Indian L.T.L. Be sure to have medal contests. This is the one line of work that will be very successful. There is a medal especially for Indians. It is aluminum and costs but a few cents." She explained that book "No. 3 of the 'Medal Contest Books' has the best recitations for children" with detailed instructions. A contest should contain eight or nine people, be officiated by three judges, and host music to accompany the events.[23]

Noting that scientific temperance instruction was already required in federally run Indian schools, Cleveland encouraged some specific methods to fulfill the curriculum. (3) She suggested experiments along with blackboard diagrams regarding alcohol, tobacco, opium, and mescal (peyote). Organizers might also form junior and senior LTL study hours every evening. She continued, "ask your superintendent to give you one evening each week for the L.T.L." (4) She suggested, "If your Indians are partly civilized you may be able to organize a W.C.T.U. among the camp Indians. In one or two places we have unions among full-blood Indian women and they are perfectly successful. If you think they are capable be sure to organize them into a union, show them how to conduct their meetings. Never omit the devotional part, for all Indians are very religious in their way, then [sic] the W.C.T.U. is a *Christian* Temperance Union." (5) She assumed everyone knew that the Interior Department banned bringing alcohol onto an Indian reservation. However, she recognized that violations were rampant and encouraged nascent undercover operations and inquiries. She suggested organizers find out how violations were happening and to report scofflaws to an "agent, inspector, or secretary of the interior." (6) She intimated that workers could benefit from light espionage on community members. She reminded the reader that there is "no secrecy in their 'teepees'" and lots of immorality and drunkenness. She closed, asking that state WCTUs send her "names and addresses of all missionaries outside of the school (for all employés of Indian schools are missionaries) that are on your reservation, and let me know how I can help you?"[24] Apparently, her efforts were effective.

At the annual convention in 1900 Cleveland reported unprecedented growth in Oklahoma Territory that year: twenty-five new unions, six hundred new members, and "four organizers in the field." Many of the new unions had healthy membership rolls but failed to pay their dues. Jail and prison work, especially that conducted by Della Jinkins in Guthrie, was successful, with "over 100 conversions." Cleveland claimed that eight towns went dry because of WCTU and Anti-Saloon League partnerships.[25] The national corresponding secretary, Susannah Fry, was able to report developments from the past year in Indian work and had been "instructed to develop our work among the Indians. To this end, Mrs. Dorothy J. Cleveland, now president of the Oklahoma Territory WCTU, was selected to carry out plans as one thoroughly conversant with that people." Considering Cleveland's experience and successes in Oklahoma, along with her firm understanding of the challenges of organizing, her selection was not surprising. Upon taking up the presidency,

Cleveland wrote to forty-nine schools in New Mexico, Washington, Minnesota, Wisconsin, California, North and South Dakota, Indian Territory, Oregon, and Idaho. "As a result, six Indian schools have held medal contests and eight were preparing for such when she reported, and L.T.L.'s have been organized in fourteen different schools. Her plan is to organize a Union among the Government employees and missionaries wherever practicable, or to put the work under the care of the nearest Union. We bespeak your help to reach these people."[26]

In 1901 in Indian Territory Rev. Dr. Murrow "made a powerful plea for Indian Territory" and read a speech, which was slated to be printed in the *Union Signal*. Indian Work was still a subcommittee of the executive committee, but committee members were serious about their charge and sent a telegram to President Theodore Roosevelt, at the request of Laura Harsha. They "recommend that no measures be taken which can imperil the existing Prohibitory law or property rights granted to the Indians by solemn treaty of the United States Government."[27] In their plea to retain all prohibitory laws in Indian country, the memorial indicated:

> It is well known that the Indian race has a peculiar and most powerful appetite for intoxicating liquors; second, that there is but a remnant of full-blood, about 40,000, in Indian Territory; that free whiskey would be the means of their being robbed of their lands and of their being exterminated very quickly. Third, that as these lands are the last they can ever own, it would be a crime for the general government to allow its Indian children to be subjected to the demoralizing influence of free whiskey which will rob them of their last landed heritage so sacredly pledged to them by treaty with the United States Government and which will destroy them very speedily, both bodies and souls.[28]

In this letter, we see laid out formally the WCTU's interpretation of a particular Indian bent toward alcohol addiction, the inevitability of the loss of an Indian land base—and thus a need to continue special protections.

By 1901 after a full year of organizing by Cleveland, Mrs. Lake "moved that the Executive Committee recommend to the Convention the creation of a department of Work Among Indians." This was almost certainly Isabel Wing Lake, secretary of Rescue Work, a division of Purity Work focused on the salvation of women who had gone down a difficult road and often been victimized by drunken men. This time, the convention agreed. Cleveland had moved Indian work to national prominence. She was able to secure $50 in appropriations and an additional $40 in "Special Appropriations" to get the department off the ground. For comparison the Work Among Colored People received $500 and Work Among Lumbermen received $150.[29]

At the 1902 annual meeting Cleveland submitted a report that introduced the department, claiming it was the first national Department of Work Among Indians—ignoring its first manifestation years earlier. It is important to note that state "agencies *received* the plan of work [emphasis added]," rather than helping to develop the plan through partnership with the national. However, she tried to connect with the state superintendents. She counted six, three of which were appointed that past year. They included (1) Northern California, led by Ada Campbell; (2) Minnesota, led by Mrs. I. F. McClure; (3) Indian Territory, led by K. Ellett Murrow; (4) Oregon, with an unnamed superintendent; and (5) Oklahoma, led by Mary E. Hokinger. While number six was not explicitly listed, Cleveland was likely counting the Southern California WCTU, whose superintendent was Mattie Black in 1902. Cleveland lauded WCTU work in schools in Arizona, North Dakota, Michigan, and New Mexico. Although the department was new, "much work has been done which has not been reported." Not long after she got all of this work underway, Dorothy Cleveland died in the summer of 1903.[30]

The office sat vacant through the next year. When the national leadership went through its roster of women who were qualified to run a department of Work Among Indians, Dorcas Spencer rose to the top. The selection revealed that the desire to have a department was not dependent upon Cleveland's individual efforts alone, nor even on specific events in Oklahoma and Indian Territory. Instead, there was a general will to affect Indian country as a whole.[31]

The Dorcas Spencer Difference

The selection of Dorcas Spencer for the national superintendent position in 1905 was not surprising. She had a long history in the WCTU and had some of the best experience in Native American communities. She was a cofounder of "The Woman's Temperance Union" in California, which came into being a month prior to the first official convention of the Woman's *Christian* Temperance Union in Cleveland, Ohio, in the fall 1874. Spencer and Emma Dibble founded the Woman's Temperance Union at the Congregational Church, Grass Valley, California on March 25, 1874. In 1879 the WCTU of California was established and a constitution adopted.[32] The first conference of northern

California (and what would become the Northern California WCTU) was held in 1880.[33] In 1883 the southern California branch broke away, forming a separate union. The rationale behind this separation was not just raw distance but also transportation realities around the geographical features of California. Some remote Native American populations in the eastern mountains were very difficult to reach. Spencer visited Inyo County, home of Death Valley and several Paiute and Shoshone communities, in 1910 after becoming national superintendent of Work Among Indians. This was the first time an "accredited" WCTU worker had been there. Inyo and San Luis Obispo Counties were better accessed by railroad from Los Angeles, and so those counties were transferred to the Southern California WCTU. In her book-length history of northern and central California WCTUs, Spencer bemoaned the "inconvenient bigness of California, as well as its rugged topography [which] has made it extremely difficult and in many cases impossible, to reach entire communities that for this reason must remain in their relation to state work very much like foreign missions."[34]

Spencer originally made a name for herself in WCTU circles as state superintendent of STI in California. The WCTU scientific temperance workers decided that *Steele's Hygienic Physiology* was the first textbook that met their standards, and they determined to make it part of the high school curriculum in districts throughout the state. Between 1885 and 1886 Spencer learned the process by which school boards adopted textbooks and began to encourage them to adopt Steele's book and their STI curriculum, starting with friendly small towns and then targeting bigger ones, like San Francisco. She and the WCTU got STI adopted across the state, through an extensive letter-writing campaign to various school boards. She developed a strategy of keeping track of districts that adopted their recommended textbooks and then convinced non-adopters that a surge of temperance instruction was happening and they should ride the wave, too. She ended 1886 as "the first state organizer."[35] In 1887 California passed an STI law, solidifying the work of her previous years' district-by-district campaign.[36]

Spencer's experience with Billy Beckwith and the closing of Fort Gaston along with her general organization and petition work marked her as someone both knowledgeable and effective in matters of Indian work. The NCIA sent a missionary to the Hoopa Valley Reservation and a church was established, largely through the urging of Spencer. "Mrs. Spencer continued her plea for the mission before every accessible denominational body for ten years when the

Presbyterian Board of Missions undertook the work." They eventually sent M. E. Chase as a missionary in 1900, and she was pastor there for many years. Spencer returned "after fifteen years and was surprised to find herself remembered gratefully by the Indians 'as the woman that sent the soldiers away.'" The "Indian man [Beckwith]" died before "his vision [was] realized, but died content in the faith that it was all coming, and in his last hours thought himself surrounded by women wearing the white ribbon—to his mind the symbol of his people's redemption." Spencer continued, referring to herself in the third person: "This was the last fieldwork of Mrs. Spencer as she was transferred to the headquarters as Corresponding Secretary. The demands of the state work now required the office to be open every day and the secretary in attendance." Apparently, the office was so respected that the corresponding secretary earned the same salary as the Northern California WCTU president.[37] Spencer described the "Work Among Indians" department, which "grew out of work reported in 1889 [on the Hoopa Reservation], and has been carried successively by Mrs. L.P. Williams, Mrs. E.M. Priddy, Mrs. M.E. Chamberlain, Miss Ella Brown and Miss Ada Campbell, until 1905 when it was taken by the national superintendent, Mrs. D.J. Spencer. An indirect help to the Indian people has resulted from the better knowledge of their condition by whites."[38]

In northern California, at the state level there were experienced people interested in Indian work who held state-level positions and encouraged Spencer's work along the West Coast. Some preceded Spencer in Indian work in California. In an addendum to the minutes from the 1889 annual convention we learn that an Indian department was established in the California WCTU that same year and that Mrs. L. P. Williams of Sacramento was appointed superintendent by the executive committee. Embedded in the presidential address of that year was a description of Indian work. Referring to the Pauline motto of the colonial-era missionaries which emblazoned the seal of Massachusetts, "come over and help us," the president wrote, "And now the Macedonian cry is heard from the real native [sic] Americans of our state. The chief of the tribe, learning something of our work, believes that the 'great women' can help his people." Then, helping to seal the legend of Dorcas Spencer, she continued, "Hearing and heeding his appeal, we sent a little woman—little when estimated by pounds and ounces, but a giant when pluck and Christian valor are taken into account— and she, with a sister worker, follows Indian Billy over a hazardous trail for many miles to a government reservation, and there found a state of affairs that affords a parallel to the Wisconsin Pineries. Plans are being matured to free these people from their present bondage, and take to them the gospel of temperance, as well as the gospel of Christ."[39]

In a report that foreshadowed the prominent role Spencer would play later, Humboldt County's report indicated that the county WCTU brought her in as an evangelistic worker. She wrote admiringly of what happened in Humboldt County, recommending their activities as a model for the rest of the state. In her words we see the future superintendent of the National Department of Work Among Indians developing her ideas. "Not the least interesting of my journeyings has been a visit to the Indian Reservation in the Hoopa Valley, which has impressed me deeply with a sense of the responsibility of the whites for the deplorable condition of these Native Sons of the Golden West. This is, perhaps, not the time or place to dwell upon the subject, but it opens before me a field of thought and effort that will not permit us to rest idly without an attempt to ameliorate these evils by an appeal to the government in their behalf."[40]

Before Spencer took over the national and the state Departments of Work Among Indians, the Northern California superintendent of Indian work in 1903 was Ada Campbell of San Francisco. Spencer, recording secretary at the time, and on the executive board, probably read Campbell's and others' reports. In this way she learned about activity in every corner of northern California, and this informed her of effective methods of working with Native American communities. Corresponding secretary Anna E. Chase commented on Butte County, which contained the town of Chico and the village of Mechoopda, stating that it was "the only county in the state having a union of native Indians, the same people have a Prohibition Alliance, both governed by Parliamentary rules[.] These Indians had a Temperance picnic July 4th with musical and literary program[s]."[41] There were twenty-six legions in California, and some local unions had conducted LTL work among Arizona Indians. In Butte County, the Bidwell Indian union had an LTL. Ada Campbell reported that she had written eighteen letters of unknown nature, distributed two hundred pages of literature, and shipped one Christmas box—a common way of donating useful goods to the tribal communities. Campbell received a report from Mendocino County indicating that Ukiah, with two hundred Indians, had a school, a church, various "temperance instruction" activities, and unfortunately, easy access to liquor.[42] In processing such information, Spencer combined her personal experiences with extensive readings and became prepared to lead the department herself for the next decade.

Spencer's understandings, accomplishments, and impact would include many aspects. First, her experience as both recording secretary and corresponding secretary led to her appreciation for and ability to compose thorough and professional reports. She knew the power of a well-written essay. As she moved into the national superintendent's position, she wrote or commissioned dozens of pamphlets to be distributed around the country in order to engender greater sympathy for Indian causes. These pamphlets were educational but were often oversimplified or biased regarding Indian religions, their legal status, and other issues. Some were condensed into briefer versions that were printed in the *Union Signal* and various state WCTU papers. Second, her travels to remote regions led her to develop robust, formalized connections with outside reform organizations and missionaries. Relying exclusively on WCTU workers to reach every remote reservation, especially in a place like California, was impossible and the WCTU would come to rely on their allies to spread the temperance message where dedicated organizers could not reach. Third, she had also come to realize that, despite various obstacles, persistent petitioning of government could lead to success in influencing legislation and enforcement of that legislation. Although she did not invent the department or all of the methods she employed, she put extraordinary energy and commitment into each of these contributions to Work Among Indians.

Missionary Boards and Reform Organizations

Across the various manifestations of national and state departments, one constant was the connection with missionary organizations. The dispersed and out-of-the-way nature of most reservations, boarding schools, and other Native American communities made it difficult to bring the organization, culture, activities, and literature of the WCTU to Indian country. Therefore, the WCTU sought help from missionaries or their spouses. Sometimes the WCTU messages came through the denominational, local, state, or federal schools. Other times WCTU workers came from unions that happened to be in a small town located near a reservation, via some enterprising woman who might also have been a missionary or a teacher.

Each major Protestant denomination had a mission wing or "board" and often a separate women's board. The white women involved in Work Among Indians often came from these boards. The WCTU's leaders reached out to missionaries to enlist their influence as additional routes to tribal audiences. K. L. E. Murrow tapped the grassroots to promote temperance by influencing the preachers in her field. The "Watch Tower" column of the *Union Signal* noted, "Murrow, of Atoka, Indian Territory, secretary of the Territorial W.C.T.U. succeeds in working the plan of securing one sermon per quarter from each pastor on the subject of temperance. It seems to me our local unions should make a strong effort to this end," suggesting that Murrow's technique in Indian Territory could be applied more broadly to the white preachers and their white congregations.[43] However, temperance preachers in Indian country tangibly influenced both white and Native American audiences.

In 1908 Spencer shared a "life sketch" of Rev. James Hayes, a Nez Perce Presbyterian minister in Idaho, written by Julia Fraser. The Nez Perce's Christianity and temperance activity had been sparked by the missionary Susan L. McBeth, who ran a Presbyterian seminary at Mount Idaho to prepare Native American ministers. Hayes was the pastor in Kamiah, Idaho, on the Nez Perce Reservation. Spencer explained that the Nez Perce had their own temperance organization and had recently held a temperance rally at Lapwai. The Nez Perce claimed they joined in the temperance cause first and Christianity followed, indicating that the demand to solve the social problems preceded their commitment to the new faith. Hayes and two other Nez Perce attended the Zayante Indian Conference in California that year. At the time the article was written, Hayes had gone to the Hoopa Valley Reservation to do evangelistic work. Hayes's transformation and participation in evangelization and temperance in other Native communities compelled Spencer to have the Literature Department put his story into a dedicated pamphlet, which they then distributed to Indian and non-Indian communities.[44]

Washington State's Department of Work Among Indians saw an early, strong relationship with missionaries, which helped spread the messages of temperance, Christianity, and other WCTU values across the state. There are two unmistakable geographic characteristics of Washington State, both of which affected Native American history and the WCTU's development there: the Pacific Coast, with its bays and magnificent island-dotted Puget Sound, and the Cascade Mountains, coming down from Canada, extending through Oregon to the California border, and dividing the state. One-third is to the west of the mountains; two-thirds are to the east, where the terrain is higher in altitude and much drier. The WCTU was divided by these geographical elements. Western Washington and Eastern Washington established separate territorial unions, Western Washington in 1884, Eastern Washington in 1887. Then, as now the Native American and non–Native American populations were greater west of the mountains, where water and other natural resources are more plentiful.

The Western Washington WCTU was in the vanguard of Indian work and created a Department of Work Among Indians at their first annual convention. Anticipating the eventual formation of a national department they declared, "Our national organization does not provide for this department, but as we have Indians among us we should seek to help them by personal visitation and conversation, and by circulating pledges and literature where appropriate." Between 1884 and 1885 the first superintendent of Work Among Indians was Mrs. B. A. (Jane) Hill of Nooksack about twelve miles up the road from the Nooksack Reservation and near Lynden, the location of the Methodist-run Stickney Indian school. The supply of illegal alcohol was apparently a major problem. The superintendent of Prison and Jail Work, Mrs. H. S. Parkhurst, worked with the Methodist and Presbyterian churches to reach out to inmates, presumably at McNeil Island Corrections Center, which operated as a federal penitentiary at the time. She noted the "U.S. Marshall told me some time ago that there were thirty-one inmates and that nearly all were in for selling whisky to the Indians." Noting the character of the men engaged in the liquor trade, "he thinks they are a very hard set and laughs at the idea of doing them good by moral suasion."[45] This trope of evil whites selling liquor to Indians was common in WCTU literature. While they were certainly violating laws, many liquor traders were frontier merchants who found the profits too attractive to ignore and thus ended up on the wrong side of the law. The WCTU Indian Work Departments had an incentive to vilify white traders so as to sell the innocence and thus the necessity of protecting Native Americans.

Eastern Washington's inaugural convention in Walla Walla in 1883 also produced a Department of Work Among Indians with their first superintendent, Mrs. A. P. Crystal of Grand Coulee, abutting the Colville Reservation.[46] In 1894 Father de Rouge commented on temperance activity at Omak Lake Mission, on the Colville Reservation, noting that the group set a good example for the whole community.[47] Although there was not a lot of activity in Eastern Washington's sparse Work Among Indians reports, there was some communication with the western union, who relayed their news. Apparently, in 1893, eastern Washington Indians had taken steps against "unprincipled whites," though these initiatives were not described in detail.[48] It does not require much imagination to understand who these whites were and what problems they caused in eastern Washington. Rickard Gwydir, Indian agent to the Colville

Reservation after 1886, was aghast at both the amount of Indian drinking and the inability to prosecute the whites who sold the alcohol. In his 1887 report to the commissioner of Indian affairs, Gwydir complained, "whiskey . . . is the greatest curse of the Indian race." It is "almost an antiquated joke to write again on it." Whites carried on illegal sales "regardless of consequences." There were many challenges to enforcement, including juries' unwillingness to accept Indian testimony, the loophole that many agents agreed that beer was "not an intoxicant," and the distance that an agent had to travel with a prisoner so as to find a commissioner to whom he could turn over the perpetrator. (The closest was Spokane Falls, sixty-five miles away.) The extreme profits one could make were so high, these weak barriers guaranteed that the infiltration by liquor sellers would continue. Gwydir was a firm believer in Christian civilization as the means to save the Indians and wrote favorably of the presence of "Rev. Mr. Eells, who with Mr. Walker, established a Protestant mission at what is now known as Walker's prairie." He also had a positive view of the Jesuits who had several missions on the northwestern reservations.[49]

At the time of the Western Washington WCTU convention of 1886, Mary J. Milroy of Olympia was superintendent of Work Among Indians, though it seems she did not attend the convention that year. In the presidential address Carrie M. White commented on department work, indicating the lukewarm feelings toward Indian work that pervaded the territory. One exception was the La Conner chapter, which she described as the "banner union." La Conner is located adjacent to the Swinomish Reservation, on the far northeastern shore of Puget Sound. White explained that the inability to organize Native American communities was due primarily to an absence of substantial Indian population near the extant white WCTU unions (and to unspecified logistical and personnel limitations). "The work among Soldiers and Sailors and that among Indians are lines that many auxiliaries have felt they did not need or could not prosecute." However, White asserted the necessity of Indian work for the territorial organization to the convention audience: "Their importance you understand so well that I need only ask that you will lend a hand to them whenever possible."[50] The Swinomish desired the kinds of temperance and purity efforts that the WCTU promised. Beginning in the 1870s the OIA lacked sufficient funding for an agent there, and the Swinomish were victimized by white alcohol dealers and men who "prostituted their women." A Catholic priest from that era, Father Chirouse, "who lived at Tulalip, occasionally visited Swinomish Reservation, mediating between Indians and White settlers when there were conflicts," though this never seemed sufficient to create social harmony.[51]

Located at the opposite end of Puget Sound from Swinomish, on the southeastern end of the Olympic Peninsula, was the Skokomish Reservation. In 1887 Sarah Maria Crosby Eells, and her husband, the Congressional minister Rev. Myron Eells, lived there. She replaced Milroy as superintendent of Work Among Indians. There was a substantial family history behind the Eellses' Indian work. The Eells brothers were the children of early missionaries to the Northwest, Cushing and Myra Eells. Myron's older brother, Edwin Eells, was the Indian agent to the Skokomish. Myron understood the anti-Indian sentiment of many white Pacific Northwest residents of the time, but he strove to impress upon them the injustice of the power structure, the white settlers' poor treatment of the Indians, and the damaging federal Indian policies. He began one speech about Indian rights to the Congregational Association of Washington and Oregon with a pronouncement of innate Indian spiritual inferiority: "Any person who has been a missionary among the Indians for any length of time knows very well that the Indian is not a saint—that his heart is naturally at enmity against God and right, and that ages of heathenism have rendered his corrupt heart still worse; and that he does not naturally love justice." He continued, "But on the other hand in comparison with the whites, he has very little power, and he knows it, hence he will bear much more from the whites than he would if he had an equal amount of power, and he will bear much more than the whites will bear from the Indians." He then proceeded to explain the many injustices against tribes across the United States, invoking Helen Hunt Jackson's recent title. He declared, "all the acts of injustice done by our government to the Indians . . . would fill volumes and make a *century of dishonor*, and are a very great obstacle to missions among the Indians, because they connect the Christian religion with the whites and with our government [emphasis added]."[52] Whether Sarah Eells herself possessed precisely these sentiments, we do not know. Although she was superintendent through 1888, she did not provide a report for either 1887 or 1888. In 1888, the lack of report was not even mentioned in the list of "missing reports."[53] However, the duo formed a partnership that supported her WCTU participation and both of their missionary efforts and it is difficult to imagine there was not some overlap in their sensibilities. However, Sarah Eells was not destined to remain in her position very long.

During the next few years the superintendent position was a veritable "hot potato" and changed hands almost every year. In 1889 Whatcom County resident Mrs. Dr. Moorehouse of the Woman's Home Missionary Society of the Methodist Episcopal Church who would soon be at Nooksack, in the same county, replaced Eells.[54] In 1890 the department was listed, but there was no superintendent. In 1891 Mrs. Hamblet of Seattle was elected, but there were no reports for 1891 or 1892. Although the reporting may have been light, activity went on. The state organizer Mary Bynon Reese reported that she had visited the Skokomish Reservation and "addressed a very intelligent company of Indian children, whose pledge cards will gladden the heart of [LTL founder] Anna Gordon at the great exposition."[55] In 1893 Clara Ansorge of Shelton, Washington (about ten to fifteen miles south of the Skokomish Reservation), was named superintendent.[56] In 1894 Eliza C. Sulliger, president of the Woman's Home Missionary Society of the Methodist Church, Puget Sound, from Chehalis, home of the Confederated Tribes of the Chehalis Reservation, was elected superintendent. Her husband, Dr. Spencer S. Sulliger, was superintendent of the "Vancouver District of the Methodist Episcopal Church."[57]

In her 1897 report Sulliger lamented the challenges of distance, which prevented her from attending the state convention. In her absence she appealed to the Almighty to bring the attendees success: "I pray for your convention a blessed time. May our God help us eradicate the curse of alcohol." Her sense of desperation and limitations with Indian Work came through clearly: "In my travelling over the district I have done the best I could with those with whom I have come into contact. I have distributed literature wherever it could be used and have done as much personal work as possible. The ladies at Mima and Shelton have been helping forward the work by sending out literature. The limited field over which I travel does not enable me to do justice to the work."[58] In 1898 Sulliger (now living in Olympia, apparently) issued one of the only substantive published reports in a decade and a half of Indian Work. Building on the themes of the prior year's scant report, she noted her limited geographic range. Transportation realities forced her to focus on "the counties lying west of the Cascade Mountains, and south of and including the counties of Thurston, Mason and Chehalis [future Grays Harbor County]." This meant her territory was limited to the area south of Seattle, in the southern portion of Puget Sound and the Olympic Peninsula. Work included "personal work" and "distribution of literature." She wrote positively of the Indian Shaker Church's abstinence message regarding alcohol and tobacco, and she left open some space for tolerance of Indigenous religious innovations: "I consider it a very inviting field to enlist the good will and work of their religious leaders in the crusade against intoxicating drink. They will do this because it is in accord with their religion."[59]

Yet, her message to the convention assumed the extinction of the Indian at the turn of the century: "The Indian is passing away very rapidly, and what we do for him must be done quickly. No missions to the heathen have been more successful than those among the Indians." Invoking the first Episcopal bishop of Minnesota, she noted:

H.B. Whipple says: "Thousands who were once wild, painted savages, finding their greatest joy in deeds of war, are now disciples of the Prince of Peace." There are Indian churches with Indian congregations, in which Indian clergy are telling the story of God's love in Jesus Christ our Savior. Where once was only heard the medicine drum and the song of the scalp dance, there is now the bell calling Christians to prayer, and songs of praise and words of prayer go up to heaven. The Christian home, though only a log cabin, has taken the place of the wigwam, and the poor, degraded Indian woman has been changed to the Christian wife and mother.[60]

For denominational missionaries like Sulliger, there was little doubt as to the trajectory of Indian life for the future. Although she would become too ill in 1903 to maintain her missionary board position, she stayed connected to the Stickney home until she died in 1911.[61]

By 1905 the Washington superintendent of Work Among Indians was A. L. Dyer Lawrence, who provided a report at the state convention. There were ten thousand Indians in the state, thirty-three different tribes, and some decent temperance work being done, especially at Tacoma. She described the compulsory education law in Washington and claimed that there was not much prejudice against Indians in the schools. "Prejudice" in WCTU usage narrowly referred to the refusal to let Native American children attend school rather than to any bias or discrimination against them by teachers or students, which undoubtedly was more widespread. She relied heavily on the missionaries' reports. "They say, as all missionaries do, that drink is the great curse among the Indians. Remember, dear Sisters, at the noon-tide hour daily especially our Brothers and down-trodden Sisters of the 'Red Men.'" The WCTU was optimistic because alcohol was banned by treaty, but still, 90 percent of cases in local reservation court "involved intoxication." That optimism ebbed later in 1905 when the US Supreme Court's decision in the *Matter of Heff* placed liquor sales to allotted Indians under the jurisdiction of state and not federal laws. For the temperance crusaders, the situation in Indian country seemed even more precarious.[62]

For several years after 1905, Superintendent Dyer was out of state, but work continued at the local and county levels. One particularly active woman was Rhoda Gaches, president of Skagit County WCTU, which also had a county Department of Work Among Indians led by Mrs. M. Jennings. There were two LTLs at the La Conner union—one for boys, run by Mr. E. Lovel, and another for girls, run by Gaches. She had a special relationship with the Swinomish Reservation, across the Swinomish Channel. Gaches was married to Baptist stalwart James Gaches, and she had been treasurer of the local Baptist church and a member of the Baptist Home Missionary Society.[63] An anonymous *White Ribbon Bulletin* author explained Gaches's role in Indian work: "In spite of the fact that Mrs. Gaches is a housekeeper, [she] is president of the Skagit County W.C.T.U. and does most of the organizing work in her county." The author went on to describe her persistence with the Native American community: "It took much time and patience to win an opening for the work" with Indians, "but it is greatly appreciated by the present superintendent of the Indian school," the Swinomish Day School, established in 1897 and in operation until 1918.[64] A Swinomish boy came regularly and picked up Gaches in a rowboat. "They are growing into temperance men and women and will help to drive strong drink from the land."[65] Gaches taught "the Indian girls at the nearby reservation singing and lace making" and was "giving them incidentally temperance teaching."[66]

Whereas most WCTU superintendents commented on their warm relationship with missionaries who welcomed their work with the Indian youth through the LTLs, Gaches eventually ran into trouble, which may have been the result of recent nationwide denominational jockeying within Indian policy circles. In 1908 the local WCTU newspaper reported that the Swinomish Reservation had an active LTL "until the new year . . . when a notice was sent Mr[s]. Gaches that the priest wished to do the teaching, so for the time it is discontinued." This was confirmed by the *White Ribbon Bulletin* reporter M. J. Jennings, who explained that, in Skagit County, "the workers had been shut out of the reservation."[67] From documents in the Seattle Archdiocese, we learn that the conflict was caused by a mixture of scheduling disputes and a desire by the priest and the Indian Office to offer religious instruction in the Indians' Catholic faith, which rubbed the Protestant Gaches the wrong way.[68] She probably pushed back,

Figure 12. "North American Indian Under the Temperance Gospel," Loyal Temperance
Legion of Swinomish Reservation, Skagit River, Washington. (Postcard photo
by O. J. Vingren, La Conner, Washington, 1907, Catalog ID # 2004.69.91.
Courtesy of Washington State Historical Society, Tacoma, WA.)

allowing anti-Catholic sentiment to creep into her temperance lessons. The diplomatic language indicating that the priest wanted to "do the teaching" belied a
deeper resentment between Protestant missionaries, their WCTU allies, and
the Catholic missionaries and Catholic Church in the United States. The dustup
between Catholic and Protestant missionaries had begun about fifteen years
earlier. Many of the reservations around Puget Sound had been Catholic strongholds. Father Chirouse was a strong presence among the Native American
communities in the region, but he was headquartered at Tulalip and only visited Swinomish infrequently. "Later, Father Hartnet moved into the area and
attended to their religious needs." He was there for thirty years, "achieving good
rapport with the community members."[69] The responsiveness and good order in
Indian Work of the Catholic missionaries was supported by federal policy.

The *Union Signal* itself described the federal government's decision to cut
funding to Indian Protestant sectarian schools. Presbyterians and Congregationalists responded by refusing government funding after 1894, the year
when funding began diminishing. Methodists, Quakers, Lutherans, Unitarians
declined funding in 1895; Episcopalians did the same in 1896. In 1895 Catholics
received $400,000, and by 1900 that number was down to $60,000. Of the
$5,903,798 million provided to sectarian schools since 1886, Catholics received

$3,959,643.[70] Protestant antipathy for the federal government's preference for Catholic participation in Indian schools bred resentment between the two camps and fueled an anti-Catholic contingency in the WCTU.

In 1908 shortly after being pushed out of Swinomish, Gaches suffered a personal tragedy when her husband died. Soon afterward, she became sick, her LTL work slackened, and she left for California to recuperate. Hattie Dunlap took the reins for Skagit County. She reported that the Central Union of Tacoma "has held one public meeting and one medal contest with eight speakers at the school on the Puyallup reservation. 38 have been converted there, and joined the Mission church. At the Stickney Home there have been 9 converted, 4 reclaimed and believing ones strengthened. Our Master says go ye into all the world and preach the gospel to every creature. Total abstinence is one step along the line of Christian service. Let us be faithful in our trust."[71] Despite all her hardships, Gaches recovered and resumed state-level leadership in Indian work in 1910 as superintendent of Work Among Indians, a position she held until about 1915 when the department began to fizzle out.[72]

The missionary connection was also strong with Montana's state WCTU leaders, especially Rev. Alice S. N. Barnes, president of the state WCTU until 1900, when her husband's ill health led her to decrease her workload temporarily. Despite stepping down from most of her responsibilities that year, she was made "honorary president and life-member of the National W.C.T.U."[73] In 1901 she became state organizer. An early member of the Montana Independent Order of the Good Templars (IOGT), Barnes was experienced with many facets of temperance work. In 1903 the *Montana WCTU Voice* was founded as an independent paper, and Barnes was made editor. She became treasurer in 1904. In 1906, with her first husband now deceased, she married C. E. Hoag and returned to the presidency in 1908, but she had already been a central figure in Work Among Indians.[74]

As early as 1904 Montana had a state Department of Work Among Indians, with Anna A. Walker superintendent. Walker traveled to the Fort Shaw Reservation School in 1904 and wrote an extensive article in *The Voice*.[75] At the 1905 convention Walker was replaced as superintendent by Barnes, who was then living in Columbus, Montana, about sixty miles west of the Crow Reservation border.[76] By 1906 Barnes had retired from her pastorate at Columbus Congregational Church, where she had worked for four years. After her marriage to Hoag, the newlyweds moved to Orr, Montana, the old name for the town near Fort Shaw, home to the Fort Shaw Indian School.[77] Barnes was also president of the Montana chapter of the Woman's Board of the Missions of the Interior of the Congregational Church. In 1908 she submitted a brief set of minutes.[78] Her 1909 report mentioned that a "picture of Miss Gordon and Mrs. Stevens [was] presented by her in [the] chapel at Fort Shaw and of work in school at Wolf Point [at Fort Peck Indian Reservation] in Northern Montana." Her presidential address describes an "enthusiastic" LTL at the Presbyterian Indian School at Wolf Point. The connections with the Presbyterian Church were particularly tight and effective. She commented that "the Temperance resolutions passed by the General Assembly of the Presbyterian church, held at Denver the last day of May, were planned for far-reaching results and harmonize fully with those passed by the National W.C.T.U. Convention held in the same city in October. These are some of the points they hope to receive by memorials to Congress." Of those listed, the most relevant was "that a prohibitory zone of 25 miles in width be established around every Indian reservation," which was an attempt to solve the problem of white border towns supplying the reservation residents with alcohol. In 1910 Reverend Hoag gave the report, by which time the Work Among Indians Department was dropped, though the Loyal Temperance Legion at Fort Shaw continued.[79]

In southern California, Mary E. Fowler dominated the superintendent position on and off for over two decades, and since this was the region of the "Mission Indians," she used preexisting mission village settlements to her advantage. In 1888, a few years after the Southern California WCTU broke away from the Northern WCTU, they formed a Department of Work Among Indians, led by Fowler who lived in San Jacinto, adjacent to the Soboba Mission of Luiseño and Cahuilla. Her location was in close proximity to dozens of other missions.[80] In 1889 a union was listed for Santa Ynez in Santa Barbara County though it is not clear if this union was entirely populated by the Chumash or if there were white members. San Diego County issued a report in 1889 that "San Jacinto Union is doing good work through that part of the County, especially in training the young, in holding public meetings, and in the Indian work."[81] Fowler laid out the current state of Indian work. She indicated that local unions included San Diego, Riverside, San Bernardino, and San Jacinto, but that only San Jacinto submitted reports (being managed by Fowler herself). She distributed literature in Spanish, including a pamphlet entitled *Satanas y el Vinatero* (Satan and the winemaker), which "seems to interest the men very much." She

hoped the pamphlet would help steer potential workers away from grape har-
vesting and other jobs in the wine industry. This was a tough sell, since vini-
culture was an important employment opportunity for Native Americans in
California. In choosing a title for her pamphlet, Fowler employed the ultimate
threat of damnation as encouragement. Helen Hunt Jackson's namesake mission was also successful. Fowler explained that the "Ramona Mission among
the Mission Indians is a very encouraging event to temperance workers among
them." The Ramona Mission even had a successful LTL that was over a year old.
She recognized the limits of local temperance workers connecting to Indian
communities and highlighted the value of having missionaries more perma-
nently involved: "The most our local Superintendents can do is to distribute literature and make individual appeals to a few. But the missionary can reach the
masses and carry Gospel temperance to them as no one else can do, and I wish
them God speed!"[82]

In 1890 the *Southern California White Ribbon* printed Fowler's report from
the October convention in Pasadena. Fowler expressed frustration with the
local unions who failed to submit reports and indicated that working through
the local unions was a dead end. She followed up on her plan to work through the
Ramona missionaries, and in this way "much more has been done to awaken
thought. . . . Temperance and Gospel Tracts, and a great deal of other helpful
literature, [in] both Spanish and English, have been sent into almost every
Indian village in San Bernardino and San Diego counties." The children especially were receptive, and she expressed confidence that temperance physiology was being taught in the schools, too. She visited Soboba often and
appealed to three "young men" in particular. "The old captain, who died a few
weeks ago, seemed to understand the true nature of the liquor business, and
to feel his responsibility in the matter. He had not permitted his people to
make wine for several years, but a new captain has taken his place and I understand that he has allowed it to be made. I trust, however, that this will be the last
year s[u]ch use will be made of their grapes." She implored her readers, "I would
urge the unions to take hold of this work among our own people. Indeed, I
believe God calls upon every union that is near a settlement of Indians to
do this work, for not only our own safety, but humanity and [C]hristianity
demand it."[83] The missionaries had been an important resource for her, but she
clearly wished that the local union members would do their duty as Christian
women rather than having to rely on the missionaries to do what should be
their work.

Missionary Ecumenism and Partnerships with Other Reform Groups

As these multidenominational missionaries and temperance supporters shared their stories in state and national publications, they contributed to a burgeoning ecumenical wave that pervaded the WCTU, and especially its Work Among Indians Department. In April 1897 the *Union Signal* reported an ecumenical atmosphere in Tahlequah. In addition to bimonthly meetings at president Tennie Fuller's house, the correspondent reported that the Tahlequah chapter had "monthly union temperance mass-meetings alternatively in the Methodist, Presbyterian, and Baptist churches." She continued, "our jail work is kept up faithfully, the ministers working with our superintendent of this department."[84] Dorcas Spencer commented on a conference in San Francisco in 1913, which had been "called by Rev. A. Grant Evans D.D., a representative of the Presbyterian Home Mission." There were representatives from the "Baptists, Episcopalians, Methodists, Presbyterian Missionary Societies," the NCIA, and the Indian Board of Cooperation. And Edward Hyatt, the state superintendent of public instruction, produced a speech that would be published as a "departmental leaflet for 'Work Among Indians.'" Spencer then referred to Rev. Frederick G. Collett and his wife Rev. Beryl Bishop Collett, heads of supervision of missionary work for the NCIA. "I have been asked if Mr. Collett was working for the W.C.T.U., in reply I would say not directly, but is certainly cooperating, as the W.C.T.U. does, with all who work for the same object."[85] By 1916 the relationship with the California Indian Board of Cooperation was much more explicit. The report stated that "a large number of Indians, by the aid of the 'Indian Board of Co-operation' visited the Exposition last year, and while there were organized as an 'Indian Auxiliary' to the Board. This gave us the names and addresses of over 300 intelligent Indians from all parts of the state, as well as some from Arizona and Nevada, and through them access to many more."[86]

Spencer employed Native American preachers' denominational journeys to emphasize the expansive tent of the WCTU and its unifying message. In a wide-ranging *Union Signal* article she commented on the tendency to highlight the worst elements of Native American development and history. She countered with numerous inspirational stories. The first was about an Arapaho Episcopal priest named Sherman Coolidge: "A good story is told of the rector of a New York church in whose pulpit Rev. Sherman Coolidge was to preach next day. He kindly took his western visitor to see the various objects of historical interest in the city, and incidentally mentioned that his forefathers came over in the 'Mayflower.' 'Ah,' said Mr. Coolidge, who is a full-blooded Arapahoe Indian, 'and mine were on the reception committee when they landed.' That was ready wit, and more,—a suggestion that the amiable weakness of ancestral pride is common to all mankind."[87]

Second, and more detailed, was the story of Edward Marsden from Metlakatla, Alaska, who was born in the "moral atmosphere of old Father Duncan's mission." Marsden, a Tsimshian, began his journey as a member of the utopian community of Metlakatla in British Columbia, led by lay Episcopal missionary William Duncan. When an Episcopal bishop moved to the area, supplanting Duncan's authority, Duncan moved the community to the United States and established "New Metlakatla." In both communities, Duncan introduced a set of rules for his Native American converts that included the abandonment of Indigenous religious practices and abstention from alcohol and gambling. When Duncan became increasingly authoritarian, especially in his attempts to constrain the education of the ambitious Marsden, the young Indian convert fled this community and became a Presbyterian pastor in his own right. According to Spencer, WCTU organizer Jessie Ackerman solicited Marsden's first temperance pledge, a source of pride for the WCTU. The movement between denominations was of little concern when compared with the commitment to temperance and the educational civilization project.[88]

The urgency of working with missionary societies led to the creation of a national WCTU Department of Cooperation with Missionary Societies. Missionary societies did not just include the "home" branches within the United States; their focus was the mission field overseas. However, the WCTU connected Indian work and missionaries in their minds, and sometimes in their fund-raising efforts. In August 1912 the Department of Cooperation with Missionary Societies sold sets of reproductions of charts and photos used at a temperance conference in Boston. Along with images from Africa, India, China, Bulgaria, there was one for the "Home Field," containing charts measuring eleven by fourteen inches with "photographs of North American Indians under the temperance gospel. In the lower picture five of the young people are wearing medals won at W.C.T.U. Medal Contests."[89] Apparently, the purchasers would be helping to fund further missionary temperance efforts while also adding tasteful décor to their homes and spreading the temperance message to guests.

The WCTU demonstrated a willingness to work with groups beyond the missionary wings of Protestant churches and their less frequent partnerships with Catholic religious orders or parish priests. The WCTU also dovetailed with broader Indian reform organizations, creating symbiotic relationships, offering their connections to tribal populations and years of insights working with communities in the remote regions of the country. In 1892 the Utes of Colorado were being threatened with removal, and the *Union Signal* printed a piece discussing the role of WCTU member and WNIA president Amelia Stone Quinton, who was working to protect them, along with Annie K. Bidwell, western vice president of the WNIA. The author attempted to spur opposition to Ute removal, based on the moral obligation of men and women to "stand between the Indian and the faithlessness of government. It is not necessary to urge white-ribboners to give their sympathy and help wherever occasion arises in the interest of the Indians against the heartless aggressions of the almighty dollar and backed up by the everlastingly persuasive rifle and bayonet."[90] Although this call to action lacked specific addresses of relevant lawmakers and a petition to sign, the author was clearly pushing members to connect with their counterparts in other organizations if at all possible. In other contexts, the partnerships were more direct.

The summer of 1906 was a challenging year for northern California. On April 18, the San Francisco earthquake rocked the city and subsequent fires ravaged it further. According to Spencer, "it is difficult to appreciate the effect of the April catastrophe on the entire state. It is felt in every line of endeavor." Banks and government offices closed. Membership in the WCTU plummeted. It was difficult to locate friends and loved ones.[91] Despite these hardships, on July 30 and 31, 1906, the Zayante Indian Conference of Friends of Indians met for the first time. This event grew out of a reform-minded group of Californians who were interested in Indian reform and who concluded that prior attempts by their respective organizations acting independently had not worked. This conference was an attempt to combine their efforts. The call to organize the group came from the NCIA branch of the WNIA, led by individuals such as the NCIA president, Mrs. T. C. (Mary Haven) Edwards, Dorcas Spencer, Annie Bidwell, Jessie Knight Jordan (wife of David Starr Jordan, president of Stanford University), Cornelia Taber, and many other religious and academic leaders. In their opening meeting they agreed to have another meeting the following year, with the following groups invited: "(a) Strong delegations of representative Indians from the various tribes. (b) Specialists and other active workers among the Indians. (c) A select company of men and women, representative of the churches and community at large." C. E. Kelsey, general secretary of the NCIA, provided an opening address entitled "The White Race and the Red in California." It was remarkably self-critical of the European conquest of California and the massacre, enslavement, and general subjugation of the California Native Americans. To counter this tragedy, the NCIA was working with Congress to appropriate money for the repurchase of lands lost; they succeeded in getting one hundred thousand dollars appropriated from the last Congress for this reason. Kelsey presented a talk, "What the Indian Needs." In the enumerated list, the fourth item was that they do not need liquor. Instead, they need the "fixity of tenure"—that is, security in land, safe from aggression, and better enforcement of liquor laws. As it stood at the time, federal Indian law did not apply to about nine thousand of the Indians in California, since they were non-reservation Indians. The state law of 1897 had been an improvement but was still difficult to enforce. Juries refused to convict saloon keepers, and drunkenness continued to be a major cause of violence.[92]

Bidwell could not attend the 1906 conference, and Spencer gave only a brief address that year. In her *Union Signal* article and report, Spencer described the 1907 Zayante Indian Conference in greater detail. Zayante, which drew its name from a local tribal name for the surrounding mountains, was a heavily Presbyterian organization that attempted to implement reforms with much more input from Native Americans than was usually sought by similar reform organizations. Spencer hinted that Friends of the Indian–type conferences in the past, like Lake Mohonk, lacked Native American participation, and the Zayante gathering attempted to remedy this obvious oversight. According to Spencer, the second Zayante had a higher number of Native American representatives from "distant reservations or 'campoodies'" than the first one. She went on to explain how inclusion of Native American delegates yielded more specific policy plans. The early twentieth century in California saw a number of challenges for Native Americans, the most problematic of which was the continued alienation from the land. Unlike allotment, where tribally held reservations were broken up by legislation, policy toward the California tribes was different since they had already suffered dispossession or were having their lands threatened in the courts, as happened at Soboba. Zayante offered some hope: Indian delegates representing seventeen thousand Indians in California attended and enumerated their requests: First, they wanted "land for our homes." Second, they wanted protection from the liquor traffic. Third, they wanted access to education, primarily through unencumbered access to the local public schools. Fourth, they asked for field physicians since the remote locations often prevented Euro-American doctors from getting to them. Fifth, they asked for legal protections limiting the biases against Indians in the courts.[93]

At the third Zayante Indian Conference at Mount Hermon in 1908, a Native American man from Ukiah, Lake County, named William Benson addressed the conference and disclosed his own troubles with alcohol and gambling but also explained how he made a living working in the vineyards three months out of the year. Another Native American man at the third conference was Robert Parish of Manchester, Mendocino County. He emphasized education and the need for lawyers, and told the story of when he tried to vote and was challenged by poll workers. Captain J. Sherwood of Sherwood, California, expressed a desire to have Christian missionaries in his community.[94] All of these ideas fit with the white reformers' existing plans for Native Americans, but the Native Americans' voices behind them strengthened the resolve of the Zayante attendees to pursue those goals.

In 1909 Spencer used the Zayante Indian Conference report to decry the lack of interest in Indian work that she observed. "It has been the grief of this superintendent that so few people knew or cared anything about Indians; and all the culture of all the schools cannot impart what personal knowledge gives. So, as yearly the representatives of both races confer together, there comes a mutual comprehension which in itself is a great gain, and the promise of greater." She went on to explain how closely the WCTU worked with the missionaries: "Nearly all the work for Indians in this state [is] now carried on by the various denominational boards of missions [and] is done in missions planted by the [Women's National] Indian Association and turned over to these boards." Spencer explained how the WCTU piggybacked on this association work. The WNIA "finds the waste places and neglected fields" and sends resources there. The latest place was the "'Hannah Bean Memorial Mission' at Bishop, Inyo county, the far off spot where a W.C.T.U. has lately sprung into life," named after Hannah Bean who had been in the San Jose WCTU and a member of the NCIA. The Paiutes at the mission had been quite isolated previously.[95] In 1910, she explained, "the Indian conference seemed to merge naturally into the work of the WCTU when its enthusiasm was at its climax, and only their kindred nature made it possible to carry so large a body, at that high pitch of interest, without a break, to the end of the sessions."[96]

In the 1910 Northern California annual report, where the Department of Work Among Indians was listed under "Evangelistic" work, President Dorr's presidential address claimed the Zayante Mount Hermon Conference was a joint effort, describing it as "the Conference of the [Women's National] Indian Association, and the Woman's Christian Temperance Union." Having attended, "my vision was enlarged, and I saw, as never before, the opportunities before us, to work for the uplift of the Indian of our State." She explained, "there are Indians in twenty-two counties, where we have the W.C.T.U." and went on to discuss "the plan presented at the conference." There would be a committee of three in each county, in addition to the county president as an ex-officio member. They would then "cooperate with the [Northern] California Indian Association" regarding alcohol issues and the "education of the young Indians of our State." She was particularly taken with the Indians' own words, especially regarding "strong drink," "the lawlessness of the saloon-keepers," and the "injustice of the courts." Then, she offered an interesting line about her racially egalitarian and evangelistic vision toward the tribes: "The thought came, 'And God is no respecter of persons—surely this [situation] is not according to His will.' I wonder if the Master is not calling to us, as He did to his disciples, that we 'cast our net on the other side of the ship.'"[97] Mount Hermon's commitment to the annual Indian conference waned shortly thereafter because of financial reasons and an increased focus on Bible study instead of what they deemed "social issues." However, the deep connections between missionaries, white ribboners, and Native Americans that occurred there solidified the goals they would pursue, placing those goals in line with the requests by the Indigenous Californians: land, liquor protections, education, medicine, and equal treatment in the courts. How these were to be operationalized would vary according to specific tribal contexts, but the framework would guide the WCTU's Indian work in the subsequent decade.[98]

Another group the WCTU connected with was the Lake Mohonk Conferences of the Friends of the Indian (LMCFI). Although the primarily male leaders of the LMCFI were prime movers behind allotment and boarding schools, they gradually moved away from supporting off-reservation schools and began promoting local schools instead. They also softened their views on Indigenous languages. While most boarding schools dealt with Indian languages by suppressing them and punishing the students for using their native tongues, this policy did not go unchallenged. As early as 1887 the *Union Signal* reported that the Lake Mohonk Conference sent a letter to the Indian commissioner criticizing restrictions against Indian languages.[99] White ribboners recognized the limitations of English-only policies, too, especially when engaging in work in distant communities. The *Union Signal* shared the speech from Rev. Charles L.

Thompson from the Presbyterian Board of Missionaries delivered at Lake Mohonk in the fall 1907. He explained that missionary zeal was not enough. Legislation against alcohol was not enough. The ideal apostle to the Native Americans would "fling himself into their lives." He explained that mission schools worked better than government schools since religious instruction was sorely needed. He continued, decrying the hard line taken toward Indigenous languages, claiming that the English only rule might be understandable in boarding schools but in mission schools the "apostles" needed to learn the language of their hosts, giving the examples of Arizona and Alaska, where Indian languages would likely persist through the next few generations. He went on to point out the essential role of Christian women among Indians: "religious uplifting of the Indians would be very incomplete if I failed to name the influence of Christian women, going among the hogans and tepees with a message to women and children, comprehensive enough to include all the physical, educational and moral needs. Than such angels of ministry there can be no mightier force for the regeneration of souls and the reconstruction of Indian society." Although he did not mention the WCTU by name, WCTU members were among the women he was referring to—and they certainly received his message as referring to them, considering the *Union Signal* reprinted his entire address.[100]

One of the main liaisons between the WCTU and the LMCFI was Amelia Stone Quinton, who was on the business committee of LMCFI and spoke frequently at the annual event. She received encouragement from US Congressman James S. Sherman from New York, who urged the women present to influence Congress, presumably because their organizations had proved their ability to do so. Regarding a prohibitory amendment to the enabling act that would allow Indian Territory to become a state, Sherman encouraged attendees: "I want to say to you women here that in my judgment it is within your power to set the fire blazing so that Congress dare not refuse your behest to incorporate in the enabling act a provision that intoxicating liquor shall be constitutionally excluded from the Indian Territory. . . . Now, ladies, start your crusade on this liquor question. Get your associations, your organizations, started throughout all the states of this Union, and let Congress hear from you."[101] Considering Quinton's leadership position (and that she spoke to the group a few speakers later), it is hard to imagine that she and other WNIA and WCTU members were not whom Sherman had in mind when he shared his encouragement. Although Lake Mohonk's platform almost always included some support for allotment, those in attendance also heard from the supporters of the California tribes who were in an impossible situation when it came to land tenure. Some were supporters or members of the WCTU. Zayante coordinator C. E. Kelsey, Quinton, and Samuel M. Brosius, the Washington agent for the Indian Rights Association, all spoke on behalf of the California tribes in their quest to have Congress return some lands to make their survival possible.[102]

The WCTU leaders were evangelical Christian idealists and women's rights advocates. However, they were pragmatic at the same time and excellent coast-to-coast networkers. These latter qualities helped them both recruit people and connect to organizations that could operationalize their vision through concrete actions in every corner of the United States, in small and remote communities. These attributes also meant that they could influence well-connected reform organizations and the congressmen and OIA officials who made policy from the top down. There were specific activities and methods they used to influence those policies.

Chapter 5

WCTU Activities, Legal Interpretation, and Enforcement

The goal of creating these multilayered networks was not to pontificate about the Indian liquor problem in the abstract. The reformers wanted to be successful on the ground. Their activities in Indian communities created a learning experience through which knowledge of Native Americans' needs, requests, and demands were processed. WCTU local and national leaders used their hard-won knowledge to influence legislation, in ways both directly and indirectly related to temperance, and they encouraged law enforcement efforts in Indian country. The focus of this chapter is on some of the smaller, state-level unions and their Indian work. In these unions and their departments of work among Indians, women employed the methods encouraged by the national organization such as literature distribution and establishing LTLs. However, the women also created innovative ways to respond to the needs of their local environments in implementing the national temperance agenda.

The main goals of the WCTU were to see woman's suffrage and alcohol prohibition at every level of government. WCTU members sought legislative protections for Indians and employed Indian men and women in suffrage fights at the state and national levels. Depending on the tribe, receiving an allotment and being deemed competent were precursors to Indian male citizenship and voting rights, up until universal Indian citizenship in 1924. WCTU members became active supporters of allotment legislation and encouraged the sometimes painstaking implementation of allotment on reservations, precisely because it would lead to their Indian allies voting their way in elections. And yet, from a Native American perspective, citizenship came with perils, including challenges to tribal identity and the potential loss of federal protections. Enforcement of legislation was also a goal of the WCTU's Indian department.

The WCTU leaders engaged in creative and aggressive prohibition enforcement methods, including running undercover operations and working with vigilante groups. What will become clear is that especially during the apex of WCTU Indian work (1900–1916), a geographically dispersed group of WCTU activists took up the challenges of organizing, lobbying, and enforcement and did their best to effect change in Native American communities and in the halls of state and federal government.

State Departments: Local Methods, Challenges, and Activities

Regardless of any individual WCTU worker's connection to missionary societies or outside organizations, they all demonstrated a commitment to legal prohibition, total abstinence, Christianity, reform of Indian policy, and the modification of Indian lifeways. In order to achieve these ends, state Work Among Indians Departments picked up on mandates and methods from the WCTU generally or the national department but often reshaped them as local circumstances dictated. Workers shared their wins, losses, struggles, and tactics in their national and state reports and newspapers. This sharing of information aided communication and understanding across racial and cultural lines, even if it did not undermine colonization itself. These voices from across the United States reveal the diversity not just between Native American communities but in drinking practices and temperance efforts. In California, for instance, the "fiestas" of the Mission Indians, surrounding older Catholic feast days, were somewhat unique, culturally, in the United States, though similar drinking bouts were common in many places. States such as Oregon and the upper midwestern states including Michigan, Wisconsin, Minnesota, North Dakota, and South Dakota had large Native American populations, but they were far away from white population centers. Distance, money, and communication problems plagued the WCTU members' work, but they tried very hard to keep Indian work going.

Although many white WCTU workers developed deeper understandings of Native American life over the decades, there was a vein of cultural hegemony and even racial superiority in the departments. From Southern California, Mary Fowler used divisive language: "Temperance work among the Indians of this State, like the same work *among our own race*, has its sun-illuminated mountaintop and its shadowed valley [emphasis added]." She complained that "the feast is the bane of Indian life: bringing among them the wine vender, the gambler and the debauchee."[1] She was optimistic, however, in the power of pledge signing and the related social pressure to keep the pledge as the means to keep a community sober. Referring to the Pechanga Band of Luiseño Indians, located near Temecula, in Riverside County, she noted, "the teacher at Pachango [*sic*] reservation writes hopefully of the out-look there. She says that the young men not only respond to her appeals to sign the pledge, but have worked so earnestly among their people to get them to sign that nearly every man, woman and child on the reservation has signed the temperance pledge. So far as she has known, only one has broken it." Mary Platt at Pechanga established a "flourishing L.T.L. and the boys and girls are very fond of their badges." Two years before Fowler's report, in 1891 the OIA recognized Platt's work and lauded her for taking over what OIA officials considered an abandoned post and starting a temperance society there.[2]

Fowler described the transformation at other nearby villages, including Potrero, "where the Moravian missionary, Rev. Wm. H. Weinland, is stationed, a good work is being done. They have temperance lessons in the school, the Sunday-school and the church. Twenty young men have signed the pledge, framed it and hung it in the church and really feel that [it] is a vow unto the Lord." And "Mrs. Salisbury, teacher of the Coahuilla school, reports much temperance work done in school and among the people; but is conscientious about asking them to sign the pledge, fearing that in temptation they may fail to keep it. She says she has seen but one drunken Indian in their village." Fowler explained that Soboba had an LTL with thirty-two people run by a Miss Noble, where the children conducted drills, wrote and read temperance essays, and "are as proud of their badges as their little white brothers and sisters." Fowler reported that Noble also spoke about temperance to patrons at a fiesta where she observed lots of drunken Indians, but she observed that during the next day's festivities there were fewer drunks. Fowler provided a rich and thorough report, though it reiterated some claims from previous years. Beneath the surface of mundane platitudes and hopeful reports of sobriety, there was a more profound vision of Native American change over time: "I submit this report with the hope that the coming year would bring much more to show that even the Indian 'world does move.'"[3] Thus, Fowler both reinforced stereotypes of Native American civilizations being stuck in amber and challenged them, slightly.

From 1897 until 1900 there was no Southern California WCTU Department of Work Among Indians, but there were county ones. Fowler, who had been state superintendent, now presided over Riverside County Department of Work Among Indians, where around ten smaller Native American communities existed, including Morongo, Agua Caliente, Santa Rosa, Cabazon, Augustine, Torres-Martinez, Pechanga, Cahuilla, Ramona, and Soboba. San Bernardino County occasionally had a Department of "Indians, Foreigners and Colored People," but the superintendent position was often vacant. In 1900 the Riverside County department was under Mattie Black, also of San Jacinto, who stayed in the position.[4] Black's dedication earned her the superintendent position of the state Department of Work Among Indians when it was reestablished in 1902. Mary A. Kenney's 1902 presidential address revealed that "one Union caused the investigation by the Government of an Indian Agent selling liquor to Indians, and put a stop to it." She also mentioned several other direct appeals to the government against reservation corruption and alcohol.[5]

Oregon took baby steps in its Indian work before the second phase of national Department of Work Among Indians in the twentieth century. There was no state department from 1889 through at least 1894, but in 1889 the Young Women's Work branch was taking an interest in Indian communities. "A Christmas box, in which the young ladies took great interest, was sent to the Indians of the Alaska Mission."[6] In 1895 Oregon's state WCTU appropriated three dollars for Indian Work. In preparation for the national meeting the president Narcissa White-Kinney indicated, "each delegation at the National would be expected to rise and sing a verse. She spoke of the first hymn translated into Chinook by Whitman and Spaulding." At a time when boarding schools were trying to exterminate Indian languages, sometimes through force, this show of respect suggested a more tolerant method of conversion among white ribboners there. Amid such developments, there was pressure to reduce the large number of departments in the Oregon WCTU, especially when more populous states like New York and Pennsylvania had far fewer departments than Oregon.[7] Although none of the troves of records for the Oregon WCTU contained the annual meeting minutes for the years 1898–1904, the *Northwest White Ribboner*, the joint newspaper covering Montana, Oregon, East and West Washington, and Idaho printed some of their meeting reports. One author reported that Mrs. M. Fullilove was superintendent of Work Among Colored People and Indians and "had been faithful in her branch." "Mrs. Jean Morrow, of Malheur county, from the Warm Springs Indian reservation, gave a fine, carefully prepared paper on 'The Government of Inferior, or Subject' Race, So-Called" at the Oregon state convention in 1900.[8] Yet, by 1905, there was no Department of Indian Work and none until 1915.

In Michigan workers made earnest attempts to reach out to Native American communities, but distance and lack of personnel were perennial challenges. Fannie McCourt's Twelfth District, in the Upper Peninsula, reported on the assistance she received from E. L. Calkins, who spent "seven and one-half weeks in the district, doing most valuable services. She organized a few new unions. Munising, Manistique, L'Anse, Iron River, and Calumet. She spent several days at the Indian camp meeting where 200 signed the pledge and a union was organized, of the tribe of the Ojibways. These sisters have been doing excellent work and were most heartily welcomed to this great sisterhood which embraces all nations and tribes under its white flag of purity."[9] In 1907 the Twelfth District report commented on the poor condition of the district, the illness of the district president, and other challenges resulting in the editor's weak report. Many unions were disbanded because of "removals of efficient workers" in the Upper Peninsula.[10]

In 1911 North Dakota received a compliment from Spencer, who declared it "easily the banner state for Indian work." It was the "only state in which the WCTU employs a special missionary for Indians," Jessie McKenzie.[11] The *North Dakota White Ribbon Bulletin* provided greater detail of McKenzie's work. She had traveled in 1909 to various Indian schools around the region, "introducing our temperance teaching among the children." She spent the winter of 1909–1910 in Bismarck and began a correspondence with various school and governmental officials. She diplomatically sought and received the approval of both the commissioner of Indian Affairs in DC and Governor John Burke. "Later, she re-visited Fort Berthold reservation, [and] did some work at Fort Trotten, [Spirit Lake Reservation]."[12] A year later, the corresponding secretary reported that shortly after the last annual convention she stayed on another two months. "She visited the Turtle Mt. Reservation and persuaded 14 of the Dunseith [Turtle Mountain Chippewa] Indians to sign the pledge. She began work on Ft. Totten Reservation but was obliged on account of her health to give it up," and she moved to San Diego to recover. In her absence, temperance activity continued in North Dakota, especially in the schools, but flagged without McKenzie's energy and organizing ability.[13]

In Minnesota, not much Indian work was happening in the nineteenth century, but activity picked up in the 1900s. In 1902 the WCTU central committee established a Work Among Indians Department, naming as superintendent I. F. McClure of Hubbard, near the Leech Lake Reservation, and allocating four dollars. In an early report McClure lamented her challenges but also shared how state superintendents navigated their duties. "My appointment came in March, when I was on a sick bed in the hospital. It was April before I could take up the work, and through some misunderstanding I did not receive postage until June 17th. However[,] I did what I could. I wrote to National Superintendent for instructions and in the meantime studied the state minutes and a county map of the state to get myself located. I received a roll of circulars which she had gotten out, [and the] 'Plan of Work.'" McClure was disappointed that specific Indian work "was simply not in existence yet." She tried to influence the government and sought valuable information from federal officials: "I then wrote to commissioner of Indian affairs in Washington, D.C. for the Indian agent's report. Here I learned the name of each and every Indian agent and school teacher on the reservations." She wrote to White Earth, Red Lake, and Leech Lake Reservations and learned the bad news about alcohol there. Even experienced agents were surprised at the gravity of the situation, noting that the women's drinking was as bad as the men's. She wrote letters, called for locals to establish superintendents for this work, and explained that she needed the missionaries' help, donors' money or fund-raisers to pay for an organizer to go there to "try to get the Indian women interested in the W.C.T.U. and L.T.L. work, so that they can help the children to grow heavenward, and away from this giant evil."[14]

In 1903 McClure reported "meager" results, but she was personally very active. She wrote seventy-two letters, "two postals, and sent out 33 'plan of work' circulars; 41 programs for Indian entertainment; 30 responsive readings. Also distributed 50 pages literature." There was, by this point, an Indian union at Morton with sixteen members, near the Lower Sioux Reservation, which received regular visits from the nearby Redwood Falls union. There were lots of violations of liquor laws, but only eleven indictments. McClure went to Leech Lake on August 28, 1903, but because of some miscommunication she never met with any Native American residents. She was able to meet with "the courteous and genial Dr. L. M. Hardin" who gave her information and support to do more work. She developed the idea of selling some of the Indians' "bead work and lace" to make money to support this work. "For the sake of Him who died for *humanity* (not just white folks) dear sisters, arouse and put your armour on and do something quick." She wanted to help the children in the Indian schools who are "a bright intelligent lot of children."[15] The new Fifteenth District superintendent, Louisa Defenbaugh, accompanied McClure to Leech Lake, to the village of Walker, and told a similar story of minimal accomplishment. However, she claimed, "it was not a failure altogether, as we got much needed information." Defenbaugh wanted to send "Miss Robbins" of Minnesota there, presumably as an organizer.[16]

In 1904 there were five young women in the Morton Union all of whom wore the white ribbon, the outward symbol of their commitment. They held eight public meetings that year. McClure was disappointed that this modest number was out of a total population eight hundred and complained of "the indifference or seeming indifference, of the White Ribbon sisterhood, toward the work that I have tried faithfully to do what I could, for you know how the dear Lord spoke in such loving praise of the 'widow's mite.'" She distributed a lot of literature, providing a one-year subscription to the *Young Crusader* for an Indian school reading room. McClure noted, "one Indian school uses the L.T.L. Manuals for text books in physiology, having one hundred copies in use in the school." Several school superintendents told her that intemperance was getting worse and they were very encouraging of WCTU help. "Remember there are human souls to save, and we are responsible for our brothers' souls."[17]

In 1906 McClure visited the Indian schools at White Earth and Leech Lake with Minnie Green, superintendent of Young Women's Work. They had great success with pledge signing and connected with teachers and students. McClure also visited an unnamed Indian "camp" and distributed literature there, too.[18] In 1907 she lamented that "since the United States Court has decided that the Indian is an American citizen, the saloonkeeper fearlessly deals out liquor over the bar; and also allows women and children admittance to the saloon and *sells them liquor* [emphasis in original]."[19] This was almost certainly a reference to the 1905 US Supreme Court decision *Matter of Heff* (1905), which indeed declared that Indians who accepted allotment were citizens and thus free to purchase alcohol just like whites and which would soon turn Minnesota into a site of conflict over how to legally prevent Indians from acquiring alcohol.[20] The removal of legal restrictions made McClure more anxious to reach out to tribal communities and she begged the state WCTU for workers. She personally visited Park Rapids three times, Hubbard twice, and Bemidji once. She was excited about the new leaflets that were being produced by the national organization but humbly asked to be replaced as superintendent as the work was becoming too much for her.[21]

In 1908 the office was vacant, but by 1909 Mrs. D. W. (Myra J. Calhoun) Longfellow had taken over and got to work. She had the temperance pledge and one of McClure's leaflets translated into Chippewa.[22] In 1910 Longfellow proclaimed the benefits of a new policy, implemented by special agent William Johnson concerning alcohol. Johnson had begun using treaties between the United States and the Indian tribes, which often contained language prohibiting alcohol from Indian reservations in perpetuity. The treaties did not mention nullifying these restrictions if the land was sold or otherwise alienated by the Indians. Following this line of legal logic, local unions urged local governments to shut down saloons that sat on land previously held by tribes under the treaties. Longfellow explained:

> One union from district no. 5 (Pipestone) reports some work done. "One saloon closed." This is in answer to a new question on our report blank, viz: Have the Indians near your union been benefitted by the enforcement of the treaty law? We have all been encouraged to note the good work done this last year by the bringing to light and enforcement of the original treaty with Minnesota Indians, which prohibited the sale of liquor within certain limits of their reservations. Let us rejoice in this good work done, and hope that very soon our own people may share also in this protection.[23]

From 1911 through the department's demise in 1919 there was little statewide outreach to specific communities. However, in 1916, the state central committee contacted commissioner of Indian Affairs Cato Sells, "commending [the OIA] for their work in closing the saloons under the provision of the treaty with the Indians and the hope that its scope will be extended."[24] Like many states and the national itself, the WCTU appeared to have moved beyond organizing in Native American communities and was focusing on larger-scale federal policies that might have an impact at the local level. Leading up to that moment, however, the WCTU's outreach could be less legalistic and policy-oriented and could be fun as well as culturally relevant.

Medals, Ribbons, Banners, and Fairs

The material culture of WCTU work was powerful. Native American participants in the WCTU made banners and gave them as gifts to other WCTU unions and displayed them in parades and other events. Organizers employed an array of visual and tactile materials during their recruitment efforts. Workers tweaked traditional (or more recently traditional) celebrations and added a temperance spin—even when some of those locations were the site of drinking binges and debauchery. In 1912 the commissioner of Indian Affairs,

Robert G. Valentine, reported on his efforts to stop drinking and gambling: "By the gradual modification of Indian dances and fiestas, and leavening of them with agricultural fairs, I feel that a step has been made in the right direction, which will result in much benefit to the Indians."[25] Valentine's technique fits into what Clyde Ellis describes in his study on the Southern Plains pow-wows. "From the beginning the Indian agricultural fairs featured traditional tribal entertainment, including dog and horse racing, gambling, and, of course, dancing. Envisioning the fairs as venues for promoting the agricultural and industrial programs that lay at the heart of assimilation policy makers hoped to attract Indians to a combination of educational programs and wholesome entertainment."[26]

The WCTU made similar efforts to create "wholesome" social events. Some of these came with national organizers into the complicated world of the Dakota territories. North and South Dakota shared a long border, with two reservations lying in both—Lake Traverse and Standing Rock. Although there was much commonality between North and South Dakota, their state organizations were quite different. While North Dakota had lots of activity, South Dakota had a harder time getting going, and it took a national organizer to get that done. Between South Dakota statehood in 1889 and 1910 there was little Indian work; the WCTU in general had trouble holding conventions there, and these tended to be in the far eastern portion of the state, where the white population was located, quite distant from Native American communities. In 1911 there was some inkling of Indian work. The Twelfth District Timber Lake Union, on the border between the Cheyenne River and Standing Rock Reservations, reported, "there are many Indians near by whom we hope to reach. Pray for us."[27] Between 1911 and 1915, conventions were held only sporadically.

In 1915 the WCTU in North Dakota reached out to Standing Rock and other reservations with a variety of material strategies that seemed to foster interest. The North Dakota *White Ribbon Bulletin* published a piece, "An Indian W.C.T.U. Convention." Around 1915 the Reverend F. L. Watkins organized a WCTU at Standing Rock and invited national workers to assist him. It is unclear how a male, non-member of the WCTU could officially organize a union within the by-laws of the organization, but perhaps there was a dispensation when it came to Indian work on the Plains. Lillie B. Bowers used a set of "stereopticon pictures" to educate viewers about the effects of alcohol. Watkins indicated that an Indian representative had asked him to get Bowers "to attend their joint Enforcement League and W.C.T.U. Convention to be held at Cannon

Ball July 1,2,3." According to Bowers, "They wrote, 'We are so happy that you will come and give us your pictures show.'" Bowers described a very large event, two miles outside of Cannon Ball, where two hundred tents (probably teepees) were set up outside of a "hall" where the convention was to take place. It was a rich and colorful scene:

> Some were decorated with paintings of animals, racing horses, etc. Some were beautifully decorated with beads, porcupine quills and little bells that would jingle every time the wind blew. Everybody was there, men, women, children, ponies, and dogs. For five days and nights I lived with the Indians, ate their food, attended their feasts and observed their ways of work along temperance and religious lines. I was indeed surprised to find the Indians, only 35 or 40 years advanced from savagery, carrying on a temperance convention according to parliamentary rules. Both old and young, men and women, seemed equally interested. From 75 to 200 seriously attended to the business of the convention at every session beginning Friday evening and continuing through all of Saturday and Sunday.[28]

Bowers listed the officers, presumably of the Enforcement League, since these were all men—unless this was a bizarre WCTU indeed. "Mr. Tomahawk is the president. He is a fine-looking man and much interested in the work." Others listed were Mr. Bear, Mr. Flyingearth, and many others. She had an interpreter, Mr. Ignecious [sic] Ironrude. "He is well educated and I felt that my lectures and all that I said were being fully understood through his fine ability to interpret and when necessary translate reading from the slides." Despite the gains, Bowers was upset at the Indians' use of tobacco: "A large proportion of the Indians, including women and girls, smoke cigarettes, even the christens [sic] and temperance workers." She even complained that in the midst of an anti-alcohol and anti-tobacco stereopticon lecture, many in her audience were smoking. Despite these transgressions, they were overall well disposed to her message and "three communities agreed to take up the L.T.L. work. Mr. Tomahawk urged them to do so." Shifting gears, she noted, "Sunday the Catholics, Congregationalists and Episcopalians held a church service together, the Congregational minister preaching the sermon. Rev. Arthur Tibbets is a full Indian Congregational minister doing good work all through that part of the reservation." A telling observation was that "the women had told me they wanted a meeting alone, so I asked the women to remain a little after the men were gone.

In a minute the men were gone. I asked if they wished to ask questions about the work. They said they would like to have me suggest" a topic. She apparently provided the women with guidance in conducting their union.[29]

There was another feast with meat and Indian bread. A chief's wife was preaching, probably in Lakota since the writer did not understand the content of her message. She noted that there were already plans for the next temperance festival the following year at Shields, North Dakota, on Standing Rock Reservation. She continued, speaking directly to the white readers: "You will be helped; you will help them. And may we all pray and work that civilization of the Indians may not mean the taking up of the white man's sins, but a real pure uplift to all the Indian tribes, and that they may become a real vital help toward the [C]hristianization of the world. . . . The next day, July 5, they celebrated." There was dancing, with the men and women separated. She closed, suggesting that, at white dances, the dancers were not so well behaved.[30]

The WCTU used the goodwill it garnered through participation in fairs and other events to encourage Indians to help pursue equal suffrage and national prohibition. Describing the situation in South Dakota, Lora La Mance posited that there were four major "troubles" in South Dakota's reform campaign. Number three on the list was that "South Dakota has the Indian. Between 20,000 and 30,000 Indians live in the state. Some of them, like the Santees, are quite civilized. They dress in white man's garb, go to church and send their children to school. Most of the Indians have been given allotments of land." There was still a fear from their 1890 suffrage setback and from politicians manipulating Indians to get votes. "Politics are beyond an Indian's ken," she flatly declared. Despite her prejudices, La Mance realized that a major campaign, using the Indian fairs and the attractive material culture, could win Indian men to their side.[31]

The preparations for the upcoming Fort Yates Indian fair indicate how the event fitted into the plan to encourage support from Native American men for suffrage and national prohibition: "It is planned to send a special representative of the W.C.T.U. to main Indian fairs. Here the W.C.T.U. representative will come face to face with 4,000 or 5,000 Indians. She will hold conferences with Indian agents, boss farmers and missionaries and map out a campaign adapted to attract and hold our Indian citizens. Indian medal contests will be held, a W.C.T.U. exhibit given, temperance stereropticon slides used, speeches made and cartoons, buttons and badges given out galore. A badge is dear to an Indian's heart. The brighter, bigger and showier it is the better he likes it." La

Mance intimated that there was potential for connecting with other states to create a network of missionary–Native American supporters throughout the Midwest. She noted there was to be a "mission camp meeting at Cannonball, North Dakota where fifty-six Presbyterians and Congregational missionaries to the Indians in Montana, Nebraska and North and South Dakota will be in attendance, together with 4,000 of their Christian converts, the very Indians in these campaign states." She continued, "Elizabeth Preston Anderson, National W.C.T.U. recording secretary and president of the North Dakota W.C.T.U. has already been invited to go to Cannonball and help plan campaign work among Indians. It is hoped she will also attend the Indian fair at Ft. Yates." There were many upcoming fairs on reservations, including Pine Ridge, Cheyenne River, and Rosebud. Spencer had provided the medals, but there was a need for "thousands of small suffrage badges for the Indian women, thousands of suffrage buttons for the men." La Mance closed by appealing for funding, which could be sent to state treasurer Mrs. L. E. Safford, of Milbank.[32]

Lillie B. Bowers planned to attend an Indian missionary meeting as a WCTU representative from September 6–10, 1916, and another Indian fair at Fort Yates on September 21–23, 1916. "This will be an opportunity to speak for prohibition and equal suffrage to thousands of Indians who will vote on these important issues in November."[33] It ended up being a banner year for Indian work, largely conducted by La Mance. The national organization took notice. In September 1916, the board noted, "The Government holds a series of five fairs at different points on the reservation for the benefit of the Indians, and Mrs. La Mance is engaged in this work of visitation at this time[;] she is presenting on the subject of prohibition and suffrage."[34] There had been substantial legwork done in preparation for this work in terms of fund-raising and procuring supplies. David C. Cook, presumably the prominent Sunday school material publisher, "donated 5,000 prohibition buttons for the Indians. Badges were also donated. . . . Mrs. Pease of Syracuse, N.Y. donated 12,500 post cards. Through the efforts of Mrs. La Mance, the sum of $312 was also obtained for the work among Indians." In her quantitative summary of her five months' work in South Dakota from June 1 to November 1, 1916, La Mance indicated that she had traveled 3,000 miles to get there and another 5,613 miles within the state. She had organized seventeen unions and one LTL, had given sixty-four school addresses and conducted twenty-one dedicated "Indian talks and 12 conferences with Indians," had attended three fairs and raised $353.11 "for Indians" and an additional $206.25 for the Indian cause.[35]

La Mance's work was inspiring to the attendees at the WCTU convention. Ruby Jackson, the recording secretary from Ipswich, South Dakota, in the Eighth District, equidistant from Standing Rock/Cheyenne River and Lake Traverse Reservations, delivered a report on La Mance's efforts "among the Indians. We all felt much encouraged with the report and felt that Mrs. La Mance had made a great deal of sentiment for our amendments, which would crystalize into votes by Nov. 7."[36] Clearly La Mance was able to inculcate the union with a more pragmatic and inclusive view of Native Americans— instead of the Indians receiving vile statements from disenfranchised women. La Mance was able to get more South Dakota women to see the value in recruiting Native American men as allies who could vote in the dual suffrage and prohibition fight.

Ruby Jackson's printed report described the tireless work of La Mance and the impressive spectacles of the Indian fairs themselves. Jackson began by emphasizing La Mance's impact on men, noting that she had been "called 'a queen among women' by some men who heard her." At the time of the report La Mance was at the Rosebud Fair, "where she gives the lecture 'John Barleycorn' with pictures. Mr. Pinkerton of Mission shows the pictures while Mrs. La Mance talks." There were about five thousand attendees at the Fort Yates fair on the Standing Rock Reservation, but Jackson estimated that two-thirds of the Native Americans were from South Dakota, which makes sense, since most of the reservation lies within the boundaries of South Dakota. At the Standing Rock and Cheyenne Reservation fairs, the WCTU hired "two good men" to do some outreach and organizing and WCTU members were working with the superintendent at Lower Brule Reservation but had made little contact with Santee Reservation. The male workers submitted reports, which the WCTU printed in the annual report. It is unclear why the WCTU women relied so heavily on men for outreach at these fairs, but they were effective surrogates. The men were further supported by the Clarence True Wilson Methodist Temperance Society, which sent along an array of temperance literature.[37]

The Fort Yates report described the material culture of the WCTU spectacle at the fair. the Reverend E. B. Tre Fethren of Ipswich, South Dakota, did the "W.C.T.U. publicity work." He brought a thirteen-foot banner, accompanied by the artwork of an Indian artist named Jos. W. Taylor of Poplar, Montana, on the Fort Peck Indian Reservation. Taylor, who may have accompanied him to the event, painted scenes that illustrated the effects of "liquor, tobacco, and vice" on the community. Whether these were for sale or for display only is not indicated in the sources. Many Indian visitors to the hall were impressed by the pictures, and Tre Fethren distributed many picture postcards and "'South Dakota Dry 1916' buttons, badges, posters, and leaflets." Amid a spectacle of "races, bronco-busting, and tumbling," Tre Fethren spoke through an interpreter, pressing for Indian volunteers to take up temperance work and start LTLs. He gave away what was left of his buttons and other materials and "urged the voters to be sure to vote for a dry South Dakota on November 7. There were over 300 members of the Standing Rock Temperance League. It seems probable that the Indians will roll up a larger proportion of dry votes on November 7 than will the whites."[38]

The WCTU sent Rev. Godfrey Matthews to the Cheyenne [River] Agency Fair and he offered a thorough and lively report. After a harrowing train ride from Mobridge to LaPlant, Matthews boarded a Ford limousine bound for the agency where the fair was to be held. He rode alongside Indians on horseback taking in the sights of "the curling Missouri. . . . In yonder bend lies the Agency with its fine farm buildings, its schools, the hospital and dormitories for the school children and the many pleasant homes of the Federal officials. Over the whole scene is the amber glory of a Western sunset whose colors no artist can ever truly catch. Into this scene the Indian fits by nature and we who are born in the 'civilized' places are out of keeping. He, the Indian is the lord of this scene by right." Matthews set up a space in the exhibit hall with his WCTU materials. He described a shockingly strong demand for the WCTU ribbons, so much so that he had to manage their distribution:

> Ribbons there were but few and Indians there were very many and all the Indians would wear a ribbon, and some of them would have worn them all, so it was for the Paleface to say that he who would wear a Red Ribbon must introduce twenty other Indians to me and let me stick a button on him: and he who would wear a Purple Ribbon must introduce ten others and he who would wear a Green should introduce five. So the bloodless warfare started and the ribbons were all disposed of in an incredibly short space of time, and after their disposal I found myself no longer a center of interest.[39]

He gathered up more political buttons and went out to the fairgrounds and roused up a discussion about the problems with whiskey and tried to convince the audience of the importance of the November 7 election. He indicated that the young people were literate and were excited to get their hands on the temperance literature. They were of great use since "they helped with a few words in the native tongue so that the older people might understand what it was that we were about." He got rid of all his materials in about three hours. For the rest of the day and the early part of the next, "we spent all our time in talking to responsible Indians, Federal Police Officers, Government officials, and Christian Indians, and found to our glad surprise that although the Indian voters on the Cheyenne are not a great number, only 50, they would all vote in favor of the Prohibition amendment, that the teaching of temperance lessons in the Federal schools is disposing the mind of the Indian in the right way, that the government is tireless in ridding the reservation of the nefarious whites who think that profit made by selling fire water to the Indian is a just profit." As he closed, he borrowed some of the Indians' own rhetorical devices of tying physical warfare to the battle against drink: "May He who has in him the blood of ancient warriors learn to fight the holy warfare and hand in hand with his brother, the white, help us to make the whole United States dry of the liquor, and clean of all unrighteousness."[40]

After the fair season La Mance summarized her experiences, writing admiringly of Indian regalia at the fairs. She stood agape at the artistry of the men and women and guiltily admitted to trying to buy a beaded tobacco pouch. The irony of a temperance worker procuring a tobacco pouch was not lost on her, and she assured the reader it was for its sheer beauty that she was interested. In another example, she explained, "here would be a small boy, his trousers so stiff with beads he had to stand up because he could not sit down in the gorgeous things. . . . Three or four months his mother worked steadily on that vest and the cuffs that go with it. The snow-white buckskin is porcupine quill worked in with US flags, stars, and roses, in colors so vivid that a rainbow looks like a faded rag. A peacock would hide his head from shame if he were to behold one of these magnificent small boy vests." Her description contrasts with the usual WCTU authors' bragging about Native American women wearing the white ribbon or other WCTU paraphernalia. Instead, La Mance described the dress she witnessed as assertions of Indigenous craftsmanship, though adorned with some syncretic elements like the American flag. All of this cultural persistence did not diminish the apparent enthusiasm for the temperance message expressed by some of the attendees, and La Mance was pleased with the spark that had occurred on several communities during her visit, including Standing Rock, Eagle Butte, Greenwood, Crow Creek, Pine Ridge, and Lower Brule Reservations. "Never did a state campaign at fairs as has South Dakota this fall." She counted nine fairs where Indians had been "largely or almost wholly in attendance," and these have "been a great influence. It has particularly helped us reach the Indians who have a vote."[41] For her, the Native Americans of the Dakotas were much needed voters in the fights for suffrage and prohibition, regardless of their state of assimilation. Indeed, there was much that was admirable in their traditions.

Music was an essential part of any local temperance work, inside and outside of the schools and inside and outside of Indian work. With the Methodist roots of the organization and that denomination's strong tradition of hymnology, it is no surprise that hymns were commonplace. The WCTU's use of bands came out of both the martial aspects of the early LTL and the need to attract attention in late nineteenth- and early twentieth-century America. In a long description of a trip to California, the *Union Signal*'s editor-in-chief wrote glowingly of Rancho Chico and of Bidwell's generosity and musicality. "One of her latest gifts to them was a set of instruments for their 'brass band,' and Miss Gordon and I can testify that they make good music, for we had a serenade on the evening the day we arrived." At the Sunday church service, Maggie Lafonso sang for the delegation.[42] Maggie's brother, Elmer Lafonso, honored Spencer's Indian department at the national convention. The minutes described Lafonso as "an educated Indian from Bidwell Ranch, Chico, California, who had favored the audience with very choice vocal music."[43] Another commentator tied the musical activities of the Native Americans at Chico to temperance, explaining, "the Indian band was a feature of public celebrations in Chico, particularly of temperance celebrations."[44]

In Oregon, music and other arts were part of both regular and special events in Indian work. On October 7, 1915, the state WCTU voted to reestablish the Department of Work Among Indians, with Esther A. F. May of Pendleton as superintendent.[45] On March 6, 1916, the recording secretary noted that May was "getting all information she can about the methods of work among the Indians, finds the schools are teaching the [bad?] effect of alcohol and will do all she can to press the work."[46] At the October convention in Pendleton that year, the minute-taker noted that "A feature of the evening was the singing by a quartette composed of Rev. William Wheeler, Allan Patawa, and William Barndhardt—all Indians and Rev. J. M. Cornelison Missionary to Umatilla Indians. This was much enjoyed by the delegates. Another pleasant surprise was the presentation of a beautiful Indian robe to our president Mrs. Kemp, by the Umatilla County W.C.T.U." In the Work Among Indians report, May indicated that "Indians are interested in and demand up to date things, their interested [*sic*] demonstrated by the Umatilla Indians who sang and talked for us during the convention."[47] The songs, the handmade gifts for visiting guests and temperance dignitaries, all indicate a great deal of planning prior to the meetings and festivities on the part of Native American temperance participants. They did not just show up to meetings because it was expected of them. Weeks of practicing their instruments and learning new songs, sewing robes and banners, painting of temperance-related scenes—everywhere from Puget Sound to the Northern Plains to New York State—indicate a commitment to temperance that was far from perfunctory.

Land, Legislation, and Dry Campaigns

Spencer commented that many Native American temperance supporters saw citizenship, legal protection, and private land ownership and the resultant taxation as all being bound together. In a 1910 Northern California report, Spencer began by lamenting the failure of local unions to share much of their activity. However, some women on reservations had been active in law enforcement activities. "Several [unions] have taken active part in the prosecuting of men for selling liquor to Indians. There is better observance of the law after a few men are sent to State's Prison for violating it." Spencer's activities included spreading literature and going to local unions' events, missionary meetings, schools, clubs, and churches. She went to "the Piutes of Inyon [*sic*] County" over the summer, who, she explained, "have never lived in reservations and are more self-reliant." She noted that they lived in a climate conducive to not needing substantial housing. "Many own lands. I found 43 Indian names in the delinquent tax list, but was assured that all would pay up as soon as informed of the delinquency." Her observation indicates that she had examined the county property tax lists. She went further, claiming that they "love to pay taxes, as they fancy they are more surely entitled to legal protection." They soon acted upon that citizenship. "A few Indians in Plumas County cast their first vote for a dry county. In Mendocino County, twenty-six Indians are pledged to vote dry when the saloon question comes to vote."[48]

Christianity, citizenship, economic progress, and education were tightly related in California. In 1912 Spencer shared her recent experiences in Northern California, where she traveled with Frederick G. Collett and Beryl Bishop Collett, both Congregational ministers and the NCIA heads of missionary activity. They had started a year and a half earlier living with the tribe at "Cachil Dehe," or Colusa Rancheria. It was a weeklong trip through three counties to

Rancho Chico. The Colletts then "visited the towns and villages along the Sacramento River, taking with them a quartet of Indian singers, and held special
Thanksgiving services. Three of these, when children, had been refused admittance to the district schools of the county because they were Indians, but their
father moved to a place where they were allowed to go to school and they are
now an object lesson in Indian progress." A fourth, a man from Rancho Chico,
trained at the Ohio State Normal Training School and shared his "rich baritone
voice" with his audience.[49] In a later state annual report, Spencer explained that
she had spoken there, the residents were very receptive, and she admired "how
lustily they joined in the battle cry, 'California's going dry' and how those men
are studying hard to be able to read and understand the constitution in order to
help make it dry."[50]

In Arizona in 1909, Spencer shared how white WCTU laborers were brought
to bear on legislative issues and social activism. In discussing events at Yuma,
now Fort Yuma Quechan Tribe, she covered the reservation and their history
with the Supreme Court's affirmation of their ownership over their land, but
she decried the recent congressional act, which provided only "entirely inade-
quate" five-acre allotments to individuals. She implored the IRA and the NIA
(they dropped the "Women" from the title in 1901) and other "friends of the
race" in the WCTU to petition the Secretary of the Interior Richard Ballinger to
make allotments of at least ten acres, since smaller ones would not be productive in the arid Southwest.[51] WCTU support for larger allotments indicates that
they were not seeking complete disenfranchisement of Indians of their land but
were trying to fulfill the goal of having them be secure, landed citizens—albeit
as private rather than communal landholders. The WCTU officials were not
naïve, however. They knew that without financial security the Native American
landowners were imperiled by access to alcohol, and swindlers would take their
land away from them.

The WCTU supported further protections of those tribes as they theoreti-
cally entered full equality. Margaret Dye Ellis provided a legislative report, indicating that "important temperance legislation was also secured for the new
states, Arizona and New Mexico, viz.; 'That without the consent of the United
States and the people of the state, the sale, barter, or giving of intoxicating liquors
to Indians, and the introduction of liquors into the Indian country are forever
prohibited.' This provision also embraces all land that may hereafter be allotted,
sold, or reserved for a period of twenty-five years—which means that 25,000
square miles of territory have been placed under Federal prohibition for a

period of twenty-five years."[52] Particular restrictions against alcohol distribution to Indians were welcome but insufficient.

According to WCTU observers, the prohibition law in Arizona had a very positive effect on Indian people throughout the state and at the Fort Yuma Indian School, across the river in California. A major difficulty in enforcement of prohibition laws on Indian reservations was a result of limited understanding of how smuggling worked and how permeable the boundary around Indian country really was. There was a strong feeling that expansion of laws might be the answer. Walter G. West, agent to the Southern Utes in Colorado, was having a hard time stopping the bootlegging on the reservation perpetrated by Mexicans. The *Union Signal* article speculated that statewide prohibition would help the Utes.[53] A year later, the paper printed a story about the Colorado Indians' new mobility throughout the state—owing, in part, to the new statewide prohibition laws. The author indicated that such activity "was discouraged when Colorado was wet," because Indians who traveled off the reservation to Denver to testify in federal liquor cases would get served alcohol in bars and end up in legal trouble themselves. With statewide prohibition, there was less possibility of that happening. The same thing was true of the Indians in Minnesota, where the tribes benefited from statewide prohibition. "Some of them are starting bank accounts." The anonymous author suggested that even anti-prohibition papers had to concede that some good came of the move.[54]

There were unanticipated perils of citizenship when it came to alcohol, however. In 1904 Oregon WCTU member Lucia H. Faxon Additon shared the observations of "Mrs. Rev. J. A. Speer, superintendent of Indian work at Warm Springs reservation," in which Speer indicated that an Umatilla man wrote a friend at Warm Springs asking that his citizenship be taken away, "so that their people could not get whisky just like white men."[55] Withdrawal of citizenship as a goal never took hold within WCTU leadership and was probably only a rhetorical device even among the Indians purportedly saying it, in order to emphasize the vulnerability that citizenship brought. Instead of launching a widespread campaign to rescind citizenship, white and Native American WCTU workers sought to mobilize Indian citizens to vote dry. According to the Oregon president, Jennie Murray Kemp, "the Tutilla Temperance Society of the Umatillas was active in the 1914 Oregon Dry Campaign and not one vote was cast against prohibition by these people."[56] Regarding a recent referendum, the Oregon recording secretary Madge J. Mears claimed that "out of 60 voting on the prohibition question, only one voted wet."[57]

In Idaho the WCTU sought Native American support in the dry campaign, but without a lot of sympathy for other elements of Native American political life. In 1910 the Southern Idaho WCTU had established a Work Among Indians department, led by Eva West of Blackfoot, about fifteen miles from the center of the Fort Hall Reservation of the Shoshone and Bannock tribes. Over the course of her career as state superintendent, she grew in her understanding of the predicament of Indians, the complicated nature of their citizenship status, and difficulties of liquor law enforcement. In 1911 she submitted her first report, though it lacked the refined writing style of many other WCTU officers. In it she fastidiously followed the questionnaire Spencer distributed to all superintendents. West listed the tribes in her jurisdiction, including the Shoshoni, Lemhi, and Bannock. This listing excluded those in the separate Northern Idaho WCTU jurisdiction, where the Kootenai, Nez Perce, and Coeur d'Alene Reservations lay. But it also excluded the Duck Valley Reservation at the far southwest of the state, on the Nevada border, home to the Shoshone Paiutes. According to West, none of the tribes "own land, pay taxes, or vote." They were in the midst of the allotment process, and the "title still remains in the government." She noted the poor housing on the reservations, which contained few frame houses. There had also been a tuberculosis epidemic that kept one-third of the children out of school. She claimed that most Native Americans in her district were church attendees. Unfortunately, liquor was easily obtained, and she claimed to have reached out to school officials about LTLs and the establishment of medal contests. In terms of religion, she noted both Christian and "heathen" services on the reservation. She attempted to visit the school at Ross Fork but was not able to do so for unspecified reasons. "I haven't been able to find any of the W.C.T.U. with Indian superintendent [sic]. We devoted one day in our W.C.T.U. studying the Indians. . . . We have the Indians here and find it hard to do anything with them." She revealed a certain level of ignorance of the WCTU's Indian work overall and even of the tribes themselves. In this sense, West was not a natural candidate to do the work in the way that Spencer, Bidwell, Lydia Pierce, and others were.[58]

In 1912 West submitted a spare, staccato report about the state of Indian affairs touching on the allotment process, their nontaxpayer status, and the religious denominations active in the communities. The Presbyterian mission was at Fort Hall; Episcopalians held "chapel service every day and preaching on Sundays." The alcohol law was enforced but sometimes circumvented. "I have suggested the Loyal Temperance Legion whenever feasible. It is hard to get the Indians to sign the pledge as they seem to be afraid of losing their land and homes." This was a telling fear, hinting that there was resistance to the WCTU because of prior land losses during treaties, unethical lease deals, and other written agreements with whites.[59] In 1913 there was no report. However, the brief report submitted in 1914 showed a bit more knowledge of the state. The Nez Perce were reoriented to the Southern Idaho WCTU, and West explained that the Nez Perce was "the only tribe that vote."[60] In one of the last reports of Indian work from Idaho, West commented that about twenty-six hundred Indians lived in Idaho: "many live in tents, but some aspire to better conditions and have autos and telephones. About 100 can vote. There are missions among them, but little has been done the last two years along special temperance lines."[61] Indian temperance took a step forward, however, with changes in the general temperance law in Idaho.

When statewide prohibition went into effect in Idaho in 1916, the *Union Signal* shared the positive effects of statewide prohibition in Indian country that had been reported by agency farmer Charles West (unrelated to Eva, it seems). Working on the Coeur d'Alene Reservation, he was interviewed by the Spokane, Washington, *Spokesman Review*. Since January 1, when prohibition went into effect in Idaho, there were almost no Indians jailed. He was able to get agricultural clubs and organizations going. M. D. Colgrove, the Indian agent, organized a fair association and made a "deal" with the village of Plummer to provide a fairground.[62] In other words, the prohibition age was looking auspicious for economic development in Indian country in Idaho.

Enforcement

Attempts to enforce anti-alcohol laws on reservations led, for some defendants, to nail-biting journeys through the federal court system. WCTU officers discussed decisions as they were handed down. One consequential case was *George Dick v. United States*, decided by the US Supreme Court on February 24, 1908. The case originated when Dick, an Umatilla from Washington State sold whiskey to a Nez Perce in Idaho who had accepted allotment and was thus a citizen. Dick was convicted; a federal court overturned the conviction; the case then landed in the Supreme Court where they upheld his original conviction based on the 1893 treaty with the Nez Perce, which stipulated that alcohol would be prohibited from lands held by the Nez Perce at the time of the treaty, even after the lands were allotted or sold to whites. The Dick decision stated:

> But this case does not depend upon the construction of the federal liquor statute, considered alone. That statute must be interpreted in connection with the agreement of 1893 between the United States and the Nez Perce Indians. By that agreement, as we have seen, the United States stipulated that the lands ceded by the Nez Perce Indians, and those retained as well as those allotted to the Indians (which embraced all the lands in the original reservation) should be subject, for the limited period of twenty-five years, to all federal laws prohibiting the introduction of intoxicants into the Indian country.[63]

The ruling opened a whole set of possibilities for stopping sales in any region where an Indian treaty had some kind of alcohol restrictions, even if the title to the land was no longer held in common by the tribe.

State and national WCTU workers followed the events closely. In the 1908 Idaho state presidential address, A. A. Garlock commented on the 1893 treaty with the Nez Perce and the Supreme Court decision to enforce it as "one of the greatest victories for the temperance forces." Garlock walked her audience through the facts of the case and the decision: George Dick, "a half-breed belonging to Umatilla, Oregon, was arrested for bringing liquor onto the Nez Perce Reservation." He was indicted and convicted in 1905 and given a sentence of one and a half years from Idaho federal court. His attorney appealed, and Dick was ordered to be released by the US Circuit Court of Appeals, arguing "Federal authority over the reservation ceased when the lands were opened for settlement." In the period between the release and the reassertion of conviction, "the county commissioners began issuing licenses for the Nez Perce reservation, and about thirty saloons had gone there and established places of business with costly and permanent fixtures. Upon the decision of the highest court they were obliged to close up and move on."[64]

Spencer used this victory of the decision to point out the trouble in other western states and territories where loopholes, ambiguities, or proximity to white towns invited scofflaws to operate. She implored members, along with the Friends of the Indian, to participate in letter-writing campaigns to the Committee on Indian Affairs to recommend passing HR 17426, introduced by Michigan congressman Edward L. Hamilton, which would amend the current law, outlaw the introduction of alcohol "under any pretext whatever into the Indian country, or in or upon any reservation," and make it so "anyone selling liquor within twenty-five miles of such a reservation shall be punished by fine and imprisonment." The law was supported by Ex-Governor L. C. Hughes of Arizona in the same article.[65] In 1909 the WCTU reported that the Nez Perce, empowered by the *Dick* decision, were spurring the government to tighten restrictions. "One thousand Nez Perce Indians in the panhandle of Idaho will join the prohibition forces in the fight against the rum shops in Nez Perce County when the campaign is started to make the district part of the arid zone. The Nez Perce treaty contains a clause for absolute prohibition inserted by the United States government at the urgent request of the chieftains, who declared that they would not otherwise ratify the compact, as they had watched the effect of rum on their people."[66]

One of the more creative enforcement efforts in 1905 was from Susie McKellop, superintendent of petition and legislation in Indian Territory. McKellop's department did not do much legislative work, focusing instead on distributing petitions that would keep Indian Territory dry rather than lobbying for specific laws. For assistance, McKellop and the territorial president went to the Anti–Horse Thief Association (AHTA) for help with petition distribution. The AHTA was a vigilante organization that became popular after the Civil War. Their law and order ethos and knowledge of criminal enterprises made them useful allies in the prohibition fight and separate statehood. She explained, "[I] had printed 900 petitions, of these I sent 600 to A.H.T.A. sub-orders and the rest to unions and ministers." Nine out of ten petitions came back from AHTA, but only a few from most of the unions. She "secured pretty good results from among the Colored people of the Creek Nation, a good number of fine petitions being filled. All of these I sent to Mrs. Margaret Dye Ellis at Washington."[67] Considering the AHTA's skill set, one wonders whether the Indian Territory WCTU employed the AHTA vigilante services in intimidating or ferreting out bootleggers in addition to using them for petition distribution and signature collection.

Although some Native American and white women had been able to turn festivals and fairs into temperance-oriented events, at many of them the drinking continued. In 1908 at the Pima Agency "intemperance" came in the form of excessive drinking of tiswin, a traditional corn or saguaro-based fermented beverage. Observers noted that there was only one habitually drunken Indian near the agency, but there was a great deal of festival-related binge drinking, which was accompanied by violence and other crime. One of the most aggressive WCTU members was also a federal Indian agent in Southern California, Clara True. She was superintendent at the Potrero Indian School and was charged with supervising several Mission Indian reservations throughout Southern California. At Palm Springs Reservation, "an organized attempt was made to introduce and sell liquor during the fiesta, as had been done in previous years; but with great energy and courage Miss True, assisted by Special Agent R. S. Connell, who was in the neighborhood at the time, thwarted the attempt by gamblers and 'boot-leggers' to violate the law. This was not brought about without a violent struggle, during which one of the boot-leggers was seriously wounded."[68]

True was brave, tough, and creative, and the WCTU made the most of her story. In 1909 the *Union Signal* ran a feature about her, comparing her legendary success with the poor results of her predecessor, who only got one arrest and that was of a Chinese immigrant who could not vote and thus had no political sway. True had achieved nearly a dozen arrests in the past year and did so by engaging women as undercover agents at fiestas to come up with evidence so she could make arrests. Spencer recounted the harrowing tales of True being shot at, witnessing many other shootings, and stepping in to stop alcohol-fueled violence on the five reservations under her supervision. The story emphasized not only her hardiness but also her condescending view of Native Americans. The story quoted True as saying, "Indians are like children . . . I manage the Indians by kindness and persuasion, and I carry a revolver as common sense dictates."[69] She was not the only temperance worker who engaged in undercover operations. In January 1915 Spencer commented on events at Cachil DeHe, where the federal government "tardily gave a parcel of land, enough to build homes for the band" and where the Colletts established a school. Whiskey crept into the community, and the Colletts got creative with their investigation. The missionaries, financed by WCTU money, transported an Indian from another reservation to go undercover and acquire evidence against the whiskey traders, leading to the arrest of ten men who were then tried in federal court. According to Spencer, the Colusas thanked the Colletts for their work.[70]

In order to prevent some of the feared perils of Indian citizenship and independence and to improve her own abilities to enforce the law, Clara True sought the support of WCTU matriarch Annie Bidwell. On March 5, 1913, True wrote to Bidwell on New Mexico WCTU letterhead after moving from California to Espanola, New Mexico. The two had been at Mount Hermon together, and now True was asking for her support in pursuing a higher appointed position in the

Indian Office. She explained that Pueblo citizenship was a major upcoming challenge in New Mexico because of an imminent Supreme Court decision. She warned Bidwell: "The franchise will be a reason for activity among those who are base enough to wish to corrupt the Indian vote. We sincerely wish to do all we can to keep the Pueblos from being debauched and as we shall most likely vote on state prohibition in 1914, it is vital that we try to take care of the Indian vote and use it for the defense of the Indians against their worst enemy." True expounded on her credentials. She spoke Spanish. She employed Indians on her family's ranches and had "organized some temperance work among some of the tribes. I had the sta[t]e convention of the W.C.T.U. come to one of my Indian villages last August. I sent six delegates from one of the villages to the previous state convention in Las Vegas, and one of my Indian communities has a day at the state Chautauqua next August. You will see that I have not been idle all this time I have been out of department work." She explained, "financially, I can ill afford to go back to Indian work." She now had responsibilities for her mother's care and that of the New Mexico ranches. In closing, she asked Bidwell to support her appointment as assistant commissioner of Indian affairs. True noted that Secretary of the Interior Franklin Lane was "a California man" so Bidwell might have some influence with him. Bidwell honored True's request with a handwritten letter to Lane.[71] Unfortunately for True, she never received the position and stayed in New Mexico managing the ranches.[72]

The WCTU tried other means of influencing the Indian Office. In November 1912 the *White Ribbon Ensign* criticized embattled Commissioner of Indian Affairs Robert G. Valentine, who would soon resign his post. Valentine had been in trouble since early 1912 when he issued a controversial mandate that "religious garb" not be worn in Indian schools. Reports swirled that he had resigned as early as July1912, but he later attacked the reports and remained in his position for a few more months. In September of that year it was discovered that he personally brought alcohol into Oklahoma Indian communities, and Congress and the Department of Justice were going to investigate and probably charge him. The accusations came via an anonymous tip to the congressional committee months earlier. Fortunately for Valentine, the charges were eventually dropped but not until his actual resignation that same month.[73]

Wherever possible the WCTU supported agents who would vigorously enforce prohibition laws and castigated those who did not. In November 1912 one state paper's headline read "Reservations Dry" referring to the acting commissioner of Indian Affairs' policy that reservations be "kept absolutely 'dry'"—making it a violation for Indian Office employees to bring even personal stashes of alcohol with them. The story referred to the "Late" commissioner Valentine who had actually taken a drink with "agency employees."[74] Cato Sells, appointed in May 1913 by President Wilson, required his personnel to take an abstinence pledge and engaged in other efforts to keep his agency dry, to the applause of the *Union Signal*.[75] In 1915 Spencer delighted in Commissioner Sells's new mandate for six thousand federal employees to pledge "total abstinence." Sells even had a temperance pledge composed for Indians, which his employees were to distribute: "The following pledge is ordered to be presented for signature and explained to all Indians, including school children: 'I hereby promise that I will not use intoxicating liquors as a beverage, and that I will do everything that I can to protect my people from this great evil.' Systematic plans are made for a certified record of all signatures, with a report six months later fully showing the results of the work, as to how many keep the pledge, how many fail, and the consequences following in each individual case. Would not that be as good for whites?"[76] For all of their commendable efforts, none of these commissioners or their agents was as effective—or as celebrated by the WCTU—as special agent William Johnson.

William "Pussyfoot" Johnson

As Johnson became known for vigorous enforcement of federal laws, the WCTU began treating him like a temperance celebrity—and for good reason. Johnson's boss, the commissioner of Indian Affairs, bragged about his arrests, confiscations, and brash methods. Cases against him ended up in the US Supreme Court and helped shape federal Indian law in years to come. His work had a secondary effect of advertising the continuing validity of Indian treaties at a time when many whites were trying to discount them. In August 1906 Johnson was appointed one of several special officers to Indian country. This hiring spree was funded by recent federal laws that earmarked money to investigate and punish anyone violating laws against the distribution of liquor to Indians. He was initially appointed to Indian Territory, and he quickly observed a slew of problems: the backlog of federal court cases dealing with alcohol violations, the complicity of railroad companies in an illegal whiskey trade, and the sale of full-strength beer labeled as low-alcohol beer. He was armed with expanded powers from the newest Indian Appropriations Act, which increased the authority of Indian agents to seize materials used in smuggling alcohol onto Indian reservations. He then used the authority to auction anything employed in smuggling, including horses, wagons, harnesses, and saddles. In 1907 he made 491 arrests in the whiskey trade—a conservative estimate according to the commissioner—and then went after gamblers, closing down 49 gambling houses and securing 52 convictions of gamblers and 7 arrests for murderers connected to these vice activities. In retaliation, smugglers and liquor purveyors put a bounty of three thousand dollars on his head. The bounty was not just criminal bluster; the work was truly dangerous. That year two of his men and a "posseman" were killed, along with ten bootleggers.[77] Even if the WCTU did not put Johnson in the field themselves, they ran a public relations campaign supporting his vigorous methods, and they broadcast the court victories associated with his aggressive work.

Johnson was operating in a briar patch of legal uncertainties, all stemming from the question of how federal laws against distributing alcohol to Indians applied to those Native American individuals who had accepted allotments. Apart from the *Dick* case, a few other legal precedents were established by the courts during this time. Preceding the *Dick* decision in 1908 was the *Matter of Heff* (1905), which declared unconstitutional an 1897 federal law stating that federal liquor restrictions against Indians applied to allotted Indians, amending the 1887 Dawes Allotment Act that made Indian allottees citizens, thus not subject to protective federal laws.[78] Declaring the law unconstitutional—and thus void—meant that allotted Indians were subject to the laws of the state, not the federal government in the matter of criminal liquor laws. This opened up liquor sales in regions with large numbers of Indian allottees, to the chagrin of the WCTU.

This was not the end of the issue, however. Not only was the unfolding *Dick* case going to give force to preexisting treaties that excluded alcohol even after allotments, in 1906 the Burke Act promised a solution to the *Heff* exclusion of Indians who received allotments from federal alcohol laws. The Burke Act or "Forced Fee Patenting Act" declared that individuals were subject to assessment by the secretary of the interior to be "competent and capable" before being granted "fee simple patents" along with the accompanying citizenship and liberation from federal alcohol laws. This extended the period of time until federal alcohol restrictions no longer applied to an individual allottee.[79] What all of this meant is that, during the decade between 1897 and 1908, there was an ever evolving and contested patchwork of laws and jurisdictions regarding the selling of alcohol to Indians, whose citizenship statuses varied markedly. Since Johnson's first appointment was Indian Territory, which had territorial prohibition, the illegality of most forms of alcohol there was largely undisputed. His methods, however, were far more controversial.

In February 1907 the *Union Signal* ran a front-page feature story on Johnson under the headline "The Beer Period Is Over." The story recounted the details of the circumvention of the law and Johnson's investigative methods beginning in September 1906. The piece explained how smugglers acquired low-alcohol licenses and then illegally dispensed full-strength beer and whiskey. It then explained how Johnson consulted with Professor George L. Holter, a chemist at Oklahoma Mechanical and Engineering College, and Professor Lewis, a bacteriologist, to determine the alcohol content of samples he acquired. He worked with railroad companies to tighten enforcement of restrictions on shipping alcohol-related materials through Indian Territory. He smashed beer bottles at Ardmore and arrested a postmaster for bootlegging (after being unsuccessfully sued by the same man for destroying his shipment of cider). The article claimed that the thirty Indian policemen were aided by his aggressiveness, whereas previously they could not do much to stop the trade. In the coming months the *Union Signal* updated readers with similarly glowing reviews accompanied by exciting stories.[80]

On July 1, 1908, the Interior Department transferred Johnson to Utah, where he would be in charge of investigations on all Indian reservations in the country. The *Union Signal* detailed Johnson's arrests in Idaho, noting that they were on the "old Nez Perce reservation," suggesting that he was consciously using the *Dick* decision to focus and justify his arrests.[81] The WCTU gave the strongest endorsement it could of Johnson's activities, and in 1909 at their annual meeting, they officially recommended cooperation with Johnson in his "effort to enforce laws" against alcohol sales to Indians. Johnson very clearly realized that the *Dick* decision, which gave binding authority to the treaties that banned alcohol in territories once held by Indians, offered a powerful strategy. Treaties could be used as a way of creating prohibition territory without any legislative action at all.[82]

Historian Sabine Meyer's work on prohibition in Minnesota only minimally recognizes Johnson's role in developing this strategy there, where he applied preexisting treaties with anti-alcohol provisions in various Chippewa/ Ojibwe and Dakota treaties. Referring to the strategy of using treaty provisions to seek prohibition in those regions Meyer suggests, "it was not clear who had initiated this government investigation, but it ignited a fierce battle in Minnesota and Washington, D.C. between 1909 and 1915, fought by the state's Prohibition Party, the ASL, the lawyers and the breweries and distilleries, the special agents of the Indian bureau, Congress, Presidents William Howard Taft and Woodrow Wilson, and the courts." The credit or blame has to fall to Johnson, however. In its own publication, the ASL explained, "as a result of the operation of Chief Special Officer Johnson, of the Federal Indian Affairs Department, two entire 'dry' counties have been added to the no-license territory of Minnesota during 1909."[83]

A *Union Signal* article explained how that government investigation got its start. In 1914 Eva Emerson Wold discussed the role of Native American treaties in the prohibition fight. Wold suggested that a Minnesota prohibitionist pointed out the treaties to Johnson in 1909. Wold further explained the recent Supreme Court decision, *Johnson v. Gearlds*, which concluded that an 1855 treaty was "still operative and that the sale of liquor within a large territory of 'ceded' Indian land in northern Minnesota can be stopped by the government. This covers an area of 16,000 square miles where two hundred saloons are operating. Over one-fifth of the state is made dry by this ruling." There were many other treaties that, if also operable, would lead to prohibition throughout the state, including urban areas. The state's "liquor organ, *Both Sides*," suggested the liquor industry would seek congressional action to abrogate the treaties.[84]

In 1911 Colorado WCTU president Adrianna Hungerford delivered an address that celebrated Johnson's five years of Indian work and lamented his recent removal from his post: "He has been the most fearless and successful law-enforcement official in this country, but the political ring resented his aggressive efforts and Mr. Johnson has been compelled to resign." A temporary court injunction against the closings would further delay the saloon-killing enterprise, but this would soon be lifted.[85] His removal did not erase the effects of his career as a special agent. In 1916 the *Union Signal* commented on progress in the largely Ojibwe town of Bemidji, Minnesota, where, after a year of enforced prohibition because of the Supreme Court's ruling, twenty-four saloons closed. There was a large increase in bank deposits, and all but two saloon buildings were occupied by new businesses.[86] There was great optimism, and the paper even suggested that an 1854 treaty with Michigan and Wisconsin Indians held promise for making those states dry, too.[87] The general trend of expanding "white" regions of the country continued through national Prohibition. Pussyfoot was vindicated, as were the members of the WCTU—if only temporarily, through 1933.

The overall thrust of the WCTU agenda was the inclusion of Native American women and men into sobriety, citizenship, and the political process. They worked with each other to create cultures of temperance in Native American communities via methods ranging from pledge signing, to music, to material culture. They became partners in legislative and law enforcement battles. These multipronged approaches were powerful, to be sure, but as the WCTU recognized in its overall efforts, children and education were the most important place to begin.

Chapter 6

Temperance in Indian Schools

The WCTU inserted itself into Native American day and boarding schools in both the curricular and the extracurricular realms. Owing in part to their lobbying for federal and state legislation, members often succeeded in getting scientific temperance instruction lessons and textbooks into the classrooms. In addition, the WCTU's signature Loyal Temperance Legions and Young People's Branches joined with like-minded "general improvement societies" and literary clubs at the schools to form an important and overlooked aspect of the Indian school experience. Shortly after taking over the position as superintendent of the Department of Work Among Indians, Spencer addressed the *Union Signal's* readers. She counted 253 Indian schools throughout the country and affirmed that the general patterns, challenges, and needs were similar to those in California Indian schools. As a rule, teachers were amenable to WCTU input and other assistance from reformers. They were happy to incorporate STI ideas, and they used LTL manuals and other literature if they were provided with them.[1] Although WCTU activity in the schools began before her tenure and could occur independently from the national office, Spencer amplified these efforts to make sure all Native American children were exposed to WCTU teachings about alcohol and ideas about Native American progress.

The WCTU started with the young captive audiences to promote various activities, but there was genuine support among the children in the fight against alcohol abuse. Children felt this suffering directly, often having had challenging experiences in their homes where alcohol abuse was present. While there was a clear sentiment among the boarding school promoters to "Kill the Indian and Save the Man," there was more to the WCTU's impact than that. At first blush, the genuine pride in the successes of leaders—ministers, teachers, professionals, successful farmers, and industrious laborers—were simply the signs of the death of their "Indianness." Temperance clubs in schools promoted

Christianity by including hymns, Christian-themed poems, religious speeches, and prayers in their activities, much as mainstream LTLs did. However, there was a heavy dose of "survivance" below the surface of the Native American children's participation in the clubs—and in their continued support for those clubs as they grew older. In Gerald Vizenor's creative formulation, "the nature of survivance is unmistakable in native stories, natural reason, remembrance, traditions, and customs and is clearly observable in narrative resistance and personal attributes, such as the native humanistic tease, vital irony, spirit, cast of mind, and moral courage. The character of survivance creates a sense of native presence over absence, nihility, and victimry."[2] While Native American students, professionals, and officeholders wore—often quite literally—the trappings of Euro-American civilization, those involved with temperance were also rejecting the most detrimental parts of the colonial enterprise: alcohol abuse, "debauchery," and succumbing to white trickery, all of which led to the loss of property, loss of self-esteem, and other indicators of social, cultural, and political decline. In this sense, they were able to move beyond physical or cultural "extinction" and offer a voice in their futures if they remained sober. Although Vizenor has been mostly concerned with Native American storytelling and other types of narratives, within even the sterile accounts of WCTU reports and articles one can perceive that "sense of native presence over absence, nihility, and victimry."[3]

More than many other reform organizations at the time the WCTU articulated the specific problems with the public schools' treatment of Native Americans. Often, the schools simply denied admission to children from local tribes. The national Department of Work Among Indians distributed their "blanks" or surveys to their state superintendents and asked about discrimination and access to public schools. From these, we learn why the WCTU thought it necessary to maintain a system of missionary, state, and federal schools. The Work Among Indians department became an explainer to the WCTU readership about the predicament of Indians' lack of access to public schools. Yet, they only scratched the surface of the generational trauma, abuse, and even deaths of students that occurred within the walls of the Indian schools, especially the boarding schools.

The WCTU reached out to Indian schools and attempted to affect law, policy, and curriculum. The children's and young adults' activities included meetings, prayers, secular songs and hymns, pledge signing, and recitations. The WCTU used the LTL medal contests, academic rituals and traditions such as valedictory addresses, student newspapers and yearbooks, scholastic speeches, to prepare future leaders. From this perspective, it can be seen that this was not "Education for Extinction," as in David Wallace Adams's formulation, but was, from the WCTU's perspective, education for survival as US citizens, which inevitably included some loss in tribal identity.[4] Yet, in the appreciation for tribal traditions seen in some speeches, the call for more day schools instead of off reservation boarding schools, the pressure to include Native Americans in mainstream public schools, and the occasional critiques of existing boarding schools, the WCTU anticipated the Indian New Deal proposals under John Collier and other later critics of turn-of-the-century Indian policy who called for an end to the boarding schools and who ushered in the push for self-determination.

The idea of starting with Native American children in a religious or cultural conversion campaign was nothing new, but it was particularly powerful for the WCTU's Indian work. The boarding school experiment itself—beginning with colonial era schools, and reaching its apogee in Richard Henry Pratt's Carlisle Indian Industrial School in Pennsylvania—was based on the idea of assimilating Indian individuals by extracting them from their Indian surroundings as youngsters when they were malleable and their English language acquisition abilities were sharpest. In order to shape the way these schools administered to the youth, the WCTU started at the top of the Indian Office hierarchy.

As with alcohol laws in Indian country, the federal government had jurisdiction over education policy within federally administered boarding schools and contract schools (those run by missionary groups who contracted with the federal government and received funding from Washington). The government did not have the same level of oversight when it came to tribally run schools, state public schools, or denominationally run schools. Generally, the Indian Office supported STI laws and policies. Since at least 1881 the WCTU had been trying to get scientific temperance taught in all Indian boarding schools under the jurisdiction of the federal government. They had even formed a committee to meet with Hiram Price, commissioner of Indian affairs, to convince him to make it part of the curriculum in all public schools in Indian Territory. Price responded very favorably and wrote a letter back to the committee indicating that "the suggestion meets my hearty approval, and books of that character will be included in the supplies for Indian schools to be purchased next Spring."[5] This was not an empty promise. Price ordered that a copy of the federal STI law, with key excerpts, be sent to all agents and superintendents of schools, and they were directed to comply. He made sure that STI textbooks were supplied, too.[6] From that point on, state and national WCTU leaders in Indian work made special efforts to ensure such literature was available at Indian schools.

In the summer of 1881 the corresponding secretary Caroline B. Buell from New York wrote to several federal officials with Indian education responsibilities; she included "Temperance Textbooks" and a request to incorporate them into the Indian schools. She received letters in return from D. B. Dyer, Indian agent at the Quapaw Agency, and Helen W. Ludlow, writing on behalf of General Samuel Chapman Armstrong from the Hampton Normal and Agricultural Institute in Virginia. Dyer promised to read the books and to "try to introduce them into our schools." He promised, "it is of vast importance that the work should be understood, and pushed here among the Indians, who never had an enemy equal to 'Alcohol.' I am safe in saying that it has cost them more trouble, and brought them nearer to starvation and ruin than any other one thing." Ludlow noted that she was a temporary surrogate for Armstrong, but she provided insights into temperance work at Hampton. "We have a Temperance society in the school every year, and employ an intelligent colored man, who has considerable education in the North, to do special work in the school and the neighborhood holding meetings, etc. We are to have next year a resident lady physician from the Philadelphia Medical College—Miss Waldron, who has charge of the New Haven training school for nurses. She will teach physiology and hygiene, and this special branch of such instruction would naturally come under her direction."[7]

The temperance movement received support from Captain Pratt himself. In 1885 Carlisle had a temperance society with over one hundred members. Pratt reported to the OIA that they had adopted the WCTU-approved *Alcohol and Hygiene* as a textbook. He expected the curriculum and the teachers to "embrac[e] nearly all that element which carries weight on account of intelligence or moral force. The instruction and example of the teachers are supplemented by the use of temperance papers and leaflets."[8] Teacher training dovetailed with partnerships with other organizations, too. The Haskell Indian School student newspaper, the *Indian Leader*, reported that at the "Middle-West Series of Institutes for Indian Service Teachers," Mr. Larson delivered a talk on alcohol, its effects, and temperance pledges, and temperance societies, giving an early plug for participation in groups such as the WCTU.[9]

State workers tried to ensure that WCTU members and school administrators were aware of legal responsibilities regarding STI. In 1905 in Michigan, in the annual presidential address, Anna S. Benjamin noted that the recent federal legislation required STI to be taught in schools under federal jurisdiction, including Indian schools.[10] In 1910 the New York Work Among Indians superintendent, Marian G. Peckham reported that Lydia Pierce "has lately visited all the government schools for the Indians in the interest of Scientific Temperance Instruction and then wrote to the authorities requesting the use of the Gulick textbooks in the schools as more modern and up to date." She also had "urgently requested the state commissioners of Indian schools in New York to use their authority in enforcing the Scientific Temperance Instruction law."[11] The apex of STI, the Frances Gulick Jewett volumes were lauded as the best student volumes about alcohol and were based on the latest physiological information.[12] In California, where many schools were not under federal jurisdiction, Governor Hiram W. Johnson wrote to the white ribboners in 1915, rejoicing with them that the state had passed an STI "measure . . . as determined by science" that added to an existing state law.[13] Such efforts, along with the politicians' and appointees' communications with WCTU officials, reveal the temperance workers' impact and the respect they enjoyed among the government officeholders.

The passage of laws and support from state officials and federal administrators did not eliminate the concerns of the WCTU leaders. During visits to Indian schools they made informal inspections to ensure compliance. Around the same time as Spencer's overview of Indian schools, the editor in chief of the *Union Signal*, Lillian M. Stevens, described the Phoenix Indian School in Arizona. According to her report of the journey through the Southwest with Anna Gordon, they visited the "United States Indian Industrial Training School," which, she noted had seven hundred pupils, putting it in the top ten in terms of size in the country of such Indian schools. She observed Helen S. Goodman, superintendent Charles W. Goodman's wife, and her sister Shannon "and nearly all of the fourteen teachers, wearing the white ribbon. We were gratified to learn that the law and the gospel of temperance instruction is observed in the school."[14] A similar report came from a visit to Riverside, California, where five miles outside the city sat the Sherman Indian School. Stevens noted, "we were pleased to find the teachers in full sympathy with the W.C.T.U., and as we went into the fifth grade classroom the teacher said she had just given a lesson in physiology on the effect of alcohol, and the pupils were eager to learn all about it."[15] Though it would have been difficult for Stevens to gauge the genuineness of their eagerness, we may surmise that the reception of the lesson was at least somewhat positive. This happy sentiment could be misleading, however. WCTU officers learned from Flora Harvey, principal of the Phoenix Indian School that the children had conducted a successful medal contest in a city church, meaning their organizational and oratorical skills were strong. Despite their development, WCTU observers suggested that they longed for traditional practices and the observers detected a hint of sadness in the students: "The Indian pupils seemed happy at their work and in the school room, but somehow I imagined that the rug-weaving suited their fancy better than the pillow-case making."[16]

Although the federal officials in the Indian office and the founders of the boarding schools generally had the same assimilative ends as the WCTU, the members of the Department of Work Among Indians, preferred—or came to prefer—inclusion of Indian children into the public schools. From the WCTU leaders' perspective, the boarding schools were a necessary evil and not the ideal method for bringing children into mainstream society. The Work Among Indians department acted as both lobbyist to government officials and explainer about schools to the WCTU readership, who would, in turn, do the work on the ground. Through these activities we see the concerns felt by white progressives about Native Americans' access to the education system. In 1904 Annie Bidwell wrote a letter to Senator George C. Perkins in support of a bill submitted by the NCIA, auxiliary of the WNIA. Bidwell, the western vice president of the WNIA, explained that the California tribes' lack of reservation land and absence of wardship status meant that they were denied all access to schools, except in rare cases of benevolent landowners. In the nearby public schools there was a great deal of prejudice. For instance, when the Colusa attempted to go to public school, the local whites immediately stopped attending. Bidwell herself had to teach at a makeshift day school at Rancho Chico. She assured readers that when some Indians went to Chico State Normal School and other public schools, in contrast to some stereotypes of the chaotic Indian behavior, the students performed extremely well. Bidwell even suggested that the Mechoopda's family values might have benefited the students within the classroom environment, stating, "filial obedience is implicitly demanded by the Indians which is the foundation of their deportment in school."[17]

In 1905, after taking her position as superintendent, Spencer explained why Indian children should be placed in public schools. "Many of these children could and should be placed in the public schools, and might be so placed without detriment to the white children. This is often done in the west, but race prejudice excludes them from many district schools where they are enumerated in the school census, and the white children have the benefit of the Indians' share of school funds." She expressed optimism about the future, however. "These suggestions are offered in the hope that somewhere these outcast people may be made to feel that they are included in the human interests of life, their self-respect raised, and their better nature reached." Distance and isolation posed another challenge to reaching children, and she explained why the small local schools were the best place to reach children with the temperance message. "It is easier to approach the Indians in schools than those outside. In all the western states there are scattered very small bands of Indians, too small to justify a government school, and these present a special object of missionary interest, and are the worst neglected of all peoples. Nobody knows or cares how they live."[18] Over the next few years, the WCTU could claim some partial victories. In 1912 Spencer celebrated that the "reports from all the states indicate that the Indians are benefitting by the efforts being made for their improvement. They live in better houses and are slowly taking on the civilization of their white neighbors. Indian children in some communities are being allowed to attend the regular public schools. The government Indian schools, however, are being built up, and scientific temperance instruction is now a requirement in all of them. Many of the Indian children are being sent away from home to school."[19]

In 1913, in the pages of the Northern California *White Ribbon Ensign*, Spencer forcefully articulated her position on getting more Indian children into the public schools. "Court decisions have declared that the Indian is a man, with the same rights, under the law, as a white man. One of these, is the education of children. The Federal schools are insufficient and it is not the policy of the government to increase their number, but the government is ready to share with the state the expense of schools for Indians." She provided instructions on how local districts should pursue funding and then declared, "the Indian problem must be solved by the state and the county, by means of schools." There were barriers, however, as she explained that fifteen hundred Indian kids out of thirty-eight hundred school-age children in California were excluded from public schools because of "race prejudice." To improve this condition, she advised WCTU members to take a cue from the Colusa county school, where seventeen Native American children attended. "At Colusa Rev. F. G. Collett did this; himself, Mrs. Collett and Thomas Odock, Captain of the band of Indians living there being the 'Trustees of the District.'" She also expressed great promise in working with the Indian Board of Cooperation, which had just elected "Prof.

Kroeber of the University of California" as president, and he has the "special object of establishing public schools for Indian children." Edward Hyatt, state superintendent of instruction, was also a member of the board and would be helpful in this regard, too.[20]

In 1916 Spencer also offered practical advice by reprinting an "official statement" from Hyatt. In very pragmatic terms, he addressed the "trustees and superintendents" of public schools and reminded them that "it is possible to get a considerable addition to the funds of rural schools by taking in the Indian children when it is possible to do so. When the number and names of the Indian children who are likely to attend are known, the trustees should make a contract with the Indian Bureau, at Washington, D.C. Write to the Hon. Cato Sells, commissioner of Indian Affairs, asking for blanks and instructions." He provided detailed directions and then a warning: "Sometimes a district is so prejudiced against Indians that it is not possible to make any harmonious arrangement. Usually, however, a handful of timid Indian children is of no possible detriment to a school. They are always obedient and tractable, and do the best they can." And then, he offered a powerful reminder, "The Indian has been here longer than we have and he must live with us always. It is our duty to give him a chance to learn how to do that living. We can give him a chance better in the public school than anywhere else. That is our great melting pot. In the case of the Indian, we get extra cash for the melting." Spencer followed Hyatt's reprinted words with her own, urging WCTU members to pursue additional educational funding as a way to begin to crack white prejudice.[21]

Despite their hope to reach every school in Indian country, the WCTU made their greatest impact in the boarding schools. The outreach launched by WCTU education advocates had racist overtones, but their views were certainly more benevolent than those who complained about retired warriors voting. Organizational efforts among children often brought out the better angels of the progressives' ambivalent nature. When the 1890 woman's suffrage campaign failed in South Dakota and the WCTU members took out their frustrations in print on the Native Americans who had acquired suffrage, there were nonetheless countervailing energies expended toward Native American children. In 1900 Emma L. Swartz compiled a history of the Dakota WCTU, which included some deeper insights into the WCTU members' thinking. "In May, 1894, a most excellent convention was held in Milbank," located near the Lake Traverse Reservation. "One of the most pleasant features of this convention was a gold medal contest. An Indian girl, Miss Emma Vanderheyden, was presented with the medal." There was some joy in this girl's success amid the overall animosity toward Native Americans in the Dakotas that was openly expressed at that time. While it is difficult to trace the future life of the young girl, an Emma E. Vanderheyden is listed as a laundress in 1903 for the Winnebago School in Nebraska, operated by the OIA, and she had been there since at least 1901.[22] Aside from the isolated examples of Native American children participating in WCTU activities that delighted WCTU leaders otherwise uninvolved in Indian Work, we must examine the more systematic efforts to spread temperance messages to the Indian schools.

Unlike the cases in the major off-reservation schools like Carlisle, Hampton, and Haskell where administrators were already tied into temperance and reform circles, how did these condescendingly sympathetic WCTU women seek to win over smaller, more remote schools' administrators, teachers, and children? The executive committee of the Colorado WCTU established a state department of Work Among Indians in 1903, led by Floretta Shields of Cortez, Colorado, adjacent to the Ute Mountain Reservation.[23] In 1905, though no longer superintendent, Shields wrote the annual report, highlighting the three Indian schools in the state: Fort Lewis, Ignacio on the Southern Ute Reservation, and Grand Junction.

In line with the national directives, Shields "subscribed for the *Union Signal* and *Crusader Monthly* for each of them." She received replies from the superintendent at Fort Lewis who wrote, "'I have enjoyed reading the *Signal*; it is used in the school room.' 'We get some helpful things out of the *Crusader Monthly*.'" In the winter 1904–1905, the secretary of the Young People's Branch (YPB), Rose A. Davidson, visited Fort Lewis and Ignacio. "At the former place she showed stereopticon views of 'Ten Nights in a Bar Room,' and as she told the story it was interpreted to the audience." *Ten Nights in a Bar Room*, a popular play and eventually a film, was a common entertainment in temperance circles as it depicted a series of violent alcohol-fueled incidents where innocent people are injured or killed. The story was intended to scare any inebriates into taking and keeping the abstinence pledge. Shields continued, "many of the parents were present as it was during the holiday season." At Ignacio, Davidson had given "a miscellaneous program; One number was 'Uncle Sam,' prepared by Mrs. Mary J. Hunt in the interest of the S.T.I. The Indian children represented the different countries and sang patriotic songs. The teachers were persuaded to take up L.T.L. work. One of them reported in July that 'some sixty children take part in the L.T.L. but none are yet pledged.'"[24]

The stereopticon show was a big hit, not just with the children at Ignacio, but with the "Old Indians [who] came from several miles around to see the pictures of 'Ten Nights in a Bar Room,' but the story had to be interpreted for them as they speak very little English." Indian parents were there for the holidays from their reservation, "one hundred and fifty miles away to spend Christmas week with their children in the school." They walked there over a period of days and weeks. At Fort Lewis they ate with their children and slept in the "old guard house." She continued, "these old Indians combine in their dress the savage and civilized styles. The women wear bright colored calicos and the men dress something as white men do except the coat, and both sexes wrap themselves in blankets or shawls and wear a good supply of beads and trinkets. This tribe, so famous for the production of Navajo blankets, is more gentle and docile than the Utes who make up the Ignacio school." Davidson commented on the universality of humanity, in what she likely thought were generous terms: "As I sat in the midst of their Christmas celebration, crowded on one side by an Indian mother with her papoose and on the other by a half-breed Indian teacher, as clean and intelligent and refined as a white lady, and watched the children enjoying their toys and candy, I realized anew that God has made of one blood all races."[25]

A few months later, Davidson produced another report on her work with Shields, who was living on the Southern Ute Reservation, about a full day's journey to Cortez. We get a glimpse of the lengths Shields went to in order to accommodate the Southern Utes. "She has a large room built on her house especially for the Indians. Here the days [sic] school, Sunday School, and sewing classes meet. Some married men come here to learn to read and write."[26] The following year the LTL superintendent Hattie M. Doughty reported that the Ignacio Indian School legion had seventy members and had submitted their three dollars in dues. Superintendent of Work Among Indians A. J. Martindale claimed, "The children old enough all go to government school. Some white people favor the education and some oppose it," suggesting some of the same prejudices against Indians in the schools. Although no information was forthcoming from Fort Lewis, Martindale noted that at the Grand Junction school a "temperance lesson is taught once a month." Martindale was there and "a great many pledge signers were secured." There was a major problem, however, with the proximity to the whites' town. "The boys go to town whenever they want to and the shoemaker employed there gets drunk almost every Saturday. I do not think the superintendent makes any attempt to prosecute the saloonkeepers."[27] The latter statement contrasts with the reports by others regarding other regions in Colorado at this time.

In 1907 Colorado's superintendent of Work Among Indians had been replaced by Augusta J. Whitney of Palisade, about ten miles east of the Teller Institute in Grand Junction.[28] In November 1907 Whitney commented on the Methodist Episcopal pastor Rev. J. Q. Vermillion's speech about temperance, calling to "the church people to vote for a dry town." According to Whitney, she and many in the congregation thought this was a great idea since a ring of dry territory around schools and reservations would be helpful in keeping the reservation population and especially students away from liquor. If a day's walk could not procure alcohol, then they might simply abandon the quest. There was further advice to unions near reservations and schools—namely, to "visit them and, if possible, organize a temperance society among them; they enjoy belonging to something of the kind and want to wear a badge proclaiming them members." She lamented that the federal government was shifting from boarding to day schools in the next two to three years, making the temperance lessons even more urgent because they could bring the temperance lessons home for the rest of their people.[29]

By 1910 E. W. A. Fiske of Grand Junction was Work Among Indians superintendent and reported that there were only 360 Indians on reservations and 210 in government schools. The Utes and Apaches "own their own land, some of which is tillable, some is not because of the lack of water." There were 71 students at Ignacio, a nongovernment school apparently, and 210 at Teller in Grand Junction. She claimed that "there is no prejudice and the Indian children receive the same attention in the schools as white children." They went to Sunday school and had the same STI books in public and government schools. In contrast to the prior report, "the Indians can not get liquor easily and when they do, prosecutions are made and the law is enforced."[30] Fiske covered the coming transfer of the Teller Institute's property to the state of Colorado, but there was some question about what was to happen to the children if it closed. She noted that the final deal would likely be that the state provide some type of schools for the Indians. "Superintendent Burton of Teller Institute very kindly consented to allow our W.C.T.U. to conduct an L.T.L. class of pupils. The boys and girls very eagerly accepted the literature I gave them. I shall be very glad to supply missionary societies with the excellent literature sent out by the National Superintendent of Indian Work."[31] The Indian school closed in 1911, and the commentary on the Colorado Indian communities faded away too.[32]

The pattern of distributing literature, creating special programming with WCTU organizers, lobbying teachers, and organizing LTLs was followed all over the country. In 1910 Mary Fowler submitted a thorough Indian Work report that emphasized activity in the schools. "I have sent a personal letter to each of the teachers in the Indian schools of the state, urging them to introduce the S.T.I. work in their schools; and have also sent them the manuals and other literature. I have sent a roll of blanks to every county president." She heard back from Will H. Stanley, "superintendent of many villages," who assured her that temperance instruction was in all of the schools. Sherman Institute, Martinez, Coahuilla, and Soboba, Fowler's "own village," all reported temperance instruction in the classrooms. She delighted in the "prompt replies from the teachers of Indians in regard to temperance among them."[33]

In 1912 Rhena E. G. Mosher, national YPB secretary, worked at the Wahpeton Indian School, near the Sisseton Reservation, during a three-week session in North Dakota. The students there were from all over North Dakota. She "reorganized the Y.P.B. with 46 members," which suggests that Wahpeton had already had one that may have dissolved. At the school, "a government official was so impressed by Miss Mosher's address, that he promised to arrange for a special temperance day in all Indian schools, the W.C.T.U. [was asked] to provide the program." She had already established a YPB at Jamestown College and conducted a "reorganization of the Antler Y.P.B." and gave nineteen addresses overall. "Miss Nelie [sic] Osmun was employed at last convention to do Indian work. She began by visiting Turtle Mountain reservation, where she discussed Scientific Temperance Instruction with the teachers. She organized local unions at Fessenden and Deering, and re-organized at Drake. . . . Later in the year she visited Ft. Berthold and Bismarck Indian Schools making addresses and distributing literature. We are glad that through Miss Osmun's efforts, we have been able to do something for the Indian work this year."[34]

At Fort Shaw Indian School, Montana, similar developments occurred with LTL work. Around 1904 Montana began printing its own paper, the *Montana WCTU Voice*, which gave a thorough account of events there. Anna A. Walker, the state Work Among Indians superintendent, described her visit to the school during "commencement exercises," which coincided with Memorial Day. Walker and her family received a warm reception and they listened to many of the commemorative speeches at the veterans' plot in the cemetery. The Fort Shaw band provided music, and 340 Indian boys and girls marched in orderly fashion to lay flowers on the graves of the dead. Walker offered a lengthy description of the grounds and the industrial education, and she boasted of the basketball team's talent, but she mentioned no LTL or explicit temperance work, probably because this was one of the first outreaches by the WCTU to the school. Apparently, this was the first visit for Walker, but she was planning for her future visits already.[35] Although the *Voice* indicated that the state dropped the Work Among Indians department in 1907, by 1910 the Presbyterian-run industrial school at Wolf Point, on Fort Peck Indian Reservation in Montana, had held three medal contests and paid their dues; the paper also described Fort Shaw as being active, and they still had a union there as late as 1914.[36] Thus, the LTLs seemed to outlast an official department of Work Among Indians in Montana.

One of the most remarkable LTL stories comes from Wisconsin. State departments of Work Among Indians were very active in forming LTLs and running medal contests. Some of these were at boarding schools, some at day schools, and some outside of schools were simply reservation LTLs associated with a WCTU chapter. Wisconsin's Indian LTL work occurred in the opposite way: the state LTL spearheaded the Indian work for the state. Wisconsin's WCTU was divided up into congressional districts, later into local unions, and developed a very strong state LTL. In the First Congressional District, one unnamed union had a Department of Work Among Indians in 1892. An Indian union emerged in the Fifth Congressional District consisting largely of members from the Brothertown community, whose history lent itself to Christian temperance work.[37] The Brothertown and Stockbridge Indian communities in Wisconsin were the descendants of primarily Algonquian-speaking groups that were forced to relocate from the East Coast during the Removal Era. The Brothertown, specifically, were refugees from the Mahicans, Mohegans, Pequots, Narragansetts, Montauks, and Delawares. The Stockbridge were refugees from a Massachusetts mission community. Both groups lived among the Oneidas in New York until moving to Wisconsin in the nineteenth century.[38]

By 1892 the Wisconsin LTL was a source of pride for the entire WCTU. Wisconsin members preserved an editorial by Willard in the *Union Signal* that shows this. Referring to LTLs she declared, "We cannot express the delight we feel in the progress that is being made in this direction. Wisconsin leads the van." Annie J. Bradbury, state LTL superintendent had established the state's legion a year earlier and had been energetic in her efforts. Eighty people, mostly teenagers, attended an LTL convention, along with "adult teachers" and local LTL superintendents. Bradbury was a stickler for parliamentary rules, and the event contained parliamentary drills for the up and coming leaders. Marion R. Barker, superintendent of the Brothertown LTL supervised the class of 1892, which included five Brothertown Indian graduates: Ruby LaPrairie, Vernie Scott, Carrie Amel, Jennie Amel, and Jessie Amel. They did not get to attend the graduation ceremony, unfortunately. According to the unpublished minutes of the LTL convention, "Graduates were expected from Brothertown and other places, but were unexpectedly delayed."[39]

In the annual report of that year, the corresponding secretary explained Barker's formation of the first Indian Loyal Temperance Legion in February 1892. "It is conducted by a blind lady, a member of the Stockbridge Union and a resident of Brothertown." Other descriptions were more laudatory: "The Fifth District, Woodbridge Division, had no L.T.L. at our last Convention. A brave and blind woman, with no W.C.T.U. in place to support her, organized Co. A in Brothertown last February. Several Indian children are members, and a little Indian girl is to sing at the L.T.L. Convention and some are expected to take their diploma."[40] The 1893 state LTL convention was held in Ashland, in the far north of Wisconsin, on the shores of Chequamegon Bay on Lake Superior and next to the Bad River Ojibwe Reservation. The proximity of the convention to the Ojibwe community was part of the inspiration for the LTL to expand their Indian Work beyond the Brothertown chapter and create a dedicated Department for Work Among Indians. It would not be a traditional Department of Work Among Indians, under the umbrella of Organization or Evangelistic Work, but specifically under the LTL. The organizers explained their commitment to Indian Work: "because on these shores once wandered the Indians free in their wild life, and 8000 of them still claimed Wisconsin as their home." The conference held one of their day's events on Madeline Island, "in a little Indian church." They noted "an added inspiration was given to the work by the presence of a former missionary among the Indians and a most interesting [unidentified] Chippewa Indian to whom we were introduced. They brought to us a revelation of the great need for [C]hristian work among this neglected portion of Wisconsin's children." The committee was also to "confer with the Indian Agent of Ashland." The committee was to include "Mrs. Campbell, Mrs. Barkley, Florence [Shores], John Boothby, Mrs. Topping, and Charles [D]rake." They also agreed to invite Reverend Wheeler on the "excursion to Madeline Island, and talk upon the Indian Question."[41]

Native Americans in Wisconsin in 1893 seemed to participate vigorously in the Flower Missions, a type of WCTU work where the children visited hospitals and infirmaries to bring flowers and cheer up patients. The Fifth District president, Julia M. Knowles, reported joyfully, "The Flower Mission Superintendent has brightened several sick rooms with what the Indians are pleased to call "The Smiles of the Great Spirit."[42] A spur to action came in 1894 from a report that reprinted a speech given at the Ashland LTL convention in 1893 by Jonathan Boothby of Hammond. From Boothby's paper entitled "The Indian and Firewater," the audience learned that "though the Government is doing much toward providing common school advantages for our dusky brethren, *no one* is doing anything, so far as could be ascertained, to keep intoxicating liquor from them." This was certainly an overstatement as there were federal laws prohibiting sales on reservations. Boothby's research was conducted by sending about thirty letters to various unnamed authorities. He declared longingly, "oh, if you could know what an evil liquor is in the homes of these Indians." He went on to describe "some of the depredations perpetrated by them when under the influence of liquor." Not surprising for a young man in a WCTU educational club, he advocated focusing on young people in both legislation and education: "a long step, and one that would not be so likely to slip backward, would be to take from those young people the temptations that must beset them, in some cases on the way home from school by way of the saloon, and to help them to live without tobacco. This means faithful, earnest teaching along the lines of temperance, purity and self-control; this is our own L.T.L. teaching." The LTL speech triggered action among the WCTU leadership: "From this paper we learned that very much needs to be done for the Indians of Wisconsin, and our State Society started a fund for raising money with which to be able to do something when we felt sure what it ought to be."[43]

At the fourth annual LTL convention in Racine in 1894, Barker of the Brothertown LTL gave an address about the Brothertown Indians, "played the accompaniment to 'I am the Child of a King,' which was beautifully sung by Wilde Sears, the little Indian girl from her Legion." At the same meeting, during the election of officers, Ruby La Prairie was elected vice president-at-large of the state LTL, and meeting participants then developed plans of work. They approved the committee on Indian Work, which included "Mrs. Campbell, Mrs. Shores, Mrs. Barkey, Mr. Peterson, Jennie Pugh, Mrs. Barker, Riley Chase, [and] Charles Drake." They also agreed to a declaration: "We recommend that the members of the State L.T.L. watch for and endeavor to execute the plans of work in the interests of the Indians, which will be published in *The Motor* and *The Rush-Light*."[44]

In the annual address to the fourth LTL convention the president, Robert M. Davis, commented on Indian Work and its placement in the organization's framework:

> Work in the Indian Department will necessarily be done principally through the state organization instead of through local Legions. It is a new department as yet and but little work has been done along this line, although there is hope that in the years to come much good can be accomplished. In the year just past there has been a more marked interest in the Indian's welfare and his cause is becoming the cause of the most advanced thinkers and philanthropists everywhere. The nation is beginning to see that while the Indian himself is not what he might be, yet he must be treated as a man, and only through such treatment can his condition be materially improved. Probably what is needed just now as much as anything is education and enforcement of the laws on our statute books for his protection. As the most of us are neither voters nor teachers, the most we can do is to agitate the subject thoroughly and keep it prominent in all our public meetings.[45]

Since this department was to be under the state LTL, and not the state WCTU more broadly, this may have limited its influence and longevity. This department of work was one of four under the LTL, along with the Departments of Books and Reading, Mercy, and the state LTL organ, the *Rush-Light*. By 1895 they had established a special "Indian Reading Course," run by Lillian Wilson of Delvan, Wisconsin. "To the Assistant Superintendents of Books and Reading," wrote state senior LTL superintendent Mate H. Topping, directing advice to the local unions. Among the recommendations were both of Helen Hunt Jackson's works, *Century of Dishonor* and *Ramona*, which "are good to inform us about the treatment and nature of the Indian."[46]

In 1896 no representatives were sent from Brothertown, which suggests the organization began to flag when Superintendent Barker moved out of town. Nonetheless, the group declared in their plan of work "that Indian missionary work be prosecuted." In the *Rush Light*'s report on the same conference, it was noted, "Mrs. Bradbury's wish that we should help educate one Indian girl is worthy of our attention."[47] In 1897 the presidential address noted that Wisconsin has the second largest Indian population of any state in the Union but has not done much except develop the reading course. That the reading course was intended primarily for white outreach to the Indians (rather than for Indians themselves) was evident. "The reading of the Indian course should inspire within us a greater desire for the civilization and Christianization of the Indians."[48] By 1900 Indian Work—or at least reporting on it—came to a halt.

In 1903 there was a reinvigoration of Indian Work, however, this time in Keshena on the Menominee Reservation, about seventy miles north of Brothertown. Bertha Dyer, the LTL superintendent and a teacher in the school supervised the group and the senior LTLs around the state, aiming to "furnish them manuals, leaflets, *Crusader Monthly*, and pay their state dues." Dyer also presented a paper entitled, "Work Among Wisconsin Indians," followed by discussion at the annual LTL convention that July in Darlington. A subsequent article indicates the paper was actually read by Lois Russell; apparently Dyer was not able to attend. The Keshena LTL was officially recognized by the state LTL at that convention following Dyer's speech. The report on the convention following it noted that "the department of Work among Indians being added with Miss Grace Alsop of Brooklyn, [Wisconsin] Superintendent," which suggests that the department had slipped out of existence in recent years.[49] By the 1904 convention it seems that Grace Alsop had married and was now Mrs. Grace Anderson, though Lois Russell of Racine was soon to take over superintendent duties, which she fulfilled through at least 1907. By 1909 the department seems to have withered again as it was no longer listed in the program.[50]

The classroom and school grounds were not the only locations that concerned the WCTU. Like the reservations themselves, on- and off-reservation schools were endangered by proximity to white towns. Since the legal and citizenship statuses of certain southwestern tribes were ambiguous, the legality of selling alcohol to them was, too. Border towns with loose law enforcement and looser morals were dangerous places for students. It was not just the consequences for individuals from alcohol abuse that concerned the WCTU, it was the threat for the whole "civilization" enterprise itself. A few incidents of drunken children in the local saloons might threaten the Indian reform enterprise by damaging public relations between the tribes and the white population. At one Indian Board of Commissioners meeting, Joseph J. Janney shared insights he had received from missionaries Rev. Walter C. Roe and his wife Mary W. Roe who had recently solicited funds from the Lake Mohonk Conference attendees to build a facility for the Cheyenne and Arapaho communities in Anadarko to sell their wares. Mary Roe had been hearing from Indian country about the problem of children drinking in the white towns, from the saloons in

Anadarko to the settlements outside the Riverside Indian School. Janney was confounded and exclaimed:

> When I go to Buffalo and visit the Exposition, and spend a half hour in the Indian village, and see the Indian lowered to the level of dime-museum freak, I am led to believe that the present peril to the Indian is not altogether in the ration question or the reservation question, or even in the education question, but it may be largely in the fact that he is being paraded over the country, clothed in blanket and bears' claws and paint, and exhibited for the entertainment of the idle and igno-rant; and that he is becoming increasingly the victim of the avarice of the rumseller.[51]

This fear of what was happening to Indian children in close proximity to white towns threatened the reformers' work and contributed to the WCTU's pursuit of statewide and federal prohibition. The *Union Signal* quoted a piece written by "Chief Special Officer Henry A. Larson of the United States Indian service, [that] the Southern Utes, the only Indians in Colorado, will be materially bene-fitted by state-wide prohibition," because they were deeply involved in bootleg-ging. His optimism came from what happened in Indian communities that were surrounded by dry towns and regions. Larson shared that "the superinten-dent of the Fort Yuma school, in California, which is just across the river from Yuma, Ariz., reports that the change in the Indians is nothing short of wonder-ful since Arizona's prohibition law went into effect the first of the year." Since it went into effect in 1915, the prohibition law had transformed a school whose students had previously made their way to the saloons in the border town of Yuma, Arizona.[52]

Within the confines of the schools, however, the WCTU's focus was not on pursuing new laws but on education and shaping the minds and behavior of the youth. Historians are fortunate to have some of the essays, speeches, and arti-cles produced by Native American students, undoubtedly with the help of their teachers or other adult mentors. Within these joint efforts with uneven power relations we can nonetheless see the students' views and the ideas that they were being encouraged to internalize. The children's assignments placed alcohol, temperance, Native American history and culture, and Euro-American tradi-tions into a broader narrative of progress. Even in today's comparatively demo-cratic classroom, it is difficult to discern when a student's written words reflect their own deeply held beliefs and when they are ideas that are borrowed from the instructor. Power relationships often steer students to give the teacher what they want to hear, a trend that was stronger with the students writing or speaking at an Indian boarding school. At some point, even mimicked words shape the young minds of the speakers and writers who express them. Furthermore, many of the young people whose words survive were campus leaders such as officers of the temperance society and commencement speakers. Therefore, they were not among the most rebellious sorts. Regardless of whether we can discern disingenuousness of the students' beliefs, we must recognize that the assignments below are not a representative sample of all the students' ideas. What they tell us is still valuable as they provide insights into the ideas the school staff tried to inculcate and the values that at least some students likely took away.

In September 1876 at the Tunesassa School on the Allegany Reservation, a student named William C. Hoag wrote an essay on the civilization process. He opened with the declaration that "it is very nice to be part of a temperance society, and what a pity it is for so many people to be intemperate[. S]ometimes boys and girls like to drink cider and wine and keep on drinking[. A]fter a while they want something stronger and if they do not stop they soon become drunkards then they keep on drinking and drinking till they sometimes lose their lives by it." He continued, "When men are drunk they abuse their wives and children & often drive them out of the house [&] sometimes burn the house. They often get into a fight and get hurt very badly or get killed or run over by [train] carse[.] that is the last of them and they are lost for ever the bible says no drunkard shall enter the kingdom of heaven."[53] Hoag was one of the temperance movement's success stories as he went on to become president of the Seneca Nation of Indians later in the century.[54]

It is unclear if Hoag's essay was for a class or an extracurricular project for the student temperance club. Although he refers to being a member of a temperance society, it is not clear what this actually meant. The LTL had not been created yet. The Six Nations Temperance League had been in existence since the 1830s and was probably the organization he was describing. By the 1890s a student temperance society had been formed, called the Tunesassa Temperance Workers, which produced *Temperance Echoes*, the precursor to *Tunesassa Echoes*, the handwritten club newsletter. Additional information from the student organization is scarce since a fire destroyed the main building and the records inside in 1886. By January 1891 the Temperance Workers met and Lydia, Fred, and "Baby Edward" Pierce visited the organization and seemed to do so regularly. Haudenosaunee families were quite involved at Tunesassa.

The minutes from later meetings listed the recent visitors: "Parents or relatives from this reservation who have visited pupils since school began are James and Electra Crouse, William and Clarissa Lee, Hiram and Libbie Watt, Eliza Curry, Ida Curry, Eliza Redeye, Sara Snow, Hiram Jacobs and wife, Sylvester and Malinda Crouse, Harry Pierce, Mary [last name missing], also Gibson and Eliza Pierce, and Charles and Mary Gordon of Cornplanter's [Reservation, Pennsylvania]."[55] Although it is not clear how often children went home, this regular stream of visitors seems to contrast with boarding schools across the country where parental visits were more tightly circumscribed. Historian Brenda J. Child documents the cruel policies and individual bureaucrats' decisions at most schools that kept Indian children from traveling home to visit their families.[56] At Tunesassa, however, proximity made such visits possible.

In 1891 the new superintendent of Tunesassa, James Henderson, initiated the Society for General Improvement for the students. Historian Lois Barton, who taught at the school decades later, suggested that the society was "patterned, no doubt, after the literary society he had become familiar with at boarding school." Perhaps the Temperance Workers' focus seemed too narrow to Henderson, or he thought that linking literary pursuits with other activities would bring increased participation. Whatever the reasons for altering the student club, the new organization met every other Saturday and produced the handwritten *Tunesassa Echoes* every term. They kept fairly consistent minutes, which provide insight into the children's activities and the ideas to which they were exposed.[57] The Society for General Improvement absorbed the membership of the Temperance Workers organization.[58] At the first meeting, Henderson presided and worked out some logistics with the students. They adopted a constitution, and the students developed the motto "Temperance at all times, humanity to every living creature, general elevation of morals." Officers included president, secretary, and editors of the paper, plus a standing committee to fill vacancies as needed. The president appointed an individual who was responsible for the temperance pledge and keeping track of signatories. The first officers were Jesse John, president; Lillie Jimeson, secretary; Crawford Nephew, curator. James Henderson and Theodore Gordon were listed as "Assisting Committee." Mary R. Batten and John Snyder were editors.[59]

At the next meeting the officers were shuffled around. Reflecting Quaker values of gender parity, "It was thought best that there should be some of both sexes appointed on the Assisting committee. And Mary McGirr was appointed in place of James Henderson." They read declamations, essays, and excerpts from *Tunesassa Echoes*.[60] By the June 19 meeting, Jesse John had left school and Henderson filled in as president, again. Quaker egalitarianism between ages and genders of individuals suggested that students and faculty were, on paper at least, equals. Male and female students shared power and extraordinary steps were taken to assure equal representation among the officers. The club was subject to the fluid nature of student enrollment at all Indian schools. By November 4, 1892, several people left the school; at least one went to Carlisle. By the May 6, 1893 meeting, thirty-two students were there at the start of the meeting. Notably, Felix Scott was elected president at this meeting. Eight years later, Scott's essays would be read to the Philadelphia Yearly Meeting and he would stand as commencement speaker during the formal spring exercises.

The former president of the Society for General Improvement at Tunesassa, Felix Scott composed an essay, which he probably read at a temperance meeting, entitled, "Alcohol Talk" in which he discussed the destructive impact of alcohol in anthropomorphic form. The main character bragged, "I can make a strong man stagger and throw him on the floor. . . . I can make him strike his wife, scold and handle his children roughly. I make a man bad by degrees." Shifting from the social disorder to individual degradation, the subject continued: "he loses his education and self-restraint and he is now ready to do anything or commit any crime." Quoting Proverbs 23:29, the villain of the story declared: "The Bible gives warning; who hath woe? Who hath sorrow? Who hath contentions? Who hath babbling? Who hath wounds without cause? Who hath redness of eyes? They that tarry long at the wine." He then shifted to the physiological, which reflected the state of scientific temperance instruction of the time. "I make many people believe that I make them warmer when they are cold. I do not do any such thing. I only bring the blood to the surface [of] the body which makes them feel warmer by making the heart beat faster. On the contrary the body really gets colder as the heat comes to the surface it is more easily eradiated."[61]

Alcohol was thus an impediment to social order, God's will, and good health. The internalization of the scientific temperance views aligned with the overarching assimilative mission of the Society for General Improvement. The students had a more complicated view of the role of Tunesassa and acculturation, however. In 1902 Scott, the first diploma recipient from the school, read an essay at the "closing exercises." He opened his speech, "The Outlook for the Indian," with this statement: "At the present time our people are intensely interested in the question of citizenship." He suggested multiple perspectives: "Some of us favor it, believing that we are able to place ourselves at the side of the white man; that we are as strong and are able to do everything that he does under the same conditions. We long to have the right to vote, and to take part in the destiny of the greatest nation of the world." In contrast, he offered that "some of us believe that we are not able to be placed on the same footing as the white man; that we are not educated enough to see into the facts and truths of everything . . . and that it is impossible to break off from the idea that we are free, and have been placed here independent, absolutely independent, by the Creator." While acknowledging varying opinions of self-worth, he clearly pointed to a sense of equality of abilities between whites and Native Americans and a sense of patriotic citizenship. At the same time, the phrase "independent, absolutely independent, by the Creator" suggests distinctiveness of American Indians. Remarkably, the young man's speech synthesized the three competing forces at work in the minds of so many Native American leaders at the time: resisting prejudice, seeking full political equality in the nation, and yet still maintaining self-determination and sovereignty alongside that equality. He closed with the mantra of acculturation: "The only thing left for us to do that we may live happily in the years to come, is to prepare ourselves so that we can live as the white people, and adopt as our motto, 'we must educate, we must educate, or we must perish.'"[62]

The substance of the speech was similar to those at other schools. David Wallace Adams has said of commencement exercises:

> Such carefully orchestrated ceremonies were designed to strengthen support for Indian education among white citizenry. But there was also a more profound purpose to commencement rituals: it was their last opportunity to impress upon graduates the deep meaning of their school experience. Two themes permeated commencement rhetoric: Indians had arrived in a state of savagism but now returned thoroughly civilized. . . . Second, commencement offered a ceremonially sanctified opportunity for passing on philosophical truisms and heartfelt advice . . . the travails ahead would be numerous. Only moral courage, stiff backbones, and right attitudes could carry the day.[63]

In Scott's speech we see those two themes strongly presented. How much the children's writings were entirely the result of indoctrination and how much their own willing acceptance of the education they received is difficult to discern. Views like Felix Scott's met the approval well enough to be included in the public addresses by students to others, but it is likely that after a decade at Tunesassa the words reflected the student's own beliefs, too.

Such assignments and activities were present all across the nation's schools. In April 1891 the *Southern California White Ribbon* shared a letter from Julian Lugo, an Indian boy from Soboba, to "Mr. alcohol" in what was likely an assignment based on the educational technique of "personification." In this assignment, students were to cast alcohol as a character and orient their feelings, thoughts, and emotions toward the inanimate object.

AN INDIAN BOY'S LETTER

Soboba February 13, 1891

Mr. alcohol,

I am going to write you a short letter[.] I am going to say something[.] You may all the time be alive and never die you have no body[,] no eyes[,] and you can't talk. You look like water but I don't like you because you make men drunk and poor and unhappy. . . . Well Mr. alcohol you live in saloons and the bad men see you and you call all the boys there but you can not catch me for I am a temperance boy.—Julian Lugo

Fowler included this in the report submitted to the paper, the result of a recent LTL project. She had, in December 1890, "with the assistance of Miss Noble, the teacher in Soboba, . . . organized a Loyal Temperance Legion in the government school. We had fifteen active members the first day, and the numbers are increasing at every meeting. [We] meet twice a month, and at our last, some of our boys had tried to write some temperance papers." She planned to share the successes of these schools with other schools and hopefully make connections with the local San Jacinto LTL, too.[64]

Temperance clubs at boarding and day schools took a few different forms. Some were not labeled LTLs and thus did not report directly to the state or national headquarters, but they were influenced by the overall WCTU program and were often referenced by WCTU Work Among Indians superintendents when they reported on their accomplishments. One school that had varied temperance offerings was the Hampton Institute, originally founded to educate African Americans but which eventually accepted Native Americans, too. In the 1880s and 1890s, at Hampton, there was a "temperance club" and a distinct

"Winona" club, named after a Mdewakanton Sioux chief's daughter. One Indian agent described the "service at Winona [Lodge,] which is something between a Sunday school and a family talk." There was a temperance committee, which guided all temperance work at the school. The Native American and African American children had segregated clubs.[65] However, the temperance committee held monthly regular meetings where both African Americans and Native Americans participated. The committee, with the aid of the school, helped organize the "Holly Tree Inn," a temperance establishment near the school that served nonalcoholic refreshments—a place to go instead of saloons. The temperance committee also supported the White Cross movement, which was related to the "Band of Mercy," the WCTU department that specialized in teaching kindness to animals.[66] Initiatives like the Holly Tree Inn were antidotes to the bad influence and the temptations in the communities around day and boarding schools—often white ones. In Pechanga Village on the Temecula Reservation, the students suffered from the problem of proximity to white saloons. However, an "efficient teacher" with a Sunday temperance society helped provide them with a healthy diversion on Sunday afternoons.[67]

In the case of the temperance club at Tunesassa, we get one of the clearest glimpses of Lydia Pierce's work with children and a club's day-to-day temperance activities. Lydia and her husband, Fred Pierce, visited the school frequently, sometimes bringing their young children, Edward and Alva, along with them. When the boys reached school age, they attended Tunesassa, too. Students signed temperance pledges, sang temperance songs, made public admissions of their transgressions, and in many other ways sought to promote abstinence from alcohol, tobacco, foul language, cruelty to animals, and other vices. Many of these goals matched precisely with the WCTU's efforts to inculcate Native Americans with the organization's values and to encourage assimilation into the capitalist workforce of the broader society. While Edward was at the school, the temperance club became a family affair. Even after he departed, Lydia Pierce remained an active participant at Tunesassa for the next decade. In 1913 the Tunesassa WCTU boasted "thirty members; has had eight public meetings and three medal contests, one being for a gold medal."[68] The involvement of parents was not unique to Tunesassa, though the level of parental involvement was peculiar. D. H. B. Evans, the teacher at the school on the Lummi Reservation in Washington, reported on August 26, 1892, that a "temperance literary society has been formed in which both scholars and their parents have taken a very great interest, the membership reaching nearly 200."[69]

Pledge signing was a feature of the WCTU that extended into the LTLs. Students described pledge-signing events as joyous occasions, and the signers' fealty to their pledges was policed by the students. At Haskell in 1914, the *Indian Leader* reported happily that at an LTL meeting Alice Wise, wife of Haskell superintendent John R. Wise, read the pledge, which was signed by five new members.[70] At Tunesassa members began most meetings by reciting the temperance pledge, though in May 1909 it was decided to recite the pledge only at the start of the school year. Children who kept the pledge would, when asked as a group, raise their hand or shout out, "kept it!" Invariably it seemed that "most had kept the pledge" at any given meeting. Those who did not, however, were subjected to palpable public shame.[71]

Religious conversion was a key part of the experiences of students in boarding schools, and the temperance groups provided an audience for mission work. However, there was room for religious tolerance. OIA agents, mainline Christian missionaries, and WCTU officials could write respectfully of the Native innovations, especially if there was some temperance sentiment among the group, as was the case with the Indian Shaker Church. In 1895 Frank Terry, superintendent of Chehalis Boarding School, in Chehalis, Washington, emphasized that Indian Shakers were a Christian organization, "for they accept Christ as the Son of God and the Savior of men, and they acknowledge the Holy Scriptures as the Word of God."[72] The story of the Jamestown, Washington, Indian Shaker Church made it all the way to Kansas where the *Indian Leader* lauded the Jamestown Indians who were celebrating statewide prohibition and noted that the tribe had many Shaker Indian Church members, whose powerful temperance ideology spurred them to action.[73] Religious leaders were commonly guest speakers and some of these came directly from the WCTU. National evangelist Etta Shaw spoke to the Haskell temperance groups and argued that the Bible was the foundation of both common law and the US legal system and claimed that the liquor business violates biblical law and all traditions stemming from it. Thus, according to this WCTU official, there was effectively a biblical injunction against drinking and the liquor trade.[74] The Haskell paper also communicated the possibility of personal redemption. In a story about the WCTU on campus, the reporter described a Mr. De Bruyn, a "missionary from the Winnebago reservation" who spoke about being a saloon keeper and drinker, but he eventually found his salvation and shared with students his "conversion to Christ and his earnest efforts since then to wipe out this dreadful curse and to bring men to his Saviour."[75]

Music was an essential part of temperance activities in the boarding schools. In 1906 President Lillian Stevens recounted her trip to Indian Territory. As they arrived in Bartlesville she noted with delight, "we found ourselves surrounded by boys and girls who merrily greeted us with L.T.L. songs." At the Cherokee National Female Seminary she explained, "before we said 'Good-by' to them they sang for us, 'We are Out for Prohibition.' Many of them are natural musicians, and we have never heard this popular prohibition song sung to better effect than by these 200 Cherokee maidens. Their principal promised that they will soon organize a Y.W.C.T.U."[76] At Haskell the LTL convened regularly, sang songs, and often met in the music room. The *Indian Leader* reported in 1915 that the children sang "Onward Temperance Soldiers" as a common feature of their regular meetings. A "musical number was then given by Nelson Wauls and Elijah Bayhylle, after which all repeated the Twenty-third Psalm and sang 'For Your Country Stand.'"[77]

Student newspapers themselves were part of temperance activity, too. Students reported the news of temperance activities from all across the nation. Historians of Indian boarding school experiences have commented how the mingling of students from many different tribal communities contributed to a pan-Indian identity.[78] One part of that pan-Indian experience came from the sharing of temperance-related developments from across Indian country. In this way, students "nativized" the temperance message beyond singular tribes or communities and made the fight for prohibition (and not just drinking) seem like part of the American Indian shared experience. The *Indian Leader* did a particularly robust job with promoting the common cause of temperance. In what was most likely a reprint from the *Indian's Friend* the author discussed Umatilla chief, Captain Shumkin, who was a proponent of total abstinence. Shumkin exclaimed, "one by one it is striking down our strong men and young people. If it is continued we shall soon be a race of old women."[79] The *Indian Leader* reported on government officials' temperance work, too. Reporters recounted Cato Sells's visit to Rosebud, where he encouraged the Lakota living there to join the temperance society.[80] One 1915 *Indian Leader* issue lauded Henry A. Larson, chief prohibition enforcer in Indian country, and explained how prohibition is helpful to Indians, noting that Arizona decreased arrests after the state went dry.[81] In April 1915 the paper dedicated an entire essay to the subject of prohibition.[82] Another story described the Santee Indian Agency's transformation under Charles E. Burton. Superintendent since 1914, Burton took it over, renovated the place, and instituted a temperance campaign; many people took the pledge, though a few violated it.[83] Thus, the temperance writing in the newspaper not only served the prohibition and total abstinence efforts but acted on behalf of the federal Indian Office, as well.

The *Union Signal* celebrated the work of these students' anti-alcohol writings, reprinting their articles and essays. One student, on the surface at least, had internalized all the key lessons of the WCTU's LTL work: committing to personal temperance, bringing the message back home to the reservation, and supporting prohibition at state and national level to protect the tribal communities. In 1915 the *Union Signal* described an essay, "written by a seventh-grade pupil, . . . [which] tells of a strong determination to lead his people in a victorious war against John Barleycorn." This student wrote, "I am ready to be one of Gideon's 300 to fight against our common enemy—alcohol—so that I will not be a beggar. . . . I will gladly remember that I have lived in the prohibition state of Kansas, and that the people there have taught me not to take any kind of drink. I am going to try hard to fight this liquor away from my people back home. So that we might have prohibition among the Indians there, like Kansas." He described the loss of his parents to alcohol and the violence associated with drinking in his community.[84]

The general literary activities of the temperance clubs, improvement societies, and LTLs, with their Christian moral tones, were practice for the pinnacle of WCTU young people's activities, the medal contests. Many of the essays reprinted elsewhere were likely the products of these events. Drafting and delivery of the medal contest speeches were clear preparation for future political action. Spencer provided explicit instructions about organizing medal contests in Indian schools and demonstrated her understanding of the hierarchies in such institutions. "The medal contest may be introduced in many schools," but it was important to contact the superintendent of the school as the first step— "as the teachers, however well disposed, can only act under his direction."[85] Medal contests were usually organized by the LTLs, which were almost always supported by educational leadership. The contests consisted of young people giving speeches on the great social issues of the day (not just limited to temperance and prohibition topics); prizes were given depending on the age of the students and the sophistication of the speeches prepared. Contests could be "silver medal contests," "gold medal contests," or, very rarely, "diamond medal contests."[86] Even in the broader white society the idea was that the boys in these groups would eventually take on the mantle of voting citizens in the republic, maybe even becoming elected officials. The women of the WCTU—who still could not yet vote—could influence the future leaders of the society through these educational means. Then, as adults, the boys would promote suffrage and temperance. As the LTL motto went, "Tremble King Alcohol Because We Shall Grow Up."[87]

In western New York, all of the WCTU officers worked together to organize six "silver medal contests" for Indian children, both those enrolled in the boarding schools and those not enrolled. In 1910 the Six Nations Temperance League held their annual meeting at Allegany. Charles Doxon (Onondaga), president of the Temperance League and a Hampton Institute graduate himself, presided over the activities. There was a silver medal contest with eight girls involved. The winner was a Tunesassa student, "Lorene Neffew," who the WCTU minutes described as "a sweet voiced Indian maiden."[88] Lorene was a long-standing member of the General Improvement Society, giving a recitation, "No One Will See Me," as late as January 12, 1917.[89] Although most of the Tunesassa participants were girls, boys were also always involved. In fact, LTLs and the medal contests echoed a Haudenosaunee tradition of future male leaders of the society being groomed and selected by the elder women.[90] Among the Haudenosaunee, where oratorical skills were so valued, this was a way of connecting traditions of the children to the contemporary message of Christian temperance.[91] With the declamations, recitations, reading of the pledges not just at the meetings but at commencement and other ceremonies, these children were not only fulfilling a trait valued among Americans in the public arena, they were valued skills within Iroquois communities, too.

Seneca children gained local and national recognition for their abilities. The *Union Signal* described a 1911 gold medal contest at Tunesassa that had seven silver medal winners, four boys and three girls. A student named Henry Sutton won with a speech entitled, "The Court of Last Appeal." Lydia Pierce presided over the event, and state superintendent of Work Among Indians, Marian Peckham attended along with a local businessman.[92] The students honed their skills off-reservation, too. In 1914 the *Indian Leader* reported that one of their alumnae, Evelyn Pierce (Seneca) from Versailles, New York (Cattaraugus) "won a gold medal offered by the Indian Office, Washington, D.C." with a piece entitled, "Citizenship: The Viewpoint of a Haskell Graduate." Her speech was based on a thorough essay with specific details about the 1906 Burke Act and discussed temperance as being part of the good character needed for citizenship.[93] By 1915 medal contests were commonplace. The WCTU reported two medal contests at an unnamed Indian school in New Mexico and three more in

Arizona. They were being performed from New York to Southern California and from Oklahoma to Washington State. Through the temperance and boarding-school presses, white women and Native American students were hearing about their activities.[94]

One season when non-Indigenous and Native American LTLs connected across distance was Christmastime. WCTU unions engaged in many instances of small-scale philanthropy, putting together Christmas boxes and other donation packages for Native American schoolchildren or their communities. These also served the purpose of encouraging Indian children to celebrate the Christian holiday. Indian LTLs were often the recipients of charity from other LTLs or unions throughout a given state. In 1905 the Morris Industrial School in Minnesota had an active LTL and received scrapbooks made by LTLs from as far away as South Troy, Minnesota, over two hundred miles away.[95] Writing about California, Spencer explained that in 1909, around Christmas "Alameda, Lodi, The Corcoran Y's, and San Francisco L.T.L.'s sent generous boxes of gifts to needy bands of Indians at Christmas."[96] A few years later Spencer commented on the "Indians Christmas." Beginning December 1, she had begun receiving boxes "filled with comforts for the Christmas celebration of the Colusa Indians," from donors in San Francisco and Melrose. Boxes would be delivered to other rancherias throughout California. The spread of Christianity had been successful in Butte County, and the Colletts had traveled to "the distant rancherias where the Indians as yet have no helpers, but will have some of these Christmas boxes."[97]

Students involved with temperance were expected to continue the circle back home. The mandate was that "returned students" were to influence the old neighborhood; this was a common theme. In 1897 the editors of *Tunesassa Echoes* described the founding of the Six Nations Temperance League and highlighted the relationship between the children's and the adults' organizations: "We have attended many meetings of that society[. The adults] have given us much good advice." The same article reported on the tragic violent deaths suffered by the community and caused by alcohol, noting that in 1890 railroad accidents involving alcohol had occurred on almost all of the western New York reservations. "But some of the Indians have left the strong drink and become [C]hristians and have made many churches for the purpose of holding meetings and telling them how harmful the strong drink is."[98]

Both the Six Nations Temperance League and the WCTU had clear Christian orientations that emphasized individual salvation for both the drinker and the sinner. Yet, the question of "what to do" moved from personal pledges and individual spirituality to the question of larger-scale political action. For Native Americans, many of whom were not yet citizens, political participation was not a foregone conclusion. However, their education and formative development led them to conclude that citizenship was both inevitable and desirable. Influenced by their teachers, many of the leaders of the GIS produced essays that reflected Lydia Pierce's earlier piece, which lauded the Euro-American view of progress but also placed the Indians' cultural development in a historical framework that was reminiscent of Lewis Henry Morgan's stages of development. In this sense, their historical sensibilities, which were a product of their formal education, helped reinforce the perceived backwardness of their own traditions. In this calculation, as individuals and tribes rapidly progressed through the stages toward Euro-American civilization, they had to move quickly past the white man's trap of alcohol in order to reach the full benefit of "Christian Citizenship," a concept implicit in many of the children's writings and one that was to become the title of a WCTU department.

An unintended consequence of the boarding school experience was the emergence of peyote usage as a national phenomenon. Peyote is a small cactus with hallucinogenic properties that for centuries has been ingested for ceremonial purposes in regions surrounding its natural habitat in southern Texas and northern Mexico. As a result of increasing transportation infrastructure, notably the railroads, the use of peyote spread, along with a common set of ceremonies that would eventually be codified as the Native American Church (NAC). As historian Thomas Maroukis points out, "many of the early Peyote adherents were young men who had gone to boarding school, been exposed to Christianity, and learned to speak English. The contacts and friendships they made in these schools helped spread the Peyote faith. With English as a *lingua franca*, the different groups of American Indians could use it as an 'enabling factor' in the spread of Peyotism."[99] From the 1880s onward, students in boarding schools contributed to this new development that would challenge the temperance ethos of the WCTU. Many white commentators mislabeled peyote "mescal," an unrelated plant, though one that could be used to make fermented beverages. For instance, Dr. Charles L. Zimmerman from the Ponca Agency in Oklahoma referred to "mescal" in a piece dedicated to peyote use.[100]

The November 1917 *Indian Leader* reprinted an article from the *Outlook*, summarizing the peyote issue for congressmen and urging passage of the Gandy Bill, first introduced on February 2, 1916. It would "prohibit the traffic in peyote, including its sale to Indians, introduction into Indian country, importation and transportation, and providing penalties therefor." The article explained, "Peyote, also called mescal buttons, is a cactus imported from Mexico; it produces results somewhat analogous to those produced by opium and by hasheesh." The piece admitted some supporters claimed it had medicinal qualities (namely, that it suppressed alcohol cravings), and it was used as a religious sacrament, which might offer its users first amendment protections (which the editors found laughable).[101] The division between the peyotists or members of the Native American Church and those critics of the church extended to the progressive Native American community. The conflict caused tension within the Society of American Indians itself.[102] For all of their work in the boarding schools regarding temperance and assimilation, the WCTU, missionary allies, and other reformers could not stop the momentum of the NAC. Indeed, the religious innovation was in many ways a backlash against that work and the colonial enterprise on the whole. Yet, one attraction to the NAC was the message of abstention from alcohol, whose destructiveness young people had witnessed. Alternatively to promoting wanton drunkenness, the NAC limited the use of intoxicants to the sacramental space of the church.

Before the demise of the national Department of Work Among Indians, the WCTU had made outreach to Indian schools a priority, and they had been successful in influencing curriculum, student activities, and the vanguard of young Native American assimilationists. However, as always, the written record privileges the voices of those who supported the assimilationist and—in this case—the temperance project. Those who resisted that project are muffled in the record, a fact that plagues boarding school studies generally. Likewise, we have only glimpses of WCTU activity in the boarding schools. For every Tunesassa, Sherman, or Haskell for which there is documentation, there are dozens that are not in the WCTU sources or that never printed student newspapers. There is little doubt that further temperance activity in these schools may be uncovered and reassessed in the future.

Conclusion
Christian Citizenship, Prohibition, Suffrage, and Repeal

From 1916 through the 1930s a lot changed. Women gained the right to vote with Congress's passage of the Nineteenth Amendment in 1919 and its ratification in 1920. Alcohol prohibition was achieved in 1920 only to be repealed in 1933. Congress passed universal citizenship for Native Americans in 1924. These developments were connected by the progressive impulse beneath them. However, progressive idealism shared the stage with pragmatic political considerations when Congress and the states voted to ratify amendments or Congress voted on federal laws. Although the Nineteenth Amendment was largely hailed as a victory of progressivism and was not seriously considered for repeal again, the same cannot be said for the Eighteenth Amendment. Nativism, with long historical roots but exacerbated by anti-German sentiment during World War I, fueled the passage of national prohibition. A rejection of progressivism spurred the 1920s laissez-faire capitalism that soon met the backlash of FDR and his New Deal domestic policies. By then, even reform-minded politicians had lost their taste for prohibition. Caused in part by the perceived increase in criminal syndicates, support for prohibition waned and repeal became increasingly likely.[1]

A corollary to the patriotism and nativism of the 1910s and 1920s drove changes in Indian policy. The assimilationist push directed toward immigrants included WCTU members calling for English-only education for immigrants, which drove their agenda to declare that American Indians were comfortably on the road to assimilation. The WCTU subsumed outreach to Native Americans under "Christian Citizenship" departments—or, in some state unions, departments of "Americanization." The Indian Citizenship Act of 1924—though still seen by many as wholly positive, and a move that gave Native Americans a voice in American politics—was a key piece in an assimilationist agenda that aimed to eliminate tribal sovereignty.

Although the Indian Citizenship Act was never repealed, the rabid assimilation policies that it capped were substantially modified by the commissioner of Indian Affairs John Collier, who was appointed in 1933 by President Franklin Delano Roosevelt. The tragedy of the Indian policies from the 1880s through the 1920s also fueled the backlash—epitomized by Collier—that ended the official assimilation push and replaced it with the philosophy of "cultural pluralism." Collier's cultural pluralist approach, which included protections for languages, religions, dances, and artwork, was attacked by WCTU hero William "Pussyfoot" Johnson and heroine Clara True.[2] The Indian New Deal promoted some of the ideas that the WCTU had championed earlier: day schools, traditional Indian artwork and crafts leveraged into small businesses, and participation in US-style democratic government. Some of the WCTU's assimilative dreams were stifled when Collier put the brakes on three assimilationist methods: the attacks on tribal governments, the suppression of traditional religions and Native innovations, and the rabid pursuit of allotment. In the end, Collier brought forth some tangible elements of the WCTU legacy while abandoning others.

The WCTU's decision to place the Department of Work Among Indians under another department and then let it fade away entirely presaged the larger full-inclusion or assimilation goals of the federal government's citizenship policy and the cultural and political shift toward nativism during and after World War I. Although the WCTU reveled in the victory of prohibition and woman's suffrage, the victories lessened the energy of the group's membership, while the remaining members tried to keep up their work during the dry era. The repeal of prohibition was really the end of the WCTU as a major national organization, though it persists through the present with more modest goals than national prohibition.

The story of the WCTU's diminishing fire begins in the years leading up to American participation in World War I. The WCTU's preferred wardship status for Indians was not under serious threat, even after waves of allotted Indian citizens. The Supreme Court decision *U.S. v. Nice* (1916) upheld the authority of the federal government to pass legislation intended to protect Indians, regardless of their newly acquired citizenship or voting rights. Quoting Associate Justice Willis Van Devanter, David Wilkins explains how this affected the alcohol laws: "'allottees remain tribal Indians and under national guardianship,' and Congress's power to regulate the sale of liquor is 'not debatable.'"[3] The decision coincided with the WCTU's objective: Indians should be full-fledged citizens while remaining subject to federal protections from alcohol.

The decision to have Christian Citizenship absorb Work Among Indians and outsource activities to the WNIA had been foreshadowed. In 1914, in a report on Indian work, Spencer explained that it was difficult to do temperance-related fieldwork in the summer, especially in California, since many Native Americans were away working on farms or in the vineyards. The reformers met at resorts as usual to strategize. A group dedicated to "the Missionary Educational movement" convened in Asilomar. The Mount Hermon Conference also met. "Its direct object was the federation of all organizations doing special work for Indians. Fourteen of these societies—including the various missionary groups, the Indian Association, the WCTU, and the Indian Board of Co-operation—were represented by accredited delegates. All joined in an Indian Mission council intended to secure more definite cooperation." She sounded a great note of optimism: "During the conference many evidences were given of the advancing development of the race, one of the most effective speakers being an educated Indian woman, Mrs. Mary Hale, a full blooded Thlinget from Alaska."[4]

In her annual report in 1915 Spencer provided state-by-state coverage of successes, including individual landownership and missionary victories. She declared, "the Indian outlook was never better. Conditions everywhere are improving. The positive attitude of government officials on the temperance question is doing wonders, and race prejudice is wearing out." The WCTU had successfully reached the farthest reaches of their territories, even those that had failed to produce fruit previously. Even Alaska now had a superintendent of Work Among Indians, Ruth Hawkesworth. The territory was a "new and promising field" with a total of three Native American unions. There were additional successes in Arizona and Southern California. In Northern California, there was improved absorption into the public schools. Bootlegging went on, but law enforcement had increased, including the recent apprehension of ten scofflaws who were interrupted by "the joint efforts of the Indian Board of Cooperation and the local W.C.T.U. and bound over to the Federal Court." Spencer declared that the tribes now received the white man's law, school, and church after they had "pleaded" for it in the late 1880s. State-by-state, American Indians had voted dry, improved their financial situation, and sent their children to schools. Some were even buying cars. In Oklahoma, the leadership declared that there was no department, stating that "it falls naturally under Christian Citizenship," presaging the upcoming national merger of departments.[5]

In 1916 the executive committee recommended the absorption of the Department of Work Among Indians by the Department of Christian Citizenship and the convention approved the change. In the Work Among Indians report that year Spencer declared that "this has been a good year for this department largely because the work of past years is coming to its fruition. . . . Race prejudices are fast fading out, so that with some exceptions the public schools are open to all." She explained that there had been improvements in housing and general conditions and that "their faces are set toward citizenship." She connected all of this to successful suffrage campaigns: "Equal suffrage in the western states is having its influence in the uplift of Indians, and as their women share in their aspiration for better things, their maternal instinct will make them a factor in securing them."[6] She compared the predicament of immigrants with that of the American Indians: "The children of foreign immigrants are admitted to schools and their sick to public hospitals. The Indian as a native son of the soil, wants the same rights." She closed, "the child race is approaching adolescence, and as the aboriginal people of this continent, is entitled to its place among the peoples whose intermingling characteristics go to make up this great nation."[7] Dissolution of the stand-alone department was the result of a desired and partially accomplished inclusion campaign by the WCTU rather than by a rejection of the merits of reaching out to the tribes.

This trend continued under Christian Citizenship. Indians in the WCTU voted for or supported prohibition, land rights, and equal educational access, affirming their role as good citizens. In 1917 the superintendent of Christian Citizenship Emma L. Starrett from Central City, Nebraska, reported on Native American concerns. Commissioner of Indian Affairs Cato Sells had issued his famous "declaration of policy" associated with Native American participation in World War I. Sells declared, "the time has come to discontinue the guardianship of all competent Indians and giving even closer attention to the incompetent that they may more speedily achieve competency." According to Sells, this was "the beginning of the end of the Indian problem." Starrett tied it explicitly to their participation in World War I: "That the democracy and freedom for which the Indian is giving his life in the war, shall be extended to him as well as alien races."[8] According to the historian Thomas Britten, Cato Sells's April 1917 "declaration of policy accelerated the discontinuation of federal guardianship and the bestowal of fee patents to competent Indians" by loosening requirements for "competency." The number of fee patents issued annually almost quadrupled in the subsequent years, as did land sales by Indians to whites.[9] Although the sales to whites were not necessarily what the WCTU sought, the organization supported increasing the number of "competent," independent Indians. The increased number of citizens during and after World War I was in line with the decades-long goals of the WCTU. Members of the federal government and the WCTU shared a desire to decrease their supervisory capacities. Not coincidentally, after 1917, the annual meeting minutes grow thin regarding the Indian work done under the aegis of Christian Citizenship. The *Union Signal* reported favorably on the OIA's declaration of policy that competent Indians were in charge of "their affairs."[10] It almost seemed like the WCTU's work was done.

As Native American veterans returned home, the WCTU and other reformers saw evidence of Indians' worthiness as citizens and desired universal citizenship for all Indians. However, Britten argues that it was "not reform groups or Indian participation in World War I" but political progressives such as Burton Wheeler, Lynn J. Frazier, Charles McNary, and Robert LaFollette who "pushed for passage of an Indian citizenship bill as a regulatory measure rather than as a piece of social legislation."[11] Thomas Grillot has gone further, arguing that the direct link between World War I participation and the 1924 bestowal of citizenship is largely a myth. Instead, he argues that the Citizenship Act was really a political calculation by Calvin Coolidge coupled with some political theater that nonetheless resonated culturally within Indian communities. Grillot explains that almost one month after the passage of the Indian Citizenship Act, "the Coolidge administration issued each officially recognized tribe a certificate of recognition for services rendered during the Great War." The certificate's issuance was accompanied by gift exchanges and other ceremonies all across Indian country. It helped bolster Indian support for the Republican Party. Grillot continues: "the alliance made a mark on Indian policy. Far from being a merely practical combination, it supported a redefinition of the meaning of citizenship for Indians. The act of June 2, 1924, granting citizenship to all Indians born in the United States did not subordinate citizenship to the relinquishment of tribal rights. It thus confirmed a trend started in 1916 with the *United States v. Nice*."[12]

Whether or not one accepts Britten's argument for a procedural pragmatism among moderate and progressive senators or Grillot's claim for the political opportunism of Coolidge and providing a dual meaning behind Indian citizenship, one can see the many political factions that were courting the American Indian vote to some degree. Montana, Wisconsin, North Dakota, Oregon—the states from which the senators who wrote the bill hailed—had proportionately large numbers of Indian voters, and since 1913 this mattered electorally. The factor that is overlooked by both historians is that the women reformers could also now vote and, even before that, had for decades been lobbying officials and influencing male voters. While it may be difficult to unpack the brains of the congressmen who voted for the bill or the president who signed it, the women reformers in the WCTU rejoiced at the Citizenship Act of June 2, 1924, and got to work trying to shape its impact.

At the 1924 annual meeting the WCTU reaffirmed its decision to place Work Among Indians under Christian Citizenship. "Since the United States Supreme Court has declared Indians to be citizens, they naturally come in the scope of this department." Throughout the country, Indian citizens were taking up their responsibilities. American Indian groups from ten states petitioned the federal government for "justice to be done to them in property rights, school rights, and in other ways." The author closed the report encouraging their just treatment and indicating that the WCTU's role as sharer of information would continue to be a part of that quest.[13] Not coincidentally, Lilah Lindsey, the long-time WCTU member and activist wrote a weighty legalistic manual on citizenship entitled *Study Course in Citizenship, on Federal and Oklahoma Laws, Pertaining to Women and Children* that was sponsored by the WCTU and published that same year. It was not specifically for Native Americans, but it helped all women understand laws that were especially relevant to them and their new role in the political process, in a state with a sizeable American Indian population.[14] Amid the excitement over suffrage, universal citizenship, and national prohibition, the WCTU lost its raison d'être. Also lost was their focus on American Indians as a politically distinct group.

One by one most of the state unions followed the national and subsumed their Indian departments under the departments of citizenship or Americanization. Sometimes a committed superintendent kept the work going. More often, Indian departments were either voted out of existence or faded away after the retirement or "promotion" of elderly superintendents. Michigan saw minimal outreach or other activity after 1916. The Mount Pleasant Union on the Isabella Reservation "paid all dues and then disbanded" in 1917.[15] In Minnesota some version of an Indian department was kept up for about a decade. In 1916 Frances A. Wright Hubbard, superintendent of Work Among Indians, sent a letter to Cato Sells commending him for closing saloons on reservations.[16] By 1918 there was no longer an Indian department, and the officers explained that Christian Citizenship was the most appropriate place to take up the work, since the primary need for Indians was the need to Christianize them.[17] By 1920 Wright was still "associate superintendent" of Indian work under Christian Citizenship. There was still a budget line and still money going to the Indian mission at Puposky, south of Red Lake, Minnesota. Christian Citizenship organized an Indian convocation at Red Lake, conducted in the Ojibwe language, at the Episcopal Church. By 1921 the department was listed as Christian Citizenship only—though Redwood Falls, near Morton, reported that it had some Indian members. By 1922, Stella Cussons, Stewartville Christian Citizenship superintendent, provided a lengthy report that did not mention Indians at all. Subsequent reports were silent on Native Americans.[18]

In South Dakota in February 1925 they simply encouraged an emphasis on education for Native Americans. By October there was no longer any mention of Native American work at all.[19] In 1916 the *White Ribbon* in North Dakota noted that Indian unions at Cannon Ball and Big Lake were "creating sentiment among their own people."[20] However, reporting on activity among Native Americans declined to nothing after 1917. Washington State fizzled, too. In 1917 the Eastern Washington union complained that there was not much department work at all. In 1918 there was a joint department of Christian Citizenship and Americanization and there was a shift in President Carrie Barr's language toward a more nativist tone. Western Washington stopped its Work Among Indians department around 1915 and the county ones were gone by 1916.[21] In Oregon there was still a department in 1917, led by A. F. May, but there was no report in the minutes. In 1918 there was no department, the decision having been made to put Indian work under Americanization. After 1918, other than the mention of a few unions located in towns near reservations, there was almost nothing that even hinted at an Indian presence in the organization.[22]

Evidence about Nevada's Indian work is thin. There was briefly a Work Among Indians department in 1902. Ratie Smith from Wadsworth—near the cluster of communities around Reno, including Pyramid Lake—discussed the federal law about STI being required in Indian schools, Dorothy Cleveland's plan of work, and Indian women in New York's activities.[23] The Nevada WCTU records go quiet after 1902, and not much information made it to the national records. Between 1914 and 1924 the record improves and reveals a litany of Work Among Indians superintendents and a few connections between the local

Reno union and surrounding Paiutes. The lack of detail makes analysis a challenge. By 1926, however, there was no more Department of Work Among Indians listed in the Nevada documents.[24] Wyoming's WCTU Indian Work was
even shorter lived. In Wyoming, which never seemed to have had a department
of Work Among Indians, there was a union at Riverton in 1916, on the Wind
River Reservation. There was no union listed there in 1918.[25] In Colorado, where
the unions were tightly tied to the schools, the department faded around 1912 as
the federal schools lost their support, and there were no departments of Work
Among Indians through the 1920s.

Idaho met a similar fate. In 1915 there was a report at the state convention,
but it was not printed in minutes. The transitional years 1916–1918 are missing,
but by 1919 Americanization and Christian Citizenship had merged, and there
were no Indians mentioned in their reports. In her presidential address
Emma F. A. Drake explained, "early in the history of our country when we were
anxiously trying to [C]hristianize the Indian, someone asked the best method
of saving a full-blooded Indian, and the answer came quickly from a listener,
'send after him a full-blooded Christian.' The same thing is true of our Americanization work, send after the one you would teach a full-blooded American
who knows what it means to be a live citizen of the fairest country on the
globe."[26] In a 1928 memorial to the Work Among Indians superintendent Eva
West, the Idaho convention did not even mention her Indian work.[27] At the
1917 Montana State Convention, the previous superintendent of Indian Work
Alice Hoag gave the benediction, but there was no information on outreach to
the Native American communities; the Americanization report discussed only
immigrants. In 1919 the Americanization report was decidedly anti-German
and mentioned the importance of reaching out to foreign-born women. Native
Americans were absent.[28]

In 1917 the Northern California *White Ribbon Ensign* covered the Supreme
Court decision of the previous year, declaring that deciding "their rights equal
with those of white men, has had a beneficent effect in the hopes and aspirations
of the redmen, and enhances their desire to give their children the benefit of
these rights and privileges." The author advocated that missionary societies
should be the conduit for any future temperance work. There was even a new
department, "Temperance and Missions," to organize this work.[29]

One of the pillars holding up WCTU Indian work crumbled in the spring of
1918 when Annie Bidwell passed away. In April Dorcas Spencer wrote an
extended obituary for her. She praised Bidwell, whom she had first met in 1885,

for her role in religious instruction and her efforts in preservation of the Mechoopda in their homelands. Spencer closed with an assertion of their spiritual connection: "and as she has vanished from sight, we stand more closely together in the bonds of a holy crusade."[30] Northern California's WCTU continued to honor Bidwell in the coming years. In April 1918 the *White Ribbon Ensign* described Burney O. Wilson, "the first California Indian to win an army commission" as second lieutenant. "A protégé" of Bidwell "he enlisted in the army at the outbreak of war and it was on the advice of his benefactress that he studied to win his promotion from the ranks."[31] The WCTU was happy to tie together the patriotism of Native Americans, especially those with WCTU ties, to the war effort.

Spencer tried to inform California about Indian affairs, but the information she shared dwindled. In 1924 she was still superintendent of the state Department of Work Among Indians and wrote a joyous report about Indians gaining citizenship, which would end formal discrimination in education, she proclaimed. She also promoted self-education by white WCTU members, indicating that there were, "wrongs to be righted" based on America's errors in the past. In 1925 she issued a two-page report that summarized the California Indians' history in the United States and the iniquities they had faced; she now wrote under the title of "director" of Work Among Indians. She reminded the readers that "Indians were made citizens by our law, in an Act of Congress in 1924. The Law of Christ made us Neighbors to each other long ages ago." She commented on their abilities in self-governance: "they have a gift for Parliamentary Order, and a most commendable sense of courtesy. I am proud of their meetings." In July 1927 she claimed that "every Indian in the United States is a voter now on exactly the same terms that we are voters. It is astonishing what ambitions they now have, just the same as whites. All public schools are open to them now and they avail themselves of all the opportunities they now have." In 1928 Suzanne McKelvey had taken over as Work Among Indians director in Northern California. Her report echoed Spencer's, but she also reminded readers of the barriers to voting that were facing new Indian citizens, especially the state-mandated literacy tests, but they represented a voting block desired by both parties, which gave them a voice in politics.[32]

After 1929 even that strongest of state departments crumbled. In 1930 an article about pioneer white ribboners in California described Spencer as "a member emeritus of the state executive board," an honorific title suggesting she was no longer able to maintain her former pace. The piece offered a brief biography and somehow never directly mentioned her Indian work.[33] By 1931 reports on Americanization contained nothing on Native Americans and never mentioned a Work Among Indians department.[34]

In December 1932, on the precipice of prohibition's repeal, the national president Ella Boole announced the new motto, "Advance Not Retreat!" Boole optimistically asserted that education, personal abstinence, and obedience to law would offset schemes of brewers, distillers, and vintners to increase sales of the forthcoming legal alcohol.[35] In June 1933 an unknown author listed the successes of prohibition prior to repeal, declaring of the noble experiment, "It is NOT the Failure."[36] On March 22, 1933, the American president signed the bill legalizing low alcohol beer. And in spring 1933 Dorcas J. Spencer, the cofounder of California's women's temperance work and pioneer in Native American outreach, was "promoted" to her reward. Fortunately, ratification of the Twenty-First Amendment would not happen until December 1933, so Spencer never had to witness the final repeal.[37]

In Southern California, where Mary E. Fowler had been Spencer's committed counterpart, the department followed the fate of Fowler's waning energies. In the 1916–1917 annual report, Fowler, still superintendent of an intact department, commented excitedly on all of the activities. The women at Soboba had organized a "Progressive Club." Bootleggers were being arrested. The superintendent at Needles and Pasadena reported good work.[38] In 1917 the report indicated that Work Among Indians had been combined with Citizenship "by order of the Convention to conform with the National departments," and the former superintendent was now to be "Associate Superintendent." Fowler gave the report for that year. "I wish you could see the gain in the Indian villages. There are comfortable homes, neat surroundings and charming vegetable and flower gardens. Much more attention is paid to sanitary conditions. . . . There is so little drunkenness that there have been only three prosecutions for liquor selling in the past year with two convictions, one pleading guilty." There was additional activity by Ora M. Salmons among the Pala Indians. Mrs. Blair described an Indian LTL in Inyo County. Many previously active counties had gone quiet, though some students from Sherman provided music for a meeting of Riverside, which kept its Indian work going.[39]

In 1918 Fowler, now demoted to "Associate Superintendent," provided no report and the overarching Christian Citizenship report said nothing about Indian work.[40] However, this oversight can be forgiven because of the 1918 San Jacinto earthquake, which impeded Fowler's activities. In 1919 she bragged that the Mission Indians were becoming more successful economically and that there had been good law enforcement with many pending bootlegging cases. The young Native American men of Southern California had been great patriots, and many veterans had fought alongside "our boys." She even claimed that Arizona's first enlistment was a Soboba boy. Her county of Riverside still had a dedicated Work Among Indians department, and Fowler remained in charge of it.[41] In 1920 Fowler once again lauded Indian citizenship and war effort and celebrated the recent demographic recovery of many Native American communities. She was excited about the passage of prohibition: "There is no doubt that the prohibitive law will prove a great blessing to the Indian, physically, financially, and morally." She explained Cato Sells's declaration of policy regarding competent Indians becoming citizens and tied it to patriotism during World War I. "During the war, 10,000 young Indians served their country. The Indians purchased $25,000,000 worth of Liberty Bonds. Is not that a magnificent showing?"[42]

In 1921 there was no Indian work in the Southern California WCTU convention report. Fowler had passed away in September of that year.[43] Very little mention of Indians followed in the next decade, though one report from Riverside County in 1924 indicated that a window had been installed at the recently constructed Protestant church at Sherman Institute in Arlington, and many local unions contributed funds to the memorial.[44] In 1913 in Arizona, which was always closely tied to Southern California, there was a Work Among Indians superintendent, Eva Watson, who organized at Tucson Indian Training School and distributed literature to other communities.[45] In 1916 the superintendent was Mrs. C. R. (Josephine P.) Broadhead of Phoenix, but she provided no report. After that, the record of formal Indian work by the WCTU goes silent.[46]

Although the institutional commitment to organizing Indian country waned, Native American and white women continued their legislative efforts. The Nez Perce submitted a petition to the state of Washington, boldly stating, "we . . . implore you to enact such legislation and laws as will forever stop the introduction of such liquors among our dependent tribesmen."[47] The primary form that legislative efforts took, aside from those dealing with alcohol, were those against Peyote and the Native American Church. Gertrude Bonin, secretary of the Society of American Indians, was connected to the WCTU and even attended the national convention. She "has been in daily attendance at the sessions of the committee, endeavoring to secure a provision prohibiting the use of the drug peyote." The issue was referred to a subcommittee who was deciding on the issue, and Margaret Dye Ellis encouraged readers to "send at once a brief note to Hon. Henry F. Ashurst, [Democrat from Arizona, Chair of the Committee on Indian Affairs,] United States Senator, Washington, D.C., urging the appointment of a sub-committee to consider the question of sale and use of the drug peyote and its baneful effects on Indians and our troops on the border."[48]

Senator Owen of Oklahoma "made a point of order against the amendment concerning peyote and presented a letter from delegates representing four tribes of Indians in Oklahoma in which they protested against the legislation to prohibit its use." Ashurst shared a letter from a WCTU-approved temperance author, Dr. Harvey Wiley, on the destructive power of peyote. The WCTU lauded Bonin for her continued efforts to support amendment to the bill.[49] Ultimately, the Hayden bill passed the House but failed in the Senate. "The two senators from Oklahoma, under pressure from their own constituents, persuaded their colleagues not to support the prohibition of peyote. They argued it was a First Amendment, religious freedom issue."[50] The WCTU continued its efforts to prohibit peyote to protect Indians, resolving in 1923 and 1924 annual meetings to work for it through Congress.[51]

In the WCTU's assessment, state and national prohibition laws benefited Indians. National prohibition solved some problems with the patchwork of laws that previously affected Indian country, but the bootlegging that washed over the entire country had a head start in Native communities. Much of the WCTU's coverage and legal advocacy turned to stifling the bootlegging, which had limited effect because of isolation and enforcement challenges that were even worse in America's rural areas. Temperance efforts were hampered by the steady decrease in federal funds marked for enforcement of suppression of liquor traffic on reservations. This coincided with changes in party politics in the 1920s but was also because of the assumption that universal Indian citizenship was coming and federal enforcement of national prohibition for everyone was taking center stage.

At the start of the decade, OIA officials were very optimistic about the positive impact that national prohibition would have, and they already began to see some benefits in a decrease in crime, but they also observed denatured alcohol and other dangerous intoxicants being used and sold, as happened across the country during the era. In 1924 the report of the commissioner of Indian Affairs provided a good overview of the problem of bootlegging. "The bootlegger is a cunning, resourceful, and treacherous offender, and finds the Indian an easy prey." The remoteness of the reservations, the proximity of so many Indian communities to the Canadian or Mexican borders, and the decreased budget in Indian Affairs for fighting the liquor traffic all led to the weakness of prohibition.[52] There had already been a decrease in the budget for liquor enforcement in Indian country from $150,000 in 1919 to $100,000 in 1920. The drop to $65,000 in 1921 was felt by officials.[53] The federal budget for "suppression of the liquor traffic among Indians" was down to $22,000 by 1928, and it was clear that the federal government was relying on national prohibition to stop the traffic on the reservations. The Department of the Interior report from that year indicates that there were problems in enforcing state laws on reservations. Federal citizenship still left the loophole of state laws not applying to reservation lands, and thus state law enforcement officials were unable to help in curtailing crimes there. Although the reservations' protection from state laws was indicative of Indian sovereignty to Native American leaders, it hampered daily prohibition efforts.[54]

The general interpretation of prohibition in Indian country by the WCTU was that it was a positive development for communities. The *Union Signal* reported on February 10, 1921, that Idaho Indians benefited from national prohibition. The paper wrote approvingly of a statement by Judge James L. McClear, US District Attorney for Idaho. He claimed that he used to see "10 to 50 cases in each of the three United States district courts in Idaho on the charge of selling liquor to Indians or taking liquor into the reservations before the national prohibition laws went into effect." Idaho was an early adopter of prohibition, but liquor had been brought in from adjoining states. National prohibition limited that route and resulted in McClear seeing no Indian cases in federal court after a year of prohibition.[55] However, bootlegging was a problem in other communities. The ASL paper, the *American Issue*, discussed a raid on the Onondaga Nation in 1924 involving state troopers and county sheriffs, and many Onondagas were arrested for bootlegging.[56] Emma Anderson, a state Baptist worker, impressed one meeting of the WCTU of Oklahoma with a talk about the use of liquor among Indians during prohibition. In Tulsa, "Mrs. [W. O.] Forman of East Side reported a special effort to close a bootlegging joint," and president Lilah D. Lindsey called for the attendance at the trials of bootleggers, presumably to apply peer pressure on the judge and jury to convict scofflaws. They closed a June 1923 meeting with words of thanks to President Harding for his efforts to enforce the Eighteenth Amendment and to local judges who were also dedicated to enforcement of local laws. They closed with a prayer for guidance in all their civic activity.[57]

Aside from fighting for anti-peyote legislation and supporting bootlegging prosecutions, the WCTU continued to fight for philanthropic issues on behalf of Native Americans, especially regarding land rights. While WCTU members maintained support for allotment, generally speaking, they wanted to protect individual ownership and opposed alienation of land through legislation or white trickery. Lenna Lowe Yost, legislative superintendent, reported on eight Indian delegates in Washington, DC, on behalf of the California tribes who wanted a "Court of Claims bill, designed to enable them to bring their plea for a settlement by the government of their rights under unfulfilled treaties." Their ultimate goal was to file suit in the Court of Claims for the 1851 treaty in which they had exchanged 7.5 million acres for money and goods. Since the US Senate never ratified the treaty, payments were never made, but the tribes lost their lands anyway. The article indicated that the bill was introduced to the House by Congressman Raker and in the Senate by Senator Johnson, both of California, as House Bill 4238 and Senate Bill 2235. Although the article was sympathetic, unlike their pattern during the Spencer years, the letter did not direct the readers to contact their representatives to support the bill, though that may have been implied.[58]

More controversial than the California Court of Claims Bill was the Bursum Bill dispute. Yost wrote somewhat joyfully that "The Bursum Bill . . . is evidently dead." Introduced in 1922 and initially passed by the US Senate, the bill protected the rights of white squatters on Pueblo lands in New Mexico. Her description of the bill was scathing. She explained that the Senate let it slip by to the House before they understood its implications. Once they did, they recalled it from the House. Yost credited the General Federation of Women's Clubs with being a major force in opposing the bill for what it would have done. A group of "organized friends of the Indians" produced a counter bill, but this one was not acceptable to other "Indians' friends" and failed to make it out of the Senate subcommittee on public lands. Yost commented approvingly of a newer bill introduced by Senator Lenroot, chairman of the subcommittee.[59] The outcome was the Pueblo Lands Act, which Congress passed in 1924. It was in the opposition to the Bursum Bill that John Collier, deeply influenced by Stella Atwood, began his career in Indian Affairs, as founder of the American Indian Defense Association in 1923.[60] Margaret Jacobs has noted that WCTU member and Indian agent Clara True supported the Bursum Bill, which shows a rift within

WCTU circles over Collier and the future of Indian reform.[61] The lack of a department dedicated to Indian Work meant that the WCTU organization would be relegated to a reporting role rather than continuing to be an active lobbying or organizing group.

By the middle of 1933, many things had changed. Repeal of prohibition was imminent. John Collier was installed as commissioner of Indian Affairs and would institute the Indian New Deal. The WCTU, as a major factor in American social policy, legislation, and women's association life had declined over the course of the 1920s and into the 1930s. The imminent death of the WCTU's Indian work was symbolized by the "promotions" of the giants of Dorcas Spencer, Annie Bidwell, Mary Fowler, and others. Before the decline of the organization, however, the early 1920s could be seen as victorious years for the WCTU and the members wanted to celebrate. Especially noteworthy was the year 1924, the fiftieth anniversary of the organization's founding in Cleveland. The jubilee preparations began a few years earlier. In March 1921, the national WCTU advertised its "Mobilize a Million Members" campaign, touting its members' mission work—in foreign, home, and city missions—and emphasized that "Its Activities Extend to the Indian Reservations."[62]

Amid the 1924 jubilee celebration of the National WCTU, the organization chose a curious symbol in which the mixed messages surrounding their Indian work were cast. To commemorate the event, the WCTU had minted a novelty jubilee penny paperweight. The August 28, 1924, *Union Signal* provided a full-page advertisement and description: "Jubilee Penny Paperweight: The Official Symbol of Fifty Years of Progress." The intention was for individuals and local unions to purchase the three-ounce medallions and give them to women, men, boys, and girls as awards for recruiting members, as a token of appreciation for their support.[63] On the back side were the following phrases: "National Woman's Christian Temperance Union, Organized Cleveland, Ohio, November 18, 1874," and "For God and Home and Every Land." It also depicted six American Flags, a cross, an inset with a mother and her infant child, and a star shining over it all.

On the face, were the words "Jubilee Penny" and "Sound the Jubilee" along with the years 1874 and 1924. The salient characteristic of the entire souvenir—but not mentioned or pictured in the *Union Signal* advertisement—was the profile of a Native American man, in full Plains-style warrior headdress, also on the face. The curator and art historian Cécile R. Ganteaume has explained, regarding such usages of headdresses, that their appropriation was not accompanied by any understanding of the rich tradition and meanings within the

Figure 13. Jubilee Penny Paperweight (face). This medallion was sold as a fund-raising effort intended to be given as a gift to temperance supporters. (Author's private collection.)

various Plains cultures that produced them. Nonetheless, such use had become common, even on US minted coins. By 1909, when Theodore Roosevelt's commissioned Indian-head Half Eagle Gold Coin was released, the Indian headdress had come to have "symbolic association of representations of American Indians with Liberty." Ganteaume explains that this reflected a shift, away from female figures symbolizing "Liberty" on various coins and other products, to a male, American Indian figure with a headdress representing liberty.[64] Unfortunately, I have not been able to unearth any documentation about the jubilee committee's decision to place the Indian head on the penny. The choice was timely, however, since the Citizenship Act was passed the same year as the jubilee. Although the Citizenship Act probably was not signed when the design was

Figure 14. Jubilee Penny Paperweight (reverse). (Author's private collection.)

hatched, many likely knew it was coming and hoped for its passage as a symbol of full inclusion in the United States, which occurred while WCTU members were enjoying the period of prayed-for prohibition and celebrating their fiftieth birthday. The more eschatological of them may have assumed that the millennium was upon them, too.

On the other hand, the practice of appropriating historical Indian figures at a moment when the historical past being depicted by the headdress was waning has been roundly criticized in recent years. Were the WCTU leaders celebrating American Indian histories and traditions? Or were they marking the demise of these histories and traditions on their souvenir coin? Judging from the entire history of WCTU Indian work, it is clear it was the latter. The white WCTU reformers were celebrating what they saw as Native American women, men,

JUBILEE PENNY PAPERWEIGHT THE OFFICIAL SYMBOL OF FIFTY YEARS OF PROGRESS

AWARDS
Give a Paperweight

To the members who get the most new members in September.

To the one who can answer the most questions from the W. C. T. U. catechism at county convention.

To the Boy Scouts who helped with courtesies at county or state conventions, fairs or local entertainments.

To the boys or girls of the Sunday school who write the best essays on the work of the W. C. T. U. for the past fifty years.

As souvenirs for members of contest classes who do not receive the medal.

To the men of your family to use on their desks.

To your pastor as a reminder of the long efforts of the W. C. T. U. for civic righteousness.

A W. C. T. U. BOOTH

Have a W. C. T. U. booth at every church bazaar or county or state fair. Arrange to have the booth decorated so as to show what the W. C. T. U. has accomplished in the last 50 years. Secure some interesting charts and photographs of the work. Display copies of THE UNION SIGNAL. Have a large number of pennies piled up on the counter, and sell these fine souvenirs to everyone who comes to visit the booth. If you cannot have a full booth arrange to get part of one. People will be glad to remember this great work by buying this handsome souvenir paperweight.

THIS BEAUTIFUL WORK OF MEDALLIC ART AND THE 50TH ANNIVERSARY SOUVENIR OF THE W. C. T. U. OUGHT TO BE IN THE HOME OF EVERY LOYAL WORKER AND FRIEND.

BUY A JUBILEE PENNY PAPERWEIGHT—HELP CELEBRATE—FIFTY YEARS OF PROGRESS OF THE NATIONAL WOMAN'S CHRISTIAN TEMPERANCE UNION.

THE JUBILEE SOUVENIR PENNY IS CAST IN BRONZE

It is over ten times the size of a real penny.

It is 2½ inches in circumference.

It weighs 3 ounces.

It is a Handsome and Appropriate Souvenir.

It costs you only 50 cents.

Any one will Appreciate the gift of the W. C. T. U. Jubilee Penny as a Souvenir of our Fifty Year's Warfare against the Alcoholic Liquor Traffic.

Order in quantities.

HAVE YOU THIS OFFICIAL SOUVENIR TO USE IN YOUR HOME AND PASS ON TO YOUR CHILDREN?

Price 50 cents each; $5.25 per dozen.

OBTAINING CONTRIBUTIONS

Many friends of the W. C. T. U. delight to give money to help our work. Many organizations and many business men contribute yearly to the support of our great cause. As a token of appreciation for their helpfulness, what could please them better than a Jubilee Penny Paperweight for Their Own Use?

To those who have helped us and realize what splendid results we have achieved the penny will be a reminder of the part they took in the conflict, will keep them interested in our continued activities. A Jubilee Penny Paperweight as a thank offering to those who help contribute to our success. A Jubilee Penny Paperweight on the desk of every friend.

As an Incentive
To Help
Finish the Task

THANKS FOR THE W. C. T. U.

Manufacturers, storekeepers and professional men are thankful for prohibition, because it has helped their business. Show the penny to them, and tell them that the W. C. T. U. is celebrating its Fiftieth Anniversary—Fifty years of hard work to accomplish something for humanity. They will be glad to buy a penny in appreciation of the work of the W. C. T. U. Regardless of personal opinions these men know that prohibition has helped their business.

The Governor of Louisiana, being presented with our Jubilee Penny, remarked that he possessed many paperweights but none that he prized more highly than this Jubilee Souvenir of the W. C. T. U.

National W. C. T. U. Publishing House, Evanston, Illinois

Figure 15. Jubilee Penny Paperweight advertisement. *Union Signal,* August 24, 1924, 14.

(Courtesy of Frances Willard Memorial Library and Archives, Evanston, IL.)

and children leaving the tribal age and entering one of universal citizenship in the United States, which now promised full suffrage to women. Native American women, especially those in leadership roles in the mainstream WCTU, may have welcomed those developments as practical matters but clearly demonstrated a sensitivity, appreciation, and desire to keep many Indigenous traditions alive. One wonders what the Native American women in the WCTU would have thought of the souvenir paperweight.

The WCTU should be seen as having a mixed legacy in Indian work. They often had the noblest of intentions for Native Americans: sobriety, economic success, and salvation. But these things came at the familiar costs that accompanied many reform efforts: cultural loss, ranging from the suppression of traditional dances, religious practices, economic traditions, languages (at times), to the weakening of tribal governments and autonomy and sometimes the disruption of gender roles. Yet, Native American women, children, and some men saw something attractive in the organization too: sobriety, Christian spiritual activities, prayer, music, and other rituals, generosity and exchange, oratory, and maternal care and training for future leaders through the Euro-American educational system. In these senses, coupled with the raw number of Native American people who participated in an LTL, a medal contest, a pledge signing, or one petition campaign or another, we must consider that the WCTU was not just a white women's organization; it was a Native American organization, too, though not primarily a Native American one. If the WCTU leaders were attempting to honor the organization's Native American connections, their medallion design seems strange. Might they have chosen a better symbol than the hackneyed warrior in headdress imagery?

Perhaps, instead of choosing the Plains warrior on the face of the jubilee medallion, if the WCTU wanted to reflect the authentic accomplishments of the WCTU among Native Americans during the years leading up to 1924—the STI legislation, the pledge-signing campaigns, the individuals who chose not to drink because of their efforts, their many connections to Indian youth, defenses of federal protections against liquor sales, national Prohibition, the Nineteenth Amendment, and the Indian Citizenship Act's passage—it would have been more appropriate to have the visage of someone else on the paperweight. More appropriate likenesses might have been found in the images of Jane Stapler, Lydia or Eliza Pierce, Lilah Lindsey, Tennessee Fuller, or one of the thousands of other Native American women who dedicated so much of their lives to the WCTU and the Department of Work Among Indians.

Notes

Preface and Acknowledgments

1. The term "Indian country" in this book refers to any area of the United States with an identifiable Native American community, including reservations, boarding schools, and both rural and urban areas. The term "Indian Territory" is a proper noun referring to the political entity created by the federal government to receive the tribes who were forcibly removed from their homelands in the 1830s and 1840s, now within the present state of Oklahoma. Although it lacked the governmental organization laid out by federal law that other territories like Washington Territory did, Indian Territory was a specific, defined political region.

2. Okrent, *Last Call*; Murdock, *Domesticating Drink*; Pegram, *Battling Demon Rum*; Rorabaugh, *The Alcoholic Republic*; McGirr, *The War on Alcohol*.

3. For coverage of the gradual reduction of Iroquois lands and the causes behind it, see Barbara Graymont, *The Iroquois in the American Revolution* (Syracuse: Syracuse University Press, 1975); Snow, *The Iroquois*, chs. 9–11; Hauptman, *Conspiracy of Interests*. For the Erie Canal, see Carol Sherriff, *The Artificial River: The Erie Canal and the Paradox of Progress* (New York: Hill and Wang, 1996).

4. Dunlap, "In the Name of the Home."

5. Thomas J. Lappas, "'For God and Home and Native Land': The Haudenosaunee and the WCTU, 1884–1921," *Journal of Women's History* 29, no. 2 (Summer 2017): 62–85. To simplify the notes, I have used the acronym WCTU for the full title "Woman's Christian Temperance Union" in the titles of published materials and collection names. The original styling remains in the bibliography.

Introduction

1. Prucha, *The Great Father*, 327.

2. Wallace, *Death and Rebirth*, 245, 303–4, 335. The preceding paragraph was originally published within Lappas, "Iroquois Temperance Societies."

3. Johnson, *Legends, Traditions*, 152–65. Author's personal communication with Chief Kenneth Patterson, Florence Patterson, and Dale Henry of the Tuscarora Temperance Society, Tuscarora Nation, May 6, 2011.

4. "Iroquois in Council, Aboriginal Ceremonies Interpreted for the 'Standard' by an Indian Reporter," *Post-Standard*, October 11, 1890, Temperance Movements,

Vertical Files, Onondaga Historical Association (hereafter TM-VF-OHA); William M. Beauchamp, "Indian Temperance Work," *Post-Standard*, October 20, 1902, TM-VF-OHA.

5. Fahey, *Temperance and Racism*, 6, 10–11, 13–14, 17–19, 84.

6. Bordin, *Woman and Temperance*, ch. 2.

7. Leonard, *Illiberal Reformers*, 124–27.

8. Mancall, *Deadly Medicine*, 112, 114.

9. Unrau, *White Man's Wicked Water*.

10. Prucha, *American Indian Policy*, 220–22.

11. Klein, *Grappling with Demon Rum*, 13–14, 38–41, 66–67, 97–98. 111, 116.

12. "Constitution and By-Laws of the National WCTU," *Union Signal*, November 26, 1885, 10, in Lenz and Blouin, *Temperance and Prohibition Papers* (hereafter cited as *WCTU-US* with date and page); "Constitution as Adopted," *Woman's Christian Temperance Union Annual Meeting Minutes*, 1874, 32–33, in Lenz and Blouin, *Temperance and Prohibition Papers* (hereafter cited as *WCTU-AMM* with date and page); "Constitution of the Woman's National Christian Temperance Union," *WCTU-AMM*, 1877, 215–16.

13. Thomas Lappas, "Loyal Temperance Legion," in *The SAGE Encyclopedia of Alcohol: Social, Cultural, and Historical Perspectives*, ed. Scott C. Martin, 3 vols. (Thousand Oaks, CA: SAGE Publications, 2018), 2: 816–17.

14. Leonard, *Illiberal Reformers*, 127; also 133, 141–44, 152–44.

15. Paddison, *American Heathens*, 3, 5, 44, 58.

16. Bordin, *Woman and Temperance*, 85. See also *WCTU-AMM*, 1879, 160.

17. *WCTU-AMM*, 1881, 54.

18. *WCTU-AMM*, 1882, 18.

19. *WCTU-AMM*, 1884, 5; *WCTU-US*, March 12, 1885, 1. Upon Jane Stapler's death, the *Union Signal* declared her to have been "president of the WCTU in Indian Territory since its organization in 1883." "Corrections," *WCTU-US*, May 9, 1895, 9.

20. Tomkinson, *Twenty Years' History*, 74, 159. Jones was the vice president of the WNIA. The committee was to be "a medium of communication between the two societies for mutual aid, grants of literature from that organization for our missions being of special value." *Fourth Annual Report of the Women's National Indian Association* (Philadelphia: Grant and Faires, 1884), 5, https://babel.hathitrust.org/cgi/pt?id=nyp.33433081751210;view=1up;seq=33. *Annual Report of the Women's National Indian Association* (Philadelphia: Grant and Faires, 1885), 6.

21. *WCTU-AMM*, 1886, 48. The WCTU often incorrectly shortened the name of the WNIA to Women's Indian Association.

22. *WCTU-US*, February 12, 1903, 16. See also *WCTU-AMM*, 1901, 36. The full name of the organization and the abbreviation with periods are cited so frequently throughout this work, in titles of works and within quotes, that I have taken the liberty to cite all as the modern acronym WCTU.

23. *WCTU-AMM*, 1903, 17.

24. "Work Among Foreign Speaking Peoples, Colored Peoples and Indians," *WCTU-US*, July 13, 1905, 13.

25. "Departments Merged," *WCTU-US*, December 14, 1916, 8.

26. Kimberly Robertson, "Rerighting the Historical Record: Violence against Native Women and the South Dakota Coalition Against Domestic Violence and Sexual Assault," *Wicazo Sa Review* 27, no. 2 (2012): 21–47.

27. Scott C. Martin, "Violence, Gender, and Intemperance in Early National Connecticut," *Journal of Social History* 34, no. 2 (2000): 309–25; Pamela Haag, "The 'Ill Use of a Wife': Patterns of Working-Class Violence in Domestic and Public New York City, 1860–1880," *Journal of Social History* 25, no. 3 (1992): 447–77; DeTora, "Denial, Discovery and Domestic Violence."

28. Pesantubbee, *Choctaw Women*, 110–11, 140.

29. Parman, *Indians*, 70.

30. Parman, *Indians*, 11.

31. Senier, *Voices of American Indian Assimilation*, xiii, 21. See also Jerry E. Clark and Martha Ellen Webb, "Susette and Susan La Flesch[e], Reformer and Missionary," in Clifton, *Being and Becoming Indian*, 137–59; Forbes, "Intellectual Self-Determination and Sovereignty," 11–23 (esp. 21 for a mandate to look at Native American identities among those who take on artistic forms of the colonizer).

32. Huebner, "Unexpected Alliance," 340, https://doi.org/10.1525/phr.2009.78.3.337.

33. Huebner, "Unexpected Alliance," 337–66.

34. Mathes, *Divinely Guided*, 54. See also Cahill, *Federal Fathers and Mothers*, 22–23, 44.

35. Mathes, *The Women's National Indian Association*, 40.

36. For women's roles in Indian reform and the role of women authors in that reform movement, see Baym, *Women Writers of the American West*; Mathes, *The Women's National Indian Association*; Mathes, *Divinely Guided*; Mathes, *Helen Hunt Jackson*; Edwards and Gifford, *Gender and the Social Gospel*; Bellin, *The Demon of the Continent*; Schechter, "Feminist Historiography," 153–66.

37. Tyrrell, *Woman's World/Woman's Empire*, 340n52; Izumi Ishii, "Cherokee Women and the WCTU," in Garrison and O'Brien, *The Native South*, 194. See also Ishii, *Bad Fruits*.

38. Ishii, *Bad Fruits*, 146, 147, 148.

39. Cahill, *Federal Fathers and Mothers*, 6–7, 49–50.

40. Schechter, "Feminist Historiography," 154; Gordon, *Women Torch-Bearers*, 115; Tyler, *Where Prayer and Purpose Meet*, 275. Schechter's claim seems most accurate for Mrs. Glenn G. [Agnes Dubbs] Hays, *Heritage of Dedication*, which, in my reading, does not mention Indian work at all.

41. Marsden, *Fundamentalism*, 165–67.

Chapter 1

1. Carrie Kendall Easterly, "First Annual Report for the Suffrage Department of the WCTU," *Eighteenth Annual Meeting, WCTU, Indian Territory Year Book, 1905–6*, Ardmore, September 21–25, 1905 (Wewoka: Seminole Printing, 1905), 58, in Lilah Denton Lindsey Papers, McFarlin Library, University of Tulsa (hereafter ML).

2. "Corrections," *WCTU-US*, May 9, 1895, 9.

3. Tennie Fuller, "Indian Territory," *WCTU-US*, July 8, 1897, 11.

4. Lilah Denton Lindsey, "Second Interview," 12357, interview by Effie S. Jackson, December 7, 1937, University of Oklahoma University Libraries Western History Collections, 182, 183, http://digital.libraries.ou.edu/cdm/ref/collection/indianpp/id/5213. See also Linda D. Wilson, "Lindsey, Lilah Denton," *The Encyclopedia of Oklahoma History and Culture*, http://www.okhistory.org/publications/enc/entry.php?entry=LI008.

5. Lindsey, "History," 1:1–2, February 9, 1918.

6. See "Editorial Comment," and Dorcas Spencer, "Indians and Prohibition," *American Indian Magazine* 4, no. 4 (October–December 1916): 280–81, 311–14, https://babel.hathitrust.org/cgi/pt?id=mdp.39015012189679;view=1up;seq=199; Dorcas Spencer, "Work Among the Indians," *WCTU-US*, May 27, 1915, 10.

7. Lindsey, "History," 1:4–5.

8. Joy A. Bilharz, "Cornplanter," in Barrett and Markowitz, *American Indian Biographies*, 112–15.

9. Spencer, "Superintendents: Work Among Indians," *WCTU-US*, June 6, 1911, 10.

10. Rorabaugh, *Alcoholic Republic*, 39–46; Mary Allen West, "Sketch of Benjamin Rush," *WCTU-US*, September 3, 1885, 3–4.

11. Kunitz and Levy, *Drinking Careers*, 239. For a look at the complex of genetic factors related to alcoholism, see Ehlers, Liang, and Gizer, "ADH and ALDH Polymorphisms." Ehlers et al. also argue against any general genetic propensity to drink or to become alcoholics. See also Gill, Eagle Elk, Liu, and Deitrich, "An Examination of ALDH2 Genotypes."

12. Hill, *Native American Drinking*, 30–37.

13. Fenton, *The Great Law and the Longhouse*, 219, 221.

14. "... Lies Ill on the Couch Awaiting the End," *Syracuse Herald*, [1904?], Jairus Pierce, Onondaga Individuals, Native Americans, Vertical Files, Onondaga Historical Association, Syracuse, NY (hereafter JP -OI-NA-VF-OHA). Jairus Pierce's name is alternatively spelled Jaris and Jarius in different sources.

15. "Indian Sage Dies at Home on Reservation," *Syracuse Journal*, February 16, 1923, JP -OI-NA-VF-OHA.

16. "May Leave the Church: Jarius Pierce of Reservation Has Two Squaws and May Be Disciplined," newspaper clipping, August 5, 1900, JP -OI-NA-VF-OHA.

17. "Kn-nosh-i-o-ni [sic] Lodge I.O.G.T.," *Syracuse Journal*, June 24, 1879; Kimbert, "The Only Indian WCTU."

18. Fahey, *Temperance and Racism*, 8, 12–13, 16, 19.

19. "Whisky Brings Grief to the Red Man," *WCTU-US*, September 18, 1913, 9.

20. Clemmer, "The Confederated Tribes of Warm Springs, Oregon," 152; Stowell, *Faces of a Reservation*; Philips, *Invisible Culture*; Wendt, "An Administrative History."

21. Mrs. E. C. Warren, "Report of Superintendents of Young Women's Work," *Minutes of the Seventh Annual Meeting of the WCTU of Oregon*, Salem, May 22–25, 1889 (Portland: David Steel, 1889), 54, Multnomah County Library, Portland, Oregon (hereafter MCL).

22. L. A. Nash, "Oregon," *WCTU-US*, June 23, 1892, 11.

23. Kants, "Letter from Our Indian Sisters," May 16, 1895, 9.

24. Kants, "Letter from Our Indian Sisters," May 16, 1895, 38. See also "Missionary Meeting," *Albany Daily Democrat* (Albany, OR), May 25, 1915, 1, https://www.newspapers.com/image/92907944/?terms=Jeanette%2Balter.

25. Helen Crawford, "90 Year Highlights: Oregon WCTU" (n.p.,1973), 5, Oregon Historical Society (hereafter OHS); "Minutes, State of Oregon WCTU," May 21, 1896, 34, 42, Minute Book 1894–1897, MSS 2535, Folder 1, Box 1, WCTU of Oregon Records, OHS.

26. Kants, "Letter from Our Indian Sisters," May 16, 1895, 37.

27. Emma Graves Dietrick, "A Prophetic Banner," *WCTU-US*, July 9, 1914, 13. This banner or a facsimile is located in the Six Nations Museum, Onchiota, NY.

28. Cook, "Earnest Christian Women"; Erickson, "Making King Alcohol Tremble"; Gordon, *Juvenile Work Questions*.

29. On the WCTU promotion of LTLs in Indian country, see Dorothy J. Cleveland, "Plan of Work for Indian Schools," *WCTU-US*, February 8, 1900, 13–15; "Corresponding Secretary's Notes," *WCTU-US*, February 6, 1902, 10. On the Onondaga LTL, see "New York," *WCTU-US*, March 26, 1903, 12.

30. "Notes," *WCTU-US*, May 21, 1903, 7. See also "New York," *WCTU-US*, July 2, 1903, 15.

31. *WCTU-US*, July 2, 1903, 15; personal communication with Perry Ground, a relative of Marvin Crouse; "LTL Notes," *Woman's Temperance Work* 22 (June 1905).

32. Snow, *The Iroquois*, 168.

33. Alfred, *Peace, Power, Righteousness*, 17.

34. Cook, "Earnest Christian Women," 249–67; Erickson, "Making King Alcohol Tremble," 333–52; Gordon, *Juvenile Work Questions*.

35. Prucha, *Indian Peace Medals*, 59. See also Pickering, *Peace Medals*.

36. Spencer, "Work Among Indians," *WCTU-AMM*, 1908, 235.

37. Laura E. Harsha, "Indian Territory: Faint Yet Worth Pursuing," *WCTU-US*, March 26, 1891, 12.

38. Laura E. Harsha, "Indian Territory," *WCTU-US*, May 21, 1891, 11. Ellen K. Denny was an important organizer in Indian Territory. She spent another month in Indian Territory in 1892. She witnessed the expansion of beer saloons in the wake of the court decision. See "Annual Convention Report," *WCTU-US*, November 17, 1892, 8–9.

39. "News in a Nutshell," *WCTU-US*, January 7, 1892, 11.

40. "A Day School Opened," *WCTU-US*, January 28, 1892, 12.

41. Tennie M. Fuller, "Indian Territory," *WCTU-AMM*, 1892, 221–22. In the minutes, Ellen K. Denny is misspelled as "Ellen R. Denney."

42. Pascoe, *Relations of Rescue*, xx, 34.

43. Johnson, *A Shopkeeper's Millennium*, 108.

44. Tarango, *Choosing the Jesus Way*, 3–7.

45. Marsden, *Fundamentalism*, 67, 167–68.

46. The records of students are sparse before February 24, 1886, because of a fire at Tunesassa that destroyed the school building and the record books. The books were reconstructed from memory, according to a note in the file folder, AA47, Philadelphia Yearly Meeting, Special Collections, Haverford College Library (hereafter PYMIC). "Records of Indian Children, 1888," PYMIC. Lydia Jackson's entry in the school roster lists her tribe as "O" for Onondaga, with no additional information. Her Seneca father, Jesse Jackson, attended school with the Quakers. It appears that her Onondaga mother, Lucy Jackson, was not literate. She signed the 1890s Kansas land claim document with a mark, not her signature. "New York Indians," No. 1218, 63678, Received November 11, 1901, Kansas Claim, National Archives.

47. Lydia Jackson to Carrie Brackman, March 1890, AA 47, PYMIC.

48. Lydia Jackson, "Memories of Our Fathers," January 1879, AA65: Friends' Indian School (Tunesassa) Student Essays, PYMIC. Portions of this work have been previously published in Thomas J. Lappas, "*Tunesassa Echoes* and the Temperance Struggle."

49. D. Sherman, "New York Indian Agency," October 14, 1879, in United States, *Annual Report of the Commissioner of Indian Affairs, 1879*, 124, https://babel.hathitrust .org/cgi/pt?id=mdp.39015009313555;view=1up;seq=204.

50. Benjamin Casler, "New York Indian Agency," October 13, 1882, in United States, *Annual Report of the Commissioner of Indian Affairs, 1882*, 133, https://babel.hathitrust .org/cgi/pt?id=mdp.39015009334189;view=1up;seq=219.

51. Mrs. J. Hendrick, "Cattaraugus County," *WCTU-US*, May 1, 1884, 11.

52. "New York," *WCTU-US*, September 2, 1886, 10. The article refers to her as Mrs. Theodore Perkins; Theodore Perkins was married to Frances Emily Smith Perkins, of Canandaigua, New York. "WCTU of Canandaigua," *Democrat and Chronicle* (Rochester, NY) December 7, 1883, 3, https://www.newspapers.com/image/135145766/?terms =%22Mrs.%2BTheodore%2BPerkins%22.

53. Frances W. Graham, County Corresponding Secretary, "Niagara County Convention," *WCTU-US*, April 18, 1889, 11. See also Frances Willard, "White-Ribboners of Texas and Indian Territory," *WCTU-US*, May 23, 1889, 10.

54. W. E. Yurans, "Report of Erie County," *WCTU-US*, October 9, 1890, 11–12.

55. E. S. T. Darte, "Cattaraugus County," *WCTU-US*, October 23, 1890, 11.

56. Frances W. Graham, "New York State Convention," *WCTU-US*, November 5, 1891, 10.

57. A. W. Ferrin, "Report of the Agent in New York," August 31, 1894, in United States, *Annual Report of the Commissioner of Indian Affairs, 1895*, 215, https://babel .hathitrust.org/cgi/pt?id=mdp.39015034627870;view=1up;seq=229.

58. Frances W. Graham, "New York," *WCTU-US*, May 10, 1894, 12.

59. J. R. Jewell, US Indian Agent. "Report of the Agent in New York," September 1, 1896, in United States, *Annual Report of the Commissioner of Indian Affairs, 1896*, 222–23, https://babel.hathitrust.org/cgi/pt?id=hvd.tz1n6t;view=1up;seq=237.

60. Marian G. Peckham, "Work Among Indians," *Report of the Thirty-Fifth Annual Meeting of the New York State WCTU*, 133–34 (coverless, 1908), Frances Willard Memorial Library and Archives, Evanston, Illinois (hereafter FWMLA); Emma Graves Dietrick, "Was It Worth While?" *WCTU-US*, August 29, 1912, 11; "The Annual Convention of the Six Nations," *WCTU-US*, October 27, 1910, 11; Marian G. Peckham, "New York," *WCTU-AMM*, 1910, 210.

61. Marian G. Peckham, "New York," *WCTU-AMM*, 1910, 210.

62. "Minutes," *WCTU-AMM*, 1908, 71; Wallace, *Death and Rebirth*, 241; Dennis, *Seneca Possessed Indians*, 69–70, 85, 86.

63. Dorcas Spencer, "The Indians' Outlook," *WCTU-US*, September 24, 1908, 5; Spencer, "The Indians' Appeal," *WCTU-US*, March 23, 1911, 5. Thanks to Leslie Dunlap for pointing me to the image reproduced as figure 7.

64. Graham, *Four Decades*, 21, 112.

65. Emma Graves Dietrick, "Was It Worth While?" *WCTU-US*, August 29, 1912, 11.

66. Dorcas Spencer, "Work Among Indians," *WCTU-AMM*, 1914, 151.

67. "Indians Declare for National Constitutional Prohibition," *WCTU-US*, January 29, 1914, 13.

68. This presence of Christianity had solid precedent in Iroquois society. In writing on "The Mohawk Saint" Kateri Tekakwitha, Nancy Shoemaker notes that similarities between the Jesuits' Catholicism and Haudenosaunee beliefs aided the

conversion process: "Similarities between Christianity and Iroquois religious beliefs . . . made syncretism possible." Christianity also aided Tekakwitha in gaining some power within the Native community. Shoemaker adds, "Some women may have in similar moments called upon the symbols of Christianity to assert their own identity and authority within the native community." Similarly, the WCTU offered Pierce an avenue for solving problems within Native communities. Shoemaker, *Negotiators of Change*, 58, 51.

69. "Interesting Event Among the Indians—Organization of a Good Templars Lodge," *Journal*, October 30, 1877, TM- VF-OHA; "Ko-nosh-i-o-ni Lodge, I.O.G.T.," *Journal*, June 24, 1879, TM- VF-OHA. In 1887 Oronhyateka/Peter Martin became Worthy Counselor of the Grand Templars, the organization's position akin to vice president. Fahey, *Temperance and Racism*, 10–11, 84–85, 147. In 1935, the year before she died, Pierce converted to Catholicism. "Services Held for Indian, 97," *Post-Standard*, October 1, 1936, JP -OI-NA-VF-OHA.

70. "New York," *WCTU-US*, May 1, 1884, 11.

71. Kimbert, "The Only Indian WCTU."

72. "Corresponding Secretary's Data," *WCTU-AMM*, 1901, n.p.

73. Eliza Pierce died in 1936, at the age of ninety-seven. Other places suggest the year of her birth as 1845, but the preponderance of coverage in the Syracuse papers and other places refer to the 1839 date. "Services Held for Indian, 97," *Syracuse Post-Standard*, October 1, 1936, 2, JP -OI-NA-VF-OHA. For an apparently erroneous age, see "Indian Woman, 85, Prefers to Walk When She Travels," *Post Standard*, January 4, 1931, JP -OI-NA-VF-OHA. "Indian Girl Reared in Lyon Family Has Had Successful Life," newspaper clipping [1916?], JP-OI-NA-VF-OHA.

74. "Indian Sage Dies at Home on Reservation," *Syracuse Journal*, February 16, 1923, JP-OI-NA-VF-OHA; "May Leave the Church," newspaper clipping, August 5, 1900, JP-OI-NA-VF-OHA.

75. "An Indian's Two Wives," newspaper clipping, June 30, 1886, JP-OI-NA-VF-OHA.

76. "Lies Ill on Couch, Awaiting the End," *Post Standard* (Syracuse), January 21, 1904, JP-OI-NA-VF-OHA. The newspaper is untitled in OHA; but Newspapers.com indicates date and title of paper: https://www.newspapers.com/image/9073677/?terms =%22Lies%2BIll%2Bon%2Bcouch%22.

77. For coverage and images of Jaris Pierce, see Fred Ryther Wolcott, *Onondaga: Portrait of a Native People* (Syracuse, NY: Syracuse University Press, 1986), 29, 50, 72, 85. For Jaris Pierce as opponent of allotment, see *Syracuse Journal*, March 24, 1882, 1.

78. "Old Indian War Dance of the Onondagas," *Post-Standard*, January 12, 1902, JP-OI-NA-VF-OHA; "Indian Sage Dies at Home on Reservation," *Syracuse Journal*, February 16, 1923, JP-OI-NA-VF-OHA; "Iroquois in Council," *Post-Standard*, October 11, 1890, TM-NA-VF-OHA.

79. Joanne Shenandoah, epigraph, in Mankiller, *Every Day Is a Good Day*, xxvii.

80. Thanks to John Gibson, genealogist for the Onondaga Nation for pointing out that Charlotte Thompson is the name of David Billings's wife. Personal email communication, October 29, 2012.

81. Lis Pendens, May 6, 1911, *Lydia George et al. vs. Eliza Pierce*, Onondaga County Courthouse; *George et al. vs. Pierce et al.*, 85 Misc. Rep. 105, 148 N.Y. Supp. 230 (1914);

Wilis Edgar Heaton, *The Procedure and Law of Surrogates' Courts of the State of New York* (Albany, NY: n.p., 1921–1922), 253–54; Pound, "Nationals without a Nation."

82. Graham, *Four Decades*, 21, 112.

83. "Congress Beer," *Post-Standard*, September 1, 1914, 13; Henry W. Schramm, *Empire Showcase: A History of the New York State Fair* (Utica, NY: North Country Books, 1985), 93; Anne S. D. Bates, "Fair Work Pays," *WCTU-US*, October 27, 1898, 5.

84. Susanna M. D. Fry, "Active Opposers of Scientific Temperance Instruction Laws," *WCTU-US*, March 6, 1902, 2–3; Hiram Price to WCTU, *WCTU-AMM*, 1881, cxxix. See also *WCTU-AMM*, 1894, 46–47; *WCTU-AMM*, 1895, 211–13.

85. Kimbert, "The Only Indian WCTU"; "Signal notes," *WCTU-US*, January 6, 1887, 15; *WCTU-AMM*,1881, cxxix.

86. Lindsey, "Indian Territory WCTU," 1:8, 9.

87. Lindsey, "History," 1:9, 10, 11.

88. Lindsey, "History," 1:12, 19, 20, 20. Gordon shared and Lindsey transcribed excerpts from *Union Signal* issues February 24, 1884, and December 23, 1886.

89. Lindsey, "History," 2:2, 3, 4.

90. Mathes, *Divinely Guided*, 153–76.

91. Jacobs, "Resistance to Rescue," 235–39.

92. Jacobs, "Resistance to Rescue," 233.

93. E. M. Priddy, "Indian Work," in *Twelfth Annual Report of the WCTU of California*, 1891 Oakland, October 13–16, 1891 (San Francisco: Herald of Trade Publishing, 1891), 125, 127, also 89–90, Annual Reports of the WCTU of [Northern] California]], California State Library, Sacramento (hereafter CSL). See also wife of Rev. W. B. Priddy of the Methodist Episcopal Church. "WCTU," *Ukiah Daily Journal*, 23 May 1890, 3, https://www.newspapers.com/image/31318371/?terms=W.B.%2BPriddy/. The "come over and help us" motto—dubbed the "Macedonian Cry"—came from the Macedonians' pleas that Paul heard in a dream in Acts 16:9. The motto was on the seal of the Massachusetts Bay Colony to emphasize the missionary mandate of the colony. It was used to reinforce evangelical efforts among churches in the nineteenth and twentieth centuries. See also "Rites Planned for Pioneer Teacher," *Oakland Tribune*, March 9, 1933, 9, https://www.newspapers.com/image/106449673/?terms=%22W.B.%2BPriddy%22.

94. Annie Bidwell, "Diary," Sunday, January 5, 1902, Folder 8, Box 6, Annie Ellicot Kennedy Bidwell Papers, California State University Chico (hereafter CSUC). For more on Quincy Lee Morrow, see "Pasadena Brevities," *Los Angeles Times*, January 23, 1902, 17, https://www.newspapers.com/image/380108838/?terms=Quincy%2BLee%2Bmorrow.

95. Bidwell, "Diary," January 12, 1902, Folder 8, Box 6, CSUC.

96. Bidwell, "Diary," January 21, 1902, Folder 8, Box 6, CSUC.

97. Bidwell, "Diary," January 23, 1902, Folder 8, Box 6, CSUC.

98. Bidwell, "Diary," January 25, 1902, Folder 8, Box 6, CSUC.

99. Bidwell, "Diary," January 26, 1902, Folder 8, Box 6, CSUC.

100. Superintendent of Indian Work Ada Campbell, "Indian Work," *Twenty-Fourth Annual Report of the WCTU of California, 1903*, San Francisco, October 19–23, 1903 (San Francisco: Salvation Army Print, 1903), 58, Bancroft Library, Berkeley, California (hereafter Bancroft). The county of Mendocino Work Among Indians superintendent was Mrs. M. B. Glavier of Ukiah.

101. Dorcas Spencer, "A Remarkable Conference," *WCTU-US*, September 19, 1907, 1. For Zayante, see also Mathes, *Divinely Guided*, 136, 140–45.

102. Bidwell, "Diary," December 21, 29, 1907, Folder 4, Box 7, CSUC. For baptisms, see Bidwell, "Diary," May 27, 1906, Folder 3, Box 7, CSUC.

103. Bidwell, "Diary," March 24, 1909, Folder 6, Box 7, CSUC.

104. Martha G. Tunstall to Frances E. Willard, December 31, 1885, in *WCTU-US*, March 25, 1886, 2. Her claim for an allotment was rejected. "Dawes Commission," *Muskogee Phoenix*, October 29, 1896, https://www.newspapers.com/image/5730616/?terms=Martha%2BG.%2BTunstall. See also "Petition of the National Woman's Suffrage Association to the Democratic Party in Nominating Convention Assembled," June 22, 1880, *Official Proceedings of the National Democratic Convention*, Cincinnati, June 22–24, 1880 (Dayton: Daily Journal Book and Job Room, 1882), 126–27, https://books.google.com/books?id=RdhAAQAAMAAJ&lpg=PA127&ots=3ypzPBJw2A&dq=Martha%20Tunstall%20suffrage&pg=PA126#v=onepage&q=Martha%20Tunstall%20suffrage&f=false.

105. Tarango, *Choosing the Jesus Way*, 7–8.

Chapter 2

1. Shoemaker, *Negotiators of Change*, 194–95; Perdue, *Cherokee Women*, 63, 77, 85, 191–95.

2. *WCTU-AMM*, 1877, n.p.

3. "Death of 'Aunt Tildy' Closes Half Century of Work Among Indians," *Miami News Record*, Sunday July 29, 1928, 1, https://www.newspapers.com/image/5710187/?terms=%22Joseph%2BWind%22.

4. Emeline Tuttle, "Indian Territory," *WCTU-AMM*, 1879, 53–54. See also Unrau, *Indians, Alcohol*, 4–7, 36–56.

5. J. M. Haworth, "Quapaw Agency, Indian Territory to the Commissioner of Indian Affairs," August 27, 1879, in United States, *Annual Report of the Commissioner of Indian Affairs, 1879*, 77–78, https://babel.hathitrust.org/cgi/pt?id=hvd.tz1nx7;view=1up;seq=147.

6. A. C. Tuttle to Women's [*sic*] National Temperance Union, October 26, 1879, in *WCTU-AMM*, 1879, 162–63.

7. "Indian Territory," *WCTU-AMM*, 1880, 92.

8. A. J. Birrell, "D. I. K. Rine and the Gospel Temperance Movement in Canada," *Canadian Historical Review* 58, no. 1 (March 1977): 24. Birrell credits Francis Murphy, a recovering alcoholic and devout jailhouse convert, with starting the Gospel Temperance movement in the 1870s. Murphy encouraged a legion of acolytes who traveled through the northeastern United States and eastern Canada getting converts to sign a temperance pledge and devote their lives to abstinence. Gospel Temperance was common among the Umatilla in Oregon and the Nez Perce in Washington. "Successful Gospel Temperance Meetings among Indians," *WCTU-US*, April 11, 1907, 12.

9. "Indian Territory," *WCTU-AMM*, 1880, 92.

10. Another person, Bettie Taylor (also Cherokee) was also involved, but it is not clear if she was an officeholder. Frances E. Willard, "Notes from Indian Territory," *WCTU-US*, November 29, 1883, 10.

11. Katie Ellett, "Indian Territory," February 21, 1884, *WCTU-US*, 11. Katrina Lois Ellett married Rev. Joseph S. Murrow of Atoka in 1888. "Will Preach to Old Soldiers, Rev. Joseph Samuel Murrow Distinguished Mason and Missionary, Here Today," *Daily Ardmoreite* (Ardmore, OK), July 27, 1913, 9, https://www.newspapers.com/image /171636755/?terms=Katie%2BEllett%2Band%2BMurrow.

12. "Departments and Superintendents," *WCTU-US*, April 16, 1885. Archer was well educated (studying law), and spoke at a Normal Institute convention in Nashville, impressing the author. Ada Archer was also secretary of the Indian International Fair Association. See "Cherokee Visitors," *Daily American* (Nashville), July 29, 1884, 5, https://www.newspapers.com/image/118995876/?terms=Ada%2Barcher.

13. "Indian Territory," *WCTU-US*, December 23, 1886, 11. See also Martha G. Tunstall to WCTU in *WCTU-US*, March 25, 1886, 2.

14. "Motions," *WCTU-AMM*, 1887, 64. See also "Indian Territory," *WCTU-AMM*, 1887, 116.

15. Martha G. Tunstall, "An Indian Woman to Her People," *WCTU-US*, February 17, 1887, 7.

16. *WCTU-AMM*, 1887, 116.

17. Mrs. J. A. Rogers, "Indian Territory: Interesting Notes," *WCTU-US*, March 17, 1887, 10–11.

18. "Saturday Session," *WCTU-US*, December 1, 1887, 19–20.

19. Martha G. Tunstall to *Union Signal*, "A Plea from Our Indian Sister," November 30, 1887, in *WCTU-US*, January 5, 1888, 5.

20. "Mrs. M. G. Tunstall, President of Indian Territory," *WCTU-US*, February 16, 1888, 1.

21. Mary E. Griffith to *Union Signal*, June 13, 1888, in *WCTU-US*, June 21, 1888, 5.

22. Sarah M. Perkins, "Lo! The Poor Indians," *WCTU-US*, July 26, 1888, 4.

23. Julia A. Rogers, "Work of Mrs. Perkins," *WCTU-US*, August 30, 1888, 11; Sarah M. Perkins, "Lo! The Poor Indians," *WCTU-US*, July 26, 1888, 4.

24. Francis Willard, "White Ribboners of Texas and Indian Country," *WCTU-US*, May 23, 1889, 10.

25. Kunitz, Levy, and Andrews, *Drinking Careers*, 4–5, 100.

26. "Local Liquor Men Met and Organized," *Salamanca Republican Press*, December 3, 1914, 5.

27. Lydia Pierce, "Work Among Indians," *New York State Report*, 1915, 105, FWMLA.

28. Marian G. Peckham, "Work Among Indians," *Report of the Thirty-Sixth Annual Meeting of the New York State WCTU*, 206–7, FWMLA.

29. Jewett, *Town and City*, 221.

30. Jewett, *Town and City*, 221.

31. Spencer, "Work Among Indians," *WCTU-US*, June 29, 1911, 10.

32. "Indians Declare for National Constitutional Prohibition," *WCTU-AMM*, January 29, 1914, 13.

33. "Executive Committee Report," *New York State Report, 1914*, 22, FWMLA; "Work Among Indians," *New York State Report, 1914*, 137–38, FWMLA; *WCTU-US*, September 12, 1912, 11.

34. Pierce, "From an Indian to Indians."

35. Pierce, "From an Indian to Indians."

36. Richard W. Hill Sr., "Regenerating Identity: Repatriation and the Indian Frame of Mind," in *Archaeology of the Iroquois: Selected Readings and Research Sources*, ed. Jordan E. Kerber (Syracuse: Syracuse University Press, 2007), 420.

37. Pierce, "From an Indian to Indians."

38. "Since Our Last Issue," *WCTU-US*, September 24, 1891, 1. See also *WCTU-US*, October 1, 1891, 1.

39. Population Statistics, https://www2.census.gov/prod2/decennial/documents /1907pop_OK-IndianTerritory.pdf. The white population went from 172,554 (in 1890) to 670,204 (1900) to 1,226,930 (1907). The Indian population remained relatively static, 64,456 (1890) to 64,445 (1900) to 75,012 (1907). Oklahoma Territory's white population went from 62,300 (1890) to 367,524 (1900) to 688,418 (1907); Indian population went from 13,177 (1890) to 11,945 (1900, a decrease) to 13,087 (1907). Indian Territory white population went from 110,254 to 302,680 to 538,512; Indian population went from 51,279 to 52,500 to 61,925.

40. "How I Felt When Statehood Came," (transcript) Folder 15, Box 1: Writings, Series IV, Lilah Denton Lindsey Papers, ML.

41. Jane Stapler, "Indian Territory: Annual WCTU Convention," *WCTU-US*, July 24, 1890, 10. Delegates included Mrs. Fite, Mrs. Thompson, and Miss Lobe of Tahlequah; Miss Reed of Atoka; Mrs. Harsha, Mrs. Bolander, Mrs. Long, and Mrs. Spaulding of Muskogee Union. Officers listed. Murrow and Fuller were elected as delegates to the national convention in Georgia.

42. Jane Stapler, "Address of President of Indian Territory to National Convention," *WCTU-AMM*, 1890, 390.

43. Jane Stapler, "Address of President of Indian Territory to National Convention," *WCTU-AMM*, 1890, 390.

44. Sarah Ford Crosby, "Indian Territory," *WCTU-US*, May 5, 1892, 10.

45. Sarah Ford Crosby, "Indian Territory: Convention Notes," *WCTU-US*, June 16, 1892, 12.

46. T. J. Morgan, "Sale of Liquor to Indians," in United States, *Annual Report of the Commissioner of Indian Affairs, 1891*, 74, https://babel.hathitrust.org/cgi/pt?id=mdp .39015024886684;view=1up;seq=86. See also "Judge Bryant," *WCTU-US*, August 20, 1891, 1; "Territory Imbibers," and "Beer Joints in the Territory," *Fort Worth Gazette*, Thursday, August 13, 1891, 1, www.newspapers.com/image/83550027/?terms=Judge%2 BBryant%2BParis%2BTexas%2BBeer; "Beer for Ardmore," *Our Brother in Red* (Muskogee, IT) August 15, 1891, 1, https://www.newspapers.com/image/30441299/?terms =United%2BStates%2Bv.%2BKahn%2Bbeer%2Bindian%2Bterritory; "Beer in Indian Territory," *New York Times*, September 13, 1891, https://search-proquest-com.ezproxy .naz.edu/hnpnewyorktimes/docview/94873903/fulltextPDF/FC4682549ED944E5PQ/1 ?accountid=28167. For ideas by Thomas Morgan on changing language, see "The Red Men," *New York Times*, September 12, 1891, https://search-proquest-com.ezproxy.naz .edu/hnpnewyorktimes/docview/94861166/FC4682549ED944E5PQ/2?accountid =28167. See "Editorial," *New York Times*, February 6, 1892, 4, https://search-proquest-com .ezproxy.naz.edu/hnpnewyorktimes/docview/1016062636/fulltextPDF/5A2F85939 4994D04PQ/10?accountid=28167.

47. Tennie M. Fuller, "Indian Territory," *WCTU-AMM*, 1892, 221–22.

48. *US Statutes at Large* 27 (1892) in Martin, "'The Greatest Evil,'" 47.

49. "From Mrs. Jane Stapler," *WCTU-US*, August 11, 1892, 12.

50. Tennie M. Fuller, "Indian Territory," *WCTU-AMM*, 1893, 169.

51. Sarah Ford Crosby, "Indian Territory," *WCTU-US*, January 12, 1893, 11.

52. "At South McAlester," *WCTU-US*, December 6, 1894, 6.

53. "Another veteran," *WCTU-US*, April 4, 1895, 1.

54. Kimbert, "The Only Indian WCTU," 27.

55. Baker, *The Moral Frameworks of Public Life*, 64.

56. Lindsey, "History," February 9, 1918.

57. Kants, "Letter from Our Indian Sisters," May 16, 1895, 37–38.

58. "Corresponding Secretary's Report," *WCTU-AMM*, 1895, 153; Jeanette Alter, "Indians and Temperance," *WCTU-US*, August 26, 1895, 3.

59. William J. Dowell, untitled draft, *Tulsa World*, in Folder 18, Box 2, Series III, Lilah Denton Lindsey Papers, ML.

60. Prucha, *The Great Father*, 527–33.

61. "Mrs. L. Adair," *WCTU-US*, March 4, 1886, 3.

62. Lindsey, "American Citizenship" Folder 2, Box 1: Writings, Series IV, Lilah Denton Lindsey Papers, ML.

63. Callahan, "Wynema," 271.

64. Callahan, "Wynema," 272. Craig S. Womack lambastes Callahan for her "failure to engage Creek culture, history, and politics" and sees Wynema as being "most useful as a document of Christian supremacy and assimilation." He acknowledges multiple Creek perspectives on topics like Creek Christianity and economics, recognizing that there were (and are) Creek pastors, but he criticizes Callahan for primarily using white heroes and heroines. Craig S. Womack, "Alice Callahan's *Wynema*: A Fledgling Attempt," in *Red on Red: Native American Literary Separatism* (Minneapolis: University of Minnesota Press, 1999), 107.

65. Frances Willard, "Cherry View of Our Present Situation: Our Work in the East," *WCTU-US*, March 10, 1887, 4. See also Coward, *Newspaper Indian*, 211; Deloria, *Indians in Unexpected Places*, 25.

66. Frances Willard, "Cherry View of Our Present Situation: Our Work in the East," *WCTU-US*, March 10, 1887, 4–5. See also Mathes, and Lowitt. *The Standing Bear Controversy*, 84–89, 187–91.

67. C. P. Luse, "White Earth Agency," September 1, 1882, in United States, *Annual Report of the Commissioner of Indian Affairs, 1882*, 96–98.

68. I. F. McClure, "Work Among Indians," *Minutes of the Thirtieth Annual Meeting of the WCTU of the State of Minnesota*, September 18–21, 1906 (Minneapolis: Thurston and Gould, 1906), 74–75, Minnesota History Center, St. Paul (hereafter MHC). Alternatively spelled Onigen and Orrigan in WCTU literature, the actual location is Onigum. Thanks to Mattie Harper, program and outreach manager, Native American Initiatives at Minnesota History Center for clarifying the location of Onigen/Orrigan/Onigum on Leech Lake. Email message to author, July 30, 2018.

69. Dorcas Spencer, "Work Among Indians," *WCTU-US*, June 1, 1916, 11.

70. Hauptman, "Senecas and Subdividers"; "Bill to Divide Senecas' Land," *Post Standard*, September 14, 1914. Thanks go to Michael Oberg for indicating allotment as a potential factor in Pierce's decision-making.

71. "Aliens at Reservation," newspaper clipping, April 30, 1901, TM-VF-OHA; Kimbert, "The Only Indian WCTU."

72. "New Mexico's First State WCTU Convention," *WCTU-US*, October 20, 1911, 2; also 3, 14. See also Jacobs, "Clara True," 100.

73. "Resolutions," *Report of the Indian Territory's WCTU, Sixteenth Annual Meeting*, Tahlequah, September 2–4, 1903, n.p., Proceedings of the Annual Convention of Indian Territory Woman's Christian Temperance Union, Oklahoma History Center, Oklahoma City (hereafter OHC).

74. "Resolutions," *Report of the WCTU, Sixteenth Annual Meeting*, Tahlequah, September 2–4, 1903, n.p., OHC.

75. Mary E. Fowler, "Work Among Indians," *Report of the WCTU of Southern California*, San Diego, June 13–16, 1916, 85, Southern California *WCTU* (hereafter SOCAL).

76. Charles Hill, "Temperance," August 19, 1888, in United States, *Annual Report of the Commissioner of Indian Affairs, 1888*, 173, https://babel.hathitrust.org/cgi/pt?id=osu .32435024007973;view=1up;seq=269.

77. Julia Fraser, "The Hupa Indian Story," *WCTU-US*, October 5, 1905, 5–6.

78. Dorcas Spencer, "Superintendents: Work Among Indians," *WCTU-US*, June 29, 1911, 10.

79. Fowler, "Work Among Indians," *Year Book of the WCTU of Southern California*, Long Beach, May 23–27, 1911, 83, SOCAL.

80. "Resignation of Chief Special Officer William E. Johnson," *White Ribbon Ensign*, November 1911, 5, Bancroft.

81. "Resignation of Chief Special Officer William E. Johnson," *White Ribbon Ensign*, November 1911, 5, Bancroft.

82. K. L. E. Murrow, "Questions and Replies," *Eighteenth Annual Meeting, WCTU, Indian Territory Year Book, 1905–6*, 63, Lilah Denton Lindsey Papers, ML.

83. Murrow, "Questions and Replies," 63–64.

84. Murrow, "Questions and Replies," 64–65.

85. Lillian M. N. Stevens, "Indian Territory to the Fore," *WCTU-US*, April 26, 1906, 3–4, 15.

86. "Minutes of the Executive Meeting," April 26–27, 1906, in *Official Proceedings of the 19th and 20th Annual Meetings of the WCTU of Indian Territory, Afton, October 26–30, 1906, and Tulsa, October 16–20, 1907* (Wewoka: Seminole Printing, 1907), 11, Proceedings of the Annual Convention of Indian Territory WCTU, OHC.

87. "Minutes of the Executive Meeting," April 26–27, 1906, in *Official Proceedings of the 19th and 20th Annual Meetings*, 20.

88. Mary T. Cranston, "Minutes of October 18, 1907," in *Official Proceedings of the 19th and 20th Annual Meetings*, 24–25.

89. K. L. E. Murrow, "Work Among Indians," *Official Proceedings of the 19th and 20th Annual Meetings*, 50.

90. Mabel Sutherland, "State President's Letter," *The Helper*, September 1907, 1, ML.

91. "Executive Committee," *WCTU of Oklahoma, Proceedings of Seventeenth Annual Convention*, Norman, September 19–21, 1906 (Oklahoma City: Manly Office Supply, 1906), 14, University of Oklahoma University Libraries, Western History Collections, Norman.

92. Mrs. William E. Currah, "WCTU Corresponding Secretary's Report, 1904," *Montana WCTU Voice,* November 1904, 14–15, Montana Historical Society Archives, Helena (hereafter MHS).

93. "Missoula," *Montana WCTU Voice,* December 1904, 3, MHS.

94. Lindsey, "History"; Special Correspondent, "Oklahoma and Indian Territory Unions Are United," *WCTU-US,* October 8, 1908, 12. See also "Official Roster," *Report of the WCTU of Oklahoma, Shawnee Oklahoma,* September 27–29, 1911 (Shawnee), 3, Proceedings of the Annual Convention of the State of Oklahoma WCTU, OHC.

95. On September 18, 1908, the meeting was called to order by Hutchinson, the "National Representative and State President of Kansas," and the purpose was the merger. In January 1908 at the executive meeting, Lindsey and Hillerman created plans for the merger of the unions. In the Indian Territory "President's Address" Lindsey initiated the merger at the national convention in Nashville. *Minutes and Year Book of Indian Territory WCTU and Oklahoma Territory WCTU and WCTU of The State of Oklahoma, Muskogee and Oklahoma City, 1908* (Muskogee: Muskogee Printing, 1908), 31, 80–92, Proceedings of the Annual Convention of the State of Oklahoma WCTU, OHC.

96. Mary Clark, "Report of the Comanche County Superintendent of Indians and Soldiers," *Minutes and Year Book of Indian Territory WCTU and Oklahoma Territory WCTU and WCTU of The State of Oklahoma,* 1908, 130.

97. Margaret Dye Ellis, "Our Washington Letter: Indians Appeal for Protection," *WCTU-US,* March 9, 1911, 3; Minges, *Slavery in the Cherokee Nation,* 3.

98. Margaret Dye Ellis, "Our Washington Letter: Indian Lands Seized by Grafters," *WCTU-US,* May 8, 1913, 2.

99. *Report of the WCTU of Oklahoma,* Guthrie, September 24–25, 1913, 2–4, Proceedings of the Annual Convention of the State of Oklahoma WCTU, OHC.

100. Bidwell, "Diary," January 28, 1902, Folder 8, Box 6, CSUC.

101. Lora S. La Mance, "The Empire State Out for Victory," *WCTU-US,* November 1, 1917, 15. See also Genetin-Pilawa, *Crooked Paths to Allotment,* 80–83.

Chapter 3

1. Jackson, *Century of Dishonor: The Early Crusade,* 10–11, 13, 17.

2. Bordin, *Woman and Temperance,* 85.

3. Frances Willard, "Annual Address," *WCTU-AMM,* 1877, 138.

4. Frances Willard, "Report of Committee on Work Among the Indians, Chinese, and Colored People," *WCTU-AMM,* 1880, 61–62.

5. Willard, *Woman and Temperance,* 504.

6. Utley, *The Indian Frontier,* 129–56; Prucha, *The Great Father,* 501–33.

7. Prucha, *The Great Father,* 538.

8. Willard, *Woman and Temperance,* 505.

9. Willard, *Woman and Temperance,* 509. In 1880 Hayt was ousted and replaced by Rowland Trowbridge, temporarily. The position was filled by Hiram Price in 1881. Prucha, *The Great Father,* 585–86.

10. Many progressive white women became fond of casting Sacajawea as one of what Patricia Schechter has dubbed native helpers, "figures who engaged with and

reinterpreted the workings of colonial institutions like schools and hospitals in their own and their community's interest." Schechter, "Feminist Historiography," 156.

11. Gordon, *Women Torch-Bearers*, 29.

12. Mann, *Sacajawea's People*, xv–xvii, 16.

13. Most historians agree that Sacajawea died in 1812, shortly after giving birth to a child. Eva Emery Dye's novel *The Conquest: The True Story of Lewis and Clark*, published in 1902, on the eve of the centennial of the Lewis and Clark expedition, began to reinvigorate interest in Sacajawea and triggered a wave of mythmaking. Progressive Era suffragists, keen on reform-minded literature with Indian motifs, picked up on this newly resurrected tale. Grace Hebard, University of Wyoming professor, trustee, and booster for the state, disseminated a theory that Sacajawea had fled her unhappy marriage and returned to her Shoshone people at the Wind River Reservation in Wyoming, where she died in 1884. Hebard's most thorough defense of the later death date was not published until 1933. Suffragists picked up on the potential of Sacajawea as inspiration to other women. The National American Women's Suffrage Association commissioned sculptor Alice Cooper to produce a statue of Sacajawea that was placed in Washington Park in Portland, Oregon, in 1905. See Thomas Hoevet Johnson and Helen S. Johnson, *Also Called Sacajawea*, 15; Hebard, *Sacajawea*. Sacajawea was likely related to the Lemhi Shoshone, not the Eastern Shoshone of the Wind River Reservation. See Mann, *Sacajawea's People*, xviii–xix; Martin, "The Greatest Evil," 82; "Sacajawea Historical Society: Historical Landmarks," http://www.sacagawea-biography.org/historical-landmarks.

14. "Sakakawea: The First Feminist," *Western Womanhood* 17, nos. 10–12 (December 1913): n.p., State Historical Society of North Dakota, Bismarck (hereafter SHSND).

15. Jackson, *Century of Dishonor: The Early Crusade*, 10–11; Banner, *How the Indians Lost Their Land*, 28–29; Robertson, *Conquest by Law*, 119.

16. Mathes, *Helen Hunt Jackson*, xi, xvi, 6–7, 11–12.

17. Jackson, "Winnebagoes," "The Sioux," and "The Cheyennes," in *Century of Dishonor: A Sketch*, 227, 141, 69, https://babel.hathitrust.org/cgi/pt?id=c00.319240880 25006;view=1up;seq=9.

18. Jackson, Appendix V, "Report on the Condition and Needs of the Mission Indians of California," in *Century of Dishonor: The Early Crusade*, 459, 463–64, https://babel .hathitrust.org/cgi/pt?id=c00.31924088025006;view=1up;seq=9.

See also Mathes and Brigandi, *Call for Reform*. Thanks to Mathes for pointing out the limitations of Jackson's anti-alcohol views. Email communication, January 30, 2019.

19. Jackson, *Ramona*, 92, 290.

20. Margaret E. Parker, "Mrs. Margaret E. Parker in Southern California," *WCTU-US*, April 7, 1887, 9.

21. Margaret Spencer, "Helen Hunt Jackson, 'H.H.,'" *WCTU-US*, October 25, 1888, 10.

22. Margaret Spencer, "Helen Hunt Jackson, 'H.H.,'" *WCTU-US*, October 25, 1888, 10.

23. S[amuel] H. Comings, "Savagery vs. Christianity—'Competition' v. 'Mutualism,'" *WCTU-US*, August 10, 1893, 3. See also Comings and Comings, *Industrial and Vocational Education*.

24. Thomas J. Lappas, "Native American 'Philanthropy': Family and Giving in Lakota Communities," in *Notable American Philanthropists: A Biographical Encyclopedia of Giving and Volunteering*, ed. Robert Grimm (Westport, CT: Greenwood and Oryx Press, 2002), 5–9.

25. E. M. Priddy, "Indian Work," *Twelfth Annual Report of the WCTU of California*, 1891, 125.

26. "Signal Notes," *WCTU-US*, March 23, 1893, 18.

27. Frances Willard, "Editorial Correspondence," *WCTU-US*, April 30, 1896, 4, 11.

28. Frances Willard, "Editorial Correspondence," *WCTU-US*, April 30, 1896, 4, 11. See also Jon D. May, "'The Most Ferocious of Monsters': The Story of Outlaw Crawford Goldsby, Alias 'Cherokee Bill,'" *Chronicles of Oklahoma* 77 (Fall 1999), 272–89.

29. Matilda B. Carse, "Temperance Temple Items," *WCTU-US*, March 26, 1891, 5.

30. Matilda B. Carse, "Temperance Temple Items," *WCTU-US*, March 17, 1892, 6.

31. Laura E. Harsha, "President's Address," *Report of the Indian Territory WCTU, Sixteenth Annual Meeting, Held at Tahlequah*, Indian Territory, September 2, 3, and 4, 1903, Proceedings of the Annual Convention of Indian Territory WCTU, OHC; Schechter, "Feminist Historiography," 154.

32. Abbie B. Hillerman, "President's Letter," *Oklahoma Messenger*, November 1907, 3, Lilah Denton Lindsey Papers, ML.

33. Mary Johnson, "Stillwater, September 28–30, State Convention, 1909," *Oklahoma Messenger*, October 1909, 5, Lilah Denton Lindsey Papers, ML.

34. Martha Gilmore "Literature Report," and K. L. E. Murrow, "The Evangelistic and Missionary Work Among Fullblood Indians," both in *Indian Territory 1903 Convention*, Proceedings of the Annual Convention of Indian Territory WCTU, OHC.

35. Laura E. Harsha, "Indian Territory," *WCTU-US*, December 10, 1891, 10.

36. Bidwell, "Diary," August 3, 1902, Folder 8, Box 6, CSUC.

37. "A Dark Picture of Intemperance," *WCTU-US*, September 22, 1883, 1.

38. Prucha, *The Great Father*, 685–86.

39. "And Now It Is the Indians Who Are to Have the Ballot," *WCTU-US*, February 5, 1885, 1.

40. Helen M. Gougar, "Woman Suffrage in South Dakota," *WCTU-US*, December 11, 1890, 5. "Pugilist Sullivan" was John L. Sullivan (1858–1918), a notorious drunk and the last of the bare-knuckled boxers, the first of the glove champions. Isenberg, *John L. Sullivan*, 51–53.

41. B. Sturtevant-Peet, "Annual Presidential Address," *Twelfth Annual Report of the WCTU of California*, 1891, 56–57.

42. "Indians and Women," *Southern California White Ribbon*, July 1899, 4, SOCAL.

43. "Indians Enfranchised but Women Ballotless," *North Dakota White Ribbon*, September 1916, 4, SHSND.

44. Fowler, "Work Among Indians," *Year Book of the WCTU of Southern California*, San Diego, June 4–7, 78, SOCAL.

45. "Annual Report of Superintendent of Legislation and Petition," *WCTU-AMM*, 1884, 86.

46. Fowler, "Work Among Indians," *Year Book of the WCTU of Southern California*, 1911, 83.

47. Fowler, "Work Among Indians," *Year Book of the WCTU of Southern California*, 1911, 83.

48. Nettie C. Hall, "Stray Bits from Nebraska," *WCTU-US*, November 20, 1890, 10–11.

49. Prucha, *The Great Father*, 437–47; Utley, *The Indian Frontier*, 76–81; Jackson, *A Century of Dishonor: The Early Crusade*, 152–78; Schultz, *Over the Earth I Come*.

50. "The following extract," *North Dakota White Ribbon*, January 1891, 5, SHSND; Nancy Tystad Koupal, "Marietta Bones: Personality and Politics in the South Dakota Suffrage Movement," in Johnson, ed., *Feminist Frontiers*, 69–82. For the Ghost Dance, see Demallie and Parks, *Sioux Indian Religion*, 8; Mooney, *The Ghost Dance Religion*, 843–87.

51. "A Pathetic Craze," *WCTU-US*, November 27, 1890, 1.

52. "General Miles Has Relieved General Forsyth," *WCTU-US*, January 8, 1891, 1; "An Indian War Is Virtually Ended," *WCTU-US*, January 22, 1891, 1.

53. "A Reminiscence and an Interview," *WCTU-US*, March 26, 1891, 9.

54. Coward, *The Newspaper Indian*, 161. For a more sympathetic portrayal of Sitting Bull, including his role as protector of his people and medicine man, see Utley, *The Lance and the Shield*.

55. Reverend E. B. Tre Fethren, "The Government Fair at Fort Yates, North Dakota," *WCTU of South Dakota, Minutes of the Twenty-Eighth Annual Convention*, Madison, September 20–24, 1916 (Rapid City: Rapid City Journal Print, 1916), 77–78, SHSND.

56. "Fear Is Entertained," *Pacific Ensign*, October 13, 1892, 1, Bancroft; "Four Cowboys Were Killed," *Pacific Ensign*, February 3, 1893, 1, Bancroft.

57. Deloria, *Indians in Unexpected Places*, 36–45.

58. "Sioux City does not allow," *WCTU-US*, August 13, 1891, 1.

59. "The plan of the Guajira Indians," *Pacific Ensign*, February 9, 1893, 4, Bancroft.

60. Dorcas Spencer, "Football from an Indian's Point of View," *WCTU-US*, December 28, 1905, 4.

61. De Koven Brown, "Indian Workers for Temperance," *White Ribbon Ensign*, May 1912, 1, Bancroft; Edwin Eels, "Report of Puyallup Agency," August 26, 1892, in United States, *Annual Report of the Commissioner of Indian Affairs, 1892*, 499, https://babel.hathitrust.org/cgi/pt?id=mdp.39015034627862;view=1up;seq=497.

62. Mrs. George Hill, "The Evil of the Liquor Traffic in Its bearing on the Success of Missionary Work," *WCTU-US*, April 30, 1885, 4–5.

63. "Signal Notes," *WCTU-US*, October 12, 1893, 14.

64. Mrs. E. J. Davis, "Riverside County Convention," *Southern California White Ribbon*, November 1894, 2, SOCAL. Mrs. E. J. Davis of Riverside, California, was Martha Davis, who, in 1897, filed a complaint for divorce from her husband after he was accused of rape by Mrs. Anita Moore. See "Two Sensational Complaints Filed against E. J. Davis," *Los Angeles Times*, October 10, 1897, 33, https://www.newspapers.com/image/380191437/?terms=%22Martha%2BDavis%22%2Briverside.

65. Susan S. Winans, "Industrial School and Temperance in Sitka, Alaska," *WCTU-US*, May 16, 1889, 7.

66. "Signal Notes," *WCTU-US*, August 3, 1893, 16.

67. "At Home," *WCTU-US*, September 9, 1897, 2.

68. "An Indian Outbreak," *WCTU-US*, October 13, 1898, 2; "Lo! The Poor Indian," *WCTU-US*, October 20, 1898, 9.

69. Deloria, *Indians in Unexpected Places*, 21–23.

70. Mrs. George Archibald, "A Postponed Thanksgiving," *WCTU-US*, November 28, 1889, 6; "The First Thanksgiving," *WCTU-US*, January, 27, 1902, 7.

71. Bradford and Winslow, *Mourt's Relation*, 130–35.

72. "The New World Invites the Old," *WCTU-US*, October 3, 1881, 1.

73. "Columbus and What He Found," *WCTU-US*, April 13, 1893, 17.

74. Amos B. Wells, "Wanted, Other Columbuses," *WCTU-US*, May 4, 1893, 3.

75. "Recent Results," *WCTU-US*, October 27, 1898, 1.

76. Wilbur F. Crafts, "The Question of Life and Death to Nations," *WCTU-US*, November 24, 1898, 4.

77. "Hiawatha the Great," *WCTU-US*, June 4, 1900, 7.

78. "News in a Nutshell," *WCTU-US*, December 15, 1892, 18.

79. Ellen L. Merriman, "Wineka: The Indian Girl's Rebuke," *WCTU-US*, March 5, 1885, 7. See also Trachtenberg, *Shades of Hiawatha*.

80. "The Red Man's Greeting," *WCTU-US*, August 24, 1893, 12; Simon Pokagon, "The Red Man's Rebuke (1893)" in Peyer, *American Indian Nonfiction*, 234.

81. "Signal Notes," *WCTU-US*, November 23, 1893, 20.

82. Carlos Montezuma, "The Indian of Tomorrow," *WCTU-US*, July 1, 1909, 5.

83. "America First as Usual: This Time an American Indian," *White Ribbon Ensign*, November 1927, 8, CSL.

84. For Morris Sheppard's role in prohibition, see McGirr, *The War on Alcohol*, 11–12.

85. Morris Sheppard, "Ancient History," *White Ribbon Ensign*, May 1930, 3, CSL.

Chapter 4

1. "Annual Meetings Oklahoma Territory," *Minutes and Yearbook of Indian Territory WCTU and Oklahoma Territory WCTU and WCTU of the State of Oklahoma, 1908*, 105, *Proceedings of the Annual Convention of Indian Territory WCTU*, OHC; Kracht, *Religious Revitalization among the Kiowas*, 152–67.

2. "Oklahoma: Flowers and Breezes," *WCTU-US*, April, 28, 1892, 10; Cahill, *Federal Fathers and Mothers*, 45; "Oklahoma: Flowers and Breezes," *WCTU-US*, April, 28, 1892, 10.

3. Sue Uhl Brown, "Oklahoma," *WCTU-US*, December 1, 1892, 12. See also D. B. Dyer, "Cheyenne and Arapaho Agency," August 9, 1884, in United States, *Annual Report of the Commissioner of Indian Affairs, 1884*, 74, https://babel.hathitrust.org/cgi/pt?id=mdp.39015034627771;view=1up;seq=140.

4. Other elected officials included vice president, Florence White (Claremore); corresponding secretary, Allenette Cook (Vinita); recording secretary Dell Lago (Muscogee); treasurer Laura Harsha (Muskogee). "Indian Territory," *WCTU-US*, June 20, 1895, 11. See also Chapin, *Thumb Nail Sketches*, 34. For meeting frequency and descriptions, see *WCTU-US*, August 8, 1895.

5. "News in a Nutshell," *WCTU-US*, May 16, 1895, 12. See also Chapin, *Thumb Nail Sketches*, 60.

6. "Tahlequah, Indian Territory," *WCTU-US*, February 13, 1896, 12.

7. Mrs. M. L. Hunter, "Indian Territory," *WCTU-US*, June 4, 1896, 10.

8. Mrs. M. L. Hunter, "Indian Territory," *WCTU-US*, August 6, 1896, 11.

9. "Corresponding Secretary's Report: Indian Territory," *WCTU-AMM*, 1896, 96.

10. "Minutes of the National WCTU, Post-executive Meeting," *WCTU-AMM*, 1896, 51.

11. "Corresponding Secretary's Report," *WCTU-AMM*, 1897, 191. See also "WCTU News," *WCTU-US*, June 10, 1897, 6.

12. Tennie Fuller, "Indian Territory," *WCTU-US*, July 8, 1897, 11.

13. "Current Events," *WCTU-US*, December 16, 1897, 4.

14. Tennie Fuller, "Indian Territory," *WCTU-US*, April, 21, 1898, 11.

15. Allenette Cook, "Corresponding Secretary's Report: Indian Territory," *WCTU-AMM*, 1898, 108.

16. Lulu Jones, "Indian Territory," *WCTU-US*, February 9, 1899, 14.

17. Tennie Fuller, "Indian Territory," *WCTU-US*, May 18, 1899, 11.

18. Nannie E. Oliver, "Indian Territory," *WCTU-US*, October 19, 1899, 9.

19. Minutes of the NWCTU, "Corresponding Secretary's Report," *WCTU-AMM*, 1899, 25.

20. "Indian Territory," *WCTU-AMM*, 1899, 130. See also Carolyn Thompson Foreman, "Laura E. Harsha," *Chronicles of Oklahoma* 18 (2): 182–84, https://cdm17279 .contentdm.oclc.org/digital/collection/p17279c0114/id/6515/rec/1.

21. Dorothy Cleveland, "Oklahoma Territory Report," *WCTU-AMM*, 1899, 136.

22. "Work Among Indians," *WCTU-US*, January 18, 1900, 9.

23. Dorothy Cleveland, "Plan of Work for Indian Schools," *WCTU-US*, February 8, 1900, 14, 15.

24. Dorothy Cleveland, "Plan of Work for Indian Schools," *WCTU-US*, February 8, 1900, 15.

25. Dorothy Cleveland, "Oklahoma Territory Report," *WCTU-AMM*, 1900, 134.

26. Susannah Fry, "Corresponding Secretary's Report," *WCTU-AMM*, 1900, 120.

27. "Petition to President Theodore Roosevelt," *WCTU-AMM*, 1901, 66–67.

28. "Petition to President Theodore Roosevelt," *WCTU-AMM*, 1901, 66–67.

29. "Department Appropriations," *WCTU-AMM*, 1901, 36, 178, 180. Lake lived in Chicago until around 1900. See "Meaning of Purity," *Buffalo Morning Express and Illustrated Buffalo Express*, October 28, 1897, 7, https://www.newspapers.com/image /345181075/?terms=%22Mrs.%2BLake%22%2BWCTU.

30. Dorothy Cleveland, "Work Among Indians," *WCTU-AMM*, 1902, 227–28. *Twentieth Annual Report of the WCTU of Southern California, Los Angeles, June 3–6, 1902* (Los Angeles: Commercial Printing House, 1902), 28, SOCAL. The closest extant record of Oregon's state WCTU—the 1903 minutes located in the Oregon Historical Society—lists no specific state department of work among Indians. See *Report of the Twenty-First Annual Convention of the WCTU of Oregon, Salem, October 20–23, 1903* (Albany, OR: R. A. Brodie, 1903), 3–4, OHS.

31. Leavitt and Sargeant, *Lillian M. N. Stevens*, 16, http://pds.lib.harvard.edu/pds /view/2582388?n=8&s=4&printThumbnails=no&oldpds.

32. Spencer, *A History*, 11–18. Mrs. A. B. Dibble is likely Emma Allen Dibble, who married A. B. Dibble in Grass Valley in 1854. See Oscar Tully Shuck, ed., *History of the Bench and Bar of California* (Los Angeles: Commercial Printing House, 1901), 549, https://books.google.com/books?id=t-lYAAAAMAAJ&lpg=PA549&ots =SJFGEvJjOi&dq=A.B.%20Dibble&pg=PA549#v=onepage&q=A.B.%20Dibble&f =false; Dibble's husband was judge Alfred Barrett "A.B." Dibble.

33. Gullett, *Becoming Citizens*, 18.

34. Spencer, *A History*, 99.

35. Leavitt and Sargeant, *Lillian M. N. Stevens*, 10.

36. Spencer, *A History*, 39–45, 138. The state paper was originally called *The Bulletin*. The editors changed its name to *The Pharos* since there was a competing paper known as *The Bulletin*.

37. Spencer, *A History*, 49.

38. Spencer, *A History*, 130. For more on Taber and M. E. Chase, see Cathleen D. Cahill, "Making and Marketing Baskets in California," in Mathes, *The Women's National Indian Association: A History*, 126–49.

39. R. R. Johnston, "Address of the President: Indian Work," 59, in *Tenth Annual Report, WCTU of California, 1889* (San Francisco: Bacon, 1889), Bancroft.

40. Spencer, "Organizer's Report," 146, in *Tenth Annual Report, WCTU of California, 1889* (San Francisco: Bacon, 1889), Bancroft.

41. Anna E. Chase, "Corresponding Secretary's Report," *Twenty-Fourth Annual Report of the WCTU of California, 1903* (San Francisco: Salvation Army Print, 1903), 34–35, Bancroft.

42. Ada Campbell, "Indian Work," *Twenty-Fourth Annual Report of the WCTU of California, 1903* (San Francisco: Salvation Army Print, 1903), 58, Bancroft; also Alice M. Bowman, "Loyal Temperance Legion," 47–48.

43. "Watch Tower," *WCTU-US*, August 15, 1889, 9.

44. Spencer, "The Indian's Outlook," *WCTU-US*, September 24, 1908; "Native Leadership," in Hans J. Hillerbrand, *Encyclopedia of Protestantism*, 4 vols. (London: Routledge, 2014), 3:1561–62. Leaflets from the Literature Department on Native Americans include numbers 403–6. No. 403 is the pamphlet biography of James Hayes. Lewis, *Creating Christian Indians*, 61.

45. "Plan of Work," *Minutes of the First Annual Convention of the Western Washington WCTU, Seattle, Washington, June 18–19, 1884* (Seattle: C. Hanford, 1884), 40; *Minutes from the Second Annual Convention of the Western Washington WCTU, in the Puget Sound Sanitarian and Prohibitionist, July 1885*, 82–83, both in WCTU Records, University of Washington, Special Collections, Allen Library, Seattle (hereafter UW). "Mrs. B. A. Hill" is undoubtedly Jane Hill, listed in the *U.S. Register of Civil, Military, and Naval Service*, as "assistant teacher" at Puyallup in 1875, directly below "Rev. B. A. Hill," whose occupation is listed as "teacher." Mrs. B. A. Hill was "in charge of the Indian School at Nooksack Crossing" in 1884. See the *U.S. Register of Civil, Military, and Naval Service, 1863–1959* (Washington, DC: Government Printing Office, 1876), 1:370, https://www.ancestry.com/interactive/2525/40411_1821100517 _0804-00393?pid=2346689&treeid=&personid=&rc=&usePUB=true&_phsrc =pb1244&_phstart=successSource; "Rev. B. A. Hill and wife," *Seattle Post Intelligencer*, December 18, 1884, 2, https://www.newspapers.com/image/333849633/?terms =%22Rev.%2BB.A.%2BHill%22. Mrs. H. S. Parkhurst is Harriet E. Parkhurst, wife of Rev. Henry S. Parkhurst. See also https://www.findagrave.com/memorial/5232387 /henry-s.-parkhurst; "Lodge and Church Entertainments," *Seattle Post Intelligencer*, August 16, 1896, 9, https://www.newspapers.com/image/333167434/?terms=%22Harriet %2BE.%2BParkhurst%22.

46. Myrtle McMillen, *History of East Washington's WCTU, 1883–1953, Seventieth Anniversary* (1953?), 19–20, MS 68, Folder 20, Box 3, WCTU Records, Northwest

Museum of Art and Culture, Eastern Washington State Historical Society, Spokane. See also *Report of the Thirty-Second Annual Meeting of the WCTU of East Washington, Colfax, September 18–October 1, 1915* (Cole Printing, 1915), 3, in WCTU Records, Northwest Museum of Art and Culture, Eastern Washington State Historical Society, Spokane. For more on Mrs. A. P. Crystal, see Engle, "Benefiting a City," 125n385, 161, 163. For general issues of assimilation, allotment, and resistance, see Hayes, "Colville Indians."

47. Jno. W. Bubb, "Report of the Colville Agency," August 24, 1891, in United States, *Annual Report of the Commissioner of Indian Affairs, 1894,* 314, https://babel.hathitrust .org/cgi/pt?id=mdp.39015034627870;view=1up;seq=328.

48. *Minutes of the Twelfth Annual Convention of the Western Washington WCTU, Olympia, June 4–7, 1895* (Seattle: Homer M. Hill Publishing, 1895), 27, WCTU Records, UW. Regarding sharing the minutes of East Washington with West Washington, see *Minutes of the Thirteenth Annual Convention of the Western Washington WCTU, Seattle, June 9–12, 1896,* 11, WCTU Records, UW; "Signal Notes," *WCTU-US,* October 12, 189, 143.

49. Gwydir and Dye, *Recollections from the Colville Indian Agency,* 19, also Appendix 1, "Annual Report to the Commissioner of Indian Affairs, 1887," 116–19.

50. Carrie M. White, "Presidential Address," *Report of the Third Annual Convention of the WCTU of Western Washington, Tacoma, June 16–18, 1886* (Tacoma: News Publishing, 1886), 21, WCTU Records, UW. Mary J. Milroy is listed only as "Mrs. Milroy," but this is undoubtedly Mary Milroy, wife of General Robert Huston Milroy. See "Mrs. Mary J. Milroy," *Tacoma Times,* February 24, 1904, 3, https://www.newspapers .com/image/68043179/?terms=%22Mary%2BJ.%2BMilroy%22.

51. Roberts, "Swinomish Tribal Community," 257.

52. Myron Eells, "Justice to the Indian, read before the Congregational Association of Oregon and Washington, July 14, 1883," in *Collected Writings of Myron Eells* (Portland: Himes, 1878–?), 39, 39–40, 44, in Robert Hitchman Collection, UW. See also *Report of the Fourth Annual Convention of the WCTU of Western Washington, Seattle, June 22–24, 1887* (Seattle: Press Steam Book and Job Print, 1887), n.p., WCTU Records, UW; Michael J. Paulus Jr., "Myron Eells Dies on January 4, 1907, and Leaves His Historical Collections to Whitman College," October 18, 2007, http://historylink .org/File/8336.

53. *Minutes of the Fifth Annual Convention of the WCTU of Western Washington, Laconner, June 20–21, 1888* (Seattle: Times Printing and Publishing, 1888), 5–8, WCTU Records, UW.

54. *Proceedings of the Sixth Annual Convention of the WCTU of Western Washington, Port Townsend, June 12 and 14, 1889* (Tacoma: Puget Sound Printing, 1889), n.p., WCTU Records, UW; "Puget Sound Conference," *Annual Report of the Board of Indian Commissioners for the Year 1890* (Washington, DC: Government Printing Office, 1891), https://archive.org/stream/annualreportboa59commgoog/annualreportboa59commgo og_djvu.txt.

55. Mary Bynon Reese, "West Washington," *WCTU-US,* June 16,1892, 4. See also "West Washington," *WCTU-US,* November 11, 1892, 8.

56. *Minutes of the Tenth Annual Convention of the Western Washington WCTU, Puyallup, June 6–8, 1893* (Seattle: Review Printing, 1893), 4, WCTU Records, UW.

57. "Report of Corresponding Secretary," *Minutes of the Eleventh Annual Convention of the Western Washington WCTU, Chehalis, WA, June 5–8, 1894* (Seattle: Review Printing, 1894), 32–33, WCTU Records, UW. Eliza C. Sulliger was, as of 1896, president of the Woman's Home Missionary Society of Puget Sound Conference of the Methodist Episcopal Church and was on the "Bureau for Indian and Frontier Work" with H. C. McCabe. "Puget Sound Conference," *Fifteenth Annual Report of the Board of Managers of the Woman's Home Missionary Society of the Methodist Episcopal Church, for the Year 1895–96* (1896), 161–62, https://babel.hathitrust.org/cgi/pt?id=wu.89077187623;view =1up;seq=9.

58. Eliza C. Sulliger, "Report of Indian Work," *Report of the Fourteenth Annual Meeting of the WCTU of Western Washington, June 29–July 2, 1897, Vancouver, Washington* (Seattle: Homer M. Hill Publishing, 1897), 50, WCTU Records, UW.

59. Eliza C. Sulliger, "Work Among Indians," in *Minutes of the Fifteenth Annual Convention of the West Washington WCTU, June 14–17, 1898, Centralia* (Centralia: Chronicle Press, 1898), 35, WCTU Records, UW.

60. Sulliger, "Work Among Indians," in *Minutes of the Fifteenth Annual Convention, 1898,* 35, WCTU Records, UW. For a more critical view of Whipple's assimilationist views, see George Tinker, "Henry Benjamin Whipple: The Politics of Indian Assimilation," in *Missionary Conquest: The Gospel and Native American Cultural Genocide* (Minneapolis: Fortress Press, 1993), 95–111.

61. "Bureau for Indian and Frontier Work," *Twentieth Annual Report of the General Board of Managers of the Woman's Home Missionary Society of the Methodist Episcopal Church for the Year 1900–1901* (Cincinnati: Western Methodist Book Concern Press, 1901), 120, https://babel.hathitrust.org/cgi/pt?id=wu.89077187706;view =1up;seq=122. "Mrs. Eliza C. Sulliger Dead," *Stafford County Republican* (Stafford, Kansas) February 23, 1911, https://www.newspapers.com/image/422210402/?terms =Sulliger%2C%2BOregon.

62. A. L. Dyer Lawrence, "Work Among Indians," *Twenty-Second Annual Meeting of the WCTU of West Washington, Aberdeen, October 22–26, 1905,* 57, WCTU Records, UW. See also Wilkins, *American Indian Sovereignty,* 121–23.

63. Dotty DeCoster, "LaConner Quilt and Textile Museum," posted October 17, 2011, http://www.historylink.org/File/9875.

64. Roberts, "Swinomish Tribal Community," 248–49.

65. "The Indian L.T.L.," *White Ribbon Bulletin,* December 1907, 3. See also H. B. D., "L.T.L. Column," *White Ribbon Bulletin,* September 1907, 3, both in Washington State Historical Society, Tacoma.

66. A. L. Dyer Lawrence, "Work Among Indians," *Report of the Twenty-Sixth Annual Meeting of the WCTU of West Washington, Puyallup, September 24–28, 1909,* 69–70, WCTU Records, UW.

67. M. J. Jennings, "Skagit County," *White Ribbon Bulletin,* July 1908, 2.

68. Thanks to Joshua Zimmerman of the Seattle Archdiocese for this information. D. R. Rhodes to Dr. Charles Buchanan, November 9, 1910; Bishop of Seattle, Edward John O'Dea to Charles H. Buchanan, December 28, 1910; Bishop of Seattle, John O'Dea to Rev. Charles O'Brien, December 28, 1910, all in RG700—Swinomish, St. Paul— Correspondence, General 133/3 Archives of the Archdiocese of Seattle, Washington.

69. Roberts, "Swinomish Tribal Community," 257.

70. "Signal Notes," *WCTU-US*, May 16, 1901, 16.

71. A. L. Dyer Lawrence, "Work Among Indians," *Twenty-Sixth Annual Meeting of the WCTU of West Washington, Puyallup, September 24–28, 1909*, 69–70, WCTU Records, UW.

72. "Skagit County," *White Ribbon Bulletin*, August 1909, 8, Washington State Historical Society, Tacoma; "State Superintendents" and "Skagit County," *Report of the Twenty-Seventh Annual Meeting of the WCTU of West Washington, Olympia, September 30–October 4, 1910*, 6, 20–21, WCTU Records, UW; "Loyal Temperance Legion," *Report of the Twenty-Eighth Annual Meeting of the WCTU of West Washington, Seattle, September 25–19, 1911*, 67–68, WCTU Records, UW; Rhoda Gaches, "Work Among Indians," *Report of the Twenty-Ninth Annual Meeting of the WCTU of West Washington, Burlington October 1–4, 1912*, 81, WCTU Records, UW.

73. Rev. Alice Barnes Hoag and Mrs. Matthew W. Alderson, *Historical Sketch of the Montana WCTU, 1883–1912* (Helena: State Publishing, 1912), 13, MHS.

74. The Montana WCTU's journalistic history was complicated. Prior to 1903, Montana was one of the states that published in the *Northwest White Ribboner*, a multi-state paper along with Oregon, and West and East Washington. See *Northwest White Ribboner*, November 1900, MHS. From 1903 until 1907 it had its own state paper. See *WCTU Voice*, November 1903, MHS. In 1907 the Montana WCTU began copublishing the *Real Issue* with the state Good Templars and Anti Saloon League. "Report of the Editor of Voice given. It recommended that the Montana W.C.T.U. continue the publication of its organ—the *Voice*—in connection with the I.O.G.T., as a department of the *Real Issue*. Report adopted." *Minutes of the Twenty-Fifth Annual Convention of the Montana WCTU*, Helena, October 13–14, 1908, 6, MHS. See also the *Real Issue*, "Official State Paper of the Good Templars, Anti Saloon League, and the WCTU," *Real Issue*, October 20, 1907, MHS. This paper lasted until at least 1910. See the *Real Issue*, December 1, 1910, MHS. In 1913 "the convention voted that the state should have its own paper again and made Rev. Hoag editor. We had been using space in 'The Real Issue' and 'Union Signal' for a few years." Alderson, *Historical Sketch*, 9. See *The Woman's Voice*, December 1913, MHS.

75. Anna A. Walker, "Fort Shaw Government School," *Montana WCTU Voice*, June 1904, 11–13, MHS. She gave a report at the convention in October, which was reported in *Montana WCTU Voice*, November 1904, 11, MHS; "Thursday Afternoon," *Montana WCTU Voice*, November 1905, 11, MHS.

76. "Thursday Afternoon," *Montana WCTU Voice*, November 1905, 11, MHS.

77. "Rev. Mrs. Barnes Resigns," *Montana WCTU Voice*, February 1906, 4, MHS; "Program," *Montana WCTU Voice*, September 1906, 1, MHS.

78. *Minutes of the Twenty-Fifth Annual Convention of the Montana WCTU, Helena, October 13–14, 1908*, 6–7, MHS.

79. Alice Barnes Hoag, "President's Address," *Report of the Twenty-Sixth Annual Convention of the Montana WCTU, Hamilton, Montana, August 10–12, 1909* (Helena: State Publishing, 1909), 10, 27, MHS; *Montana WCTU Minutes of the Twenty-Seventh Annual Convention, Billings, October 11–13, 1910* (n.p.: Raegale Publishing, 1910), 8, MHS.

80. *Third Annual Report of the WCTU of Southern California, 1885, Los Angeles* (Los Angeles: Commercial Printing House, 1886), 3, SOCAL; *Sixth Annual Report of the*

WCTU of Southern California, 1888 (Los Angeles: Commercial Printing House, 1888), 5, 80, SOCAL.

81. S. Whitmore, "County Report: San Diego County," 49, in *Seventh Annual Report of the WCTU of Southern California, 1889*, Huntington Library, San Marino, California (hereafter HL).

82. Fowler, "Work Among Indians," 76. See also "San Diego County," 70, both in *Seventh Annual Report of the WCTU of Southern California, 1889*, HL.

83. Fowler, "Work Among Indians," *Southern California White Ribbon*, November 1890, 3–4, HL.

84. "Indian Territory," *WCTU-US*, April 1, 1897, 11.

85. Spencer, "Indian Council," *White Ribbon Ensign*, January 1914, 5, Bancroft.

86. Spencer, "Work Among Indians: California (North)," *WCTU-AMM*, 1916, 185.

87. Spencer, "American Indians Make Good Citizens," *WCTU-US*, January 20, 1916, 13.

88. Spencer, "American Indians Make Good Citizens," *WCTU-US*, January 20, 1916, 13. See also Spencer, "Work Among Indians," *WCTU-AMM*, 1916, 184–85; Danver, "Metlakatla."

89. "The Missionary Charts, Home Field," *White Ribbon Ensign*, August 1912, 6, Bancroft.

90. "Perhaps There Is," *WCTU-US*, March 17, 1892, 9.

91. Spencer, "State Correspondence," *WCTU-US*, October 26, 1906, 10.

92. "Zayante Indian Conference of Friends of the Indian," 1906, Mount Hermon, Santa Cruz, California, July 30 and 31, 1906, 2–15, vertical files, folder "Indians General," CSL.

93. Spencer, "A Remarkable Conference," *WCTU-US*, September 19, 1907, 1–2.

94. "The Third Zayante Conference," *Indian's Friend*, September 1908, 2, https://books.google.com/books?id=Y5wyAQAAMAAJ&pg=PA134&lpg=PA134&dq=William+Benson+Ukiah&source=bl&ots=NDwBXk_png&sig=Ohaf0EsjoDshPsvEWH3u38 23uzY&hl=en&sa=X&ved=0ahUKEwjfi_KQ4NvZAhUD71MKHW2RDLYQ6AEIRj AG#v=onepage&q=William%20Benson%20Ukiah&f=false; Spencer, "Conference of Indians and Their Friends," *WCTU-US*, May 21, 1908, 3.

95. Spencer, "The Zayante Indian Conference at Mt. Hermon California," *WCTU-US*, September 30, 1909, 5, 14. Spencer erroneously and oddly refers to this as the fifth Zayante conference. The fifth was in 1910, according to the 1910 Zayante report cover, making 1906 the first.

96. Spencer, "The Indian at Mt. Hermon," *WCTU-US*, September 15, 1910, 2, 14.

97. Sara Dorr, "Presidential Address: Work Among Indians," *Thirty-First Annual Report of the WCTU of California, Berkeley, October 6–11, 1910* (San Francisco: E. L. Mackey, 1910), 5, 32, Annual Reports of WCTU of [Northern] California, CSL; Sarah Dorr, "President's Letter," *White Ribbon Ensign*, February 1911, 2, *White Ribbon Ensign* Collection, CSL.

98. Harry R. Smith, *Apart with Him* (Oakland, CA: Western Book and Tract, 1956), 26–31, http://www.ccel.us/apart.toc.html#2.

99. "The Mohonk Conference," *WCTU-US*, October 6, 1887, 1.

100. Rev. Charles L. Thompson, Presbyterian Board of Missionaries, "Give the Indians a Fair Chance," *WCTU-US*, January 2, 1908, 5.

101. Hon. James Sherman, *Proceedings of the Twenty-Second Annual Meeting of the Lake Mohonk Conference of Friends of the Indian and Other Dependent People*

(New York: Lake Mohonk Conference, 1904), 127, https://babel.hathitrust.org/cgi/pt?id=iau.31858050966427;view=1up;seq=139. See also A. S. McKennon, "The Liquor Problem in Indian Territory," in the same issue, 127.

102. S. M. Brosius, "A Plea for the Northern California Indians," *Proceedings of the Twenty-Second Annual Meeting of the Lake Mohonk Conference of Friends of the Indian and Other Dependent People*, 1904 (New York: Lake Mohonk Conference, 1904), 150–54, https://babel.hathitrust.org/cgi/pt?id=iau.31858050966427;view=1up;seq=139. See also Charles Kelsey, "Providing for the California Indians," *Report of the Twenty-Seventh Annual Meeting of the Lake Mohonk Conferences of the Friends of the Indian and Other Dependent Peoples*, 1909 (New York: Lake Mohonk Conference, 1909), 44, https://babel.hathitrust.org/cgi/pt?id=ucl.b3728481;view=1up;seq=256. Regarding Lake Mohonk and support of schools, see "General Clinton B. Fisk," *WCTU-US*, October 17, 1889, 16. Regarding Lake Mohonk's support for allotment and compulsory education, see "The Recent Lake Mohonk," *WCTU-US*, October 27, 1892, 1.

Chapter 5

1. Fowler, "Work Among Indians," *Southern California White Ribbon*, February 1893, 3, HL.

2. Fowler, "Work Among Indians," *Southern California White Ribbon*, February 1893, 3, HL. According to Horatio N. Rust in 1891, Mary Platt, Pachanga Village, Temecula Reservation, took over an abandoned post and started a temperance society. "Report of Mission Agency," September 10, 1891, in United States, *Annual Report of the Commissioner of Indian Affairs, 1891*, 224, https://babel.hathitrust.org/cgi/pt?id=hvd.tz1nxc;view=1up;seq=236.

3. Fowler, "Work Among Indians," *Southern California White Ribbon*, February 1893, 3.

4. *Fifteenth Annual Report of the WCTU of Southern California, Ventura, June 8–11, 1897* (Los Angeles: Press of T.T. Jones and Son, 1897), iii–xiii, SOCAL.

5. Mary A. Kenney, "President's Address," *Twentieth Annual Report of the WCTU of Southern California, Los Angeles, June 3–6, 1902* (Los Angeles: Commercial Printing House, 1902), 28, SOCAL.

6. Mrs. Prof. F. G. Young, "Report of Superintendents of Young Women's Work," *Minutes of the Seventh Annual Meeting of the WCTU of Oregon, Salem, May 22–25, 1889* (Portland: David Steel, 1889), 54, MCL.

7. *Minutes of the Thirteenth Annual Convention of the WCTU of Oregon, Roseburg, May 15–17, 1895* (Portland: J. F. Gotshall, 1895), 25. See also 4, 9, 12, 25, 34–35, MCL.

8. "Oregon State Convention by Washington Field Editor," *Northwest White Ribboner*, December 1900, 6, MHS. Mrs. M. Fullilove may be Mary E. Fullilove of Portland, Oregon, an African American woman and participant in the African Methodist Episcopal Church in the Northwest. See "Fifteenth Census of the United States,1930 Census," 39, 6B, https://search.ancestry.com/cgi-bin/sse.dll?indiv=1&dbid=6224&h=109761690&tid=&pid=&usePUB=true&_phsrc=pb1340&_phstart=successSource; "African M.E. Conference," *Seattle-Post Intelligencer*, May 23, 1895, 8, https://www.newspapers.com/image/332937529/?terms=%22Mary%2BE.%2BFullilove%22.

9. Fannie McCourt, "Twelfth District," *Thirty-First Annual Report of the Michigan State WCTU, Grand Rapids, June 6–9* (Bay City, MI: Jno. P. Lampert, 1905), 110–11, WCTU Records, 1874–2006, Bentley Historical Library, University of Michigan.

10. Editor, "Twelfth District," *Thirty-Third Annual Report of the Michigan State WCTU, Lansing, 1907* (Bay City, MI: Jno. P. Lampert, 1907), 92, WCTU Records, 1874–2006, Bentley Historical Library, University of Michigan.

11. "Frances E. Willard Memorial Fund," *WCTU-US*, January 19, 1911, 5, 7, 13.

12. "Report of Corresponding Secretary," *North Dakota White Ribbon Bulletin,* October 1910, 3, SHSND.

13. "From the Corresponding Secretary's Annual Report," *North Dakota White Ribbon Bulletin*, October 1911, 4, SHSND.

14. Mrs. I. F. McClure, "Work Among Indians," *Minutes of the Twenty-Sixth Annual Meeting of the WCTU of the State of Minnesota, Redwood Falls, September 15–19, 1902* (Minneapolis: Thurston and Gould, 1902), MHC 78–79, also 17, 24.

15. I. F. McClure, "Work Among Indians," *Minutes of the Twenty-Seventh Annual Meeting, WCTU, Winona, September 25–18, 1903* (Red Wing: Red Wing Advertising, 1903), 62–63, MHC.

16. Louisa Defenbaugh, "Fifteenth District," *Minutes of the Twenty-Seventh Annual Meeting WCTU, Winona, September 25–18, 1903* (Red Wing: Red Wing Advertising, 1903), 80.

17. Mrs. I. F. McClure, "Work Among Indians," *Twenty-Eighth Annual Meeting of the WCTU of the State of Minnesota, Rochester, September 23–27, 1904* (Minneapolis: Thurston and Gould, 1904), 66, MHC. The Thirty-Second District Report suggested that President Scovell help organize the Morton union in September. After Scovell's visit, the union at Morton was officially organized on February 11, 1904. The president was Louisa Hanna, the treasurer and vice president Mrs. D. A. Sherman, and the secretary Mrs. E. B. Sherman. Angie M. Harper, "Thirty-Second District" and "District No. 32," in *Twenty-Eighth Annual Meeting of the WCTU of Minnesota, 1904*, 92, 117.

18. I. F. McClure, "Work Among Indians," *Minutes of the Thirtieth Annual Meeting of the WCTU of the State of Minnesota, September 18–21, 1906* (Minneapolis: Thurston and Gould, 1906), 74–75.

19. I. F. McClure, "Work Among Indians," *WCTU Thirty-First Annual Meeting, Northfield, September 17–19, 1907* (Minneapolis: Thurston and Gould, 1907), 68, MHC.

20. Wilkins, *American Indian Sovereignty*, 121–23.

21. I. F. McClure, "Work Among Indians," *WCTU Thirty-First Annual Meeting, Northfield, September 17–19, 1907* (Minneapolis: Thurston and Gould, 1907), 68, MHC.

22. Mrs. D. W. Longfellow, "Work Among Indians," *Minutes of the Thirty-Third Annual Meeting of the WCTU of the State of Minnesota, Marshall, September 22–25* (location of conference and dates misprinted as 1908 on original cover; 1909 in rest of document) (Minneapolis: Thurston and Gould, 1909), 80, MHC. Myra and Daniel Webster Longfellow had been missionaries to Native Americans. "The Young People's Church," *Star Tribune* (Minneapolis), January 29, 1882, 7, https://www.newspapers.com/image /179049452/?terms=%22Myra%2BC.%2BLongfellow%22.

23. Mrs. D. W. Longfellow, "Work Among Indians," *Minutes of the Thirty-Fourth Annual Meeting of the WCTU of the State of Minnesota, Blue Earth, August 30–September 2, 1910* (Minneapolis: Thurston and Gould, 1910), 83, MHC.

24. "Central Committee Meetings," *Minutes of the Fortieth Annual Meeting of the WCTU of Minnesota, Owatonna, August 22–25, 1916* (Minneapolis: Thurston and Gould, 1916), 27, MHC.

25. Robert G. Valentine, "Law and Order," in United States, *Annual Report of the Commissioner of Indian Affairs, 1912*, 45, https://babel.hathitrust.org/cgi/pt?id=osu .32435064041650;view=1up;seq=51.

26. Clyde Ellis, *A Dancing People: Pow-Wow Culture on the Southern Plains* (Lawrence: University of Kansas Press, 2003), 66. See also Tara Browner, *Heartbeat of the People: Music and Dance of the Northern Pow-Wow* (Urbana: University of Illinois Press, 2002), 19.

27. "Twelfth District Locals," *WCTU of South Dakota, Minutes of the Twenty-Third Annual Convention, Aberdeen, September 16–19, 1911*, 49, South Dakota State Historical Society, Pierre (SDSHS).

28. Lillie B. Bowers, "An Indian WCTU Convention," *White Ribbon Bulletin*, August 1915, 4, SHSND.

29. Lillie B. Bowers, "An Indian WCTU Convention," *White Ribbon Bulletin*, August 1915, 4, SHSND.

30. Lillie B. Bowers, "An Indian WCTU Convention," *White Ribbon Bulletin*, August 1915, 4, SHSND.

31. Lora S. La Mance, "In the Land of the Dakotas," *WCTU-US*, August 3, 1916, 7.

32. Lora S. La Mance, "In the Land of the Dakotas," *WCTU-US*, August 3, 1916, 7.

33. Barbara H. Wylie, "From Mrs. Wylie," *White Ribbon Bulletin*, September 1916, 2, SHSND.

34. "Official Board Meeting," *WCTU of South Dakota, Minutes of the Twenty-Eighth Annual Convention, Madison, September 20–24, 1916* (Rapid City: Rapid City Journal Print, 1916), 18, SDSHS.

35. "Official Board Meeting," and Lora S. La Mance, "Five Months Work in South Dakota, June 1 to November 1, 1916," *WCTU of South Dakota, Minutes of the Twenty-Eighth Annual Convention, 1916*, 18, 76, SDSHS.

36. Pres. Anna R. Simmons, "Presidential Address," *WCTU of South Dakota, Minutes of the Twenty-Eighth Annual Convention, 1916*, 18, SDSHS.

37. Ruby Jackson, "Corresponding Secretary's Report," *WCTU of South Dakota, Minutes of the Twenty-Eighth Annual Convention, 1916*, 37, SDSHS.

38. E. B. Tre Fethren, "The Government Fair at Fort Yates, North Dakota," *WCTU of South Dakota, Minutes of the Twenty-Eighth Annual Convention, 1916*, 77–78, SDSHS.

39. Godfrey Matthews, "With the Sioux Indians on the Cheyenne River Reservation," *WCTU of South Dakota, Minutes of the Twenty-Eighth Annual Convention, 1916*, 78–81, SDSHS.

40. Matthews, "With the Sioux Indians," *WCTU of South Dakota, Minutes of the Twenty-Eighth Annual Convention, 1916*, 79, 79–81, SDSHS.

41. Lora S. La Mance, "Looping the Loop in South Dakota: From the Black Hills to the Rosebud Indian Reservation," *WCTU-US*, November 2, 1916, 6.

42. "President's Pacific Coast Itinerary," *WCTU-US*, May 25, 1905, 9.

43. "Tuesday Evening," *WCTU-US*, November 14, 1912, 6.

44. S. M. M. Woodman, "Mrs. Annie E. K. Bidwell," *White Ribbon Ensign*, March 1914, 1–2, CSL.

45. "Official Board Meeting," October 7, 1915, Minute Book 1914–1915, n.p., folder 1/2, MSS 2535: WCTU of Oregon, OHS.

46. "March 6, 1916," Minute Book 1915–1916, 23–24, folder 1/3, MSS 2535: WCTU of Oregon, OHS. See also Helen Crawford, "90 Year Highlights: Oregon WCTU" (n.p., 1973), 11, OHS.

47. "October 18, 1915," Minute Book 1915–1916, 23–24, folder 1/3, MSS 2535: WCTU of Oregon, 59–60, 68, OHS.

48. Spencer, "Work Among Indians," *Thirty-First Annual Report of the WCTU of California, Berkeley, October 6–11, 1910* (San Francisco: E. L. Mackey, 1910), 75–76, Annual Reports of the WCTU of [Northern] California, CSL.

49. Spencer, "The Red Man and Christian Citizenship," *Union Signal*, January 25, 1912, 11.

50. Spencer, "The Indians' Christmas," *White Ribbon Ensign*, January 1912, 8, Bancroft.

51. Spencer, "A Threatened Wrong to the Yuma Indians—Will You Help Avert It?" *WCTU-US*, October 14,1909, 4.

52. Margaret Dye Ellis, "WCTU Legislative Work," *WCTU-US*, December 15, 1910, 3.

53. "Colorado's Prohibition Law to Benefit Indians," *WCTU-US*, December 30, 1915, 3.

54. "Indian Life under Prohibition," *WCTU-US*, December 28, 1916, 3.

55. Additon, *Twenty Eventful Years*, 53–54, WCTU Records, Oregon State Library, Salem.

56. Jennie Murray Kemp, "President's Annual Address," *Minutes of the Thirty-Third Annual Convention of the Oregon WCTU, Pendleton, October 17–20, 1916* (Portland: Marsh Printing, 1916), 27, MPL.

57. "General Officers Meeting," March 20, 1915, folder 1/2, MSS 2535: WCTU of Oregon, Minute Book 1914–1915, n.p., OHS. This story is confirmed in the 1916 minutes by Jennie M. Kemp, "Presidential Address: Our Indian Leaders," *Minutes of the Thirty-Third Annual Convention of the Oregon WCTU, Pendleton, October 17–20, 1916* (Portland: Marsh Printing, 1916), 27, MPL.

58. Cora "Eva" West, "Department of Work Among the Indians," *Silver Jubilee Convention of the Southern Idaho WCTU, Boise, October 3–6, 1911* (Weiser, ID: American Printery, 1911), 26, 26, 27, Idaho State Archives, Idaho State Historical Society, Boise (hereafter ISHS).

59. Eva West, "Work Among Indians," *Minutes of the Southern Idaho WCTU, Twenty-Sixth Annual Convention, Nampa, September 23–25, 1912* (n.p.: Caldwell News Print, 1912), 42–43.

60. Eva West, "Indian Work," *WCTU of Southern Idaho, Minutes of the Twenty-Eighth Annual Convention, Caldwell, September 21–23, 1914*, 26, ISHS.

61. Eva West, "Work Among Indians," *Gem State Signal*, December 1916, 17, ISHS.

62. "Prohibition Good for Red Men," *WCTU-US*, April 13, 1916, 3.

63. *Dick v. United States*, 208 US 340 (1908), https://supreme.justia.com/cases/federal/us/208/340/case.html.

64. A. A. Garlock, "President's Annual Address," *Southern Idaho WCTU, Twenty-Second Annual Convention, Roswell, September 4–6, 1908* (Boise, ID: Syms York, 1908), 23, ISHS.

65. Spencer, "Hope for the Indian," *WCTU-US*, April 16, 1908, 4.

66. "One Thousand Nez Perce," *WCTU-US*, August 12, 1909, 15.

67. Susie McKellop, "Petition and Legislation," *Eighteenth Annual Meeting, WCTU, Indian Territory Year Book, 1905–6*, 67–68. The *Weekly News* was the national organ of the Anti–Horse Thief Association. For the history of the organization, see Burchill, *Bullets, Badges, and Bridles*.

68. Francis E. Leupp, *Report of the Commissioner of Indian Affairs, 1908*, 37, https://babel.hathitrust.org/cgi/pt?id=mdp.39015034627904;view=1up;seq=49.

69. Spencer, "A Woman Indian Agent," *WCTU-US*, April 15, 1909, 5.

70. Spencer, "Missions vs. Whiskey," *White Ribbon Ensign*, January 1915, 3, Bancroft.

71. Clara D. True to Annie K. Bidwell, March 5, 1913, and Annie K. Bidwell to Franklin Lane, March 17, 1913, both in file 5:4, MSS003, "Indian Affairs Correspondence, 1910–1915," CSUC.

72. Jacobs, "Clara True," 111.

73. "Indian Reservations Dry," *White Ribbon Ensign*, November 1912, 4, Bancroft. See also "Valentine Resigns," *Allentown Democrat*, July 3, 1912, 5, https://www.newspapers.com/image/68313717/; "Robert G. Valentine," *Yale Expositor* (Yale, MI) July 18, 1912, 6, https://www.newspapers.com/image/174680168/; "Indian Director Faces Serious Charge," *Journal Times* (Racine, WI), September 11, 1912, 1, https://www.newspapers.com/image/334084769/; "Valentine Not an Offender," *Washington Post*, October 30, 1912, 6, https://www.newspapers.com/image/28986211/. For Republican criticism of the handling of the case, see "Valentine Defended in Minority Report," *Evening Star* (Washington, DC) January 3, 1913, 9, https://www.newspapers.com/image/331485977/.

74. "Indian Reservations Dry," *White Ribbon Ensign*, November 1912, 4, Bancroft.

75. "No Firewater for Indian Service Officials," *WCTU-US*, August 17, 1916, 9.

76. Spencer, "The New Pledge for the Indians," *White Ribbon Ensign*, September 1915, 6, Bancroft.

77. Leupp, "Liquor Traffic in the Indian Country."

78. John Green, in Washington and Idaho, dealt with the outcome of the Supreme Court decision in the *Matter of Heff* decision. The *George Dick* case (discussed in the 1906 report) was now pending in US Supreme Court. Leupp, "Liquor Traffic in the Indian Country."

79. Wilkins, *American Indian Sovereignty*, 123.

80. "The Beer Period Is Over," *WCTU-US*, February 7, 1907, 1. For Meeks's decision allowing railroad companies to refuse beer supplies, see "Continued Success," *WCTU-US*, April 11, 1907, 12; "Signal Notes," *WCTU-US*, April 25, 1907, 16; "Indian Territory Gamblers," *WCTU-US*, June 6, 1907, 12; Associated Prohibition Press, "Summary of William E. Johnson's Indian Territory Campaign," *WCTU-US*, November 4, 1907, 2.

81. "Keeping Up the Battle for Indian Sobriety," *WCTU-US*, December 31, 1908, 15. See also Francis E. Leupp, "Suppression of the Liquor Traffic," *Report of the Commissioner of Indian Affairs, 1908*, 34, 38, https://babel.hathitrust.org/cgi/pt?id=ucl.l0061295333;view=1up;seq=50.

82. "Recommendations," *WCTU-AMM* 1909, 128. See also "Work Among Indians," *WCTU-AMM* 1909, 204.

83. Meyer, *We Are What We Drink*, 130; "Minnesota," *Anti-Saloon Year Book* (Westerville, OH: Anti-Saloon League of America Publishers, 1910), 72.

84. Mrs. Eva Emerson Wold, "Court Decision Makes One-Fifth of Minnesota Dry," *WCTU-US*, June 25, 1914, 13.

85. Adrianna Hungerford, "Presidential Address," 43. See also E. W. A. Fisk, "Indians," in *Report of the Thirty-Second Annual Convention of the Colorado WCTU, Colorado Springs, October 11–13, 1911* (Denver: Alexander and Meyer, 1911), 10, 82–83.

86. "Twelve Months in Prohibition in Bemidji," *WCTU-US*, January 6, 1916, 3.

87. "Indian Treaty May Add to Michigan and Wisconsin Dry Zones," *WCTU-US*, January 20, 1916, 13.

Chapter 6

1. Spencer, "Work Among Indians," *WCTU-US*, April 6, 1905, 10; United States, "Education: Government Schools," in *Report of the Commissioner of Indian Affairs, 1907*, 36–39, 43–45; "Education of the Indians," in *Extracts from the Annual Report of the Secretary of the Interior, Fiscal Year 1928, Relating to the Bureau of Indian Affairs* (Washington, DC: Government Printing Office, 1928), 2, https://babel.hathitrust.org/cgi/pt?id=ucl.31158001497246;view=1up;seq=260.

2. Vizenor, *Survivance*, 1.

3. Vizenor, *Survivance*, 1.

4. Adams, *Education for Extinction*.

5. *WCTU-AMM*, 1881, xxi; Hiram Price to Caroline Buell, November 28, 1881, in *WCTU-AMM*, 1881, cxxix. For "contract schools," see Prucha, *The Great Father*, 693.

6. John B. Riley, "Report of the Indian School Superintendent," in United States, *Annual Report of the Commissioner of Indian Affairs, 1886*, lxxxii, https://babel.hathitrust.org/cgi/pt?id=mdp.39015034627797;view=1up;seq=95. For more on Price's anti-alcohol bent and that of other temperance men in the Indian Office, see Prucha, *American Indian Policy*, 219–22.

7. D. B. Dyer to Caroline B. Buell, July 9, 1881, Helen W. Ludlow to Caroline B. Buell, July 2, 1881, both in *WCTU-AMM*, 1881, cxxxiii.

8. R. H. Pratt, "Report of Carlisle School," in United States, *Annual Report of the Commissioner of Indian Affairs, 1885*, 219, https://babel.hathitrust.org/cgi/pt?id=mdp.39015034627789;view=1up;seq=459.

9. "Lo! The Poor Indian," *Indian Leader*, September 1914, 7, https://babel.hathitrust.org/cgi/pt?id=wu.89060401486;view=1up;seq=27.

10. A. S. Benjamin, "Annual Address," *Thirty-First Annual Report of the Michigan State WCTU, Grand Rapids, June 6–9* (Bay City, MI: Jno. P. Lampert, 1905), 40, WCTU Records, 1874–2006, Bentley Historical Library, University of Michigan.

11. *WCTU-AMM*, 1910, 210.

12. See Jewett, *Town and City*.

13. Hiram W. Johnson to White Ribboners, April 27, 1915, in "Vice President's Letter," *Southern California White Ribbon*, June 1915, 3, SOCAL.

14. Lillian M. Stevens, "The Marvelous West," *WCTU-US*, April 27, 1905, 3.

15. Lillian M. Stevens, "In the Far West," *WCTU-US*, May 4, 1905, 3, 8.

16. Lillian M. Stevens, "The Marvelous West," *WCTU-US*, April 27, 1905, 3.

17. Annie K. Bidwell to Hon. George C. Perkins, March 11, 1904, Indian Affairs, Correspondence, Folder 3, Box 5, CSUC.

18. Spencer, "Work Among Indians," *WCTU-US*, April 6, 1905, 10.

19. Spencer, "The Indians' Advance," *WCTU-US*, November 28, 1912, 13.

20. Spencer, "The Native Sons of the Golden West," *White Ribbon Ensign*, February 1913, 4–5, Bancroft.

21. Spencer, "Indian Children," *White Ribbon Ensign*, September 1916, 4, Bancroft.

22. Emma L. Swartz, *History of the Dakota WCTU Illustrated* (Rapid City, S.D.: Daily Journal Stream Printing House, 1900), 59, in "WCTU of North Dakota History, 1900–1989," Box 1, SHSND; "Employees in Indian School Service," *Report of Commissioner of Indian Affairs, 1903* (Washington, DC: Government Printing Office, 1904), 572, https://babel.hathitrust.org/cgi/pt?id=hvd.tz1n6y;view=1up;seq=606.

23. *Twenty-Fourth Annual Convention of the Colorado WCTU, Denver, October 7–9, 1903* (Denver: Lugg and Chamberlain, 1903), 27, Norlin Library, Special Collections, University of Colorado, Boulder (hereafter NLCO). In 1904, the first report was delivered, but it was never printed in the state minutes. In the 1905 report, no superintendent is listed, but in the volume in the University of Colorado Boulder library, there is a handwritten addendum with the new superintendent: "Mrs. A. J. Martindale of Indian School Grand Junction." Despite the shift in leadership, Shields wrote the departmental report. *Twenty-Fifth Annual Convention of the Colorado WCTU, Colorado Springs, October 12–14, 1904* (Denver: Lugg and Chamberlain, 1904), 25; *Twenty-Sixth Annual Convention of the Colorado WCTU, 1905* (coverless, 1905), 4, 62–63, NLCO.

24. *Twenty-Sixth Annual Convention of the Colorado WCTU, 1905* (coverless, 1905), 4, 62–63.

25. Rose A. Davidson, "In Southern Colorado," *WCTU Messenger*, January 1905, 3, NLCO.

26. Rose A. Davidson, "In Southern Colorado," *WCTU Messenger*, March 1905, 2, NLCO.

27. Hattie M. Doughty, "L.T.L. Report," and Mrs. Martindale, "Work Among Indians," *Twenty-Seventh Annual Convention of the Colorado WCTU, Rocky Ford, September 19–21* (1906), 4, 54–55, 70, NLCO.

28. *Twenty-Eighth Annual Convention of the Colorado WCTU, Greeley, October 9–11, 1907*, 4, NLCO.

29. Augusta J. Whitney, "Work Among Indians," *WCTU Messenger*, December 1907, 7.

30. *Report: Thirty-First Annual Convention of the Colorado WCTU, Denver, October 12–14, 1910* (Denver: Alexander and Meyer, 1910), 89–90.

31. E. W. A. Fisk, "Work Among Indians," *WCTU Messenger*, October 1910, 10, 3.

32. Kimberley Gitchell [?], "Indian School to Regional Center: A History of the Grand Junction Regional Center," (unpublished, 2017).

33. Fowler, "Work Among Indians," *Report of the WCTU of Southern California, Los Angeles, May 12–16, 1910* (Los Angeles: Press of Hand and Hand, 1910), 88. Stanley was superintendent of the Soboba Reservation, He was shot by "Indians under his jurisdiction on May 2, and died on the morning of May 3." Leupp, "Law and Order," in United States, *Report of the Commissioner of Indian Affairs, 1912*, 45, https://babel.hathitrust.org/cgi/pt?id=osu.32435064041650;view=1up;seq=51. This report also deals with the resignation of William Johnson in September 1911. He was replaced by his assistant Harold F. Coggeshall.

34. "Report of Corresponding Secretary," *North Dakota White Ribbon Bulletin*, October 1912, 9, 4.

35. Anna Walker, "Ft. Shaw Indian School," *Montana WCTU Voice*, June 1904, 11–13, MHS.

36. The department was most likely established in 1902. See *Montana WCTU Voice*, November 1904, 1, 11, 12. Barnes was listed as Work Among Indians superintendent in *Montana WCTU Voice*, November 1905. See also "Work Among Indians— Department Dropped," *Montana WCTU Voice*, October 1907, 9, MHS; Spencer, "Work Among Indians," *WCTU-AMM*, 1910, 209; "Fort Shaw Government Industrial Indian Boarding School, 1892–1910," Vertical Files, MHS. By 1913 there was no Indian Department listed in Montana's latest iteration of the WCTU paper, *Woman's Voice*, December 1913, 8, but there was a Fort Shaw Union led by Mrs. W. A. Graham. *Woman's Voice*, February 1914, 3.

37. "Report of Districts," *Report of the Nineteenth Annual Meeting of the WCTU of Wisconsin, June 7–10, 1892, Madison* (Madison: Tracy, Gibbs, 1892), WHS.

38. Bieder, *Native American Communities*, 21.

39. Frances Willard, "The Young Recruits," from the *Union Signal*, n.d., Scrapbook History of Clippings and Photographs, 1890–1906, MSS 42, Vol. 1, Box 3/5, Loyal Temperance Legion Records, WHS. This must have been around 1892 as it is sandwiched between a program and report from the 1892 state LTL convention.

40. *Report of the Nineteenth Annual Meeting of the WCTU of Wisconsin, June 7–10, 1892, Madison* (Madison: Tracy, Gibbs, 1892), 71, 76, 98, WHS; "Second Annual Convention of the Loyal Temperance Legion of Wisconsin, Delvan, July 6 and 7, 1892," in Scrapbook History of Clippings and Photographs, 1890–1906, Vol. 1, Box 2, MSS 42, WHS.

41. Annie J. Bradbury, "History of State L.T.L. of Wisconsin for 1891, 1892, 1893," in Scrapbook History of Clippings and Photographs, 1890–1906, Vol. 1, Box 2, MSS 42, WHS.

42. Julia M. Knowles, "Fifth District Report," *Report of the Twentieth Annual Meeting of the WCTU of Wisconsin, May 22–26, 1893, Eau Claire, Wisconsin* (Madison: Tracy, Gibbs, 1893), 84.

43. Mrs. Mate H. Topping, "Senior L.T.L. Report," *Minutes, Presidential Address, and Reports of the Wisconsin WCTU at its Twenty-First Annual Convention, Portage, Wisconsin, June 5–8, 1894* (Evansville, WI: R.M. Antes, Steam Print, 1894), 116.

44. "Minutes of the LTL Convention," 1894, in Scrapbook History of Clippings and Photographs, 1890–1906, Vol. 1, Box. MSS 42. Box 3/5, Minute Book 1891–1895, n.p., WHS.

45. Robert M. Davis, "President's Address to the Fourth Convention of the State Loyal Temperance Legion of Wisconsin," Racine, July 11, 1894, in Scrapbook History of Clippings and Photographs, 1890–1906, Vol. 1, Box. 2, MSS 42, WHS.

46. "Wisconsin Loyal Temperance Legion Fifth State Convention," Berlin, Wisconsin, July 10–11, 1895, in Scrapbook History of Clippings and Photographs, 1890–1906, Vol. 1, Box. 2, MSS 42, WHS.

47. Temperance Workers, *Lacrosse Daily Republican*, July 8, 1896, newspaper clipping, and "Plan of Work," *Rush Light*, newspaper clipping, both in Scrapbook History of Clippings and Photographs, 1890–1906, Vol. 1, Box. 2, MSS 42.

48. Ruth A. Perham, superintendent of the Department of Books and Reading, "Books and Reading," *The Motor*, newspaper clipping in Scrapbook History of Clippings

and Photographs, 1890–1906, Vol. 1, Box. 2, MSS 42, WHS. See also Father Oderic Derenthal, "Report," July 20, 1886, in United States, *Annual Report of the Commissioner of Indian Affairs, 1886*, 252, http://digicoll.library.wisc.edu/cgi-bin/History/History-idx?type=turn&entity=History.AnnRep86.p0390&id=History.AnnRep86&isize=M; Thomas H. Savage, "Report of Green Bay Agency," in United States, *Annual Report of the Commissioner of Indian Affairs, 1894*, 328, http://digicoll.library.wisc.edu/cgi-bin/History/History-idx?type=article&did=History.AnnRep94.i0023&id=History.AnnRep94&isize=M; Thomas H. Savage, "Report of the Green Bay Agency," in United States, *Annual Report of the Commissioner of Indian Affairs, 1896*, 321, http://digicoll.library.wisc.edu/cgi-bin/History/History-idx?type=article&did=History.AnnRep96.i0023&id=History.AnnRep96&isize=M.

49. Mary J. Money, "The Thirteenth Annual Convention," newspaper clipping, and Isadore Whiting Black, General Secretary Wisconsin LTL, "Wisconsin's Thirteenth Annual LTL Convention, Darlington, July 7–8, 1903," newspaper clipping, both in Scrapbook History of Clippings and Photographs, 1890–1906, Vol. 1, Box 2, MSS 42, WHS.

50. "Minutes from LTL Convention," newspaper clipping, and "Superintendents of Departments," *1907 and 1909 State LTL Programs*, both in Scrapbook History of Clippings and Photographs, 1890–1906, Vol. 1, Box 2, MSS 42, WHS.

51. Joseph J. Janney, "Minutes," *Thirty-Third Annual Report of the Board of Indian Commissioners* (Washington, DC: Government Printing Office, 1901), 71, https://babel.hathitrust.org/cgi/pt?id=ucl.31175031093209;view=1up;seq=77.

52. "Colorado's Prohibition Law to Benefit Indians," *WCTU-US*, December 30, 1915, 3.

53. In almost all of the children's works, the original dates were composed according to the Friends' conventions. In this case, September was written "9 Mo," reflecting the Quaker education he received. William C. Hoag, September 1876, AA65: Student Essays, PYMIC.

54. Hauptman, "The Meddlesome Friend."

55. *Temperance Echoes*, vol. 4, no. 5, AA64, PYMIC.

56. Child, "Homesickness," *Boarding School Seasons*, 43–54.

57. Barton, *A Quaker Promise Kept*, 44; James Henderson, *An Autobiography of the Life and Religious Experience of James Henderson, a Minister in the Religious Society of Friends* (Ohio Yearly Meeting, 1944).

58. "Temperance Acts," ca. 1891, AA64, PYMIC.

59. General Improvement Society (GIS) Minutes, May 8, 1891, PYMIC. (The Society for General Improvement changed its name to the General Improvement Society.)

60. GIS Minutes, May 22, 1891, PYMIC.

61. Felix Scott, "Alcohol Talk," March 8, 12, 1901, Read at the Committee. AA65, PYMIC.

62. Felix Scott, "The Outlook for the Indian," March 3, 1902, AA65: Student Essays, PYMIC.

63. Adams, *Education for Extinction*, 274.

64. Fowler, "Work Among Indians," *Southern California White Ribbon*, April 1891, 2–3, HL.

65. "Hampton Normal and Agricultural Institute" and "Religious Work," in United States, *Annual Report of the Commissioner of Indian Affairs, 1887*, 265, 268, https://babel

.hathitrust.org/cgi/pt?id=mdp.39015032032370;view=1up;seq=357; S. C. Armstrong, "Report of Hampton Normal and Agricultural Institute," July 1, 1890, in United States, *Annual Report of the Commissioner of Indian Affairs, 1890*, 320, https://babel.hathitrust .org/cgi/pt?id=mdp.39015011917930;view=1up;seq=514; S. C. Armstrong, "Report of Hampton Normal and Agricultural Institute," July 1, 1891, in United States, *Annual Report of the Commissioner of Indian Affairs, 1891*, 1:605–7, https://babel.hathitrust.org /cgi/pt?id=mdp.39015024886684;view=1up;seq=619.

66. S. C. Armstrong, "Report of Hampton Normal and Agricultural Institute," in United States, *Annual Report of the Commissioner of Indian Affairs, 1889*, 375, 379, https://babel.hathitrust.org/cgi/pt?id=mdp.39015011917948;view=1up;seq=385.

67. Horatio N. Rust, "Report of Mission Agency," August 8, 1890, in United States, *Annual Report of the Superintendent of Indian Affairs, 1890*, 17, https://babel.hathitrust .org/cgi/pt?id=mdp.39015011917930;view=1up;seq=211.

68. Spencer, "Work Among Indians," *WCTU-AMM*, 1913, 211.

69. D. H. B. Evans to C. C. Thornton, August 26, 1892, in United States, *Annual Report of the Commissioner of Indian Affairs, 1892*, 507, https://babel.hathitrust.org/cgi /pt?id=mdp.39015034627862;view=1up;seq=505.

70. "Haskell WCTU," *Indian Leader*, October 16, 1914, 3–4, https://babel.hathitrust .org/cgi/pt?id=wu.89060401486;view=1up;seq=47.

71. GIS minutes, June 29, 1894, April 29, 1904, May 8, 1909, PYMIC.

72. Frank Terry, "Report of Superintendent of Chehalis School," June 30, 1895, *Report of the Secretary of the Interior*, 54th Cong., 1st Sess., 5 vols. (Washington, DC: Government Printing Office, 1896), 2:406–8, https://babel.hathitrust.org/cgi/pt?id=ucl .31158011073516;view=1up;seq=414.

73. "Indians for Prohibition," *Indian Leader*, April 1915, 20, https://babel.hathitrust .org/cgi/pt?id=wu.89060401486;view=1up;seq=322.

74. "A Strong Temperance Address," *Indian Leader*, October 2, 1914, 3, https://babel .hathitrust.org/cgi/pt?id=wu.89060401486;view=1up;seq=39.

75. "Woman's Christian Temperance Union," *Indian Leader*, June 11, 1915, 4, https://babel.hathitrust.org/cgi/pt?id=wu.89060401486;view=1up;seq=382.

76. Lillian M. N. Stevens, "Indian Territory to the Fore," *WCTU-US*, April 26, 1906, 3–4, 15. The article "That 'Organization Is the Watchword,'" *WCTU-US*, May 2, 1895, 1, indicated that Clara C. Parrish established a Somerset YWCTU at Cherokee National Female Seminary a decade earlier.

77. "WCTU Meeting," *Indian Leader* April 9, 1915, 3, https://babel.hathitrust.org /cgi/pt?id=wu.89060401486;view=1up;seq=291.

78. Child, *Boarding School Seasons*, 4.

79. "Leading Indians against Liquor," *Indian Leader*, October 16, 1914, 4.

80. *Indian Leader*, October 1914, 20, https://babel.hathitrust.org/cgi/pt?id=wu .89060401486;view=1up;seq=48.

81. "Prohibition Aids Protection of Indian Tribes," *Indian Leader*, May 21, 1915, 1, https://babel.hathitrust.org/cgi/pt?id=wu.89060401486;view=1up;seq=339.

82. "Prohibition," *Indian Leader*, April 1915, 9, https://babel.hathitrust.org/cgi/pt?id =wu.89060401486;view=1up;seq=311.

83. "Santee Indian Agency, Nebraska," *Indian Leader*, February 23, 1917, 5, https:// babel.hathitrust.org/cgi/pt?id=wu.89060401502;view=1up;seq=253.

84. "20th Century Red Man Ready to Fight 'Firewater,'" *WCTU-US*, July 29, 1915, 4.

85. Spencer, "Work Among Indians," *WCTU-US*, April 6, 1905, 10.

86. "LTL Reports: New York," *WCTU-US*, July 2, 1903, 15.

87. Cook, "'Earnest Christian Women," 249–67; Erickson, "Making King Alcohol Tremble," 333–52; Gordon, *Juvenile Work Questions*.

88. Spencer, "Work Among Indians," *WCTU-AMM* 1910, 210.

89. GIS Minutes, January 12, 1917, PYMIC.

90. Snow, *The Iroquois*, 168.

91. Alfred, *Peace, Power, Righteousness*, 17.

92. "Indian Medal Contest," *WCTU-US*, July 27, 1911, 12.

93. Evelyn Pierce (Seneca), "Viewpoint of a Haskell Grad," *Indian Leader*, September 1914, 13, https://babel.hathitrust.org/cgi/pt?id=wu.89060401486;view=1up;seq=23.

94. Spencer, "Work Among Indians," *WCTU-AMM* 1915, 172–74; "Woman's Christian Temperance Union," *Indian Leader*, March 19, 1915, 4, https://babel.hathitrust.org/cgi/pt?id=wu.89060401486;view=1up;seq=256.

95. Eva Jones, "L.T.L. Branch," and I. F. McClure, "Work Among Indians," *Minutes of the Twenty-Ninth Annual Meeting of the WCTU of the State of Minnesota, Minneapolis, September 19–22, 1905* (Minneapolis: Thurston and Gould, 1905), 70–71, 72.

96. Spencer, "Work Among Indians," *Thirty-First Annual Report of the WCTU of California, 1910*, 75–76, Annual Reports of the WCTU of [Northern] California, CSL.

97. "Butte County," *White Ribbon Ensign*, January 1912, 4, 20, Bancroft.

98. *Tunesassa Echoes*, February 5, 1897, AA64: PYMIC.

99. Maroukis, *The Peyote Road*, 34.

100. Charles Zimmerman, "Life Conservation," *Indian Leader*, October 26, 1917, 13, https://babel.hathitrust.org/cgi/pt?id=wu.89060401510;view=1up;seq=77.

101. "Peyote," *Indian Leader*, November 30, 1917, 18–19, https://babel.hathitrust.org/cgi/pt?id=wu.89060401510;view=1up;seq=132. See also Robert G. Valentine, "Suppression of the Liquor Traffic," in *Report of the Commissioner of Indian Affairs for the Fiscal Year Ending June 30, 1911* (Washington, DC: Government Printing Office, 1911), 35, https://babel.hathitrust.org/cgi/pt?id=hvd.tz1n7s;view=1up;seq=43. Cato Sells, "The Menacing Use of Liquor," in *Report of the Commissioner of Indian Affairs for the Fiscal Year Ended June 30, 1915* (Washington, DC: Government Printing Office, 1915), 12–15, https://babel.hathitrust.org/cgi/pt?id=hvd.tz1n8e;view=1up;seq=19.

102. Maroukis, "The Peyote Controversy," https://doi.org/10.1353/aiq.2013.0034.

Conclusion

1. McGirr, *The War on Alcohol*, 233–55.

2. Philp, *John Collier's Crusade*, 62.

3. Wilkins, *American Indian Sovereignty*, 135. See also Britten, *American Indians in World War I*, 45.

4. Spencer, "Superintendents: Work Among Indians," *WCTU-US*, August 13, 1914, 10.

5. Spencer, "Work Among Indians, *WCTU-AMM*, 1915, 173, 174.

6. Spencer, "Work Among Indians," 184. See also "Convention," November 21, and "Official Board Meeting," November 20, 1916, *WCTU-AMM*, 1916, 62, 84.

7. Spencer, "Work Among Indians," *WCTU-AMM*, 1916, 186, 188.

8. Emma L. Starrett, "Christian Citizenship," *WCTU-AMM*, 1917, 216.

9. Britten, *American Indians in World War I*, 149.

10. Margaret Dye Ellis, "Our Washington Letter," *WCTU-US*, May 10, 1917, 9.

11. Britten, *American Indians in World War I*, 179.

12. Grillot, *First Americans*, 168–69.

13. "Christian Citizenship," *WCTU-AMM* 1924, 192–93.

14. Lilah Denton Lindsey, *Study Course on Citizenship* (Muskogee: Bowman Press, 1924), 13–17, University of Oklahoma University Libraries, Western History Collections, Norman.

15. Norma F. Mudge, "Eighth District," *Michigan State WCTU, Forty-Third Annual Report, Kalamzoo, May 29–June 1, 1917*, 80, WCTU Records, Clarke Historical Library, Central Michigan University, Mount Pleasant, Michigan.

16. "Central Committee," *Minutes of the Fortieth Annual Meeting of the WCTU of Minnesota, Owatonna, August 22–25, 1916* (Minneapolis: Thurston and Gould, 1916), 27, MHC.

17. "Minutes, Wednesday Morning, September 18, 1918," and "Work Among Indians," *Minutes of the Forty-Second Annual Meeting of the WCTU of Minnesota, Duluth, September 17–20, 1918* (Minneapolis: Thurston and Gould, 1918), 24, 86, MHC.

18. Stella Cussons, "Christian Citizenship," *Minutes of the Forty-Sixth Annual Meeting of the WCTU of Minnesota, Saint Paul, August 29–September 1, 1922* (Minneapolis: Order of Mrs. Myra Griswold, 1922), 71, MHC.

19. "Plans for the Department of Christian Citizenship," *South Dakota White Ribbon Journal*, February 1925,11; "Christian Citizenship," *South Dakota White Ribbon Journal*, October 1925, 1, SDSHS.

20. "Local Unions," *White Ribboner* (November–December 1916): 2, SHSND.

21. Carrie M. Barr, "Presidential Annual Address," *Report of the Thirty-Fifth Annual Meeting of the WCTU of East Washington, Pomeroy, October 8–11, 1918*, 16–19, WCTU Records, Northwest Museum of Art and Culture, Eastern Washington State Historical Society, Spokane; "General Officers," *Report of the Thirty-Second Annual Meeting of the WCTU, Seattle, October 8–9, 1915* (Seattle: Davis-Peek Printing, 1915), 3, 17, WCTU Records, UW; "General Officers," *Report of the Thirty-Third Annual Meeting of the WCTU, Anacortes, November 17–20, 1916*, 3–5, WCTU Records, UW.

22. "Superintendents" and "Americanization," *Minutes of the Thirty-Fourth Annual Convention of the Oregon WCTU, Albany, October 1–5, 1917*, 11, 33, MCL; "Summary of Official Board and Executive Meeting," *Minutes of the Thirty-Fifth Annual Convention of the Oregon WCTU, Portland, October 9–11, 1918*, 18, MCL.

23. Ratie Smith, "Indian Work," *Report of the Nineteenth Annual Convention of the Nevada WCTU, Reno, October 22–23, 1902*, 4, 27, WCTU of Nevada Records, Nevada Historical Society, Reno (hereafter NHS).

24. "Work Among Indians Superintendent: Mrs. Corwin," in "Minutes of Convention, 1914," 7, Book MS/NC511/1/3, Box 1, WCTU of Nevada Records, NHS; "Indians: Mrs. Gardiner (Supt.) and Mrs. Rhorer," "Departments and Superintendents," September 6, 1917, in Book 17, Box 1, WCTU of Nevada Records, NHS; "General Officers," *1919 Yearbook and Report of the Thirty-Sixth Annual Convention of the Nevada WCTU, Reno, November 3–4, 1919*, 3, WCTU of Nevada Records, NHS; "Mrs. Earl Williams Spoke on Paquita, Indian Maiden," "Reno Local WCTU Minutes, January 17, 1921," in Book 19,

Box 1, 63, WCTU of Nevada Records, NHS; "Work among Indians: Laura Bulmer," in *Program of the Thirty-Ninth Annual Convention of Nevada WCTU*, Reno, October 19, 1922, in WCTU of Nevada Records, NHS. Laura Bulmer discusses Christmas celebrations at Indian Camp East of Reno (probably Pyramid Lake Reservation). Laura Bulmer, "Undated Work among Indians Report, [1922–1924]," 8, Book NC511/9/1, Folder 5, Box 1, WCTU Records of Nevada, NHS.

25. The Riverton union boasted seven members, led by president Mrs. Blanche Smothers, vice presidents Cora Brown, Mrs. Carr, and Mrs. Racer, along with corresponding secretary Mrs. C. E. Deardoff and treasurer Emma Stratton. *Report of the Thirty-Third Annual Convention of the WCTU of Wyoming, Casper, November 1–3, 1916* (Cheyenne: S. A. Bristol, 1916), and "Roster of Unions," *Report of the Thirty-Fifth Annual Convention of the WCTU of Wyoming* (Cheyenne: Cheyenne Printery, 1918), 10–15, both in WCTU Records, Wyoming State Archives, Cheyenne.

26. "Presidential Address," *Proceedings of the Thirty-Third Annual Convention of the WCTU of South Idaho, Boise, October 28–30, 1919*, 17, ISHS.

27. "Convention Proceedings," *Proceedings of the Forty-Second Annual Convention of the WCTU of Southern Idaho, Caldwell, September 26–28, 1928* (Boise: Oster Printing, 1928), 8–9, ISHS.

28. "October 7, 1917," and "Resolutions of 1919 Convention," in *Minutes of Annual Meetings, 1917–1923*, 6, 18, 80, MSS 160, Folder 5, Box 9, Montana WCTU Records, MHS.

29. "Dept. of Work Among Indians, *White Ribbon Ensign*, December 1917, 7, Bancroft.

30. Spencer, "In Memoriam," *White Ribbon Ensign*, April 1918, 6, Bancroft.

31. "Chico Indian First to Win Commission," *White Ribbon Ensign*, June 1918, 6, Bancroft.

32. "Superintendents of Departments" and "Work Among Indians," *Forty-Fourth Annual Report of the WCTU of California, Sacramento, October 20–24, 1924*, 139, FWMLA. "Work Among Indians," *Forty-Fifth Annual Report of the WCTU of California, Oakland, October 19–23, 1925*, 144–45, FWMLA; Spencer, "Work Among Indians," *White Ribbon Ensign*, July 1927, 8, Bancroft. See also Suzanne McKelvey, "Work Among Indians," *Forty-Eighth Annual Report of the WCTU of California, Stockton, October 22–26, 1928*, 96–97, FWMLA. "McKelvey" is alternately spelled McKelvy in WCTU records.

33. Mary Helen McLean, "Some Pioneers and Others," *White Ribbon Ensign*, October 1930, 6, CSL.

34. M. A. Todd, "Americanization," *White Ribbon Ensign*, March 1931, 2, CSL.

35. Ella Boole, "Advance Not Retreat," *White Ribbon Ensign*, December 1932, 2, CSL.

36. "It is NOT the Failure," *White Ribbon Ensign*, June 1933, 1, CSL.

37. "Woman Author, Pioneer Dies," *Oakland Tribune*, May 2, 1933, https://www.newspapers.com/image/106276337/?terms=Dorcas%2BSpencer.

38. Fowler, "Work Among Indians," *Report of the WCTU of Southern California, 1916–1917*, 85.

39. Fowler, "Work Among Indians," *Report of the WCTU of Southern California, 1917–1918, Thirty-Fifth Annual Convention, May 22–25, 1917*, 8–9, 110–11. For more on Salmons, see "Extract from Letter," *Times-Democrat* (New Orleans), January 29, 1905,

32, https://www.newspapers.com/image/152745211/?terms=Ora%2BSalmons%2Band%2BPala%2BIndians.

40. Etta Burnham Taft, "Christian Citizenship," *Report of the WCTU of Southern California, Thirty-Sixth Annual Convention, 1918–1919, Bakersfield, May 7–10, 1918*, 12, 117–18, SOCAL.

41. Fowler, "Work Among Indians," *Report of the WCTU of Southern California, 1919–1920, Thirty-Seventh Annual Convention, Santa Ana, May 27–30, 1919*, 135–36, SOCAL.

42. Fowler, "Work Among Indians," *Report of the WCTU of Southern California, 1920–1921, Thirty-Eighth Annual Convention, May 21–24, 1920*, 99–100.

43. "Riverside County," *Southern California White Ribbon*, November 1921, 7, SOCAL; *Report of the WCTU of Southern California, for the year ending May 1, 1922, Fortieth Annual Convention, May 23–26, 1922*, 30, https://www.findagrave.com/memorial/54162199.

44. Arilla Grizzle, "Riverside County," *Report of the WCTU of Southern California, Forty-Second Annual Convention, Pasadena, October 14–17, 1924*, 74.

45. Eva Watson, "Work Among Indians," *Minutes of the Twenty-Fifth Annual Convention of the Arizona's WCTU, Phoenix, December 3–5, 1913*, 25–26, FWMLA.

46. "Superintendents of Departments," *Minutes of the Twenty-Seventh Annual Convention, Arizona WCTU, Mesa, April 26–28, 1916*, 2, FWMLA. The 1917–1919 reports are missing in FWMLA, and reports for 1920 and afterward lack any information on Indian work. For more on Mrs. Rev. C. R. Broadhead, see Josephine P. Broadhead, "Indian Customs Much Improved," *Bisbee Daily Review* (Bisbee, Arizona), April 1, 1910, 3, https://www.newspapers.com/image/42284821/?terms=Josephine%2BP.%2BBroadhead.

47. "'Keep Whisky Away from Us' Indians Plead," *WCTU-US*, February 8, 1917, 2.

48. Ellis, "Our Washington Letter," *WCTU-US*, February 21, 1918, 2.

49. Ellis, "Our Washington Letter," *WCTU-US*, April 4, 1918, 2.

50. Maroukis, *The Peyote Road*, 58.

51. "Other Federal Legislation," *WCTU-AMM*, 1923, 66. The superintendent of the Legislation Department resolved to make efforts to support federal legislation to protect the Indian against "the drug peyote." Lenna Lowe Yost, "Legislative Program for 1924," *WCTU-US*, October 11, 1923, 2.

52. Charles H. Burke, "Law and Order," *Report of the Commissioner of Indian Affairs, 1924*, 21, https://babel.hathitrust.org/cgi/pt?id=uc1.31158001497246;view=1up;seq=33.

53. Cato Sells, "Suppression of the Liquor Traffic," *Report of the Commissioner of Indian Affairs for the Fiscal Year Ended June 30, 1920*, 46–47, https://babel.hathitrust.org/cgi/pt?id=hvd.tz1n79;view=1up;seq=526.

54. Roy West and Charles H. Burke, "Law and Order," *Extracts from the Annual Report of the Secretary of the Interior, Fiscal Year 1928, Relating to the Bureau of Indian Affairs*, 21, https://babel.hathitrust.org/cgi/pt?id=uc1.3115800149724;view=1up;seq=279.

55. "National Dry Law Helps Enforcement of Dry Laws on Reservations, *WCTU-US*, February 10, 1921, 3.

56. "Indian Reservation Raid," *American Issue* (New York edition), November 22, 1924, 5, 8, SOCAL.

57. R. Mobley [?], "November 1, 1921," 29, *Secretary's Book*, WCTU Collection, Box W-27, University of Oklahoma University Libraries, Western History Collections,

Norman; "January 23, 1923" and "June 21, 1923," Federated WCTU of Tulsa Typescript Minute Book, n.p., Folder 19, Lilah Denton Lindsey Papers, ML.

58. Lenna Lowe Yost, "California Indians Ask Pay for 7,500,000 Acres Ceded to the United States under Eighteen Treaties of 1851," *WCTU-US* March 16, 1922, 2.

59. Lenna Lowe Yost, "Friends of Pueblo Indians Guarding Legislation," *WCTU-US*, March 1, 1923, 2.

60. Prucha, *The Great Father*, 799–800.

61. Jacobs, "Clara True," 111.

62. "Mobilize a Million Members," *WCTU-US*, March 17, 1921, 7.

63. "Jubilee Penny Paperweight: The Official Symbol of Fifty Years of Progress," *WCTU-US*, August 24, 1924, 14.

64. Ganteaume, *Officially Indian*, 102–3.

Bibliography

Archives and Special Collection Libraries

Bancroft Library, Berkeley, California (Bancroft)
    Annual Reports of the WCTU of [Northern] California
    White Ribbon Ensign/Pacific Ensign

Bentley Historical Library, University of Michigan, Ann Arbor
    WCTU Records, 1874–2006

California State Library, Sacramento (CSL)
    Annual Reports of the WCTU of Southern California
    Annual Reports of the WCTU of [Northern] California
    White Ribbon Ensign
    Sherman Bulletin

California State University, Chico (CSUC)
    Annie Ellicot Kennedy Bidwell Papers, 1888–1903

Clarke Historical Library, Central Michigan University, Mount Pleasant
    Mount Pleasant Indian School Records
    WCTU Records

Eastern Washington State Historical Society, Northwest Museum of Art and
        Culture, Spokane
    WCTU Records

Frances Willard Memorial Library and Archives, Evanston, Illinois (FWMLA)

Haverford College Library, Special Collections, Philadelphia
    Philadelphia Yearly Meeting (PYMIC)

Hazelden-Pittman Archives, Center City, Minnesota
    Scientific Temperance Instruction

Huntington Library, San Marino, California (HL)

Idaho State Historical Society, Idaho State Archives, Boise (ISHS)
    Women's [*sic*] Christian Temperance Union papers MS 36

McFarlin Library, Special Collections, University of Tulsa (ML)
    Lilah Denton Lindsey Papers
    The Helper

Minnesota History Center, St. Paul (MHC)
  WCTU Collection

Montana Historical Society Archives, Helena (MHS)
  Montana WCTU Records, 1883–1976

Multnomah County Library, Portland, Oregon (MCL)
  Annual Meeting Minutes of WCTU of Oregon

Nevada Historical Society, Reno (NHS)
  WCTU of Nevada Records

New York State Library, Albany

Norlin Library, Special Collections, University of Colorado, Boulder (NLCO)
  Colorado WCTU Papers, 1878–1975

Oklahoma History Center, Oklahoma City (OHC)
  W. P. Campbell Collection
  Proceedings of the Annual Convention of Indian Territory WCTU
  Proceedings of the Annual Convention of the Oklahoma Territory WCTU
  Proceedings of the Annual Convention of the State of Oklahoma WCTU

Onondaga Historical Association, Syracuse, New York (OHA)
  Individual Name Files
  Vertical Files

Oregon Historical Society, Davies Family Research Library, Portland (OHS)
  WCTU of Oregon Records, MSS 2535

Oregon State Library, Salem
  Thomas C. Battey Papers
  Choctaw Nation Papers
  Joseph Samuel Morrow Collection
  Peter Perkins Pitchlyn Papers
  WCTU Records

Rush Rhees Library, University of Rochester

San Diego History Center
  WCTU Records

South Dakota State Historical Society, Pierre (SDSHS)
  Women's [sic] Christian Temperance Union of South Dakota, 1890–1991

Southern California WCTU, Los Angeles, California (SOCAL)

State Historical Society of North Dakota, Bismarck (SHSND)
  WCTU of North Dakota Records, 1882–2010

Tonawanda Reservation Historical Society, Tonawanda Band of Seneca, Tonawanda,
  New York

University of Oklahoma University Libraries, Western History Collections,
  Norman (OUL)

University of Washington, Special Collections, Allen Library, Seattle (UW)
  Lucy Gearhart Papers
  Pacific Northwest Scrapbook Collection

Robert Hitchman Collection
WCTU Records

Washington State Historical Society, Tacoma (WSHS)
White Ribbon Bulletin
William White Papers
WCTU of Olympia
WCTU of Puyallup

Wisconsin Historical Society Archives, Madison (WHS)
Loyal Temperance Legion Records
WCTU Records

Wisconsin Historical Society Library, Madison (WHS)
WCTU, Wisconsin Annual Meeting Minutes

Wyoming State Archives, Cheyenne (WY)
WCTU Records

Books, Articles, Theses, and Dissertations

Ackerman, Lillian A. *A Necessary Balance: Gender and Power among Indians of the Columbia Plateau*. Norman: University of Oklahoma Press, 2013.

Adams, David Wallace. *Education for Extinction: American Indians and the Boarding School Experience, 1875–1928*. Lawrence: University of Kansas Press, 1995.

Additon, Lucia H. Faxon. *Twenty Eventful Years of Oregon Woman's Christian Temperance Union, 1880–1900*. Portland: Gotshall, 1904.

Ahern, Wilbert H. "Indian Education and Bureaucracy: The School at Morris, 1887–1909." *Minnesota History* 49, no. 3 (October 1984): 82–98.

Alderson, Mary Long. *Thirty-Four Years in the Montana Woman's Christian Temperance Union, 1896–1930*. No publication information, 1930. MHS.

Alfred, Taiaiake. *Peace, Power, Righteousness: An Indigenous Manifesto*. 2nd ed. New York: Oxford University Press, 2009.

Anderson, Gary L., and Kathryn G. Herr. *Encyclopedia of Activism and Social Justice*. 3 vols. Thousand Oaks, CA: Sage, 2007.

Armstrong, Kimberly E. "A Failed Uncle Tom's Cabin for the Indian: Helen Hunt Jackson's Ramona and the Power of Paratext." *Western American Literature* 52, no. 2 (2017): 129–56.

Armstrong, William H. *Warrior in Two Camps: Ely S. Parker, Union General and Seneca Chief*. Syracuse, NY: Syracuse University Press, 1989.

Atwood, A. *Glimpses in Pioneer Life on Puget Sound*. Seattle: Denny-Corvell, 1903.

Bahr, Diana Meyers. *The Students of Sherman Indian School: Education and Native Identity since 1892*. Norman: University of Oklahoma Press, 2014.

Bailey, Hannah J., and Women's National Indian Association (US). *Temperance Work for Indians*. Publications of the Women's National Indian Association (Philadelphia: Women's National Indian Association, 1901). https://babel.hathitrust.org/cgi/pt?id=ucl.31175035180275;ql=Temperance%20Work%20for%20Indians.

Baird-Olson, Karren, and Carol Ward. "Recovery and Resistance: The Renewal of Traditional Spirituality among American Indian Women." *American Indian Culture and Research Journal* 24, no. 4 (December 2000): 1–35.

Baker, Paula. *The Moral Frameworks of Public Life: Gender, Politics, and the State in Rural New York, 1870–1930.* New York: Oxford University Press, 1991.

Banner, Stuart. *How the Indians Lost Their Land: Law and Power on the Frontier.* Cambridge, MA: Harvard University Press, 2005.

Barrett, Carole A., and Harvey Markowitz, eds. *American Indian Biographies.* Pasadena, CA: Salem Press, 2005.

Barton, Lois. *A Quaker Promise Kept: Philadelphia Friends' Work with the Allegany Senecas, 1795–1960.* Eugene, OR: Spencer Butte Press, 1990.

Bauer, William J. Jr. *We Were All like Migrant Workers Here: Work, Community, and Memory on California's Round Valley Reservation, 1850–1941.* Chapel Hill: University of North Carolina Press, 2009.

Baym, Nina. *Women Writers of the American West, 1833–1927.* Urbana: University of Illinois Press, 2011.

Bays, Daniel H., ed. *Foreign Missionary Enterprise at Home: Explorations in North American Cultural History.* Tuscaloosa: University of Alabama Press, 2009.

Bays, Daniel H., Laurie F. Maffly-Kipp, Alvyn Austin, Jay S. F. Blossom, Edith L. Blumhofer, Jay R. Case, Scott Flipse, Mark Y. Hanley, Nancy A. Hardesty, and Kathryn T. Long. *Foreign Missionary Enterprise at Home: Explorations in North American Cultural History.* Tuscaloosa: University of Alabama Press, 2003.

Bellin, Joshua David. *The Demon of the Continent: Indians and the Shaping of American Literature.* Philadelphia: University of Pennsylvania Press, 2001.

Bellin, Joshua David. *Medicine Bundle: Indian Sacred Performance and American Literature, 1824–1932.* Philadelphia: University of Pennsylvania Press, 2008.

Bieder, Robert E. *Native American Communities in Wisconsin, 1600–1960: A Study of Tradition and Change.* Madison: University of Wisconsin Press, 1995.

Birrell, A. J. "D. I. K. Rine and the Gospel Temperance Movement in Canada." *Canadian Historical Review* 58, no. 1 (March 1977): 23–42.

Bliss, Edwin Munsell, Henry Otis Dwight, and H. Allen Tupper, eds. *The Encyclopedia of Missions: Descriptive, Historical, Biographical, Statistical.* 2d ed. New York: Funk and Wagnalls, 1910. https://babel.hathitrust.org/cgi/pt?id=njp.32101078252838;view=1up;seq=7.

Blocker, Jack S., Jr. *Alcohol, Reform, and Society: The Liquor Issue in Social Context.* Westport, CT: Greenwood Press, 1979.

Blocker, Jack S., Jr. *American Temperance Movements: Cycles of Reform.* Boston: Twayne Publishers, 1989.

Board of Home Missions of the Presbyterian Church in the United States. *Reports of the Missionary and Benevolent Boards and Committees to the General Assembly of the Presbyterian Church in the USA.* No publication information.

Boettcher, Graham Corray. "Domestic Violence: The Politics of Family and Nation in Antebellum American Art." PhD dissertation, Yale University, 2006.

Bonnell, Sonciray. "Chemawa Indian Boarding School: The First One Hundred Years, 1880–1980." Master of Arts in Liberal Studies, Dartmouth College, 1997.

Bordin, Ruth B. *Frances Willard: A Biography.* Chapel Hill: University of North Carolina Press, 1986.

Bordin, Ruth Birgitta Anderson. *Woman and Temperance: The Quest for Power and Liberty, 1873–1900.* Philadelphia: Temple University Press, 1981.

Bradford, William, and Edward Winslow. *Mourt's Relation or Journal of the Plantation at Plymouth*. New York: Garret Press, 1969.

"Bright Eyes (Instha Theamba), Mrs. T. H. Tibbles." *Ioway Cultural Institute*. N.d. http://ioway.nativeweb.org/history/bright_eyes.htm.

Britten, Thomas. *American Indians in World War I: At Home and at War*. Albuquerque: University of New Mexico Press, 1997.

Brummitt, Stella Wyatt. *Brother Van*. New York: Missionary Education Movement of the United States and Canada, 1919.

Brummitt, Stella Wyatt. *The Last Decade of the Woman's Home Missionary Society of the Methodist Episcopal Church*. N.p., 1940.

Bruni, John. *Scientific Americans: The Making of Popular Science and Evolution in Early-Twentieth-Century U.S. Literature and Culture*. Cardiff: University of Wales Press, 2014.

Burchill, John K. *Bullets, Badges, and Bridles: Horse Thieves and the Societies That Pursued Them*. Gretna: Pelican, 2014.

Burgess, Larry E., and Laurence M. Hauptman. *The Lake Mohonk Conference of Friends of the Indian: A Guide to the Annual Reports*. New York: Clearwater Press, 1975.

Burich, Keith R. *The Thomas Indian School and the "Irredeemable" Children of New York*. Syracuse, NY: Syracuse University Press, 2016.

Cahill, Cathleen D. *Federal Fathers and Mothers: A Social History of the United States Indian Service, 1869–1933*. Chapel Hill: University of North Carolina Press, 2011.

Callahan, Sophia Alice. "Wynema." In *Native American Women's Writing, c. 1800–1924: An Anthology*, edited by Karen L. Kilcup, 268–72. Oxford: Blackwell, 2000.

Carpenter, Cari M. "Tiresias Speaks: Sarah Winnemucca's Hybrid Selves and Genres." *Legacy: A Journal of American Women Writers* 19, no. 1 (2002): 71–80.

Carter, Harvey L. *The Life and Times of Little Turtle: First Sagamore of the Wabash*. Urbana: University of Illinois Press, 1987.

Caswell, Harriet S. Clark. *Our Life Among the Iroquois Indians*. Boston: Congregational Sunday School and Publishing Society, 1892.

Chalcraft, Edwin L., and Cary C. Collins. *Assimilation's Agent: My Life as a Superintendent in the Indian Boarding School System*. Lincoln: University of Nebraska Press, 2004.

Chandler, J. D. *Hidden History of Portland, Oregon*. Charleston, SC: History Press, 2013.

Chapin, Clara C., ed. *Thumb Nail Sketches of White Ribbon Women, Woman's Christian Temperance Union*. Chicago: Woman's Temperance Publishing Association, 1895.

Cherokee National Female Seminary. *Catalogue of Cherokee National Female Seminary, 1883, Tahlequah, Cherokee Nation, Indian Territory*. N.p., 1883.

Cherrington, Ernest Hurst, ed. *The Anti-Saloon League Year Book, 1910*. Westerville, OH: Anti-Saloon League of America, 1910.

Child, Brenda J. *Boarding School Seasons: American Indian Families, 1900–1940*. Lincoln: University of Nebraska Press, 1998.

Child, Brenda J. *Holding Our World Together: Ojibwe Women and the Survival of Community*. New York: Penguin Books, 2013.

Clemmer, Janice White. "The Confederated Tribes of Warm Springs, Oregon: Nineteenth Century Indian Education History." PhD dissertation, University of Utah, 1980.

Clifton, James A. *Being and Becoming Indian: Biographical Studies of North American Frontiers.* Prospect Heights, IL: Waveland Press, 1993.

Clifton, James A. *The Pokagons, 1683–1983: Catholic Potawatomi Indians of the St. Joseph River Valley.* Lanham, MD: University Press of America, 1984.

Coleman, Michael C. *American Indian Children at School, 1850–1930.* Jackson: University Press of Mississippi, 1993.

Coleman, Michael C. "The Mission Education of Francis La Flesche: An American Indian Response to the Presbyterian Boarding School in the 1860s." *American Studies in Scandinavia* 18, no. 2 (1986): 67–82.

Colman, Julia. *Alcohol and Hygiene: An Elementary Lesson Book for Schools.* New York: National Temperance Society and Publication House, 1883.

Comings, Samuel Huntington, and Lydia Jane Newcomb Comings. *Industrial and Vocational Education, Universal and Self Sustaining (Pagan versus Christian Civilizations).* Boston: Christopher Publishing House, 1915. http://hdl.loc.gov/loc.gdc/scd0001.00295013813.

Cook, Minnie A. *Apostle to the Pima Indians: The Story of Charles H. Cook, the First Missionary to the Pimas.* Tiburon, CA: Omega Books, 1976.

Cook, Sharon Anne. "'Earnest Christian Women, Bent on Saving Our Canadian Youth': The Ontario Woman's Christian Temperance Union and Scientific Temperance Instruction, 1881–1930." *Ontario History* 86, no. 3 (September 1994): 249–67.

Cook, Sharon Anne. "Educating for Temperance: The Woman's Christian Temperance Union and Ontario Children, 1880–1916." *Historical Studies in Education* 5, no. 2 (September 1993): 251–77.

Coward, John M. *The Newspaper Indian: Native American Identity in the Press, 1820–1890.* Urbana: University of Illinois Press, 1999.

Crawford O'Brien, Suzanne J. *Coming Full Circle: Spirituality and Wellness among Native Communities in the Pacific Northwest.* Lincoln: University of Nebraska Press, 2013.

Danver, Steven L. "Metlakatla: Native Leadership and White Resistance in an Alaskan Mission Community." *Journal of the West* 46, no. 4 (Fall 2007): 40–47.

Davis, Janet M. *The Gospel of Kindness: Animal Welfare and the Making of Modern America.* New York: Oxford University Press, 2016.

Davison, Kathleen. *Fort Totten: Military Post and Indian School, 1867–1959.* 2nd ed. Bismarck: State Historical Society of North Dakota, 2010.

Del Mar, David Peterson. *Beaten Down: A History of Interpersonal Violence in the West.* Seattle: University of Washington Press, 2002.

Deloria, Philip J. "Four Thousand Invitations." *Studies in American Indian Literatures* 25, no. 2 (2013): 23–43.

Deloria, Philip J. *Indians in Unexpected Places.* Lawrence: University Press of Kansas, 2004.

Demallie, Raymond J., and Douglas R. Parks. *Sioux Indian Religion.* Norman: University of Oklahoma Press, 1987.

Dennis, Matthew. *Seneca Possessed: Indians, Witchcraft, and Power in the Early American Republic.* Philadelphia: University of Pennsylvania Press, 2010.

DeTora, Lisa. "Denial, Discovery and Domestic Violence: A Consideration of Domestic Violence, as Represented across Disciplines, from the 19th Century to the Present in American Culture." PhD dissertation, University of Rochester, 2000.

Donehoo, George Patterson, Dorcas Spencer, and Woman's Christian Temperance Union. *The Real Indian of the Past and the Real Indian of the Present.* Evanston, IL: Issued by the Department of Work Among Indians, 1912. https://babel.hathitrust .org/cgi/pt?id=uc1.31175032014873;view=1up;seq=3.

Dunlap, Leslie Kathrin. "In the Name of the Home: Temperance Women and Southern Grass-Roots Politics, 1873–1933." PhD dissertation, Northwestern University, 2001.

Edwards, Wendy J. Deichmann, and Carolyn De Swarte Gifford, eds. *Gender and the Social Gospel.* Urbana: University of Illinois Press, 2003.

Ehlers, Cindy L., Tiebing Liang, and Ian R. Gizer. "ADH and ALDH Polymorphisms and Alcohol Dependence in Mexican and Native Americans." *American Journal of Drug and Alcohol Abuse* 38, no. 5 (September 2012): 389–94.

Ellis, Clyde. *A Dancing People: Pow-Wow Culture on the Southern Plains.* Lawrence: University of Kansas Press, 2003.

Ellis, Clyde. *To Change Them Forever: Indian Education at the Rainy Mountain Boarding School, 1893–1920.* Norman: University of Oklahoma Press, 2008.

Emmerich, Lisa E. "Helen Hunt Jackson and Her Indian Reform Legacy." *Journal of American History* 78, no. 2 (September 1991): 688.

Engle, Nancy Arlene Driscol. "Benefiting a City: Women, Respectability and Reform in Spokane, Washington, 1886–1910." PhD dissertation, University of Florida, 2003.

Engs, Robert Francis. *Educating the Disfranchised and Disinherited: Samuel Chapman Armstrong and Hampton Institute, 1839–1893.* Knoxville: University of Tennessee Press, 1999.

Erickson, Judith B. "Making King Alcohol Tremble: The Juvenile Work of the Woman's Christian Temperance Union, 1874–1900." *International Journal of Suicide and Crisis Studies* 18, no. 4 (1988): 333–52.

Fahey, David M. *Temperance and Racism: John Bull, Johnny Reb, and the Good Templars.* Lexington: University Press of Kentucky, 1996.

Fear-Segal, Jacqueline, and Susan D. Rose, eds. *Carlisle Indian Industrial School: Indigenous Histories, Memories, and Reclamations.* Lincoln: University of Nebraska Press, 2016.

Fenton, William N. *The Great Law and the Longhouse: A Political History of the Iroquois Confederacy.* Norman: University of Oklahoma Press, 1998.

Fisher, Linford D. *The Indian Great Awakening: Religion and the Shaping of Native Cultures in Early America.* Oxford: Oxford University Press, 2014.

Forbes, Jack D. "Intellectual Self-Determination and Sovereignty: Implications for Native Studies and for Native Intellectuals." *Wicazo Sa Review* 13, no. 1 (1998): 11–23.

Forrest, Earle R. *Missions and Pueblos of the Old Southwest.* Cleveland, OH: Arthur H. Clark, 1929.

Fouberg, Erin Hogan. *Tribal Territory and Tribal Sovereignty: A Study of the Cheyenne River and Lake Traverse Indian Reservations.* New York: Garland Publishing, 2000.

Fraser, Julia. *The Modern Apostle to the Indians.* Work Among Indians Department Leaflets, No. 403. Evanston, IL: National W.C.T.U., 190[?]. https://babel.hathitrust .org/cgi/pt?id=uc1.31175032015235;q1=The%20Modern%20Apostle%20to%20 the%20Indians.

Frick, John W. *Theatre, Culture and Temperance Reform in Nineteenth-Century America.* Cambridge: Cambridge University Press, 2008.

Fry, Maggie Culver. *Cherokee Female Seminary Years: A Cherokee National Anthology, Biographical and Autobiographical Narratives Told against Historical Background.* N.p.: Rogers State College Press, 1988.

Gaeng, Betty Lou. *Chirouse: The Reverend Father Eugene Casimir Chirouse, a Pioneer in Oregon and Washington Territories.* N.p., 2011.

Gallup-Diaz, Ignacio, and Geoffrey Plank, eds. *Quakers and Native Americans.* Leiden: Brill, 2019.

Ganteaume, Cécile R. *Officially Indian: Symbols That Define the United States.* Washington, DC: National Museum of the American Indian, 2017.

Garbutt, Mary Alderman. *Victories of Four Decades: A History of the Woman's Christian Temperance Union of Southern California 1883–1924.* 1924. Reprint, [California?]: [Woman's Christian Temperance Union of Southern California?], 1966.

Garrison, Tim Alan, and Greg O'Brien. *The Native South: New Histories and Enduring Legacies.* Lincoln: University of Nebraska Press, 2017.

Genetin-Pilawa, C. Joseph. *Crooked Paths to Allotment: The Fight over Federal Indian Policy after the Civil War.* Chapel Hill: University of North Carolina Press, 2012.

Genzoli, Andrew. "How Christmas Prairie Received Its Name." *Humboldt Historian* 50, no. 6 (1992).

Gill, K., M. Eagle Elk, Y. Liu, and R. A. Deitrich. "An Examination of ALDH2 Genotypes, Alcohol Metabolism and the Flushing Response in Native Americans." *Journal of Studies on Alcohol and Drugs* 60, no. 2 (1999): 149–58.

Goeman, Mishuana. *Mark My Words: Native Women Mapping Our Nations.* Minneapolis: University of Minnesota Press, 2013.

Goodykoontz, Colin Brummitt. *Home Missions on the American Frontier, with Particular Reference to the American Home Missionary Society.* 1939. Reprint, New York: Octagon Books, 1971.

Gordon, Anna A. *Frances E. Willard: A Memorial Volume.* Chicago: Woman's Temperance Publishing Association, 1898. https://archive.org/details/francesewillardm 00gord.

Gordon, Anna A. *Jubilee Songs.* Evanston, IL: National Woman's Christian Temperance Union Publishing House, 1923.

Gordon, Anna A. *Juvenile Work. Questions Answered.* Chicago: Woman's Temperance Publishing Association, 1891.

Gordon, Anna A. *Marching Songs for Young Crusaders. No. 2, Temperance Songs for the Cold Water Army.* Chicago: Woman's Temperance Publishing Association, 1890.

Gordon, Anna A. *Songs of the Young Women's Christian Temperance Union.* Chicago: Woman's Temperance Publishing Association, 1889.

Gordon, Elizabeth Putnam. *Women Torch-Bearers: The Story of the Woman's Christian Temperance Union.* Evanston, IL: National Woman's Christian Temperance Union Publishing House, 1924. 2nd ed. [Montana?]: Kessinger, 2007.

Graham, Frances W. *Four Decades: A History of Forty Years' Work of the Woman's Christian Temperance Union of the State of New York.* New York: Salvation Army Press, 1914.

Graham, Frances W., and Georgeanna M. Gardenier. *Two Decades: A History of the First Twenty Years' Work of the Woman's Christian Temperance Union of the State of New York.* Oswego, NY: Press of R. J. Oliphant, 1894.

Graymont, Barbara. "New York State Indian Policy after the Revolution." *New York History* 57, no. 4 (October 1976): 438–74.

Greer, John. "Brief History of Indian Education at the Fort Shaw Industrial School." Master's thesis, Montana State University, 1958.

Grillot, Thomas. *First Americans: U.S. Patriotism in Indian Country after World War I.* New Haven: Yale University Press, 2018.

Guernsey, Alice M. *Home Missions on the Border.* New York: Woman's Home Missionary Society, n.d.

Guinda Indian Industrial School. *The Guinda Indian School.* Guinda Indian Industrial School, 1913. https://babel.hathitrust.org/cgi/pt?id=nnc2.ark%3A%2F13960%2Ft17m47185;q1=The%20Guinda%20Indian%20School.

Gullett, Gayle Ann. *Becoming Citizens: The Emergence and Development of the California Women's Movement, 1880–1911.* Urbana: University of Illinois Press, 2000.

Gwydir, Rickard D., and Kevin Dye. *Recollections from the Colville Indian Agency, 1886–1889.* Spokane: Arthur H. Clark, 2001.

Hadley, Richard Ernest. "An Analysis of the Southern California Woman's Christian Temperance Union, 1920–1938, As an Expression of Progressivism." Master's thesis, University of Southern California, 1970.

Hale, Frederick. "The Confrontation of Cherokee Traditional Religion and Christianity in Diane Glancy's Pushing the Bear." *Missionalia* 25, no. 2 (August 1997): 195–209.

Hansen, Karen V. *Encounter on the Great Plains: Scandinavian Settlers and the Dispossession of Dakota Indians, 1890–1930.* Oxford: Oxford University Press, 2016.

Harmon, Wendell E. "A History of the Prohibition Movement in California." PhD dissertation, University of California, Los Angeles, 1955.

Hauptman, Laurence M. *Conspiracy of Interests: Iroquois Dispossession and the Rise of New York State.* Syracuse, NY: Syracuse University Press, 2001.

Hauptman, Laurence M. "The Meddlesome Friend: Philip Evan Thomas among the Onöndowa'ga', 1838–1861." In Gallup-Diaz and Plank, *Quakers and Native Americans.*

Hauptman, Laurence M. "Senecas and Subdividers: Resistance to Allotment of Indian Lands in New York, 1875–1906." *Prologue* 26 (1994): 86–99.

Hayes, Susanna Adella. "The Resistance to Education for Assimilation by the Colville Indians, 1872 to 1972." PhD dissertation, University of Michigan, 1973.

Hays, Mrs. Glenn G. [Agnes Dubbs]. *Heritage of Dedication: One Hundred Years of the National Woman's Christian Temperance Union, 1874–1974.* Evanston, IL: Signal Press, 1973.

Hebard, Grace Raymond. *Sacajawea: A Guide and Interpreter of the Lewis and Clark Expedition, with an Account of the Travels of Toussaint Charbonneau, and of Jean Baptiste, the Expedition Papoose.* Glendale, CA: A. H. Clark, 1967.

Heizer, Robert F. *The Destruction of California Indians: A Collection of Documents from the Period 1847 to 1865 in Which Are Described Some of the Things That Happened to Some of the Indians of California.* Lincoln: University of Nebraska Press, 1993.

Helleson, Linda Louise. "The Lake Mohonk Conferences of the Friends of the Indian, 1883–1916." Master's thesis, University of Denver, 1974.

Heykes, Benjamin Nelson. "White Ribbon Women and the Golden Gate of Heaven: Religion, Nature, Region, and the Women's Christian Temperance Union of California." Master's thesis, Graduate Theological Union, 2012.

Hill, Richard W., Sr. "Regenerating Identity: Repatriation and the Indian Frame of Mind." In *Archaeology of the Iroquois: Selected Readings and Research Sources*, edited by Jordan E. Kerber, 420. Syracuse: Syracuse University Press, 2007.

Hill, Thomas. *Native American Drinking: Life Styles, Alcohol Use, Drunken Comportment, Problem Drinking, and the Peyote Religion*. Los Angeles: New University Press, 2013.

Hillerman, Abbie. *History of the Woman's Christian Temperance Union of Indian Territory, Oklahoma Territory, State of Oklahoma, 1888–1925*. Sapulpa, OK: Jennings Printing and Stationery, 1925.

Hinken, Susan Elizabeth. "The Woman's Christian Temperance Union of Oregon, 1880–1916." Master's thesis, University of Portland, 1987.

Hoag, Rev. Alice Barnes, and Mrs. Matthew W. Alderson. *Historical Sketch of the Montana Woman's Christian Temperance Union, 1883–1912*. Helena: State Publishing, 1912.

Hollister, Ovando James. *Words and Deeds: The Mormons and Temperance: How the Lamb Roils the Stream for the Wolf*. [Salt Lake City?]: n.p., 1884.

Holtby, David V. *Forty-Seventh Star: New Mexico's Struggle for Statehood*. Norman: University of Oklahoma Press, 2016.

Holzhueter, John O. *Madeline Island and the Chequamegon Region*. Madison: State Historical Society of Wisconsin, 1974. https://ebookcentral-proquest-com.ezproxy.naz .edu/lib/naz-ebooks/reader.action?docID=3417341&query=&ppg=1.

Horton, Sidney. "Senecas and Their Neighbors: An Ethnographic and Historical Portrait." PhD dissertation, State University of New York at Buffalo, 2010.

Hubbard, Jeremiah. *Grand River Monthly Meeting of Friends: Composed of Indians*. Carthage, MO: Press Book and Job Printing House, 1886.

Huebner, Karin L. "An Unexpected Alliance: Stella Atwood, the California Clubwomen, John Collier, and the Indians of the Southwest, 1917–1934." *Pacific Historical Review* 78, no. 3 (August 2009): 337–66.

Hull, Mary H. *Columbus and What He Found*. Chicago: Woman's Temperance Publishing Association, 1892.

Hyer, Sally, Joseph Abeyta, and Margaret Szasz. *One House, One Voice, One Heart: Native American Education at the Santa Fe Indian School*. Santa Fe: Museum of New Mexico Press, 1990.

Inter-State Publishing Company. *An Illustrated History of Skagit and Snohomish Counties; Their People, Their Commerce and Their Resources, with an Outline of the Early History of the State of Washington*. Chicago: Interstate Publishing, 1906.

Irwin, Mary Ann., Robert W. Cherny, and Ann Marie Wilson. *California Women and Politics: From the Gold Rush to the Great Depression*. Lincoln: University of Nebraska Press, 2011.

Isenberg, Michael T. *John L. Sullivan and His America*. Urbana: University of Illinois Press, 1994.

Ishii, Izumi. *Bad Fruits of the Civilized Tree: Alcohol and the Sovereignty of the Cherokee Nation*. Lincoln: University of Nebraska Press, 2008.

Jackson, Helen Hunt. *A Century of Dishonor: The Early Crusade for Indian Reform*. Edited by Andrew F. Rolle. New York: Harper Torchbooks, 1965.

Jackson, Helen Hunt. *Century of Dishonor: A Sketch of the United States Government's Dealings with Some Indian Tribes*. Boston: Roberts Brothers, 1891. https://babel.hathi trust.org/cgi/pt?id=c00.31924088025006;view=1up;seq=9.

Jackson, Helen Hunt. *Ramona: A Story*. Boston: Roberts Bros., 1884. Reprint, Boston: Little Brown, 1905.

Jackson, Helen Hunt, and Valerie Sherer Mathes. *The Indian Reform Letters of Helen Hunt Jackson, 1879–1885*. Norman: University of Oklahoma Press, 2015.

Jacobs, Margaret D. "Clara True and Female Moral Authority." In *The Human Tradition in the American West*, edited by Benson Tong and Regan A. Lutz. Wilmington, DE: Scholarly Resources, 2002.

Jacobs, Margaret D. "Resistance to Rescue: The Indians of Bahapki and Mrs. Annie E. K. Bidwell." In *Writing the Range: Race, Class, and Culture in the Women's West*, edited by Elizabeth Jameson and Susan H. Armitage, 230–51. Norman: University of Oklahoma Press, 1997.

Jacobs, Margaret D. *White Mother to a Dark Race: Settler Colonialism, Maternalism, and the Removal of Indigenous Children in the American West and Australia, 1880–1940*. Lincoln: University of Nebraska Press, 2009.

Jacobson, Lori L. "Agencies and Associations: Women Writing Indian Reform in Nineteenth-Century America." PhD dissertation, State University of New York at Buffalo, 2007.

Jaimes, M. Annette. *The State of Native America: Genocide, Colonization, and Resistance*. Boston: South End Press, 1992.

Jameson, Elizabeth, and Susan H. Armitage. *Writing the Range: Race, Class, and Culture in the Women's West*. Norman: University of Oklahoma Press, 1997.

Jewett, Frances Gulick. *Town and City*. Boston: Ginn, 1909.

Johnson, Elias. *Legends, Traditions and Laws of the Iroquois, or Six Nations, and History of the Tuscarora Indians*. 1881. Reprint, New York: AMS Reprints, 1978.

Johnson, Paul E. *A Shopkeeper's Millennium: Society and Revivals in Rochester, New York, 1815–1837*. New York: Hill and Wang, 2004.

Johnson, Thomas Hoevet, and Helen S. Johnson. *Also Called Sacajawea: Chief Woman's Stolen Identity*. Long Grove, IL: Waveland Press, 2008.

Johnson, Yvonne, ed. *Feminist Frontiers: Women Who Shaped the Midwest*. Kirksville, MO: Truman State University Press, 2010.

Johnston, Carolyn. *Cherokee Women in Crisis: Trail of Tears, Civil War, and Allotment, 1838–1907*. Tuscaloosa: University of Alabama Press, 2003.

Johnston, Carolyn. *Voices of Cherokee Women*. Winston-Salem, NC: John F. Blair, 2013.

Kants, Lizzie. "Letter from our Indian Sisters." May 16, 1895. In *Minutes of the Thirteenth Annual Convention of the Woman's Christian Temperance Union of Oregon, Roseburg, May 15–17, 1895*, 37–38. Portland: J. F. Gotshall, 1895. Annual Meeting Minutes of Woman's Christian Temperance Union of Oregon, MCL.

Kelsey, Penelope Myrtle. *Tribal Theory in Native American Literature: Dakota and Haudenosaunee Writing and Indigenous Worldviews*. Lincoln: University of Nebraska Press, 2008.

Kelsey, Rayner Wickersham. *Friends and the Indians, 1655–1917.* Philadelphia: Associated Executive Committee of Friends on Indian Affairs, 1917.

Kidwell, Clara Sue. "Bright Eyes: The Story of Susette LaFlesche, an Omaha Indian." *Journal of Ethnic Studies* 2, no. 4 (January 1975): 117–22.

Kilcup, Karen L. *Native American Women's Writing, c. 1800–1924: An Anthology.* Oxford: Blackwell, 2000.

Kimbert, Victor Gage. "The Only Indian WCTU in the State." *Sunday Herald,* July 20, 1902. Miscellaneous Vertical Files, Temperance Societies, OHA.

Klein, James Edward. *Grappling with Demon Rum: The Cultural Struggle over Liquor in Early Oklahoma.* Norman: University of Oklahoma Press, 2008.

Kracht, Benjamin R. *Religious Revitalization among the Kiowas: The Ghost Dance, Peyote, and Christianity.* Lincoln: University of Nebraska Press, 2018.

Kreider, Marie L., and Michael R. Wells. "White Ribbon Women: The Women's Christian Temperance Movement in Riverside, California." *Southern California Quarterly* 81, no. 1 (1999): 117–34.

Krouse, Susan Applegate, and Joseph K. Dixon. *North American Indians in the Great War.* Lincoln: University of Nebraska Press, 2007.

Kugel, Rebecca, and Lucy Eldersveld Murphy. *Native Women's History in Eastern North America before 1900: A Guide to Research and Writing.* Lincoln: University of Nebraska Press, 2007.

Kunitz, Stephen J. and Jerrold E. Levy. *Drinking Careers: A Twenty-Five-Year Study of Three Navajo Populations.* New Haven: Yale University Press, 1994.

Laird, W. David. "Apostle to the Pima Indians: The Story of Charles H. Cook, the First Missionary to the Pimas." *Arizona and the West* 19, no. 4 (December 1977): 386–87.

Lappas, Thomas J. "Iroquois Temperance Societies: Facing Modernity on the Western Reservations in the Nineteenth Century." *Topos: Bilingual Journal of Space and Humanities* 1 (2011): 37–49.

Lappas, Thomas J. *"Tunesassa Echoes* and the Temperance Struggle: A Family Tradition at Tunesassa Quaker Indian School, Allegany Indian Reservation across Generations." In Gallup-Diaz and Plank, *Quakers and Native Americans,* 158–76.

Larner, John W. *Guide to the Scholarly Resources Microfilm Edition of the Papers of the Society of American Indians.* Wilmington, DE: Scholarly Resources, 1987.

Laubach, David Charles. *American Baptist Home Mission Roots, 1824–2010.* Valley Forge, PA: American Baptist Home Mission Societies, 2010.

Leavitt, Gertrude Stevens, and Margaret L. Sargeant. *Lillian M. N. Stevens: A Life Sketch.* 1921. http://pds.lib.harvard.edu/pds/view/2582388?n=8&s=4&printThumbnails=no&oldpds.

Lentz, Andrea D., and Francis X. Blouin. *Temperance and Prohibition Papers: A Joint Microfilm Publication of the Ohio Historical Society, Michigan Historical Collections and Woman's Christian Temperance Union.* Sponsored by the National Historical Publications and Records Commission, Columbus. Microfilmed by the Ohio Historical Society, 1977. Microfilm.

Leonard, Thomas C. *Illiberal Reformers: Race, Eugenics, and American Economics in the Progressive Era.* Princeton, NJ: Princeton University Press, 2017.

Leupp, Francis E. "Liquor Traffic in the Indian Country." *Report of the Commissioner of Indian Affairs to the Secretary of the Interior,* 30–36. Washington, DC: Government Printing Office, 1907. https://babel.hathitrust.org/cgi/pt?id=osu.32435064041759;

view=1up;seq=36.Levack, Brian P. *The Oxford Handbook of Witchcraft in Early Modern Europe and Colonial America*. New York: Oxford University Press, 2014.

Lewis, Bonnie Sue. *Creating Christian Indians: Native Clergy in the Presbyterian Church*. Norman: University of Oklahoma Press, 2003.

Lindsey, Donal F. *Indians at Hampton Institute, 1877–1923*. Urbana: University of Illinois Press, 1995.

Lindsey, Lilah Denton. "History of Indian Territory WCTU." Vols. 1–2. In Folder 17, Box 2, Series III, Lilah Denton Lindsey Papers, ML.

Lönnberg, Allan. "The Digger Indian Stereotype in California." *Journal of California and Great Basin Anthropology* 3, no. 2 (1981): 215–23.

Maddox, Lucy. *Citizen Indians: Native American Intellectuals, Race, and Reform*. Ithaca, NY: Cornell University Press, 2005.

Mancall, Peter C. *Deadly Medicine: Indians and Alcohol in Early America*. Ithaca, NY: Cornell University Press, 1995.

Mandell, Daniel R. "'Lo, the Poor Indian': Native Americans, Reality and Imagery." *Reviews in American History* 38, no. 3 (September 2010): 407–13.

Mankiller, Wilma Pearl. *Every Day Is a Good Day: Reflections by Contemporary Indigenous Women*. Golden, CO: Fulcrum, 2011.

Mann, John W. W. *Sacajawea's People: The Lemhi Shoshones and the Salmon River Country*. Lincoln: University of Nebraska Press, 2004.

Maroukis, Thomas C. "The Peyote Controversy and the Demise of the Society of American Indians." *American Indian Quarterly* 37, no. 3 (2013): 159–80.

Maroukis, Thomas C. *The Peyote Road: Religious Freedom and the Native American Church*. Norman: University of Oklahoma Press, 2014.

Marsden, George M. *Fundamentalism and American Culture: The Shaping of Twentieth-Century Evangelism, 1870–1925*. Oxford: Oxford University Press, 1980.

Martin, Jill E. "'The Greatest Evil': Interpretations of Indian Prohibition Laws, 1832–1953." *Great Plains Quarterly* 23, no. 1 (January 1, 2003): 35–53.

Martis, Kenneth C. *The Historical Atlas of Political Parties in the United States Congress, 1789–1989*. New York: Macmillan, 1989.

Masson, Erin M. "The Women's Christian Temperance Union 1874–1898: Combating Domestic Violence." *William and Mary Journal of Women and Law* 3, no. 1 (1997): 163–88.

Mathes, Valerie Sherer. *Divinely Guided: The California Work of the Women's National Indian Association*. Lubbock: Texas Tech University Press, 2012.

Mathes, Valerie Sherer. *Helen Hunt Jackson and Her Indian Reform Legacy*. Austin: University of Texas Press, 1990.

Mathes, Valerie Sherer. "Susan Laflesche Picotte, MD: Nineteenth-Century Physician and Reformer." *Great Plains Quarterly* 13, no. 3 (June 1993): 172–86.

Mathes, Valerie Sherer. *The Women's National Indian Association: A History*. Albuquerque: University of New Mexico Press, 2015.

Mathes, Valerie Sherer, and Phil Brigandi. *A Call for Reform: The Southern California Indian Writings of Helen Hunt Jackson*. Norman: University of Oklahoma Press, 2015.

Mathes, Valerie Sherer, and Phil Brigandi. *Reservations, Removal, and Reform: The Mission Indian Agents of Southern California, 1878–1903*. Norman: University of Oklahoma Press, 2018.

Mathes, Valerie Sherer, and Richard Lowitt. *The Standing Bear Controversy: Prelude to Indian Reform*. Urbana: University of Illinois Press, 2003.

Mattingly, Carol. "Woman's Temple, Women's Fountains: The Erasure of Public Memory." *American Studies* 49, no. 3/4 (Winter 2008): 133–56.

May, Jon D. "'The Most Ferocious of Monsters': The Story of Outlaw Crawford Goldsby, Alias 'Cherokee Bill.'" *Chronicles of Oklahoma* 77, no. 3 (September 1999): 272–89.

McClary, Andrew. "The WCTU Discovers Science: The Women's Christian Temperance Union, Plus Teachers, Doctors and Scientific Temperance." *Michigan History* 68, no. 1 (January 1984): 16–23.

McGirr, Lisa. *The War on Alcohol: Prohibition and the Rise of the American State*. New York: W. W. Norton, 2016.

McKenzie, Fayette Avery. *The Indian and Citizenship*. Title 2472. Washington, DC: Society of American Indians, 1912. https://babel.hathitrust.org/cgi/pt?id=mdp.39015016465893;view=1up;seq=3.

Mead, Rebecca J. *How the Vote Was Won: Woman Suffrage in the Western United States, 1868–1914*. New York: New York University Press, 2004.

Meeker, Ruth Esther. *Six Decades of Service, 1880–1940, a History of the Woman's Home Missionary Society of the Methodist Episcopal Church*. [Cincinnati, OH]: [Steinhauser], 1969.

Merriam, C. Hart, and Northern California Indian Association. *The Indian Population of California*. San Jose: Northern California Indian Association, 191[?]. https://babel.hathitrust.org/cgi/pt?id=nnc2.ark:/13960/t9g48n88b.

Methodist Episcopal Church. *Minutes of the Cincinnati Annual Conference of the Methodist Episcopal Church*. Vol. 12. Cincinnati, OH: Western Methodist Book Concern Press, 1899.

Meyer, Sabine N. *We Are What We Drink: The Temperance Battle in Minnesota*. Urbana: University of Illinois Press, 2015.

Miles, Tiya. *The House on Diamond Hill: A Cherokee Plantation Story*. Chapel Hill: University of North Carolina Press, 2010.

Miller, David Reed. *The History of the Assiniboine and Sioux Tribes of the Fort Peck Indian Reservation, 1600–2012*. 2nd ed. Poplar, MT: Fort Peck Community College, 2012.

Minges, Patrick N. *Slavery in the Cherokee Nation: The Keetoowah Society and the Defining of a People, 1855–1867*. New York: Routledge, 2003.

Mintz, Steven. *Moralists and Modernizers: America's Pre–Civil War Reformers*. The American Moment. Baltimore: Johns Hopkins University Press, 1995.

Minutes and Year Book of Indian Territory WCTU and Oklahoma Territory WCTU and Woman's Christian Temperance Union of The State of Oklahoma. Muskogee: Muskogee Printing Company, 1908. OHC.

Minutes of the General Assembly of the United Presbyterian Church of North America. Pittsburgh: United Presbyterian Board of Publication, 1904.

Minutes of the Iowa Yearly Meeting of Friends. Oskaloosa, IA: Herald, 1889.

Mitchell, Timothy. *Intoxicated Identities: Alcohol's Power in Mexican History and Culture*. New York: Routledge, 2004.

Mitchinson, Wendy. "The Woman's Christian Temperance Union: A Study in Organization." *International Journal of Women's Studies* 4, no. 2 (March 1981): 143–56.

Montezuma, Carlos, and Woman's Christian Temperance Union. *The Indian of Tomorrow: An Address*. Chicago: Ruby I. Gilbert, 1888. https://babel.hathitrust.org/cgi/pt?id=ucl.31175032015284;view=1up;seq=3.

Mooney, James. *The Ghost Dance Religion and the Sioux Outbreak of 1890*. 1896. Reprint, Lincoln: University of Nebraska Press, 1991.

Moore, O. E. *The Story of the Temperance Congress Auxiliary to the California Midwinter International Exposition, 1894*. San Francisco, CA: R. R. Patterson, 1894. https://babel.hathitrust.org/cgi/pt?id=ucl.31158010727609;view=1up;seq=14.

Morton, Marian J. "Temperance, Benevolence, and the City: The Cleveland Nonpartisan Woman's Christian Temperance Union, 1874–1900." *Ohio History* 91 (August 1982): 58–73.

Murdock, Catherine Gilbert. *Domesticating Drink: Women, Men, and Alcohol in America, 1870–1940*. Baltimore: Johns Hopkins University Press, 2002.

Neuman, Lisa Kay. *Indian Play: Indigenous Identities at Bacone College*. Lincoln: University of Nebraska Press, 2014.

Nicholas, Mark A. "A Little School, a Reservation Divided: Quaker Education and Allegany Seneca Leadership in the Early American Republic." *American Indian Culture and Research Journal* 30, no. 3 (September 2006): 1–21.

Northern California Indian Association. *The Fifth Zayante Indian Conference: Mount Hermon, California, August 9, 1910*. N.p., 1910. https://babel.hathitrust.org/cgi/pt?id=ucl.31175031701819.

Official Proceedings of the 19th and 20th Annual Meetings of the Women's [sic] Christian Temperance Union of Indian Territory, Afton, October 26–30, 1906, and Tulsa, October 16–20, 1907. Wewoka: Seminole Printing, 1907.

Okrent, Daniel. *Last Call: The Rise and Fall of Prohibition*. New York: Scribner, 2010.

O'Leary-Siemer, Clare Denise. "Roots of the New Mexico Women's Movement: Missionaries and the New Mexico Woman's Christian Temperance Union." Master's thesis, University of New Mexico, 1997.

Osburn, Katherine M. B. "A Necessary Balance: Gender and Power among Indians of the Columbia Plateau." *Journal of American Ethnic History* 25, no. 2/3 (Winter/Spring 2006): 289–93.

Ostrander, Gilman Marston. *The Prohibition Movement in California, 1848–1933*. Berkeley: University of California Press, 1957.

Paddison, Joshua. *American Heathens: Religion, Race, and Reconstruction in California*. Berkeley: University of California Press, 2012.

Parker, Dorothy R. *Phoenix Indian School: The Second Half-Century*. Tucson: University of Arizona Press, 2017.

Parman, Donald Lee. *Indians and the American West in the Twentieth Century*. Bloomington: Indiana University Press, 1994.

Pascoe, Peggy. *Relations of Rescue: The Search for Female Moral Authority in the American West, 1874–1939*. New York: Oxford University Press, 1990.

Pearson, Arnold, and Esther Pearson. *Early Churches of Washington State*. Seattle: University of Washington Press, 1980.

Pegram, Thomas R. *Battling Demon Rum: The Struggle for a Dry America, 1800–1933*. Chicago: Ivan R. Dee, 1998.

Perdue, Theda. *Cherokee Women: Gender and Culture Change, 1700–1835*. Lincoln: University of Nebraska Press, 1999.

Pesantubbee, Michelene E. *Choctaw Women in a Chaotic World: The Clash of Cultures in the Colonial Southeast*. Albuquerque: University of New Mexico Press, 2005.

Peyer, Bernd C., ed. *American Indian Nonfiction: An Anthology of Writings, 1760s–1930s*. Norman: University of Oklahoma Press, 2007.

Philips, Susan Urmston. *The Invisible Culture: Communication in Classroom and Community on the Warm Springs Indian Reservation*. New York: Longman, 1983; Prospect Heights, IL: Waveland Press, 1993.

Phillips, Kate. *Helen Hunt Jackson: A Literary Life*. Berkeley: University of California Press, 2003.

Philp, Kenneth R., ed. *Indian Self Rule: First-Hand Accounts of Indian-White Relations from Roosevelt to Reagan*. Boulder: University Press of Colorado, 1986.

Philp, Kenneth R. *John Collier's Crusade for Indian Reform, 1920–1954*. Tucson: University of Arizona Press, 1977.

Phoenix Indian School. *Views of United States Indian School, Phoenix, Arizona*. Phoenix: Native American Press, 1915. https://babel.hathitrust.org/cgi/pt?id=njp.32101078162441;view=1up;seq=1.

Pickering, Robert B., ed. *Peace Medals: Negotiating Power in Early America*. Tulsa, OK: Gilcrease Museum, 2011.

Pierce, Lydia. "From an Indian to Indians" [1915?]. Blue Publications Binder, FWMLA, Evanston, IL.

Pinhey, Thomas K., Daniel A. Lennon, and Nicholas A. Pinhey. "Consumer Debt, Alcohol Use, and Domestic Violence in Guam." *Pacific Studies* 20, no. 4 (December 1997): 51–60.

Pollack, Adam J. *John L. Sullivan: The Career of the First Gloved Heavyweight Champion*. Jefferson, NC: McFarland, 2006.

Pound, Cuthbert W. "Nationals without a Nation: The New York State Tribal Indians." *Columbia Law Review* 22, no. 2 (1922): 97–102.

Presbyterian Church in the USA. *The American Indian and Missions*. New York: Presbyterian Board of Home Missions, 1918.

Presbyterian Church in the USA. *Annual Report of the Committee of Home Missions*. New York: Mission Rooms, 1871–1918.

Presbyterian Church in the USA. *The Pacific Coast Alaska, Washington and Oregon, California*. New York: Home Missions of the Presbyterian Church in the USA, 1913.

Pripas-Kapit, Sarah. "We Have Lived on Broken Promises." *Great Plains Quarterly* 35, no. 1 (2015): 51–78.

Proceedings of the Annual Meeting of the Lake Mohonk Conference of Friends of the Indian. New York: Lake Mohonk Conference, 1887–1910.

Proudfit, Joely, and Nicole Quinderro Myers-Lim. *On Indian Ground: California*. Charlotte, NC: Information Age Publishing, 2017.

Prucha, Francis Paul. *American Indian Policy in Crisis: Christian Reformers and the Indian, 1865–1900*. Norman: University of Oklahoma Press, 1976.

Prucha, Francis Paul. *The Great Father: The United States Government and the American Indians*. Lincoln: University of Nebraska Press, 1995.

Prucha, Francis Paul. *Indian Peace Medals in American History*. Norman: University of Oklahoma Press, 2000.

Prussing, Erica. "Warriors and Survivors: The Culture of Sobriety in Northern Cheyenne Women's Narratives." PhD dissertation, University of California San Diego, 1999.

Prussing, Erica. *White Man's Water: The Politics of Sobriety in a Native American Community.* Tucson: University of Arizona Press, 2011.

Purdy, John Lloyd. *Writing Indian, Native Conversations.* Lincoln: University of Nebraska Press, 2009.

Putman, Edison Klein. "The Prohibition Movement in Idaho, 1863–1934." PhD dissertation, University of Idaho, 1979.

Putnam, John. "Racism and Temperature." *Pacific Northwest Quarterly* 95, no. 2 (2004): 70–81.

Qoyawayma, Polingaysi. *No Turning Back: A True Account of a Hopi Woman's Struggle to Live in Two Worlds.* Albuquerque: University of New Mexico Press, 2003.

Ramsey, Robert E. "'My God Eddie, What Will We Do?' The Ramsey Family's Experiences on the Pima Indian Reservation, 1926–1964." *Journal of Arizona History* 42, no. 1 (March 2001): 23–38.

Rawls, James J. *Indians of California: The Changing Image.* Norman: University of Oklahoma Press, 1984.

Reid, Gerald F. *Kahnawà:Ke: Factionalism, Traditionalism, and Nationalism in a Mohawk Community.* Lincoln: University of Nebraska Press, 2004.

Remele, Larry. *Fort Totten: Military Post and Indian School, 1867–1959.* Bismarck: State Historical Society of North Dakota, 1987.

Reuter, Dorothy, and Ronald A. Brunger. *Methodist Indian Ministries in Michigan, 1830–1990.* N.p.: D. Reuter, 1993.

Riney, Scott. *The Rapid City Indian School, 1898–1933.* Norman: University of Oklahoma Press, 2014.

Robbins, Louise Barnum, ed. *National Council of Women of the United States: History and Minutes of the National Council of Women of the United States, Organized in Washington, D.C., March 31, 1888.* Boston: E. B. Stillings, 1898.

Roberts, Natalie Andrea. "A History of the Swinomish Tribal Community." PhD dissertation, University of Washington, 1975.

Robertson, Lindsay G. *Conquest by Law: How the Discovery of America Dispossessed the Indigenous Peoples of Their Land.* New York: Oxford University Press, 2005.

Rorabaugh, W. J. *The Alcoholic Republic, an American Tradition.* New York: Oxford University Press, 1979.

Routh, E. C. *The Story of Oklahoma Baptists,* 1932. http://baptisthistoryhomepage.com/ok.bapt.routh.ch5.murrow.html.

Rowley, Maxwell C. "Grave Yard Prairie." *Humboldt Historian* 29, no. 4 (August 7, 1981): 13.

Ruby, Robert H., and John A. Brown. *John Slocum and the Indian Shaker Church.* Norman: University of Oklahoma Press, 1996.

Rush, Benjamin. *An Inquiry into the Effects of Ardent Spirits upon the Human Body and Mind: With an Account of the Means of Preventing, and of the Remedies for Curing Them.* Boston: James Loring, 1823.

Sakiestewa Gilbert, Matthew. *Education beyond the Mesas: Hopi Students at Sherman Institute, 1902–1929.* Lincoln: University of Nebraska Press, 2010.

Sampson, Martin J., and Skagit County Historical Society. *Indians of Skagit County*. La Conner, WA: Skagit County Historical Society, 2014.

Schechter, Patricia A. "Feminist Historiography, Anti-Imperialism, and the Decolonial." In *Empire's Twin: US Anti-Imperialism from the Founding Era to the Age of Terrorism*, edited by Ian Tyrrell and Jay Sexton, 153–66. Ithaca, NY: Cornell University Press, 2015.

Scheuerman, Richard D., and Michael O. Finley. "Chief Cleveland Kamiakin and 20th-Century Political Change on the Colville Reservation." *Pacific Northwest Quarterly* 101, no. 1 (Winter 2009/2010): 17–27.

Schultz, Duane P. *Over the Earth I Come: The Great Sioux Uprising of 1862*. New York: St. Martin's Press, 1992.

Schultz, John L., and Deward E. Walker Jr. "Indian Shakers on the Colville Reservation." *Washington State University. Research Studies* 35, no. 2 (March 1967): 167–71.

Scott, Anne Firor. *Natural Allies: Women's Associations in American History*. Urbana: University of Illinois Press, 1991.

Senier, Siobhan. *Voices of American Indian Assimilation and Resistance: Helen Hunt Jackson, Sarah Winnemucca, and Victoria Howard*. Norman: University of Oklahoma Press, 2003.

Sheriff, Carol. *The Artificial River: The Erie Canal and the Paradox of Progress, 1817–1862*. New York: Hill and Wang, 1996.

Shoemaker, Nancy. "From Longhouse to Loghouse: Household Structure among the Senecas in 1900." *American Indian Quarterly* 15, no. 3 (1991): 329–38.

Shoemaker, Nancy. *Negotiators of Change: Historical Perspectives on Native American Women*. Hoboken: Taylor and Francis, 2012.

Silverman, David J. *Red Brethren: The Brothertown and Stockbridge Indians and the Problem of Race in Early America*. Ithaca, NY: Cornell University Press, 2015.

Simonsen, Jane E. *Making Home Work: Domesticity and Native American Assimilation in the American West, 1860–1919*. Chapel Hill: University of North Carolina Press, 2006.

Smith, R. J. *Salamanca, New York: White Man's City, Red Man's Land*. 2nd ed. N.p., 2007.

Snow, Dean R. *The Iroquois*. Oxford: Blackwell, 1994.

Spencer, Dorcas J. *Birth Control: Morality and Habits of a Primitive Race*. Chicago: International Purity Association, n.d.

Spencer, Dorcas J. *Cornplanter: A Seneca Chief*. Evanston, IL: National WCTU, 190[?]. https://babel.hathitrust.org/cgi/pt?id=ucl.31175032015177.

Spencer, Dorcas J. *A Cry of Mother Love from the Depths*. Evanston, IL: National WCTU, 190[?]. https://babel.hathitrust.org/cgi/pt?id=ucl.31175032015052.

Spencer, Dorcas J. *Hints and Helps for Work among the Indians*. Work Among Indians Department Leaflets, No. 401. Evanston, IL: National WCTU, 190[?]. https://babel.hathitrust.org/cgi/pt?id=ucl.31175032014998.

Spencer, Dorcas J. *A History of the Woman's Christian Temperance Union of Northern and Central California, Written by Request of the State Convention of 1911*. Oakland: West Coast Printing, 1911. https://babel.hathitrust.org/cgi/pt?id=nncl.cu55542 034;view=1up;seq=5.

Spencer, Dorcas J. *The Indian Problem*. Work Among Indians Department Leaflets, No. 408. Evanston, IL: National WCTU, 190[?]. https://babel.hathitrust.org/cgi/pt?id=ucl.31175032014782.

Spencer, Dorcas J. *What Shall We Do for the Indians.* Work Among Indians Department Leaflets, No. 400. Chicago: Ruby I. Gilbert, 190[?]. https://babel.hathitrust.org/cgi/pt?id=uc1.31175032014931.

Spude, Catherine Holder. *Saloons, Prostitutes, and Temperance in Alaska Territory.* Norman: University of Oklahoma Press, 2015.

Stanton, Elizabeth Cady, Susan Brownell Anthony, Matilda Joslyn Gage, and Ida Husted Harper, eds. *History of Woman Suffrage in Six Volumes, 1900–1920.* New York: J. J. Little and Ives, 1922.

Starr, Emmet. *Early History of the Cherokees: Embracing Aboriginal Customs, Religion, Laws, Folk Lore, and Civilization.* 1917. Reprint, Baltimore: Clearfield, 2011.

Starr, Emmet. *History of the Cherokee Indians and Their Legends and Folk Lore.* Oklahoma City: Warden, 1921.

Steele, Joel Dorman. *Hygienic Physiology, with Special Reference to Alcoholic Drinks and Narcotics, for the Use of Junior Classes and Common Schools.* New York: American Book, 1884.

Steele, Joel Dorman. *Hygienic Physiology: With Special Reference to the Use of Alcoholic Drinks and Narcotics: Being a Revised Edition of the Author's Fourteen Weeks in Human Physiology.* New York: American Book, 1901.

Stokes, Claudia. *The Altar at Home: Sentimental Literature and Nineteenth-Century American Religion.* Philadelphia: University of Pennsylvania Press, 2014.

Stowell, Cynthia D. *Faces of a Reservation: A Portrait of the Warm Springs Indian Reservation, Text and Photographs.* Portland: Oregon Historical Society Press, 1987.

Sturtevant, William C. *Handbook of the North American Indians.* Washington, DC: Smithsonian Institution, 1978.

Swatzler, David, and Henry Simmons. *A Friend among the Senecas: The Quaker Mission to Cornplanter's People.* Mechanicsburg, PA: Stackpole Books, 2000.

Taber, Cornelia. *California and Her Indian Children.* San Jose: Northern California Indian Association, 1911.

Tarango, Angela. *Choosing the Jesus Way: American Indian Pentecostals and the Fight for the Indigenous Principle.* Chapel Hill: University of North Carolina Press, 2014.

Taylor, Graham D. *The New Deal and American Indian Tribalism: The Administration of the Indian Reorganization Act, 1934–1945.* Lincoln: University of Nebraska Press, 1980.

Taylor, Melanie Benson. *Reconstructing the Native South: American Indian Literature and the Lost Cause.* Athens: University of Georgia Press, 2011.

Thorne, Tanis. "The Death of Superintendent Stanley and the Cahuilla Uprising of 1907–1912." *Journal of California and Great Basin Anthropology* 24, no. 2 (2004): 233–58.

Tiedke, Kenneth E. *A Study of the Hannahville Indian Community, Menominee County, Michigan.* East Lansing: Michigan State College, 1951.

Tinling, Christine I. *About Ourselves: Lessons in Hygiene for the Loyal Temperance Legion.* Evanston, IL: National Woman's Temperance Union, 1914. https://babel.hathitrust.org/cgi/pt?id=mdp.39015071819838;view=1up;seq=3.

Tinling, Christine I. *A Handful of Hints: Outline Lessons for Loyal Temperance Legion Leaders.* Evanston, IL: National Woman's Christian Temperance Union, 1913. https://babel.hathitrust.org/cgi/pt?id=mdp.39015071819697;view=1up;seq=3.

Tollefson, Kenneth D. "In Defense of a Snoqualmie Political Chiefdom Model." *Ethnohistory* 43, no. 1 (1996): 145–71.

Tomkinson, T. L. *Twenty Years' History of the Woman's Home Missionary Society of the Methodist Episcopal Church, 1880–1900.* Cincinnati: The Woman's Home Missionary Society of the Methodist Episcopal Church, 1903. https://babel.hathitrust.org/cgi/pt?id=wu.89077022747;view=1up;seq=7.

Toner, Deborah. *Alcohol and Nationhood in Nineteenth-Century Mexico.* Lincoln: University of Nebraska Press, 2015.

Tonkovich, Nicole. *The Allotment Plot: Alice C. Fletcher, E. Jane Gay, and Nez Perce Survivance.* Lincoln: University of Nebraska Press, 2012.

Trachtenberg, Alan. *Shades of Hiawatha: Staging Indians, Making Americans, 1880–1930.* New York: Hill and Wang, 2010.

Trafzer, Clifford E., and Matt Sakiestewa Gilbert. *Indian School on Magnolia Avenue: Voices and Images from Sherman Institute.* Corvallis: Oregon State University Press, 2012.

Trefzer, Annette. *Disturbing Indians: The Archaeology of Southern Fiction.* Tuscaloosa: University of Alabama Press, 2007.

Trennert, Robert A. *The Phoenix Indian School: Forced Assimilation in Arizona, 1891–1935.* Norman: University of Oklahoma Press, 1988.

Twenty-Second Annual Report of the Board of Indian Commissioners, 1890. Washington, DC: Government Printing Office, 1891.

Two Bulls, Marty. "Pine Ridge's Sun Dance Dilemma: Sacrifice or End Alcohol Prohibition?" August 9, 2013. https://indiancountrymedianetwork.com/culture/health-wellness/pine-ridges-sun-dance-dilemma-sacrifice-or-end-alcohol-prohibition.

Tyler, Helen E. *Where Prayer and Purpose Meet: The WCTU Story, 1874–1949.* Evanston, IL: Signal Press, 1949.

Tyrrell, Ian. *Reforming the World: The Creation of America's Moral Empire.* Princeton, NJ: Princeton University Press, 2010.

Tyrrell, Ian. "Temperance, Feminism, and the WCTU: New Interpretations and New Directions." *Australasian Journal of American Studies* 5, no. 2 (1986): 27–36.

Tyrrell, Ian R. *Woman's World/Woman's Empire: The Woman's Christian Temperance Union in International Perspective, 1880–1930.* Chapel Hill: University of North Carolina Press, 1991.

Tyrrell, Ian R., Jay Sexton, and Peter S. Onuf. *Empire's Twin: U.S. Anti-Imperialism from the Founding Era to the Age of Terrorism.* Ithaca, NY: Cornell University Press, 2015.

Unger, Samuel. "A History of the National Women's [*sic*] Christian Temperance Union." PhD dissertation, Ohio State University, 1933.

United States. *Annual Reports of the Commissioner of Indian Affairs to the Secretary of the Interior.* Washington, DC: Government Printing Office, 1871–1933.

Unrau, William E. *Indians, Alcohol, and the Roads to Taos and Santa Fe.* Lawrence: University Press of Kansas, 2013.

Unrau, William E. *White Man's Wicked Water: The Alcohol Trade and Prohibition in Indian Country, 1802–1892.* Lawrence: University Press of Kansas, 1996.

Utley, Robert M. *The Indian Frontier of the American West, 1846–1890.* Albuquerque: University of New Mexico Press, 1984.

Utley, Robert M. *The Lance and the Shield: The Life and Times of Sitting Bull.* New York: Ballantine Books, 1993.

Vizenor, Gerald Robert, ed. *Survivance: Narratives of Native Presence*. Lincoln: University of Nebraska Press, 2008.

Wallace, Anthony F. C. *The Death and Rebirth of the Seneca*. New York: Knopf, 1970.

Wanken, Helen M. "'Woman's Sphere' and Indian Reform: The Women's National Indian Association, 1879–1901." PhD dissertation, Marquette University, 1981.

Wells, Mildred White. *Unity in Diversity: The History of the General Federation of Women's Clubs*. Washington, DC: General Federation of Women's Clubs, 1953. https://babel.hathitrust.org/cgi/pt?id=mdp.39015012098292;view=1up;seq=9.

Wendt, Bruce Howard. "An Administrative History of the Warm Springs, Oregon Indian Reservation, 1855–1955." PhD dissertation, Washington State University, 1989.

Wilbert H. Ahern. "Indian Education and Bureaucracy: The School at Morris, 1887–1909." *Minnesota History* 49, no. 3 (1984): 82–98.Wilkins, David E. *American Indian Sovereignty and the U.S. Supreme Court: The Masking of Justice*. Austin: University of Texas Press, 1997.

Willard, Frances E. *Woman and Temperance; or, The Work and Workers of the Woman's Christian Temperance Union*. 1888. Reprint, New York: Arno Press, 1972.

Willard, Frances E., Carolyn De Swarte Gifford, and Amy R. Slagell. *Let Something Good Be Said: Speeches and Writings of Frances E. Willard*. Urbana: University of Illinois Press, 2007.

Willard, Mrs. Eugene S. *Kin-Da-Shon's Wife: An Alaskan Story*. 3rd ed. New York: Fleming H. Revell, 1892.

Wilson, Dorothy Clarke. *Bright Eyes: The Story of Susette La Flesche, an Omaha Indian*. New York: McGraw-Hill, 1974.

Womack, Craig S. *Red on Red: Native American Literary Separatism*. Minneapolis: University of Minnesota Press, 1999.

Woman's Christian Temperance Union. *The Pathfinder; or, National Plans for Securing Scientific Temperance Education in Schools and Colleges for the Women's Christian Temperance Unions of the United States*. New York: A. S. Barnes, 1885.

Woman's Christian Temperance Union, Department of Scientific Temperance Instruction, and Mary H. Hunt. *A History of the First Decade of the Department of Scientific Temperance Instruction in Schools and Colleges, of the Woman's Christian Temperance Union*. Boston: Washington Press, 1892.

Woman's Home Missionary Society. *Annual Report of the Board of Managers of the Woman's Home Missionary Society of the Methodist Episcopal Church*. Cincinnati, OH: Western Methodist Book Concern Press, 1882. https://catalog.hathitrust.org/Record/005921815.

Woman's Home Missionary Society. *Our Work in Red Man's Land*. New York: Methodist Episcopal Church, [192?].

Wood, William. "The Trajectory of Indian Country in California: Rancherias, Villages, Pueblos, Missions, Ranchos, Reservations, Colonies, and Rancherias." *Tulsa Law Review* 44, no. 2 (2008): 317–64.

Woodland Cultural Centre, Brantford, Ontario, July 27–December 17, 2001, and Royal Ontario Museum, March 2–August 4, 2002. *Mohawk Ideals, Victorian Values: Oronhyatekha, M.D.* n.d. https://ecommons.cornell.edu/handle/1813/52441.Woods, Betty Jane. "An Historical Survey of the Woman's Christian Temperance Union of Southern California, as It Reflects the Significance of the National W.C.T.U. in the

Woman's Movement of the Nineteenth Century." Master's thesis, Occidental College, Los Angeles, 1950.

Worley, Ramona Cameron. *Sacajawea, 1788–1884: A New Examination of the Evidence.* Lander, WY: Mortimore Publishing, 2011.

Yohn, Susan M. *A Contest of Faiths: Missionary Women and Pluralism in the American Southwest.* Ithaca, NY: Cornell University Press, 1995.

Zanjani, Sally Springmeyer. *Sarah Winnemucca.* Lincoln: University of Nebraska Press, 2001.

Index

CPSIA information can be obtained
at www.ICGtesting.com
Printed in the USA
BVHW041652311022
650761BV00005B/134